安藤忠雄の建築 2

Tadao Ando 2
Outside Japan

2008年1月25日　初版 第1刷発行

著者……安藤忠雄

発行者……遠藤信行

デザイン……太田徹也

プリンティングディレクション……高柳　昇

印刷・製本……株式会社東京印書館

発行所……TOTO出版
（TOTO株式会社 文化推進部）
〒107-0062 東京都港区南青山1-24-3
TOTO乃木坂ビル2階
[営業] tel:03(3402)7138
fax:03(3402)7187
[編集] tel:03(3497)1010
URL:http://www.toto.co.jp/bookshop/

ISBN978-4-88706-286-3

安藤忠雄の建築　2

Tadao

TADAO ANDO 2 Outside Japan

First published in Japan on January 25, 2008

TOTO Shuppan (TOTO Ltd.)
TOTO Nogizaka Bldg., 2F,
1-24-3 Minami-Aoyama, Minato-ku,
Tokyo 107-0062, Japan
[Sales]Telephone: +81-3-3402-7138 Facsimile: +81-3-3402-7187
[Editorial]Telephone: +81-3-3497-1010
URL: http://www.toto.co.jp/bookshop/

Author: Tadao Ando
Publisher: Nobuyuki Endo
Book Designer: Tetsuya Ohta
Printing Director : Noboru Takayanagi
Printer: Tokyo Inshokan Printing Co., LTD.

Ando 2

Outside Japan

Tadao Ando 2 Outside Japan

目次
Contents

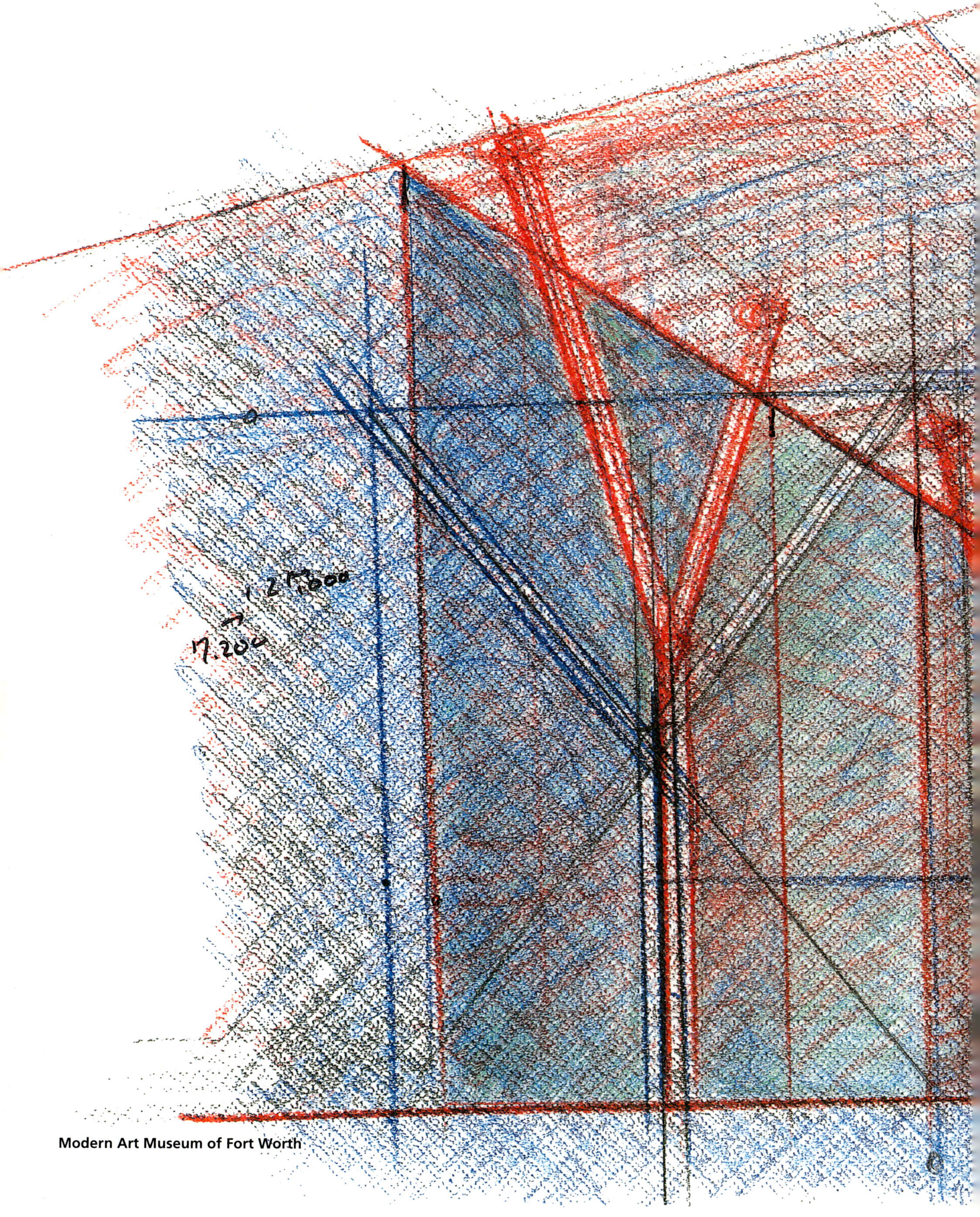

Modern Art Museum of Fort Worth

Tate Gallery of Modern Art

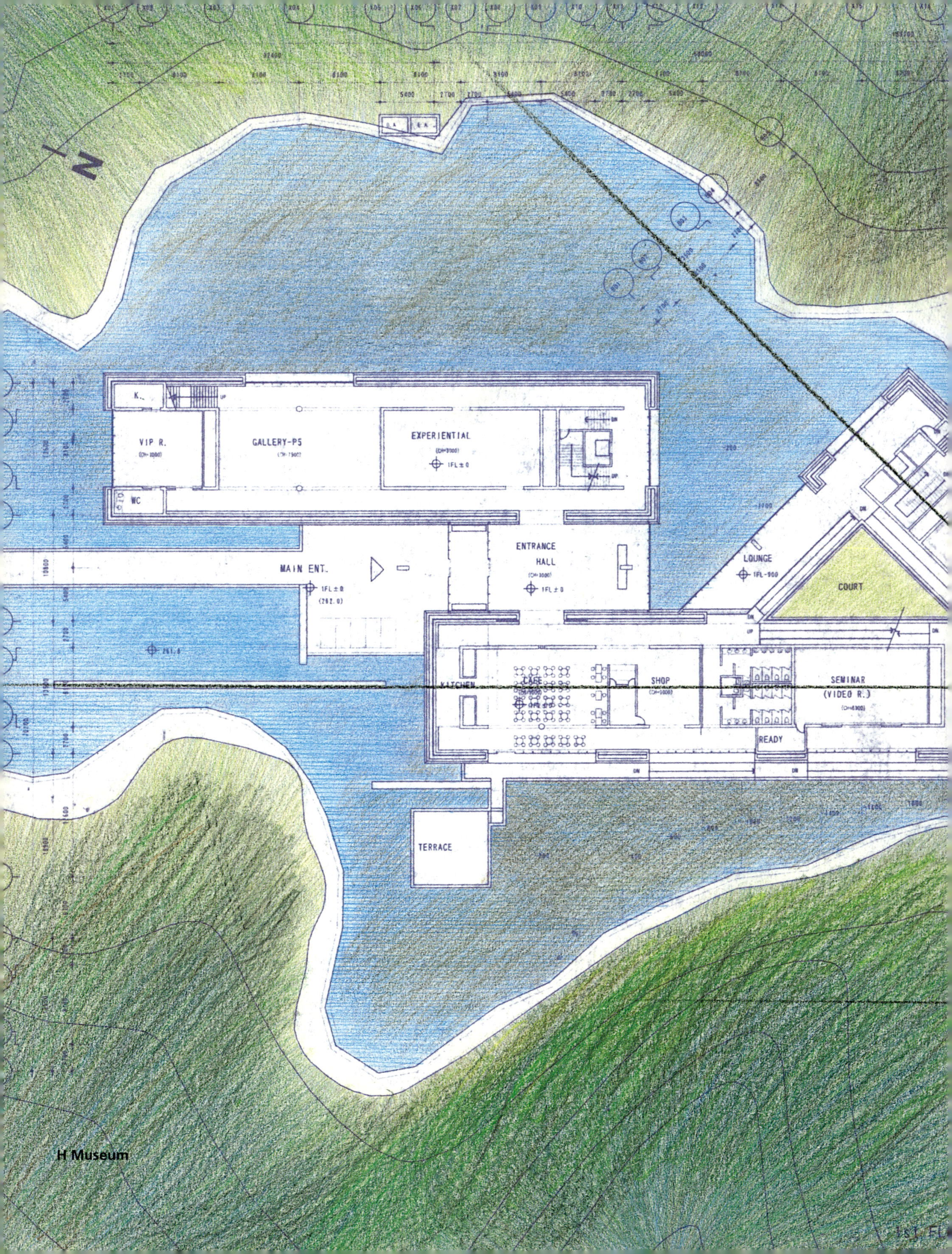
VIP R.
WC
GALLERY-P5
EXPERIENTIAL
MAIN ENT.
ENTRANCE HALL
LOUNGE
COURT
KITCHEN
CAFE
SHOP
SEMINAR (VIDEO R.)
READY
TERRACE

H Museum

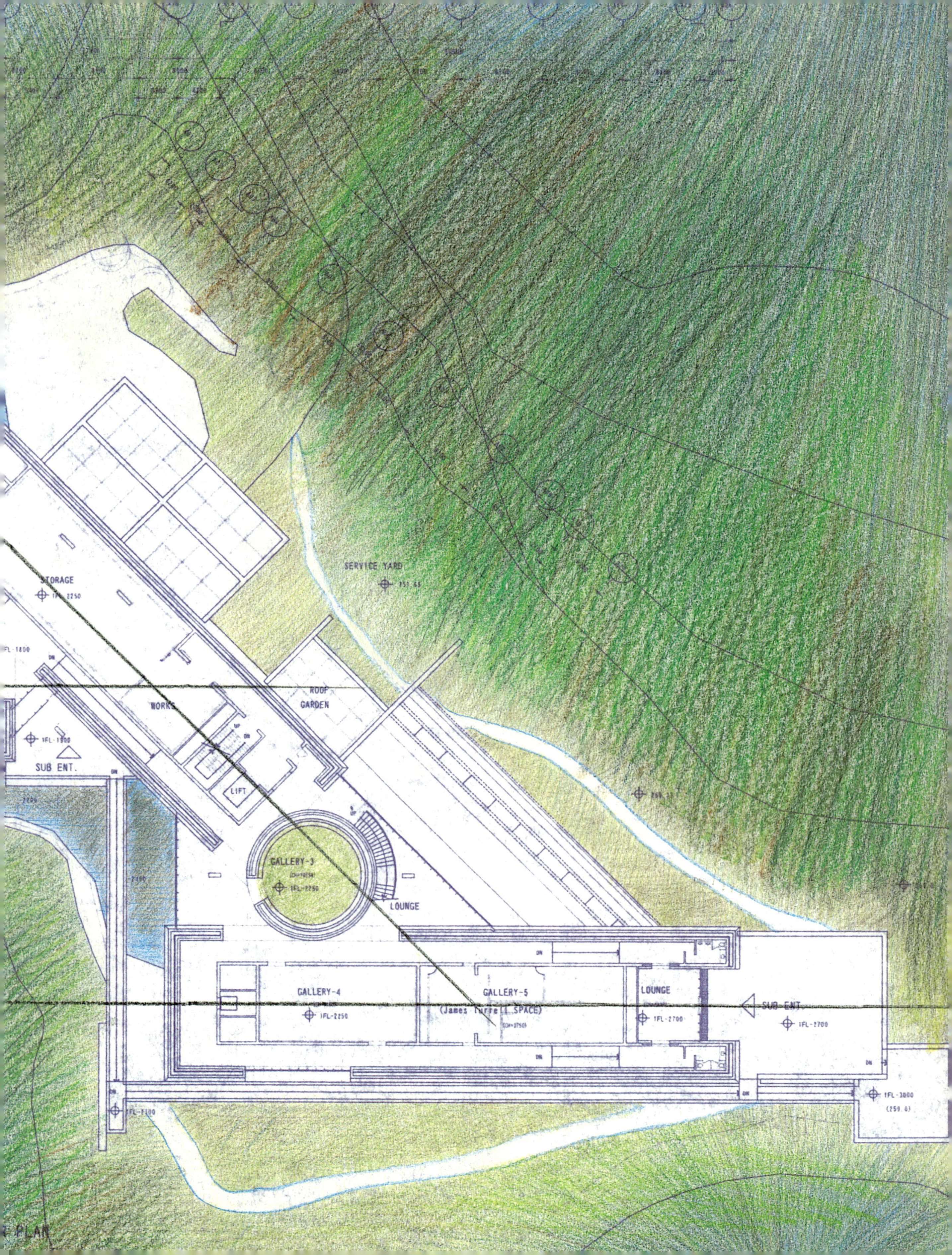

STORAGE
WORKS
SUB ENT.
LIFT
ROOF GARDEN
SERVICE YARD
GALLERY-3
LOUNGE
GALLERY-4
GALLERY-5
(James Turrell SPACE)
LOUNGE
SUB ENT.
PLAN

海外での仕事

安藤忠雄

アブダビ海洋博物館プロジェクトのスタート

2007年1月、アラブ首長国連邦(UAE)の首都アブダビが、沖合いの島サアディヤット島の開発プロジェクトを正式に発表した。自然環境と文化が楽しめる「文化島」を目指すプロジェクトで、その中核となる文化地区は、ミュージアムやシアターなど、5つの文化施設を中心に構成される。その設計者として、フランク・O・ゲーリー、ジャン・ヌーヴェル、ザハ・ハディドとともに私が参加することになった。

私が担当するのは、砂漠の国ながら、海とともに暮らすアブダビならではの生活文化を紹介する海洋博物館である。プロジェクトの性格上、新たに生まれる建築には場所に根差したある種のシンボリズムが期待された。それに対し、私は矩形平面のヴォリュームから、海風を受けた船の帆のふくらみをなぞるようにシェル状のヴォイドをくり抜いたかたちの建築を提案した。

造形をそれ単体として見たならば、単純な幾何学によるオブジェに見えるかもしれない。しかし、それがサアディヤット島の海際で、海を取り込むようにつくられた水庭の上に浮かべられたとき、なだらかな曲面に覆われたヴォイドの空間は、雄大な海景を身近に引き寄せる装置となる。

アブダビ政府は、このかたちのない自然の営みをモチーフとする建築の提案を受け入れ、プロジェクトは2012年竣工を目標に、実現へと向けて動き出した。

若い日の憧れ

仕事を通じて、初めて海外との直接の接点をもったのは、1971年に大阪梅田の地下街でカフェOS2001のインテリアを手がけたときだ。チャレンジのつもりでイタリアの建築雑誌『DOMUS』に紹介資料を送ると、それが翌々月号に掲載された。世界で最も華やかな建築雑誌であった『DOMUS』に取り上げられたことは、独学で建築の世界に飛び込み、厳しい現実にもまれていた当時の私に大きな希望を与えてくれた。

それから30年余り。現在、私の事務所では複数の海外プロジェクトが同時進行している。ヨーロッパ、アメリカに中南米、スリランカ、中国、韓国、台湾、そしてアラブ圏に至るまで、それぞれにまったく異なる風土を背負った場所での建築だ。

遠く離れた場所から仕事の機会が与えられることは光栄なことであるし、それがコンペを闘った結果ならば誇らしくもある。だが、この状況を若い頃の夢がかなったと単純に喜んでいるかというと、否である。それはこの10数年間にわたる海外プロジェ

クトの経験から、それがいかに困難な仕事かを心底実感しているからだ。

距離の問題

ともかく、問題は現場と自身との距離だ。いくら情報技術が進歩し、世界のグローバル化が進もうとも、結局建築はあるひとつの場所に一から組み上げていく土着の産物であり、あくまで現場でつくるものだ。E-mailなどの情報メディアは、単純なデータを伝えるのには便利な道具であるが、最も重要なその場所の空気をすくい取ることは難しい。頻繁に現地を訪れることができない海外でのプロジェクトには、そうしたリアリティの欠如という面で、身近な場所での建築に比べ、決定的ともいえるハンディがある。

物理的な距離以上に厄介なのが、文化的な距離だ。いうまでもなく建築とは、社会的な生産行為であり、その土壌となる文化、伝統、国民性、社会のシステムが異なれば、当然その建築のプロセスも変わってくる。未経験の環境での予期せぬ事態が次々に起こってくる。

例えばイタリアでの仕事では、歴史都市らしく、日本と比して開発に関わる法手続きに驚くほどの時間がかかる。FABRICAにおいては、アイディアを出してから完成まで、結局10年以上の時間を要した。加えて現地の職人たちの仕事に向かう姿勢も文字通りの職人気質で、いったん仕事を始めると工期などおかまいなく、自分が納得できるまで手を止めようとしない。それを頼もしく思う反面、プロジェクトの時間が読めないという怖さが終始あった。

裁判社会がそのまま反映されたアメリカでの仕事も驚きだった。とにかく契約の度に弁護士が登場し、簡単に済む話を変に複雑にして、プロジェクトの進行を妨げる。民主国家らしく、物事をひとつ決めるごとに関係者を集めての会議を開きたがるのにも閉口した。フォートワース現代美術館のときは、コンペから完成までの5年7カ月の間に、総計30回は大阪―フォートワース間を往復している。移動の費用を担うクライアント側の経済的負担も相当のものだったはずだ。

距離を埋めるのに膨大なエネルギーが費やされる、国際プロジェクトはつくり手とクライアント双方に、余程の覚悟がないと成り立たない。

社会的なギャップとして、単純な建築技術のレベルの問題もある。アルマーニ・テアトロの工事の際には、全体のスケジュールは驚くほどスムーズに進行しながら、現地ミラノの施工レベルの予想外の低さに泣かされ、ついにはコンクリートの打ち直しという事態まで生じてしまった。結局、日本から馴染みの左官職人に来てもらうことで、

何とか事は収まったのだが、このとき改めて日本で建築のキャリアを積んでくることができた自身の幸運を思い知った。

技術力だけでなく、勤勉さ、チームワークと、どれをとっても間違いなく日本の建設業は世界最高レベルにある。その強力なサポートのない海外での仕事の際、私はいつも最初の体制づくり、チーム編成に最も神経をすり減らす。ここを怠ると、ちょっとしたトラブルであっという間にプロジェクトは転覆してしまう。

もちろん、物事がスムーズに動いていかないのは建築の常であり、建築の悪戦苦闘のプロセスは海外でも日本でも同じだ。しかし、海外での仕事の場合、日本にいる私はそのトラブルに即座に対応ができない。また、臨場感がないために、ときに重要な判断を間違えることもある。この状態は非常にストレスだ。複数の現場でトラブルが重なったときなど、海外での仕事はもう止めようかと思いかけたことも何度かあった。

だが、そうして海外はもう懲り懲りといいながら、新しい仕事の依頼があると、結局引き受けてしまう。「つくりたい」という欲望が抑えられない。

アブダビの計画を打診されたときも、あまりの遠さとプロジェクトのスケールの巨大さにリアリティを感じられないまま、半ば建築のトレーニングのつもりでスタディを開始した。しかし、現地を訪れ、場所の空気を身体で掴んでいくうちに、徐々に熱は増していき、気がつけばアトリエの地下には1/50の巨大なスタディ模型がいくつも並ぶようになっていた。

海外での建築を続ける理由

後の苦労を知りながら、それでもなお海外での仕事を諦めないのはなぜか。説明するために、まず私の建築に対する姿勢を語ろう。

当たり前のことだが、それぞれの建築には、地形、歴史、文化的経緯、人々の生活習慣に至るまで、必ず場所ごとに固有のコンテクストがある。それに対し、私は新たな仕事に向かう度、素材から工法技術、造形表現など、原点に立ち帰って異なるアプローチでの建築の組み立てを試みる。かつて20世紀モダニズムがインターナショナルスタイルと称し、すべての場所の建築を単一普遍の枠組みに押し込めようとしたような一般解としての建築ではない、海洋国アブダビと歴史国家イタリアと、それぞれにまったく個別の解答を探していく。

確かに、アブダビという未知の環境での仕事には、さまざまな意味でリスクが伴う。距離のハンディを埋めるために費やされるエネルギーも、かつてないほど膨大だろう。しかし、砂漠の国の海際というダイナミックな立地環境、求められるスケールは、とも

に私にとっては未経験のテーマだ。何よりそこには、発展目覚しい国家のシンボルをひとつの都市建築で表現するという、得がたいテーマがある。

かつてルイス・I・カーンが、インドの激しい風土との出会いの中でバングラデシュ国会議場をつくり上げたように、あるいは無名のヨーン・ウッツォンが、紆余曲折のプロセスを経てシドニー・オペラハウスというひとつの建築で都市の顔をつくり上げたように——異なる世界との出会いは、ときに建築家にとって、新たな建築の地平を切り拓くチャンスになる。

人間との出会い

場所の差異ばかりではない。仕事を通じてのさまざまな人間との出会いも、困難なプロセスを乗り越える大きな原動力だ。

まずはクライアント。遠く日本にいる私に声をかけて、建築をつくろうとする彼らは、それだけで十分ユニークといえるのだが、ともに仕事をする中で次第に明らかになるその素顔は、さらに個性的で魅力的だ。

FABRICAのプロジェクトを通じて、私にイタリアの建築文化の懐の深さを教えてくれたルチアーノ・ベネトン。優美さと機能性を備えたアルマーニのファッションさながら、詩的に建築の永遠性を語る一方で、実務にも長けた一面を見せ、私を感服させたジョルジオ・アルマーニ。サンタフェの砂漠の真ん中での住宅の設計を依頼してきたトム・フォード。10数年前に住宅の設計を依頼してきてから、いまだ理想の敷地を求め探し続けているカール・ラガーフェルド。時代の流れに敏感な一流のデザイナーたちとの共同作業は、大いに私の感性を刺激してくれる。

企画から完成までの長い時間を乗り越え、ともに闘った同士として思い浮かぶのは、ピューリッツァー美術館のピューリッツァー夫妻、ランゲン美術館のマリアンネ・ランゲン夫人とカール・ハインリッヒ・ミュラー氏、そしてパラッツォ・グラッシのクライアントであるフランソワ・ピノー氏だ。

ピューリッツァー美術館は、現代アーティストのリチャード・セラ、エルスワース・ケリーと建築家である私とが、プロジェクトの初期段階から顔を合わせ、双方に妥協することなく対話を重ねながら、一から美術館を組み立てていくという稀有な企画だった。それが10数年の時間を経て実現まで導かれたのは、やはりクライアントの途切れぬ情熱があってこそだったと思う。

ランゲン美術館は、世界有数の環境美術館インゼル・ホンブロイッヒの延長線上に構想されたミュージアム公園の一部をなす計画で、その構想のあまりの壮大さに、正

直私は実現はかなわないだろうと半ば諦めかけていた。しかし、プロジェクトのスタートから6年目、立案者であるカール・ハインリッヒ・ミュラー氏にマリアンネ・ランゲン夫人が救いの手を差し伸べ、2002年ついにプロジェクトは動き出し、2年の工事期間を経て、2004年に奇跡のような完成のときを迎えた。

パラッツォ・グラッシは、パリのピノー財団美術館の計画中断の後、急遽スタートが決まったプロジェクトだった。セガン島と決別し、ヴェニスを選択した際のフランソワ・ピノー氏の決断の早さ、実現に漕ぎつけるまでの圧倒的な行動力は忘れがたい。

残念ながら、ピューリッツァー氏、ランゲン夫人は、建物の完成を見ぬまま他界してしまったが、ともあれ幾多の障害を乗り越え、プロジェクトを完遂させたのは、彼ら個人の思いであったことは間違いない。

同時代のライバルと

国際コンペやアブダビのような大きなプロジェクトで顔を合わせる同時代の優れた建築家との対話も、海外に出てこその特典だ。アブダビでも、ゲーリー、ヌーヴェル、ハディドと仕事をともにする。第一線で活躍する建築家の仕事に共通するのは、世界各国で建築をつくり続けている彼らの精神、肉体の強靭さだ。1年に1回会うだけでも、大変な刺激を受ける。

ヌーヴェルは、セーヌ川岸のアラブ世界研究所での鮮烈なデビューから20年余り、常に新しい建築のイメージを生み出しながら、一定した高い空間の質と独自性を保ち続けている。その活動の力強さ、スピード感は一層凄みを増しているのでないか。ルーヴルのアブダビ・ブランチの計画でも、敷地全面を覆うドーム状のフィルターの下に、かつての土地の風景を再現させるという、非常にポエティックで美しい建築イメージを提案している。

ゲーリーは、1979年のロス近郊の自邸に衝撃を受けて以来、私にとって常に大きな存在であるとともに、敬愛する友人である。ゲーリーが求め続けた建築表現の自由は、20世紀の最後、ビルバオ・グッゲンハイム美術館において華々しく開花した。グッゲンハイムのアブダビ・ブランチの計画は、大スケールでのビルバオの変奏のようにも見えるが、聡明なゲーリーのことである。その裏にはきっと意表をつくアイディアを忍ばせていることだろう。

国際コンペを闘うときでも、コンペティターに彼らの名前を見つけると、自身のアイディアを練っていく一方で、無意識にヌーヴェルならどうするか、ゲーリーならどうするか、レンゾ・ピアノなら……と、彼らの建築を考えてしまう。国際社会を建築で

闘っていくには、そんな緊張感のある関係が必要なのかもしれない。

建築における創造とは

海外での仕事を手がかりに、私の建築がいかにプロジェクトごとの場所と人間との出会いによっているかを書いてきた。これは70年代頃に流行った、いわゆるコンテクスチュアリズム（文脈主義）の考え方といえるのかもしれない。こういうと「それならば建築家の個性、オリジナリティはどこにあるのか」という反論があるだろう。

誤解を恐れずにいえば、私は建築において、ゼロからの創造、発明とは存在しないものだと考えている。例えば、20世紀初頭の近代建築の歴史的名作、シュレーダー邸を取り上げてみよう。オランダの慣習的な街並みに突如出現した、3原色を使った線と面による抽象表現は、まさに前衛であり、建築における革命だった。しかし、それが家具デザイナーから出発した建築家ヘリット・トーマス・リートフェルトひとりの創造であるかというと、そうではない。その背景には、終生リートフェルトのパトロンとして支援し続けたシュレーダー夫人（シュレーダー邸のクライアント）の存在があり、一方で当時ピエト・モンドリアン、ファン・ドゥースブルフらが展開していた芸術運動デ・ステイルの影響がある。ちなみに、モンドリアンに抽象への目覚めのきっかけを与えたのはピカソのキュビズムだ。20世紀初頭、さまざまな分野で新しい表現世界を模索する運動が発生していた、当時の時代の空気も考えねばならない。

シュレーダー邸以降のリートフェルトが、何ら後世に残るような建築をつくれなかったという事実は象徴的である。時代と社会、そして人間。さまざまな個性の幸運な出会いが、あの名作を生んだ。

無論、建築は状況に応じて、偶然の産物としてできるわけではない。重要なのは、つくり手である主体が、そこから何をすくい取り、いかに応えられるかということ——その発見と対話の過程で、自己批評の精神をもって前進していくことこそが、私の考える“創造”だ。

異国の地での仕事は、必ず私に豊かな“世界”との出会いと、そこからの新たな“創造”の機会をもたらしてくれる。その挑戦の喜びと感動があるから、私は懲りずに海外での仕事を続けている。

Work Overseas

Tadao Ando

The Start of the Abu Dhabi Maritime Museum Project

In January 2007, Abu Dhabi, the capital of the United Arab Emirates (UAE), formally announced a project to develop Saadiyat, an offshore island. The aim of the project is to create a "culture island" where visitors can enjoy both the natural environment and culture; the cultural district which is to be the core of the project will be composed of five cultural facilities such as museums and theaters. The participating architects are Frank O. Gehry, Jean Nouvel, Zaha Hadid and myself.

I am in charge of a maritime museum, which will introduce the close relationship of everyday life and culture in this country of deserts to the sea. Because of the nature of the project, there was hope that the new building would have a certain symbolism rooted in the place. My response was to propose a volume with a rectangular plan from which a shell-shaped void, resembling a wind-filled sail, had been scooped out.

The form, by itself, may seem like a simple geometrical object. However, when it is suspended over a water court that has been designed to incorporate views of the sea, on a seaside site on the island of Saadiyat, the void space, defined by gentle curves, will become a device drawing the grand seascape closer to the observer.

The Abu Dhabi government accepted this architectural proposal with an ephemeral motif based on natural phenomena, and the project has begun to move forward with completion expected in 2012.

Dreams of Youth

My first direct contact through work with the world overseas came when I designed the interior of Cafe 0S2001 in the underground mall of Umeda in Osaka in 1971. Seeing it as a chance to test myself, I sent introductory material on the work to the Italian architectural magazine Domus: it was published two months later. Having a work published in the most brilliant architectural magazine in the world was an enormous encouragement to someone who was self-educated in architecture and struggling against harsh reality, as I was.

Thirty years have passed since then. My office is simultaneously engaged in multiple overseas projects. The projects are in Europe, the United States, Latin America, Sri Lanka, China, Korea, Taiwan and the Arab world. They are buildings for places with entirely different climates.

It is an honor to be given an opportunity to work in a distant land, and specially a source

of pride when the commission is won through a competition. However, though this may seem like a youthful dream come true, I cannot entirely rejoice in my present situation. That is because I have become fully aware from experience with overseas projects in the last ten years or so of the difficulty of such jobs.

The Problem of Distance

The problem is the distance between myself and the site. No matter how much information technology has advanced and globalization has progressed, a building is ultimately an indigenous product assembled from scratch in a certain place; it is created on the site. Information media such as e-mails are convenient tools for communicating simple data, but capturing the atmosphere of a place, which is such an important thing, is difficult. Overseas projects that cannot be frequently visited have this, perhaps decisive, disadvantage, compared with projects closer at hand—there is about them not as much reality of this kind as I could hope for.

Even more troublesome than physical distance is cultural distance. Needless to say, creating a building is a social, productive act. If the cultural, traditional, national and social systems that are the basis for that act are different, the architectural process too will differ. Unexpected situations arise in quick succession in environments in which one has no experience.

For example, an amazing amount of time must be spent in Italy going through legal processes to get approval for a project in a historic city, compared with Japan. FABRICA ultimately required over ten years between initial conception and completion. In addition, local craftsmen in Italy take great pride in their work; once they begin, they work until they are satisfied with what they have done, no matter what the construction deadline may be. One can rely on the quality of their work, but it makes difficult to know how much time a project will take.

I have also been surprised by the way jobs in the United States reflect the litigious nature of American society. Lawyers show up each time a contract is signed; simple matters are made needlessly complex, hindering the progress of a project. I have also been dumbfounded by the eagerness to gather all those involved in the project each time something needs to be decided; no doubt that is a reflection of the democratic nature of the country. For the Modern Art Museum of Fort Worth, I made a total of 30 round trips between Osaka and Fort Worth in the five years and seven months it took from the competition to completion. Paying all these travel costs must have been a considerable expense for the client.

Enormous amounts of energy are consumed to cover distance. An international project demands great commitment on the part of both the architect and the client.

There also problems stemming simply from differences in level of building technology. In the construction of the Armani/Teatro, the project as a whole proceeded according to schedule to my surprise. However, the standard of construction in Milan was unexpectedly low; it reached the point where concrete had to be re-cast. In the end, the problem was resolved by having plasterers with whom we were familiar flown in from Japan, but the incident made me realize how fortunate I was to have spent so many years practicing in Japan.

Japanese builders are unquestionably among the best in the world in skill, industry and teamwork. Whenever I work overseas without the benefit of their support, I take the greatest care in organizing the project team. If I fail to give that matter sufficient thought, the slightest problem can capsize a project.

Of course any building project is bound to run into problems, and the process is as much a struggle in Japan as it is overseas. However, as I am usually in Japan, I am unable to respond immediately to trouble in an overseas project. I also make errors of judgment at times on important matters because I am at a remove. It is an extremely stressful situation. I have thought a number of times of no longer taking on overseas work, especially when troubles occur simultaneously on multiple sites.

Nevertheless, I end up accepting new commissions despite repeated declarations that I have had enough. My desire to create is simply too strong for me to turn down work.

When I was first approached about the Abu Dhabi project, it was so distant and enormous in scale, it did not seem real. I began making studies, thinking of it to some extent as a form of architectural training. However, as I visited the site and began to absorb the atmosphere of the place, my enthusiasm gradually grew. Before I knew it, a number of huge study models at 1:50 scale were arranged in the basement of my atelier.

Reasons for Continuing to Work Overseas

Why do I continue to accept overseas work, when I know it will mean so much trouble? Before I answer, let me first explain my approach to architecture.

Obviously, each place has its own distinctive context that is the sum total of its geography, history, cultural circumstances and the everyday customs of the people. Each time I take on a new job, I attempt to start afresh with respect to such things as materials, construction methods and forms of expression and to assemble the building by a different approach. I seek, not general architectural solutions that are the result of trying to fit buildings everywhere into a single, universal framework such as the one adopted by twentieth-century modernism and referred to as the International Style, but solutions, each unique to a certain place, be it the

maritime emirate of Abu Dhabi or the historic state of Italy.

Certainly, work in an unfamiliar environment such as that of Abu Dhabi carries various risks. The amount of energy consumed in trying to overcome the disadvantages of distance will no doubt be greater than ever before. However, working in such a dynamic environment, one near the sea in a desert country, or on such a scale is a new experience for me. Above all, this project represents a rare opportunity to create through a work of urban architecture a symbol for a country undergoing remarkable development.

For an architect, an encounter with a different world is a chance to open up a new architectural horizon, just as Louis I. Kahn did in creating the National Assembly in Bangladesh out of his encounter with the harsh climate of the Asian subcontinent, or as the then-little-known Jorn Utzon did in creating through a tortuous process a new city symbol with his Sydney Opera House.

Encounters with People

It is not just the difference of places. Encountering diverse people through work enables me to get through difficult processes.

First, there are the clients. Asking an architect in far-off Japan to participate in a project certainly suggests someone who is out-of-the-ordinary; on closer acquaintance over the course of a project, I usually find the client to be a unique, attractive human being.

Through the FABRICA project, Luciano Benetton taught me the nobility of spirit of architectural culture in Italy. Giorgio Armani, as might be expected from his elegant yet functional fashions, spoke poetically of the eternal in architecture but showed his business acumen as well. Tom Ford asked me to design a house in the middle of the desert in Santa Fe. Since asking me to design a house over ten years ago, Karl Lagerfeld has continued to search for the ideal site. Collaboration with first-rate designers sensitive to the trends of the time has greatly stimulated my own sensibility.

Kindred spirits with whom I worked long years on projects from planning to completion include Joseph and Emily Rauh Pulitzer of the Pulitzer Foundation, Marianne Langen and Karl-Heinrich Muller of the Langen Foundation, and François Pinault, the client for Palazzo Grassi.

The Pulitzer Foundation for the Arts was an unusual project in which the contemporary artists Richard Serra and Ellsworth Kelly and I, the architect, engaged in repeated face-to-face discussions from the start and designed the museum from scratch without compromising our individual visions. It was thanks to the passionate commitment shown by the client that the

project was completed after ten years.

The Langen Foundation is part of a museum park conceived as an extension of Hombroich Island, one of the leading contemporary art museums in the world. The concept was so grand, I was not entirely confident it would ever be realized. However, six years after the start of the project, Marianne Langen extended help to Karl-Heinrich Muller who had conceived the original proposal. The project finally got underway in 2002 and was completed after two years of construction work in 2004. In light of all the difficulties that had to be overcome, the completion of the project was virtually a miracle.

The decision to start Palazzo Grassi was made shortly after the François Pinault Foundation for Contemporary Art project in Paris was discontinued. I will long remember the decisiveness Pinault displayed in choosing to quit Seguin Island and selecting Venice and his remarkable energy in bringing the project to completion.

Joseph Pulitzer and Marianne Langen unfortunately did not live to see the completion of their respective projects, but their dreams undoubtedly enabled the projects to overcome many obstacles and achieve realization.

Contemporary Rivals

Working overseas brings opportunities to meet and converse with excellent contemporary architects in international competitions or large projects such as the one for Abu Dhabi. In Abu Dhabi, I will be working with Gehry, Nouvel and Hadid. Architects on the leading edge who continue to work in different countries of the world all have tenacity and stamina. Meeting them is stimulating, even if it may happen only once a year.

Since his remarkable debut with the Arab World Institute built by the Seine two decades ago, Nouvel has continued to create spaces of high quality and originality while producing new architectural images. He seems to be displaying even greater power and speed in his activities lately. In his project for the Abu Dhabi branch of the Louvre, he has proposed an extremely poetic and beautiful architectural image: the re-creation of the landscape that once existed there under a dome-shaped filter covering the entire site.

Gehry's own house built in 1979 in a suburb of Los Angeles made a huge impression on me, and ever since, he has been for me an enormous presence and a friend whom I hold in high esteem. His long pursuit of freedom of architectural expression bore fruit in the splendid Guggenheim Museum Bilbao at the end of the twentieth century. The project for the Abu Dhabi branch of the Guggenheim may suggest a variation on Bilbao at a grand scale, but Gehry is an architect of great intelligence. No doubt he has hidden in it some extraordinary idea.

When I find their names among those invited to participate in an international competition, I find myself wondering, as I develop my own ideas, what Nouvel, or Gehry, or Renzo Piano would do under these circumstances. This sense of rivalry may be necessary in competing in architecture internationally.

Creation in Architecture

Using my work overseas as a point of departure, I have discussed how my architecture is a response to the places where the projects are located and the people I encounter. This is similar to the approach popular in the 1970s called contextualism. One might ask, where then is the individuality or originality of the architect in such an approach?

Though my statement may be open to misinterpretation, I believe nothing is entirely newly created or invented in architecture. Examine, for example, the Schröder House, the masterpiece of modern architecture from the early twentieth century. This work of abstract expression, composed of lines and planes in three primary colors and inserted into an otherwise conventional Dutch townscape, was indeed avant-garde and revolutionary for architecture. However, it was not created solely by Gerrit Rietveld, the furniture-designer-turned-architect. The house would not have been possible without the presence of Rietveld's lifelong patron and client, Mrs. Schröder. Rietveld was also influenced by De Stijl, the art movement founded by Piet Mondrian and Van Doesburg. It might also be mentioned that Mondrian in turn was made aware of the importance of abstraction by Picasso's Cubism. We must take into consideration the atmosphere in the early twentieth century, when various movements were seeking new modes of expression in different fields.

It is quite revealing that Rietveld was unable to create any building of lasting architectural importance after the Schröder House. That masterpiece was the product of a number of fortunate encounters between individuals at a certain time and in a certain society.

Of course architecture is not an accidental product created in response to circumstances. The important thing is what the architect makes of those particular circumstances. To undertake this process of discovery and dialogue, willing to engage in self-criticism, but always eager to press forward, is my idea of "creation."

My work in foreign countries will inevitably lead to new encounters and new opportunities for "creation." It is because of the joy and excitement of that challenge that I continue to engage in work overseas.

2001年9月11日、早朝のニューヨークを襲った〈テロ〉は、数多くの尊い人命とともに、都市にとっても最も重要な〈記憶〉を一瞬にして奪った。1世紀前に岩盤の上に誕生した近代都市ニューヨークの富と繁栄のシンボルの破壊——それは同時に20世紀的世界を形づくってきた価値観そのものを真っ向から否定する行為だった。その行為の思想的背景を問う以前に、いかなる理由があったとしてもその蛮行を許すことはできない。単なる破壊と報復の連鎖からは何も生まれはしない。

事件の根幹は結局異文化間の対立、即ちグローバル・スタンダードという名のアメリカ型資本主義経済およびそれと表裏一体の消費文明の繁栄と伝播を善とする価値観と、それに対して自らのアイデンティティ、宗教的なバックボーンを守ろうとした地域共同体の価値観との衝突にあったことをわれわれは認識し、後世に伝えていかねばならない。それは追い詰められた人々の、精一杯の抵抗だった。生命の宿る奇跡の星・地球の表層にせめぎあって住みついている私たち人間が、いかにしてともに集って生きていけるか。互いの存在を認め合いながら、世界でひとつの共同体を営んでいけるかを、今、われわれは真剣に考えねばならない。

そのときに、失われた都市の空白を埋める〈モニュメント〉は建築であるべきではない。そこは、鎮魂と反省のための場所として、あらゆる経済活動から切り離された場所であるべきだろう。

われわれは、グラウンド・ゼロに、鎮魂の墳墓の造営を提案する。球体の一部にして底面の直径は200m余りの、緩やかな大地のふくらみともいうべき〈モニュメント〉の計画である。経済によるグローバリゼーションではなく、人間の対話による"ただひとつの地球"へ——との思いを込めて、地球の赤道半径との比率から、球体の半径を割り出した。未来に受け継がれるべき場所の記憶が、再び経済の波に呑まれてしまわないことを願っている。

グラウンド・ゼロ・プロジェクト
Ground Zero Project

2001-02
アメリカ合衆国 ニューヨーク
——New York, U.S.A.

As well as a large number of precious human lives, the terrorist attack that struck New York on the early morning of September 11, 2001, instantaneously extinguished what is most important for a city: its "memory." The destruction of the symbol of wealth and prosperity of modern New York, founded on solid bedrock a century ago, was simultaneously an act utterly negating the values that have shaped the 20th century world. Before questioning the ideological background of this act, such barbarity should never be permitted for any reason. Nothing will arise from a chain of mere destruction and retribution.

Having recognized that the root of the event was ultimately a confrontation between different cultures, that is to say, a collision between the values of the global standards of the American-model capitalist economy, with its concomitant prosperity and propagation of a culture of consumption, and the values of a regional community attempting to abide by its own identity and religious spine, we must convey this to future generations. It was the final act of resistance by a cornered people. How can we human beings cohabit while in competition for the surface of the earth, a miraculous planet brimming with life? While acknowledging each other's existence, we must now think seriously about how a single community can be maintained in the world.

Then this "monument" buried in the lost blank margin of the city should not be architecture. As a place for introspection and reflection, it should be a place detached from all economic activities.

At Ground Zero, we propose building a tomb for the repose of souls. A piece of a sphere with a resulting base diameter of 200m, the plan is a "monument" that could be described as a gentle swelling of the earth. It embodies the desire for "just one earth" through dialogue between people, not through economic globalization, and the radius of the sphere was calculated as a ratio of the equatorial radius of the Earth. I hope that the memory of this place that must be passed on to the future will not once again be engulfed by the economic tide.

大地のゆるやかな膨らみとして計画された
鎮魂のモニュメント。墳墓のスケールは、
地球の赤道半径との関係で決められている。

A monument for the repose of souls, designed as a gentle swelling of the earth. The scale of the tomb was determined in relation to the equatorial radius of the globe.

New York

木でつくられたグラウンド・ゼロの模型。高密度の都市の空白として存在する祈りの場。

Wood model of Ground Zero. A place existing for prayer as a blank space in the dense city.

地球に生きる

三宅理一（建築史家）

世界との触れ合い

安藤忠雄はまぎれもなく世界をリードする建築家である。みずからが生を受け過去60年に渡る長い人生を送ってきた故郷大阪をこよなく愛し、誰よりも大阪のために貢献してきたことは間違いない。その点では、大阪に登場した傑出した建築家であり、大阪人はそのことを誇りに思ってよい。同時に彼は日本の地が培ってきたすぐれた感性を建築に結実させた類稀な人物であり、現代日本文化を代表する人物である。彼の作品が提示する繊細かつ大胆な表現は、浄土教の寺院や茶室がかたちづくってきた美の世界の彼方に位置している。そのような日本の最もよい部分を引き継ぎつつも、彼は狭い意味でのナショナリストではない。今世界で起こりつつあるもろもろの出来事に対して常に心を砕き、ヒューマニティ溢れるまなざしで世界を包み込みながら、素早い決断で行動を起こす意志の人でもある。

事実、彼は世界のトップビジネスマンも羨むようなスピードで世界中を駆け巡り、世界のあちこちで仕事をこなしてきた。古都ヴェネツィアからネパールの山奥まで、彼の行動範囲は大きく、建築という世界共通の言語を通してやさしく人々に語りかける。世界を代表するリーダーたちと付き合いながらも、辺境のどのように貧しい人であっても同じ態度で接し、人々の安寧と幸福を実現しようと努力するのである。

私が関心を抱いているのは、このように世界に確固とした地盤を確立した安藤忠雄が、日本を出て世界との直接的な触れ合いを始めたのはいつ頃のことであり、どのような動機によるのだろうか、ということである。日本の建築家は、丹下健三がそうであるように、モダニズムの早い段階で国際的な知名度を達成し、世界各地で仕事をするようになっているが、建築というどちらかというと狭いプロフェッションに留まらずに、まさに地球市民を進んで実践している安藤忠雄の場合は、もっと異なった背景があったに違いないと思うからである。1941年生まれの彼は、不幸な第二次大戦の時代に生まれ、同年齢の伊東豊雄や長谷川逸子と同様に、戦後のもののない時代に育ち、敗戦を契機に政治体制が一気に変わった日本という国に対して錯綜した感情を抱いて青年時代を送ったはずである。強いていえば、国家とかアカデミズムという上部構造に依拠するのではなく、日々の身の周りで体験し触れ合う人々のリアリティから出発し、自身の言語を構築してきたに違いない。その点が丹下健三とは決定的に異なるのである。

安藤が、日本での仕事の蓄積の上に、海外からの依頼で初めて仕事をこなしたのは、相次いで手がけたドイツのヴィトラ・セミナーハウス（1993）とパリのユネスコ

Living on Earth

Riichi Miyake (Architectural Historian)

Contact with the World

Tadao Ando is beyond a doubt one of the leading architects of the world. He loves Osaka, the city in which he was born and where he has spent the 60-odd years of his life, and has made an enormous contribution to that city. He is the most distinguished architect to have ever emerged from Osaka, and the people of the city can take great pride in that fact. At the same time, he is a rare individual who has given architectural expression to the superb sensibility nurtured by his native land and a representative figure of contemporary Japanese culture. His works, bold yet delicate, belong to the same world of aesthetics as Jodo-sect temples and tea houses. Although he carries on what is best in Japan, he is not a nationalist in any narrow sense. He is always concerned about events happening around the world today and displays great humanity in his view of the world; at the same time, he is a person of great determination and decisive action.

He is constantly on the move around the world at great speed, doing work in many different places. His sphere of activity stretches from the ancient city of Venice to a place deep in the mountains of Nepal. He speaks gently through architecture, the common language of humankind. His attitude is the same, whether he is with world leaders or with the poor in some remote region. Ando works to achieve peace and happiness for people.

When did Ando, who has thus firmly established his position in the world, begin to venture outside Japan and come into direct contact with the world, and what moved him to do so? Japanese architects such as Kenzo Tange gained global reputations at a relatively early stage of modernism and have worked in various parts of the world. However, Ando is much more than an architect—he is truly a citizen of the world. I feel that he is different in background from those architects whose activities are focused strictly on their professional field. Like Toyo Ito and Itsuko Hasegawa, he was born in 1941 during World War II and raised in the impoverished postwar period. In youth he must have had mixed feelings about Japan, for the country experienced a complete change in its political system after defeat in World War II. Instead of depending on some higher organization or structure such as the state or the academy, he began from the reality of his immediate environment and everyday experience and constructed his own language. It is in that that he differs decisively from someone like Tange.

Having already produced a body of work in Japan, Ando received two successive commissions which became his first overseas work: the Vitra Seminar House (1993)

瞑想空間(1995)である。前者はフランク・ゲーリー設計の美術館に近接して端正な佇まいを見せる打ち放しコンクリートのコンプレックスを計画し、後者はユネスコ本部の庭園に瞑想空間のためのパヴィリオンをつくった。だから、クロノロジカルには1990年代の初めが彼の海外での活動の始まりとされるのであるが、世界のどの地においても土地と人々を対象として強いメッセージを送っている彼の態度を眺めていると、もっと早い段階から彼は世界に対して独自の見方をもち、彼なりの貢献を行ってきたと考えた方がよさそうである。彼がまだ若い頃、ボクシングを生業としていた話は有名だが、私にはその頃から、彼の世界に対するまなざしが形成されていたように思えて仕方ない。あるとき、安藤がふと漏らした「あの頃は海外に行くチャンスというのは限られていて、ボクシングの試合で海外に出るのがてっとり早かった」という言葉が、奇妙に説得力をもって迫ってくる。その頃の安藤はすでに建築を志した青年であり、頭の中を去来する古今東西の建築がまさに遠い彼方の約束の地として彼を惹きつけていたに違いない。その飢えにも似た気持ちが彼をボクサーとなし、その上で建築を修めさせるに到る原動力であったのではないだろうか。

1960年代当時、日本の若者は、日本国内の閉塞的な状況に嫌気がさして、さまざまな手立てを使って海外を目指していた。アルバイトで貯めた資金を元手にシベリア鉄道でヨーロッパに向かう者、東南アジアや中近東でその日暮らしの仕事をしながら、ゆっくりと西に向かうもの、キューバの革命にあこがれてカリブ海を目指す者など、いかに日本を離れて異文化の地に到り着くかが大きなテーマであった。エスタブリッシュメントに与し、国家のパトロネージのもとで海外を往復していた丹下健三の世代とは動機が根本的に異なっていた。そのようなときに安藤は、それこそ名もなきボクサーとして鞄ひとつでタイに渡り、その足でアジアとヨーロッパの建築をつぶさに見て回った。この地べたを這う貴重な体験こそが、彼の人間性をかたちづくり、土地と人間に対する尊厳の念を培ったのではないだろうか。訪れた土地で人々の生活を見聞し、風土の中に展開する建築と風景の一切合切をスケッチブックに必死に描きとめている安藤の姿が容易に想像できるのである。建築を単なる物理的なモニュメントとみなすのではなく、それを構想し支えてきた地元の人々との交感の上に、敬虔なる巡礼者としての純粋性に到達したに違いない。肉体を酷使した荒々しい行の上に一点の曇りもない美の世界に到り着く、行者の世界をみずから追体験してみたのである。シトー会の建築に限りない共感を抱く安藤は、単にル・コルビュジエの影響でそのル・トロネ修道院に辿り着いたのではなく、自身の遍歴の必然的な帰結として純粋なる石の建築に巡り会うのである。建築を学び始める最初の頃から、このように世界に対するまなざしを培い、様式や技術だけでは語れない

in Germany and the UNESCO Meditation Space (1995) in Paris. The former is an exposed concrete complex of dignified appearance adjacent to an art museum designed by Frank Gehry, and the latter is a pavilion for meditation in the garden of the UNESCO headquarters. Strictly speaking, therefore, he began his activities overseas in the early 1990s. However, what he does is to send powerful messages that have land and people as their subject, no matter where in the world he may be working. In all likelihood, therefore, he developed his own perspective on the world and began to contribute in his way to that world much earlier. His early career as a boxer is well-known. I believe his view of the world developed from around that time. A remark that Ando once let slip ("Opportunities to go abroad in those days were limited, and taking part in an overseas boxing tournament was a quick way to get such an opportunity") has the ring of truth. By that time, Ando already aspired to be an architect; no doubt images of the architecture of all eras and countries beckoned to him like the promised land. A hunger-like feeling made him a boxer and became the driving force that led him to pursue architecture.

Impatient with insular conditions in the country, Japanese youths tried to go abroad by various means in the 1960s. Leaving Japan behind and going to different cultures was a major theme of that period. Some, clutching funds saved up from part-time work, headed to Europe by way of the Siberian Railway; others, working as day laborers as they traveled across Southeast Asia and the Near East, gradually headed west; still others, enamored of the Cuban revolution, headed to the Caribbean. Their motives were fundamentally different from those of Tange's generation, whose members belonged to the establishment and went abroad under the patronage of the state. Ando went to Thailand as a nameless, penniless boxer and from there traveled on to examine architecture in Asia and Europe. No doubt that valuable experience grounded in reality shaped his humanity and nurtured his sense of the dignity of land and human beings. One can easily imagine him observing the way people lived in the places he visited and frantically drawing any and every building and landscape in his sketchbook. He did not see buildings simply as physical monuments; through empathy with local people who had conceived and maintained those buildings, he achieved the purity of a devout pilgrim. He experienced for himself the life of the ascetic who arrives at a cloudless world of beauty by subjecting his body to a course of rough self discipline. Ando, who is greatly attracted to Cistercian architecture, did not visit the Abbey of Le Thoronet simply because of Le Corbusier but came upon that pure architecture of stone as the natural consequence of his own travels. He can be said to have nurtured from the start of his study of architecture such a view of the world and to have intuitively understood

建築の根源的な部分を直観的に会得していたといってもよさそうである。彼の強靭なヒューマニズムの根底にはこのような伏線があるのを知ってもらいたい。

土地を読む

以上のような前提をもって安藤忠雄の国外での建築を眺めると、建築という行為が単なるクライアントに対するサービスではなく、人間の創造力の核心を指し示すものであり、それを梃子としてそれこそ地球まで動かしてみせようとする彼の強い信念が見えてくる。それを彼の建築というプロフェッションに対する責任感と理解しても構わないし、あるいは長年の経験の上に打ち立てられたヒューマニズムの発現とみなすこともできそうだ。仕事を依頼する側の人間も、そのことを期待して彼のひらめきと行動力に賭けてみたのであろう。これまでの海外の仕事は、ミュージアムの設計を依頼されるケースが多かった。それも人類の遺産ともいうべきすぐれたコレクションをもつ美術館であることが多く、施主側の安藤に対する気持ちがそれだけでもよく伝わってくるといってよい。

安藤は日本国内においても多くの美術館や博物館を手がけてきた。瀬戸内海に浮かぶ小島につくられた直島コンテンポラリーアートミュージアム（1992）は島の風光明媚な土地に埋め込まれた美しい風景式の美術館であり、世界から多くの客を呼び寄せてきた。逆に東京上野の国立国会図書館子ども図書館（2002）は狭隘で厳しい敷地条件の中でそれこそ地下も含めて内部をつくり替え、そこに小宇宙を獲得した子ども向けの博物館である。外から見れば既成の古い建造物を尊重し、ささやかな入口を設けるだけの建築であるのが、一度中に入れば、あっと驚くくらいの大胆な空間が展開する。このように敷地に課せられた条件を的確に読み取り、それが難しければ難しいほど燃えるのが安藤の性格ともいってよい。外部空間に風景としての品格を与えると同時に、内部では自律した建築の美学が自己展開することによって独自の空間に到り着く。建築が建築たる所以をとことん追い求め、建築の可能性を徹底的に切り開く安藤の姿勢は、国内外の多くに人々の賛同を得、共感を呼んだ。禁欲的といってもよい純粋な空間がミュージアムとしての可能性を一気に高めるのである。アメリカやヨーロッパのコレクターや美術館関係者が、安藤にミュージアムの設計依頼を行ったのもこのような経緯からに違いない。

例えばドイツのルール地方でデュッセルドルフ郊外のホンブロイッヒの地に環境型の新たなミュージアムの建設を考えていたアートコレクターのカール・ハインリヒ・ミューラーからの打診に対して、安藤がその情熱に強く惹かれたことが新たな美

that essence of architecture which cannot be explained merely by style or technology. Such preparations provided the basis for his tenacious humanism.

Reading the Land

If one considers Ando's work overseas with the above in mind, one begins to see that architectural design for him is not simply a service rendered to a client but an act that goes to the very core of human creativity, and that he is intent on using that as a lever to try to move the world. It can be understood as an expression of his sense of responsibility to the architectural profession or as the declaration of a humanism developed from long experience. Those who commission him no doubt wager on his energy and inspiration in hopes that it is indeed so. Many of his commissions overseas up to now have been to design museums—large art museums with superb collections that represent the assets of humankind—and that in itself shows the high expectations clients have of Ando.

Ando has also designed many museums in Japan. Naoshima Contemporary Art Museum (1992), built on a small island in the Inland Sea of Japan, is a beautiful landscape-style museum embedded in a scenic place and has attracted many visitors from all over the world. By contrast, the International Library of Children's Literature (2002) in Ueno, Tokyo, is on a small site with many constraints; by transforming the interior, including the basement, of a preexisting building, Ando was able to create a museum that is a world-in-miniature for children. He has respected the old building on the outside and added only a modest entrance. Once inside, however, visitors discover spaces of amazing boldness. Thus, Ando will read the conditions imposed on a site; the more difficult those conditions are, the greater will be the enthusiasm with which he takes up the challenge they pose. He arrives at his own distinctive space by endowing outside space with the dignity of a landscape while at the same time developing an autonomous architectural aesthetic of his own inside. Ando's stance—his dedication to the pursuit of the essence of architecture and the full development of architecture's potential—has gained him the support and sympathy of many people both inside and outside Japan. Pure spaces of an ascetic character enhance the possibilities of museums. That no doubt accounts for the commissions Ando has received to design museums from collectors and museum people in the US and Europe.

For example, Karl-Heinrich Müller, who was thinking of constructing a new environment-oriented museum in the Hombroich district outside Düsseldorf in the Ruhr region of Germany, sounded out Ando. Ando was attracted by the collector's passion

術館建設のきっかけとなった。ミューラーは、広大なホンブロイッヒの地に「インゼル・ホンブロイッヒ」と名づけられたアートコンプレックスを構想し、かつてNATO軍のミサイル基地があったこの土地一帯を取得した。その結果として、12ヘクタールにおよぶ土地のところどころにギャラリーやアトリエが配され周囲の田園風景と一体となった環境志向のエコパークが成立した。ミューラーに加えて建築家のエルヴィン・ヘーリヒや彫刻家の西川勝人らがその構想の推進役となり、1994年以降、「忘れ去られた地球の片隅」に環境芸術の足跡を刻んでいった。昨今脚光を浴びているIBAブランデンブルクの例を引くまでもなく、ドイツは近代の産業化を通して失われた環境の回復に強い意欲を燃やしており、ライン河の流域圏を形成するホンブロイッヒの地も同様の問題意識を共有する人間たちが集まって環境と芸術をつなげる運動が繰り広げられていた。

ミューラーからの依頼によって安藤がミュージアムの計画を始めたのは1994年のことであり、その2年後にはその入口をかたちづくる湾曲したコンクリート壁が築かれ、新たな建設事業のマニフェストとなった。安藤の設計は早い段階で完成していたが、その後、財団側の資金調達などに手間取り、ミュージアム本体の工事が始まるのはそれから5年を待たなければならなかった。ある意味では、彼の設計図が担保となって資金を集めるわけだが、それだけの「担保力」があり国際的な信用があるのが安藤の建築である。海外のプロジェクト、特にアート関係の企画は、当初からはっきりとした資金計画が決まって着手されることが普通の日本と異なり、このようにある種の環境運動を前提とした篤志家的なアプローチで始められることが少なくない。建築家にとっては忍耐が要求され、下手をするとプロジェクト倒れになる危険性が高いということであるが、みずからが運動の渦中にあれば、時間がかかることを厭わない。そこに登場したのが齢90歳を数えるマリアンネ・ランゲン夫人で、亡き夫ヴィクトール・ランゲンの遺志を継いで、自身のコレクションの展示施設としてこの美術館建設の継続を申し出た。ランゲン夫人はミューラーの運動に共鳴し、自身が所有する1950年来の日本美術や現代美術のコレクションを普通のミュージアムで展示するのではなく、失われた環境の再生の上に位置づけていくことに情熱を傾けた。土地と一体となったアートと建築の拠点がつくり出されるのである。従って、その拠点たるランゲン美術館は、たまたま安藤忠雄を建築家として指名したというなりゆきの話ではなく、当初から安藤忠雄でなければならない必然性があった。安藤のもつ自然と空間に対する強い直観力がこの土地の力を増幅し、いうなれば新しい風景がつくられるのである。そのアプローチは芸術家のそれと変わらない。即断を得意とする安藤がここまで忍耐強くプロジェクトの持続にこだわるのは、彼自身

for the project. Müller had conceived an art complex called Hombroich Island to be built on a large tract of land he had acquired that had formerly been a NATO missile site. Galleries and ateliers were to be distributed over a site of over 12 hectares, forming an environmentally-sensitive eco-park integrated with the surrounding pastoral landscape. In addition to Müller, people such as the architect Erwin Heerich and the sculptor Masato Nishikawa were in favor of the concept, and since 1994, works of environmental art had been created in a once-forgotten corner of the world. The much-discussed case of IBA Brandenburg is but one of the many efforts being made in Germany to restore environments lost through modern industrialization. The Hombroich district, formed by the Rhine River basin, had attracted similarly concerned people who developed a movement to link the environment and art.

Commissioned by Müller, Ando began the museum project in 1994. Two years later, he built the curving concrete wall that shapes its entrance, and it became a manifesto for the new construction project. Ando's design was finished at an early stage in the project, but the foundation had to raise funds, delaying the beginning of construction of the museum proper for five years. In a sense, his design drawings served as security for fundraising purposes. It was because Ando's architecture is trusted internationally that they could be used for such a purpose. Unlike Japan, where projects usually begin only after financial plans have been finalized, projects overseas, especially art-related projects, not infrequently begin in a philanthropic mode, premised as in this case on a type of environmental movement. Patience is demanded of an architect—there is a danger of the project falling through if things are not done right—but if the architect himself is closely involved in the movement, he does not mind it taking time. This was when the 90-year-old Marianne Langen came on the scene. She proposed to continue the construction of the museum so that, in keeping with the wishes of her late husband Victor Langen, their own art collection might be exhibited in the facility. She was sympathetic with Müller's movement and became enthusiastic about the idea of housing her collection of Japanese and contemporary art, begun in the 1950s, not in an ordinary museum but in a project that would help revive a lost environment. The goal was to create a center of art and architecture that was integrated with the land. Thus, Ando did not just happen to be named the architect of the Langen Foundation/Hombroich Museum. There was from the start an inevitability about the commission—the architect had to be Ando. Ando's power of intuition with respect to nature and space amplifies the potential of land; one might say he creates a new landscape. His approach is the same as that of an artist. Ando, who prides himself on being able to come to quick decisions, has insisted on persevering to this extent with the project because he

がこの土地に感情移入を行い、建築にみずからの生命を注ぎ込んでいるからである。ランゲン夫妻とは同志的な絆によって結ばれているといってもよいだろう。

ミュージアムが環境をつくる

インゼル・ホンブロイッヒのランゲン美術館は、プロジェクトの開始から数えて10年後の2004年にオープンした。安藤自身にとっては何度も断念しかけたプロジェクトであるに違いないが、長い時間をかけて実現に到ったというその持続力がインゼル・ホンブロイッヒの壮大な環境計画をそのまま物語っているようにも思われる。広い土地を利用して、景観が多様に変化するところは安藤のいつもの手法であるが、ここでは建築に内側のコンクリートと外側のガラス面という二重の皮殻を導入したところが特徴的である。入口の湾曲した壁を潜り抜けると水面に沿って桜の並木があり、その奥まったところにミュージムが位置している。鏡面となった水面にガラスの輪郭が投影され、建築の全体像が映し出される。当初の段階で安藤は45度の角度で接するふたつの直方体を構想したが、最後までそのジオメトリーが継続され、コンクリートの壁体の上にガラスのスキンが被さる二重皮殻となっている点が特徴的である。ガラスによって構成される透明な地表の空間から突如として地下の隠された空間に導かれるのも、安藤が得意とする方法である。地下にはふたつの並行する直方体が挿入され、その間に配された階段状となったサンクンガーデンからふんだんの光が注ぎ込み、地下という印象を与えない。美術館が要求するプログラムに対応させて地上部分を日本美術のコレクション、地下の空間を近現代美術と分節させているが、その全体をほどよくつなぎ、美術館という空間を人間の身体感覚に対応させて奥へ奥へと展開させていく。前景と後景を巧みに絡ませながら、壁や階段、ブリッジなどを配置していく。この日本の回遊式庭園を思わせるような絶妙な配置こそが安藤の建築の神髄であり、地上に展開する雄大なエコパークの風景に対置して繊細な織物のような小宇宙がかたちづくられるのである。

ミュージアムにとっての命は当然所蔵作品つまりコレクションであるが、その所蔵者たるコレクターとの同志的な関係から始まったという点では、例えばセントルイスのピューリッツァー美術館(2001)でも同様である。ピューリッツァー家は報道・文学関係のピューリッツァー賞で世界に知られており、セントルイスを代表する名家である。そのコレクションの落ち着く先を決めるにあたって、ドイツ的な環境論の世界とは大きく異なった文脈から始まったことは間違いないが、セントルイスという中西部の都市に対してどのような貢献を果たすかという使命感から計画が具体

feels himself to be in accord with the land and because he puts so much of himself into architecture. He and the Langens were kindred spirits.

A Museum that Creates the Environment

The Langen Foundation/Hombroich Museum opened in 2004, ten years after the project commenced. Ando himself must have nearly given up on the project a number of times, but tenacity ultimately enabled him to see the project to completion. In fact, the grand environmental plan of Hombroich Island itself is all about tenacity. Ando creates changes of view in diverse ways, making effective use of the extensive land, but that is a technique he has often adopted. What is new here is the introduction of a double-layer structure, with concrete inside and glass outside. Passing the curving wall, the visitor finds cherry trees lining a pool at the far end of which is the museum. The water reflects the outline of the glass and the overall image of the building. At an early stage in the project, Ando conceived two boxes connected at a 45 degree angle. That geometry, which survives in the final scheme, and the double-layer organization of the glass skin over concrete walls are what make the building distinctive. Guiding a visitor from a transparent, glass-enclosed space at ground level to a hidden space underground is another favorite technique of Ando's. Two parallel boxes are inserted into the ground, and an abundance of light enters through a stepped sunken garden situated between them, so that the space does not seem like it is underground. In response to the program presented by the museum, Ando accommodated the collection of Japanese art in the aboveground portion and the modern and contemporary artworks belowground. The parts are judiciously connected to form a whole, and the museum spaces, keyed to the senses, guide visitors deeper and deeper inside. Walls, stairways and bridges are carefully arranged, while foreground and background are skillfully intertwined. This exquisite arrangement, evocative of a Japanese tour-style garden, is quintessentially Ando. The grand landscape of the eco-park aboveground is set off by this delicate, textile-like world-in-miniature.

The artworks in its possession, that is, its art collection is naturally of vital importance to an art museum. The Pulitzer Foundation for the Arts (2001) in St. Louis and the Langen Foundation, however, are similar in that the former project also began with the forging of a close bond between Ando and the collector. The Pulitzer family of St. Louis is known throughout the world for the Pulitzer journalistic and literary awards given annually in its name. The process of determining a place to accommodate its collection of art began in a context very different from that of the environmental move-

化されてきた経緯は大変興味深い。

ピューリッツァー夫妻が自身のコレクションのためにミュージアムを構想したのは1990年代初めに遡るからホンブロイッヒ／ランゲン美術館よりも前になる。安藤は既に1991年には夫妻からその計画を打診されており、夫ジョゼフ・ピューリッツァー・ジュニアが亡くなって計画の見直しが迫られたものの、未亡人となったエミリーから1993年に敷地を変えて再度設計を依頼される。新たに選ばれた敷地は、中心部をかたちづくるミシシッピ河岸から若干北側にずれた場所で、今日では廃屋や空き地が目立つ典型的なインナーシティ現象の進んだ地区であった。アメリカの都市問題をそのまま体現したようなこの場所に貴重なコレクションをもったミュージアムをつくるという大胆なアイディアは、投資家ならば尻込みしてしまうような場所に積極的に入り込み、率先して都市文化の構築をはかるというピューリッツァー家の気概がそのまま表れたものと理解してもよいだろう。安藤が意気投合したのはまさにその点である。コレクションが街を活性化させるのに対して、建築は街を救う。

安藤の建築は、その幾何学的な整合性から閉じた建築とみられることが少なくないが、実際は正反対である。彼の建築に胚胎した強靭な構築力ゆえに、周囲に街がおのずから形成されていくということである。それも一元的な街ではない。ここで指摘しておかなければならないのは、彼の都市的な理念は、ル・コルビュジエが主導したプラン・ヴォワザン的な強権的かつ一律の再開発ではなく、きわめて控え目であるということだ。実際、外部に露出しているのは、外国人にしばしば「絹のような」と表現される柔らかなコンクリートの被膜のみで、しかも高さを抑えられて、見た眼には本当に小さな建築のようでもある。しかし門を潜ってひとたび内部に入り込めば、奥の先にまた奥が続く深遠でドラマティックな建築を体験することができる。そのような技が可能になったのも、ひとえに脆弱な日本の街並みを相手に厳しい法的規制をかいくぐりながら少しでも質の高い空間をつくろうとした彼の忍耐強い態度によるわけで、そのようにつくり上げてきた彼の一連の作品が行き着いたのは、建築の内と外を分節することで街のスケールと建築内部の空間を調整するという方法に他ならない。「閾（しきい）」を介して外と内を切り分けるやり方といってもよい。

かくして都市に対する建築の構えが、西欧の伝統的なファサード主義ではなく、閾をはっきりと表示することで領域区分の考え方に到る。その禁欲的で耐えるような姿勢が、乱雑な日本の街でも、大柄で装飾的な建築が崩壊の危機に瀕しているアメリカのインナーシティでもすこぶる有効な手段となりえたのである。何よりもじっくりと時間をかけて街並みを再生する。それも伝統的なファサードの連続を復活させるのではなく、ひとつひとつの敷地に配されたモダンでダイナミックな建築がも

ment in Germany. The family, however, had a sense of mission—a desire to contribute in some way to the Midwestern city of St. Louis—and the process by which that was fulfilled is quite interesting.

Joseph and Emily Rauh Pulitzer conceived the idea of a museum for their collection in the early 1990s, before the Langen Foundation/Hombroich Museum. The couple sounded out Ando about the plan in 1991. Although the plan was reexamined after Mr. Pulitzer died, Mrs. Pulitzer asked Ando to design the museum once more for a different site in 1993. The newly selected site was slightly north of the bank of the Mississippi River which shapes the central district. The site was in a typical inner-city district with many abandoned buildings and vacant lots. The bold idea to create a museum for the valuable collection in a place that seemed to embody many of America's urban problems can be understood as an expression of the courageous determination of the Pulitzers to go into a place most investors would shun and to take the lead in developing an urban culture there. It was on that point that Ando saw eye to eye with the Pulitzers. The collection might help revitalize the city, just as architecture might help save it.

Ando's architecture is frequently regarded as closed because of its geometrical coherence, but the truth is the exact opposite. The tenacious creative power of a building by him helps shape the city around it. And the city that is shaped is by no means one-dimensional. It needs to be pointed out that his urban doctrine is quite moderate and does not call for anything like the uniform and high-handed redevelopment of the Plan Voisin-type espoused by Le Corbusier. In fact, the only thing exposed on the outside of the Pulitzer Foundation is the soft concrete membrane that non-Japanese observers often describe as "silken." Moreover, the height is kept low, so that the museum does truly appear to be a small building. However, once visitors enter, they are able to experience a dramatic building of seemingly limitless depth. Ando developed the skill he demonstrates here by laboring to create spaces that are as high in quality as possible in fragile Japanese townscapes under severe legal constraints. In the works he created in Japan, he developed a method for reconciling the urban scale with the spaces inside the building by segmenting the architectural interior from the exterior. One might call it a method for cutting and dividing outside from inside by means of thresholds.

A building by Ando does not present a façade to the city as traditional Western buildings do. Instead, it presents a threshold that represents the demarcation of a separate domain. This ascetic, tenacious stance proved an extremely effective means, not only in Japanese cities without order, but in an American inner city district where large, ornamental buildings faced imminent destruction. He slowly and thoroughly revived

つ空間の豊かさを回復しようというのが主眼ではないだろうか。建築が街を救いうるという揺るぎない信念の背景には、時間をかけて地道に築かれてきたこのような方法論が横たわっているのである。日本であっても外国であってもそれは普遍的である。

ピューリッツァー美術館の建物は、起伏のある台地の一画に建てられており、丘の下にはテレビ局や大学、フリーメーソン本部など、やや不思議な建物が並んでいるが、広場を介して丘を登ったこの辺りはむしろ背の低い建物が似合っている。ここでもふたつの直方体を並行させ、その間に空間を配する手法がとられている。左右の高さを違えているので、非対称のヴォリュームが空間に動きを与えている。ホンブロイッヒ／ランゲン美術館ではサンクンガーデンであった空間が、ここでは池となり、コンクリートの壁を映し出す鏡としての役割が与えられている。悠久の時間の中で動くことを頑なに拒む不動のコンクリートの存在に対して、わずかの風に対しても波紋を残して音もなく揺れ動く水面の移ろいやすさが心地よい。

ジオメトリーの具現化

ホンブロイッヒ／ランゲン美術館やピューリッツァー美術館の建築が、コレクターとともに時間をかけて進めたプロジェクトであったのに対し、同じミュージアムであってもフォートワースの現代美術館は国際コンペの結果として6者の案から選ばれたもので、設計に到る経緯がまったく異なっている。コンペは1997年に実施され、安藤案が首席になった後、実施設計を経て1999年に着工し、2002年には竣工した。総床面積で14,820m^{2}を占める大規模な建築であり、その点から見ると計画から完成までが5年であったというのはむしろ短いくらいのきわめて順調な進行具合であった。別の言い方をすれば日本での公共美術館と同程度の設計施工期間で済んだということである。

この建築には日本での蓄積とアメリカでの経験が十分に反映されていた。震災後の神戸で実現された兵庫県立美術館（2001）も同じ1997年のプロポーザルで安藤の参加が決められたものであり、この頃から長方形の箱を内側にコンクリートのボックス、外側をガラスの外被とする二重皮殻の空間構成が主題となってくる。美術館であれば貴重なアートワークは外光から保護し、セキュリティの面でも十分な管理が必要である。他方、内部も公共空間の延長として開放性を保ち、周囲の都市や田園のランドスケープを採り入れる上で、ガラスの空間は大きな意味をもつ。安藤はこのガラスによって導かれる空間を、日本の伝統的な建築になぞらえて「縁」と位置づけ

the townscape. He does not revive the continuity of traditional façades; instead his chief concern seems to be to restore the richness of space of modern, dynamic buildings on individual sites. This methodology, developed slowly but steadily, is behind his unshakable conviction that architecture can save the city, in Japan or overseas.

The Pulitzer Foundation for the Arts stands on undulating high ground; motley buildings including a television station, a university and the local headquarters of the Freemasons are at the bottom of the hill, but low buildings seem to suit the area on top of the hill. Here too he has placed two boxes side by side and created a space between them. The two boxes are different in height, and the asymmetry makes the space dynamic. The space that is a sunken garden in the Langen Foundation/Hombroich Musuem is here a pool that serves to reflect the concrete walls. The slightest breeze sends ripples on the water that silently cause the reflections to waver. This flux is in pleasing contrast to the permanence and immobility of the concrete.

The Embodiment of Geometry

By contrast to the Langen Foundation/Hombroich Museum and the Pulitzer Foundation for the Arts, which are projects that were developed slowly over time together with their respective collectors, the Modern Art Museum of Fort Worth, though it too is a museum, was the result of an entirely different process, an international competition in which Ando's scheme was chosen from six proposals. The competition was held in 1997; after Ando's scheme was selected and the final design was produced, construction was begun in 1999 and completed in 2002. The museum has a total floor area of 14,820 square meters. Thanks to its smooth implementation, the project took only five years from planning to completion, which is a short period of time for such a large building. It required about the same length of time for design and construction as a public art museum in Japan.

This building reflects Ando's work in Japan and his experience in the US. Ando's participation in the Hyogo Prefectural Museum of Art (2001), realized in Kobe after the Hanshin-Awaji Earthquake, was also based on a proposal of 1997. It was around that time that he began to adopt double-layered spatial compositions: long concrete boxes wrapped on the outside by another layer of glass. Protecting valuable artworks from outside light and providing adequate security are requirements for an art museum. The glass space has significance: as an extension of public space, it is open in character and affords views of the surrounding city or countryside. Likening this glass-enclosed space to a feature of traditional Japanese architecture, Ando calls this an *en*

ているが、その種の相互貫入的な共有スペースの登場は、安藤にとってはむしろ最近のことである。大震災の後で復興を遂げた街並みに対して開き、同時に港の眺望をも採り込む必要のあった神戸の美術館と、周囲の広々とした緑溢れる風景に対してやはり一体感を生み出すことが痛感されたフォートワースとでは、条件が意外と似ていたのだろうか。外側に庇を張り出させる手法も共通しているが、これはまさしく縁の上に張り出した軒先という日本の伝統空間の現代的な解釈に他ならない。

だからといってフォートワース現代美術館が日本的であるかというと決してそうではない。何よりもこの地にはルイス・カーンによるキンベル美術館（1972）があり、その圧倒的な存在感が周囲を支配している。その敷地に隣接した約4.5ヘクタールの土地に新たな美術館を建てるということ自体が大胆な試みであるが、それゆえに設計競技に参加した建築家たちが皆カーンに対して恐怖心にも似た気持ちに襲われたことは想像に難くない。街並みがコンパクトにまとまるのではなく、モータリゼーションに伴って広くネットワーク上に展開するアメリカの都市では、文化的なコアをつくることが意外と難しい。しかし、キンベル美術館を核として整備されたフォートワースのこの一帯は、暑いテキサスの気候の中でオアシス的な風情を伴い、心身ともに人々の憩いの場所となってきた。古典的なプロポーションをもって豊かな緑の姿を現すキンベル美術館に凛とした佇まいを感じるのである。

このロケーションを与えられて安藤がいかに苦心したかは、彼の残した一群のスケッチからも窺える。当初の段階で、キンベルを構成する6本のヴォールトに対応して、それと直交する6本の直方体を並べたのもカーンへのオマージュに他ならない。その並べ方も、キンベルを中心とした軸線を設定し、1本が長く突き出した配置から徐々に変化して軸線に沿ってパブリックな部分をまとめて2本の長い直方体としていく。最終的には、6本が5本に変わり、その比例関係も5：3のプロポーションを巧みに配し、カーンの黄金比とほぼ同じ形式に近づいていく。

建築家にとってジオメオリーは、形態と空間を生み出す根本的な原理であるが、生来の直観力をもった安藤は、構築的かつ直截なかたちでそれを表してきた。日本人の建築家には珍しいといってもよい。西欧的なラショナリズム、つまりはル・コルビュジエの系譜に連なるといわれるのがこの点である。住吉の長屋（1976）から始まる長い道程は、鉄筋コンクリートという素材をもってそのジオメトリーを実体化し、空間化していく過程であった。記念碑的な意味をもつ光の教会（1989）や直島コンテンポラリーアートミュージアムを眺めてみれば、建築の大小とは関係なく、形式のもつ自律的な力でかたちを生み出し、場がつくられていくことがよくわかるだろう。その力こそがジオメトリーなのである。

(veranda) space, but this type of shared, interpenetrating space has emerged in his work only in recent times. Conditions in the two projects—the museum in Kobe, which affords views of the townscape reconstructed after the earthquake and whose program required views of the harbor, and the museum in Fort Worth, which Ando wanted to integrate with the spacious landscape outside—were unexpectedly similar. The way the roof is extended out is the same in both buildings; this is surely a contemporary interpretation of the extended roof over the veranda in traditional Japanese spaces.

That is not to say that the Modern Art Museum of Fort Worth is Japanese in character. That museum is located close to the Kimbell Art Museum (1972) by Louis Kahn, whose powerful influence is felt throughout the area. Just the idea of putting up a new art museum on approximately 4.5 hectares of land adjacent to the Kimbell was a bold one; it is not difficult to imagine all the architects who participated in the competition being intimidated by Kahn. Creating a cultural center in a city in the US in difficult, because motorization causes townscapes to develop in spread-out networks. However, the area around the Kimbell has become a place for physical and spiritual relaxation, thanks in part to its landscape which is like an oasis in Texas' hot climate. The Kimbell, with its classical proportions and verdant greenery, projects an image of great dignity.

The sketches Ando produced show how much the architect struggled, having been given this location. In the first stage, in clear homage to Kahn's building, he arranged six boxes set at right angles to Kimbell's six vaults. He established an axis centered on the Kimbell. An arrangement in which one box was extended was further elaborated so that eventually two long boxes accommodating public areas were placed parallel to that axis. In the end, the scheme changed to one with five boxes instead of six, and their proportions became 5:3, which is quite close to the golden ratio employed by Kahn.

For an architect, geometry is the basic principle generating shape and space. Ando, who has keen powers of intuition, has demonstrated that both creatively and directly. He is rare in that respect among Japanese architects. That is why he is said to belong to the tradition of Western rationalism, that is the line of Le Corbusier. The long journey that began with the Rowhouse in Sumiyoshi (1976) has been a process of giving substance to and translating into space that geometry by means of reinforced concrete. If we examine milestones on that journey such as the Church of the Light (1989) and Naoshima Contemporary Art Museum, we see that, whether the buildings are large or small, he generates shapes and creates places through the autonomous power of form. That power is geometry.

If we look at his work in Japan, Ando has often generated spaces in response, not to the uncertainties of the surrounding townscape, but to topography. However, at least in

彼の日本での仕事を眺めてみると、周囲の街並みといったやや不確定な要素以上に、建築が拠って立つ地形を手がかりとして空間を生成させていくことが多いが、ここフォートワース現代美術館に限ってみると、何よりもそれ自体がアウラを発するルイス・カーンの作品と向かい合うことによって、建築の自律的な形式が生み出されていった。「向かい合う」という受動的な言い方よりもサムライ的な語感を含む「真剣勝負」という語で読み替えた方が的確だろうか。建築家には建築家なりの強い個性があり、その究極の到達点が傑作として歴史の中に刻印される。その傑作のひとつに対比されることは名誉であると同時に、とんでもなく難しい仕事を引き受けたことにもなる。10年ほど前にニームのメゾン・カレ（紀元前19年頃）の正面にカレ・ダール（1993）を設計することとなったノーマン・フォスターの苦労が偲ばれよう。その時点で、従来実践してきたコンクリートの閉じた系から脱け出して、開放的で透明な空間を選んだのは賢明であった。この土地全体の風景を、小ぶりながら圧倒的な緊張感を漂わせるキンベル美術館を消点とした透視図法的な構図の中に組み込み、その手前に置かれた現代美術館の透明な箱がすべて奥のキンベル美術館に収斂するようにしたのである。はるかに大きなスケールを有していたにせよ、その存在が風景と溶け合うようになったといってもよい。「縁」と位置づけられる中間領域を伴った方法論の登場が、先達の影をあえて踏まないようにする安藤忠雄のやや控えめな表現に大いに貢献したことはいうまでもない。

歴史との葛藤

海外の仕事で特に安藤が労力を費やしたと思われるのは、ヨーロッパの圧倒的な歴史に直面したときであろう。歴史といっても教科書的な意味合いで通り一遍の時間の流れを指すのではなく、それこそ古代からの遺産がそこかしこに蓄積され、新しい文物の出現を頑なに拒むかのようなどこまでも保守に徹した歴史なのである。その典型ともいえるのがヴェネツィアであり、その周辺のヴェネト地方なのだ。

安藤が世界ブランドとなったベネトンのアートディレクター、オリヴィエロ・トスカーニと知り合ったのは1980年代半ばのことである。あの激しい広告戦略を展開したその人である。その後に長きに渡る付き合いの中から、ベネトン社がヴェネト地方に計画するアートスクールの設計を打診されるようになる。1992年のことである。ベネトン社は、イタリア企業の多くがそうであるように、創始者ルチアーノ・ベネトンの出身地であるトレヴィソを拠点とし、1950年代の発足から一貫して地域に根づいて発展を遂げてきた。派手やかな広告のイメージとは裏腹に、安易にミラノ

Fort Worth, he has produced an architecturally autonomous form through confrontation with a work by Kahn that has its own aura. I say "confrontation" rather than some passive form of response; it is a game in earnest—what the samurai would call "a duel with real swords." Buildings can have strong personalities, and those with the strongest personalities are the ones history labels masterpieces. To be given an opportunity to design a work that cannot help but be compared to a masterpiece is both an honor and an enormous challenge. We recall the difficulties encountered by Norman Foster in designing the Carré d'Art (1993) in front of the Maison Carré (c. 19 B.C.) in Nîmes. It was wise of Ando to depart from his established vocabulary of closed concrete forms and to choose to work in open, transparent spaces. He incorporated the Kimbell, which, though compact, is a work of tremendous intensity, into the overall landscape, making it the vanishing point for a perspectival composition. The transparent boxes of the Modern Art Museum were conceived as the foreground of a composition all converging on the Kimbell. Although his building is far larger in size, Ando managed to make it blend into the landscape. Needless to say, the emergence of a methodology of intermediate domains similar to the Japanese veranda greatly contributed to the success of Ando's relatively low-profile work, in which care was taken not to upstage the museum by Kahn.

Entanglement with History

Overseas works that confront Europe's long history has no doubt required special effort on Ando's part. By "history" I do not mean a conventional, textbook-like flow of time, but a thoroughly conservative history that hoards all assets from ancient times and obstinately rejects new culture and institutions. Venice and the surrounding Veneto region can be said to be representative of such a history.

Ando first met Oliviero Toscani, the art director of the global brand Benetton in the mid-1980s. Toscani is the man who developed Benetton's controversial advertising strategy. Their long acquaintance led to Ando being sounded out about designing an art school that Benetton was planning in the Veneto region. That took place in 1992. Like many Italian corporations, Benetton is centered in the birthplace of its founder, in this case Treviso, where Luciano Benetton was born. Since its start in the 1950s, Benetton has had its roots in the region. In sharp contrast to the flamboyant image of its ads, the company has chosen to expand production in the middle of the beautiful countryside of Treviso instead of moving to Milan. Local people take great pride in the company. The headquarters, housed in a remodeled eighteenth-century villa, is inside

に居を移したりはせず、トレヴィソの美しい田園風景の中で生産を拡大してきた歴史があり、地元の住民にとっても大いなる誇りであった。トレヴィソの町の中には、18世紀のヴィラを改装した本社があり、カルロ・スカルパやその子トビア・スカルパが一族の建築を手がけてきた。一族が所有するトレヴィソ郊外のヴィラを核として、インターナショナルなデザイン研究教育機関を設立し、ベネトンの広告部門を入れるとともに、メディアデザインの学校を整備するというのが新たに浮かび上がった目標であった。そこでベネトンのノウハウを生かして少数教育に徹した戦略的な拠点をつくり上げるのというのがトスカーニの目論みであった。会長であるルチアーノ・ベネトンに引き合わされ、会長の強い信頼を得た安藤は、最終的にその計画からデザインに関する一切を任され、古いヴィラの改装とそれに付属する新たな施設の設計を手がけることになる。田園風景の到る所に近世のヴィラが散らばるヴェネト地方であれば、既に荒れ果てていたベネトン社のヴィラは18世紀のもので、それほど大きな価値をもっていなかった。事実、文化財にも指定されていない。これを取り壊して新しい施設を建設することも可能であったが、安藤はあえてその道は選ばず、古いヴィラとその付属棟をそのまま残し、内部に全面的な改装を加えるとともに、地下を掘って新しい施設を地中に埋め込む方法をとった。その安藤の姿勢に、先人たちが育んできた歴史に対する謙虚で真摯な態度を感じるのは私だけではない。

FABRICA（2000）と命名されたこのアートスクールを構成するジオメトリーは、相互に交差するいくつかの軸線と敷地の中ほどに位置する楕円形から成立している。バロック的な動きを感じさせる空間構成である。ヴィラの背後には一面の池が設けられ、その真ん中を貫く軸線を示すかのように円柱が一列に並び、柱、水面、ヴィラの組み合わせによって小ぶりの風景式庭園をかたちづくっている。この列柱は同時にその先の地下に展開する大空間への導入部ともなっており、古典的な柱のオーダーがそのまま安藤のコンクリートの空間のリズムに対応している点がユニークだ。ここでのプランニングの手法は、同時期に手がけられた淡路夢舞台（1999）と共通しており、地表から深く掘り込まれた楕円形の中庭が全体の空間構造を支配することになる。ヴィラのエントランス部分から延びるコンクリートのテラスがやがて大階段になってこの中庭に到達する。施設の主要部分はこの中庭を囲むように展開しているが、他の安藤の建築と同様、地下にいることをまったく感じさせない。

FABRICAの用途は研究教育のための施設であり、新規に建築する部分の方が、古いヴィラの面積をはるかに凌いでいる。しかし、表に現れるのは200年近くも変わらない昔ながらのヴィラの佇まいである。安藤が心がけたのは、この伝統的な風景をそのまま残し、季節の移り変わりの中で微妙に変化する空間の襞とでも呼ぶべき

the town of Treviso; Carlo Scarpa and his son Tobia Scarpa have designed buildings for the family. The new objective was to establish an international design research and educational institution centered on a villa owned by the family in a suburb of Treviso; it would house Benetton's advertising department as well as a media design school. Toscani's aim was to make use of Benetton's knowhow and develop a strategic center dedicated to educating a small number of students. Introduced to the chairman, Luciano Benetton, Ando gained his trust and was ultimately given complete architectural responsibility for the project. He was to remodel the old villa and design a new facility annexed to the villa. Feudal-period villas are scattered throughout the countryside in the Veneto region; the Benetton villa, which was already in ruins, dated from the eighteenth century and was not of great value in itself. It was in fact not designated a cultural asset. Demolishing it and constructing an entirely new facility would have been an option. However, Ando deliberately chose not to do that. Instead, he retained the old villa and its auxiliary structures and completely remodeled their interiors; in addition he buried the newly-constructed facility underground. Ando's approach suggests an attitude of humility and sincerity toward the history of the past.

The geometry of this art school named FABRICA (2000) consists of several intersecting axes and an oval situated near the center of the site. This spatial composition has a dynamism that is almost Baroque. A pool is in the back of the villa, and a colonnade is arranged as if to trace the axis that cuts across the pond. The columns, the reflecting pool and the villa give shape to a small landscape garden. This colonnade is at the same time the entry for a large space that unfolds underground. The columns of a classical order respond to the rhythm of his concrete spaces in a way that is unique in Ando's work. The method of planning used here is similar to that employed in Awaji Yumebutai (1999), which was undertaken at the same time. The oval courtyard carved deep into the ground dominates the overall spatial structure. The concrete terrace extended from the entrance of the villa eventually becomes a grand stairway which reaches this courtyard. The main parts of the facility are organized around this courtyard, but as in other buildings by Ando, it never feels like an underground space.

FABRICA is a facility for research and education; the newly constructed portion is far larger than the floor area of the old villa. However, on the outside, the facility looks like the villa that has stood there unchanged for nearly 200 years. Ando's aim was to retain this traditional landscape and to carve into the earth what might be called a spatial fold that changes subtly in response to changes in the season. The hot sun in summer makes the building's shadows stand out; in winter, the pastoral landscape is wrapped in milky-white fog that causes walls and columns to lose depth and sets them adrift.

部分を大地に刻むことであった。夏の暑い太陽のもとでは建築の陰影を浮きたたせ、霧に包まれて乳白色に変わる冬の田園風景の中では、奥行き感を失った壁と柱が霧の中を浮遊する。本来ならばコンクリートの幾何学的な組み合わせ以上の何物でもない地下の建築が、土地の霊力を備えたヴィラと組み合わされることによって、ある瞬間に魔術的な力を与えられ人々を黄泉の国へと誘う。安藤の魅力は、それまでのイタリアには存在しなかったまったく別の空間を登場させ、ヴェネト地方の田園地帯に巧みに挿入したところにある。

このトレヴィソでの試みは、歴史的な景観との折り合いの付け方を示した点で多くの人々の注目を集めた。実際にその建築に接してみると、航空写真や配置図から窺える大規模な空間構成とは裏腹の人間的で居心地のよいきめ細やかなタッチを感じとることができる。安藤が設計期間中に常に感じていたに違いない歴史への強迫観念が、最後には見事な調和となってきれいに拭い去られているのも安藤の自信の表れといえそうだ。その結果として、彼はさらに深奥なイタリアの歴史に直接関わることになる。ヴェネツィアのパラッツォ・グラッシ再生計画(2006)である。

このパラッツォは、ヴェネツィアの中心軸ともいえるカナル・グランデに面し、18世紀半ばの建立になるロマネスク＝ビザンチン様式をまとった建物である。戦後、美術館に改装され、ガエ・アウレンティが内装デザインを手がけたが、2005年にフランスのフランソワ・ピノー財団が買収した。安藤がそのデザインに関わるのは、それまでパリ郊外のスガン島でピノー財団の現代美術館を設計していたことが直接のきっかけであった。残念ながら、パリの計画は中断されてしまったが、財団を率いるフランソワ・ピノーから改めてヴェネツィアでのデザインを提示されたときは、大いに戸惑ったに違いない。というのも、パリのスガン島計画では、セーヌ河の上にまったく新しい美術館を構想することが可能であり、空中に浮かんだ大胆な案に到り着いていたが、今度は歴史のエッセンスとでもいうべきヴェネツィアのど真ん中に、しかも装飾的な18世紀のパラッツォを現代美術館につくり直すという途方もなく難しい課題を突き付けられたからである。安藤が是とするモダニズムのコンクリートの建築など、ヴェネツィアに建てられるわけがない。自律するジオメトリーを既存の建築から発して外に展開するという方法も、密集して建築が建ち並ぶヴェネツィアでは困難である。

結果として、そこから導かれるのは、外被には一切手をつけず、内部の構成に限ってのみデザインを手がけるという手法であった。パラッツォの内部の大アトリウムをコアとして、その周りに平滑で厚みをもった内部の壁がフロア単位で積層するという構成となった。軸線と回遊がここでもキーワードとなり、上部のトップライト

This underground architecture, basically nothing more than geometrically assembled concrete, when combined with the villa and the mysterious power of the land, can suddenly take on magical powers and entice people to the land of the dead. Ando has skillfully introduced into the countryside of the Veneto region spaces of a kind never before seen in Italy.

This project in Treviso attracted a great deal of attention for the way it came to terms with a historical landscape. When one actually visits this building, one can sense a pleasant and delicate human touch that is very different from the impression given by the large spatial composition as seen in aerial photographs or the site plan. The fact that the obsession with history that Ando no doubt felt throughout the design period was in the end wiped away, leaving only a work of magnificent harmony, was surely a sign of his self-confidence. Not long thereafter, he was to come into direct contact with the very heart of Italian history in the Palazzo Grassi remodeling project (2006) in Venice.

This palazzo is a building in the Romanesque-Byzantine style, constructed in the middle of the eighteenth century on the Grand Canal, the main axis of Venice. After World War II, it was remodeled into an art museum, and Gae Aulenti did the interior design. In 2005, it was purchased by the François Pinault Foundation. Ando became involved because until then he had been designing the Pinault Foundation for Contemporary Art on Seguin Island in a suburb of Paris. The project in Paris unfortunately fell through. Ando must have been taken aback to be promptly presented by François Pinault, the head of the foundation, with another commission, this time to design the project in Venice. That is because the Paris project had offered an opportunity to conceive an entirely new art museum on the Seine, and he had developed a bold scheme seemingly floating in air. In Venice, however, he was given the extremely difficult task of turning an ornamental eighteenth-century palazzo in the middle of historic Venice into a contemporary art museum. There was no way a concrete building of modernist character that Ando might countenance could be constructed in Venice. It would also be difficult to take an existing building and develop on its exterior an autonomous geometry in the densely built up environment of Venice.

In the end, the method he adopted was to leave the exterior envelope alone and to limit his intervention to the interior composition. Smooth, thick interior walls are layered floor by floor around the large atrium inside the palazzo. Here too the keywords are 'axes' and 'circular movement.' The light entering from the skylights above serves to make each space impressive. The interior itself carries the weight of history; the result is a building within a building, with highly concentrated, inward-oriented spaces.

から落ちる光がそれぞれの空間を印象づける役割を果たしている。歴史の厚みをみずからに課すことによって、建築内部のもうひとつの建築という構図をとり、内部に向かって凝縮した空間を生み出すのである。

以上のように、安藤忠雄はこの15年ほどの間に世界に向けて積極的に乗り出し、ヨーロッパやアメリカで繰り返し新しい挑戦を行ってきた。そのためには乗り越えなければならないハードルがあちこちにあった。彼が育った日本とは大きく異なる歴史と価値観を有し、技術的にもばらつきのある国々で、デザイン的にも技術的にも一定の質を保ち続けるためには、相当の努力が強いられる。それこそコンパネのサイズから仕上げ材の種類まで、種々雑多な調整作業が必要で、日本のように一定のラインを形成していない現場において職人たちをとりまとめ、的確な指示を出していくプロジェクトマネージャーが要請される。さらに必ずしも設計図通りに動かない現場を説得し、コンセプトに沿って一定の品質と性能を保証するためには、それぞれの国で安藤の仕事を理解し、その実現のために努力を惜しまない有能な職人集団を確保することが何よりも重要である。イタリアであれドイツであれ、時間をかけてそのような努力を重ねてきた結果、安藤の建築を支えて現場から現場を動き回る職人たちが現れるようになったと聞く。コンクリートの魔術師と称される安藤の背後には、彼の思想と方法に慣れ親しみ、そのために技術革新を惜しまない多くの人々が控えているわけで、安藤の作品が世界各国で登場するようになったということは、その輪がインターナショナルに広がってきた証しでもある。建築をつくるという行為が、単なる建設ビジネスということではなく、新たな公共的な価値を生み出す持続的な作業であり、人類にとっての創造そのものであるということを世界に向けて身をもって示しているといえるだろう。

冒頭にも述べたように、安藤のまなざしは、先進国にだけ向けられているものではない。彼は何よりも、「生きる」という人類の根源的なあり方に対して直接間接に関わることが自身の使命であることをわきまえ、建築という行為をそのために捧げてきた稀有な人間である。生まれ故郷大阪であっても、歴史の凝縮したヴェネツィアであっても、あるいは遠いネパールの山間であっても、基本的な態度は変わらない。建築が無限の価値をもって人々に愛され、未来に向けて持続する力をかたちづくることの重要さを知り、それを着実に実践している。繰り返していうが、安藤忠雄の建築に対する信念を支えているのは、彼が長い人生の中で邂逅した無数の人々との触れ合いから生まれた人類に対する慈しみの心であることを知ってもらいたい。

In this way, Ando has actively ventured out into the world in the last 15 years or so and repeatedly taken up new challenges in Europe and the US. He has had to overcome many obstacles to do so. To maintain a certain level of quality of both design and construction in countries with histories and values very different from those in Japan and with varying levels of construction skills has required considerable effort. Many miscellaneous adjustments have had to be made, from the size of panels used for concrete forms to the types of finishes, and project managers able to gather together workmen on a site that does not meet a certain standard and give appropriate instructions have been needed. Above all, in order to persuade people who do not necessarily work from drawings and to assure a certain quality and level of performance in accordance with the design concept, a group of skilled workmen who understand Ando's work and do not begrudge the extra effort needed to realize it has had to be found. In countries such as Italy and Germany, as a result of time spent in such efforts, there are now said to be workmen who go from one site to the next and make Ando's work possible. The magician of concrete, which is what Ando has been called, is supported by many persons who have become familiar with and sympathetic to his ideas and methods and do not begrudge technical changes; the emergence of works by Ando all over the world means that circle of supporters is expanding internationally. He is demonstrating by example to the world that making architecture is not just a construction business but a sustained effort to generate new public values—and that for humankind, it constitutes creation itself.

As I stated at the outset, Ando is not concerned just with advanced countries. He is a rare individual who understands that his own mission, above all, is to concern himself, directly and indirectly, with life, that most basic of human conditions, and has dedicated himself to architecture for that purpose. His basic attitude is the same whether he is in his birthplace and home town of Osaka, a city as full of history as Venice, or the mountains of remote Nepal. He knows the importance of shaping the power of architecture—to embody myriad values, to win people's love and to endure into the future—and steadily translates that knowledge into action. As I have stated before, Tadao Ando's architectural convictions are based on his love of humankind, born of his contact with countless individuals in chance encounters during his long life.

ミシガン湖畔に建つシカゴ美術館は、規模、質ともに優れ、ボストン美術館、メトロポリタン美術館と並んで、アメリカを代表する美術館のひとつである。前身は1866年に創立されたシカゴ・アカデミー・オブ・デザインであり、日本の浮世絵とフランス印象派の絵画のコレクションで知られる。そのシカゴ美術館の東洋部門が新たに増設され、その一角の展示計画がわれわれに依頼された。美術館収蔵の日本の屏風および陶磁器を展示するギャラリーである。

構成は極めて単純なものとなった。まずギャラリーを2分し、その一方に1辺30cm、高さ3mの柱を16本均等に立てる。この柱は直接の視線を遮ると同時に、空間の深さや、奥行きを測る手立てとして存在する。視線の変化につれて静止していた柱は動へと転じる。時として複数の柱は重なり1本の柱となる。屏風は多目的に使われる日本の屋内空間を一時的に仕切り、場の確保を可能にするとともに、屏風によって隔てられたその室の奥行きの深さを予測させる装置でもあった。単に展示物としての屏風を見せるだけではない、それが本来置かれていた日本建築の空間の精神を継承し、現代的につくり替えた場に屏風を置くことによって、日本的空間の美学そのものを伝えることが私の主題だった。

シカゴ美術館屏風ギャラリー
Gallery for Japanese Screen, the Art Institute of Chicago

1989-92 アメリカ合衆国 シカゴ —— Chicago, U.S.A.

Built on the shore of Lake Michigan, the Art Institute of Chicago excels in both scale and quality, and along with the Boston Museum of Fine Arts and the Metropolitan Museum of Art, it is one of the most representaive art museums in the United States. Originating in the Chicago Academy of Design, established in 1866, it is well known for its collection of Japanese *ukiyo-e* and French Impressionist paintings. The East Asian section of the Art Institute of Chicago has been newly expanded, and we were commissioned for one corner of the exhibition design. This is a gallery to display the museum's collection of folding screens and ceramics from Japan.

The composition is extremely simple. The gallery was first divided in two, with sixteen identical columns arrayed in one half, each 30cm per side and 3m high. The presence of these columns obstructs direct sightlines and simultaneously provides a way to measure the length and depth of the space. Depending on changes in sightline, the stationary columns appear to move. Sometimes two or more columns overlap and become one column. Folding screens are used to temporarily partition the multipurpose interior spaces of traditional Japanese architecuture, enabling places to be defined, and they are also devices to estimate the depth of a room subdivided by these folding screens. Not wanting to merely show these folding screens as display objects, my theme was to show the aesthetics of a Japanese space by putting them in a modern environment that is a reinterpretation of the spirit of the Japanese architectural spaces where they were originally placed.

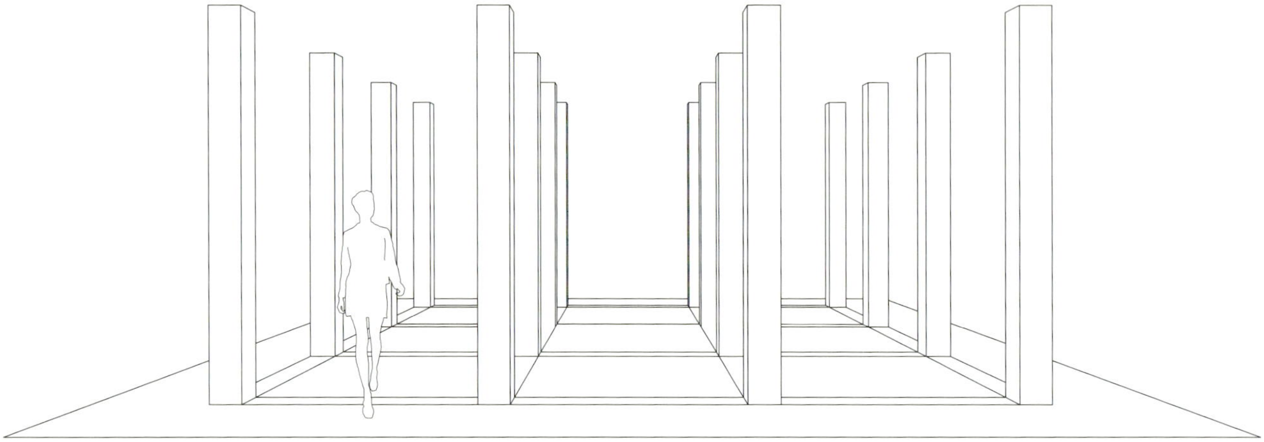

パースペクティブ・ドローイング。 Perspective drawing.

ミシガン湖岸に建つシカゴ美術館は、1866年に創立されたシカゴ・アカデミー・オブ・デザインが前身。日本の浮世絵とフランス印象派のコレクションで知られるほか、中国美術を中心に多くの東洋美術品を収蔵している。屏風ギャラリーは、1993年に増築された東洋部門の一部である。

Built on the edge of Lake Michigan, the Art Institute of Chicago was preceded by the Chicago Academy of Design established in 1866. It is known for its collection of Japanese *ukiyo-e* and French impressionism, but it also houses many works of Asian art, particularly Chinese fine art. The Gallery for Japanese Screens is part of the Asian wing added in 1993.

4本ずつ、4列に配列された漆黒の柱の中を進んでいくと、その柱の間から、金色に輝く屏風の景色、色鮮やかな打ち掛けや小袖、日本画や陶器の名品が姿を現す。華やかな展示品が、漆黒の柱と鮮やかな対比をなし、抑制された新しい美の表情を見せる。

Advancing through the jet-black columns, arranged in four rows of four, scenes on folding screens glittering with gold, vividly colored fabrics of *uchikake* and *kosode*, famous Japanese paintings and ceramics are all visible between the columns. The colorful display items make a striking contrast with the jet-black pillars, which show a new expression of restrained beauty.

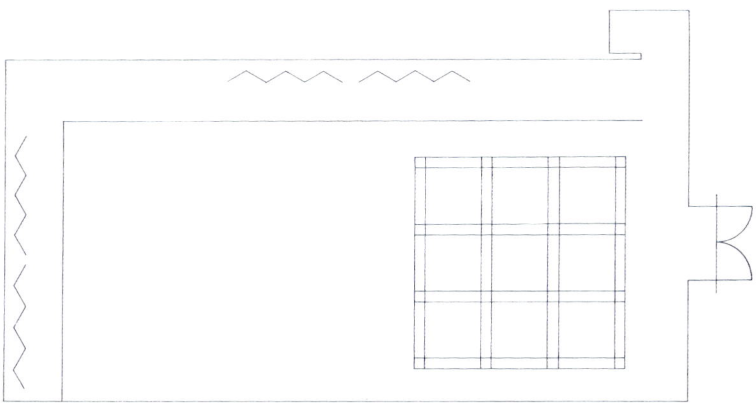

Plan 1:200

屹立する16本の柱は、展示空間を切り取る額縁であるのと同時に、その重なりによって空間の奥行きを演出する装置でもある。

The sixteen soaring pillars are like picture frames dividing up the exhibition space, and at the same time they are devices that produce spatial depth through their layering.

この建物は、ピューリッツァー賞の創設者の一族のコレクションを収蔵するとともに地域の文化的拠点となることを目指して計画された。アメリカ中部ミシシッピ川の流域に位置するセントルイス市の中心部は、郊外の開発に伴って荒廃していった。長年セントルイスの名士であったピューリッツァー夫妻はこの中心部の再開発計画に私財を投じ、自らのコレクションを含む美術作品に触れ合える文化的な核となる施設をつくり、公開することを決意した。1990年秋、ピューリッツァーさんからプロジェクトの打診を受け、翌年5月、夫妻の案内でセントルイスの敷地を訪ねた。シカゴ美術館の館長ジェイムズ・ウッドさんの紹介によるものだった。

ピューリッツァー夫妻が中心となって、新たな再開発計画が進められてきた文化地区の一角に建てられるこの建物には、地域再生を考える上でのひとつの拠点になれば、との期待も込められていた。敷地の周辺状況、要求されたプログラムから、われわれは本計画を住宅的スケールの特質をも備える空間として捉え、設計を進めた。

ここでは建物が、極力単純な構成の中で適切なプロポーションで配置され、緊張感ある内外の関係を可能にする開口部をもつよう考えた。形態や素材といった建築の要素を限定し、単純な幾何学に置き換えることで、建築の意図をより明確に示したいと考えた。建物は、2本の直方体ヴォリュームが、水庭を挟んで並行に配されるという構成からなる。これらに、それぞれ異なる高さを与え、高い方には幅と同じ天井高をもつ2層吹き抜けの細長いメインギャラリーを配し、高さを1層に抑えた低い方には、エントランスホール、ライブラリーおよび事務、研究関連の諸室を配し、さらに屋上を緑の庭とした。その長さ、高さの違いによって生じる余白部分に深い庇を設け、美術館へのエントランスおよびふたつのヴォリュームを結ぶラウンジとした。2棟に挟まれた水庭、低層棟屋上の緑の庭、それぞれに面するテラスなど、いずれの外部空間も内部のギャラリーに連続して、美術の展示の場となるよう考えられている。また、内部の展示室も内外の連続性を高め積極的に自然光を採り入れることで、時間、季節の移り変わりとともに多彩な表情を見せる自然が息づくような空間を意図した。

本計画では、その計画段階から、この美術館に作品を収めるアーティスト――エルスワース・ケリー、リチャード・セラなど――が参加し、建築家と美術作家、双方の立場から、美術館について意見、提案を交わしながら設計を進めてきた。ケリーは、何回も現場に訪れて作品の位置と内容を検討した。現代美術家の執念を感じた。セラの場合は、話を聞くたびに構想している作品の大きさが大きくなっていった。開口部の設計変更を迫ってきたことさえあった。時に意見が衝突し、なかなか前に進まないこともあったが、クライアントも含めた妥協のない対話を彼らと繰り返していくうちに、建築のレベルは徐々に高まっていった。彼らとの協同作業は、美術館の原点を考える上で、非常に有意義なものであった。美術館と美術作品、アーティスト、そして観衆との間に活発な対話が喚起され、常に刺激となりうるような場所となることを期待している。

ピューリッツァー美術館
Pulitzer Foundation for the Arts

1992-2001 アメリカ合衆国 セントルイス ―― St. Louis, U.S.A.

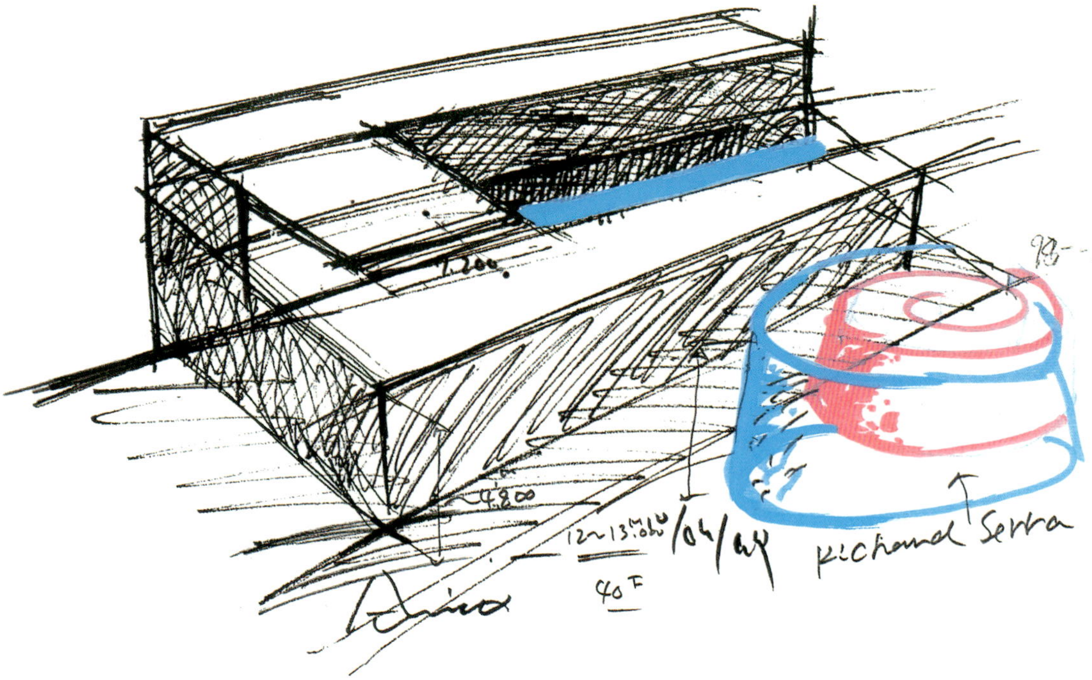

2棟のボックスが並置されただけのシンプルな構成の建築。ミニマルな形態ゆえに、初期段階からそれぞれのプロポーションを細かく検討している。

A simple architectural composition in which two boxes are placed side by side. From the outset, a detailed investigation was made of each proportion, following this minimal shape.

当初は、現敷地近くの古い工場の残る敷地で、既存建物を改修して美術館とする計画だったが、水庭を介して2棟が並列する構成へと変更された。

An old factory remained on a site close to the present site, and the first plan was to renovate it as the art museum. The composition of two parallel buildings connected by a water garden is a later design, and was implemented in altered shape.

Initially, this building was designed to house a part of the collection of the family that founded the Pulitzer Prize, as well as to become a cultural hub for the area. The core of St Louis, near the Mississippi River in the center of the USA, had been devastated as a result of suburban development. For a long time, Joseph and Emily Pulitzer, as prominent St Louisans, have invested their private assets and played a central role in this central area redevelopment. With the decision to open to the public a place to view art, although no longer purely that from their private collection, they have realized a facility that will become a cultural nucleus.

I was introduced to the Pulitzers by James Wood, director of the Art Institute of Chicago. They wrote to me about the project in the autumn of 1990 and the following March I was shown around the site in St Louis.

Occupying a corner of the developing cultural zone, this building embodies our hope that it will become a cultural hub within the regeneration of the area. Given the surrounding site conditions and the programmatic requirements, the design progressed based on our view that these spaces should have a residential-scale character.

Within a restrained composition, the building was conceived by following appropriate proportions for the layout and openings to enable a sense of tension in the relationships between inside and outside. We realized this concept by limiting the architectural elements such as forms and materials within a pure geometrical order. The building is composed of two rectangular volumes, placed parallel to each other on either side of a water garden. The two volumes are each given different heights: the taller one contains the long and narrow main gallery, a double-height space with its width the same as its ceiling height, whereas the other is one level lower in height, and contains the entrance gallery, a library, as well as offices, various support service spaces and a green rooftop garden. Deep eaves have been placed over the space produced by the difference in length between the two volumes, and this is used for the entrance to the museum and the sitting area that connects the two volumes. All of the outdoor spaces, such as the water garden contained between the two wings, the green rooftop garden on the lower wing and the terraces they face, are also continuous with the interior gallery spaces, and they may be considered as places for exhibiting works of art. With regard to the interior of the exhibition rooms, by actively bringing in natural light to enhance this interior-exterior continuity, the intention was to create spaces that breathe nature by integrating the changing effects of time and season.

From the planning stage onward, the artists Ellsworth Kelly and Richard Serra, who have provided works for the Foundation, participated in the design process, which progressed as the architects and artists exchanged opinions and proposals about art museums from our respective standpoints. Kelly visited the site several times to consider the placement and content of his work. I could sense the tenacity of this modern artist. In the case of Serra, each time I listened to him, the size of his intended work seemed to increase. Each one urged me to make changes in the design of the openings. Although our opinions sometimes came into conflict, and progress was impeded, the quality of the architecture steadily increased through uncompromising dialogues between us, and with the client. This collaborative work with them was extremely significant, making us think about the most basic elements of art museums.

In evoking a vigorous dialogue between the art museum and the artworks, the artists and the audience, we hope that the Pulitzer Foundation for the Arts will remain a place of constant stimulus.

Pulitzer Foundation for the Arts

配置図。建物と同様に、リチャード・セラの彫刻「Joe」がサイト全体を規定する重要な要素になっている。
Site plan. Like the buildings, Richard Serra's sculpture "Joe" became an important element for regulating the entire site.

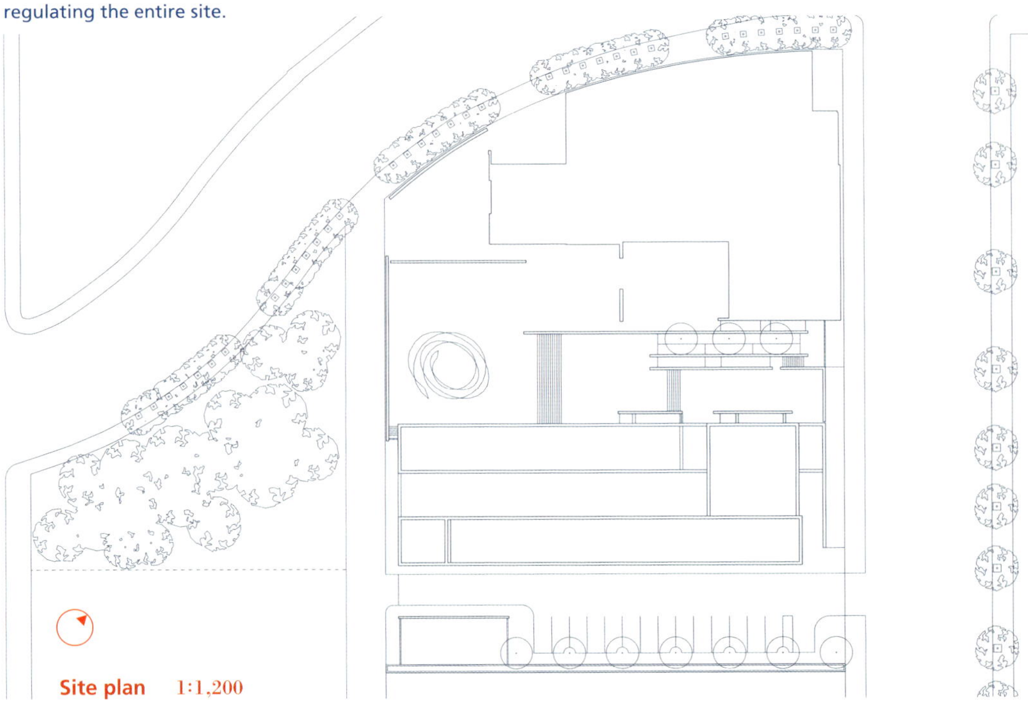

Site plan　1:1,200

北東側外観。一切開口のない、純粋なコンクリートの壁によるファサード。微妙にずらされた壁の重なり、その上にキャンチレバーで突き出された屋根スラブがつくる陰影が、内部の空間の存在をほのめかす。

Exterior view from the northeast. The façade comprises an unadulterated concrete wall utterly without openings. The shadows produced by the cantilevered roof slab projecting above the subtly shifted layered walls hint at the existence of the interior spaces.

建物西側、彫刻広場からエントランス方向に階段状のコートを見る。素材、要素の限定された、幾何学による緊張感溢れる空間。

Looking at the stair-shaped court from the sculpture plaza on the west side of the building in the direction of the entrance. A space brimming with tension due to geometry, as well as the reduced materials and elements.

右頁上:1階ロビー。左側が水庭に面したテラス。
右頁下:2階ラウンジからの眺め。

Right page above: Lobby on the first floor. The terrace facing the water garden is on the left.
Right page below: View from the lounge on the second floor.

2層吹き抜けの1階メインギャラリー。絶妙な高さで穿たれた側面の開口部が、水庭の反射光を室内に採り込み、ストイックな箱の空間に多様な表情を与える。正面吹き抜けを受けとめる壁は、エルスワース・ケリーの彫刻「Blue Black」のためにつくられた。上部に切り込まれたトップライトからの光が、アートとの出会いの空間を劇的に演出する。

The double-height gallery on the first floor. A lateral aperture at the ideal height draws light reflected from the water garden into the room, and gives diverse expressions to the stoic box space. The wall that contains the double-height space in front was made for Ellsworth Kelly's sculpture "Blue Black." The light from a skylight sliced above dramatically produces a space for encountering art.

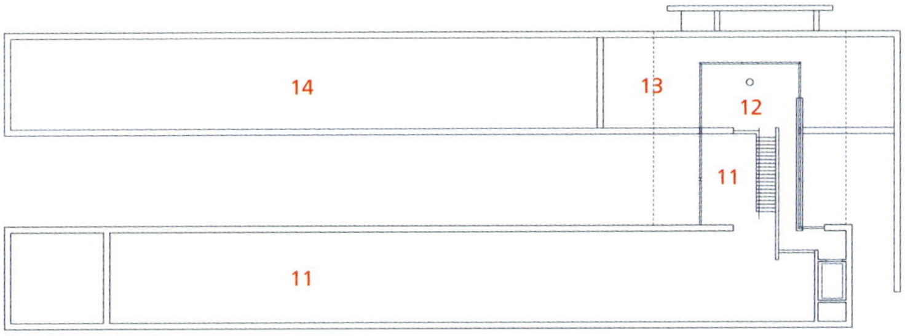

Second floor plan

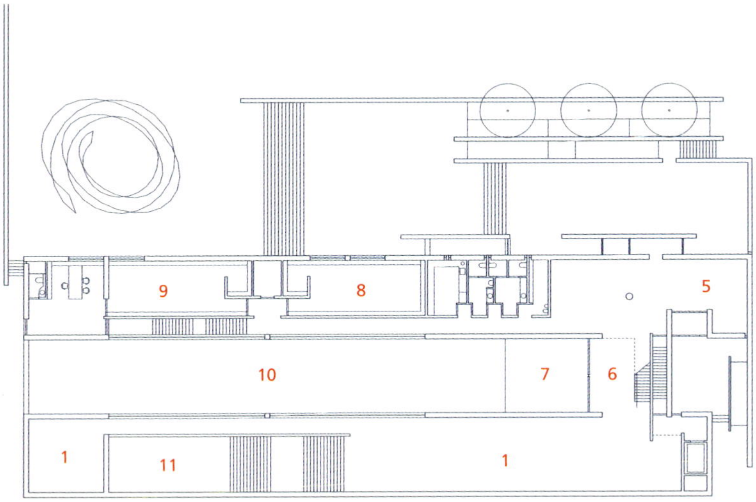

First floor plan

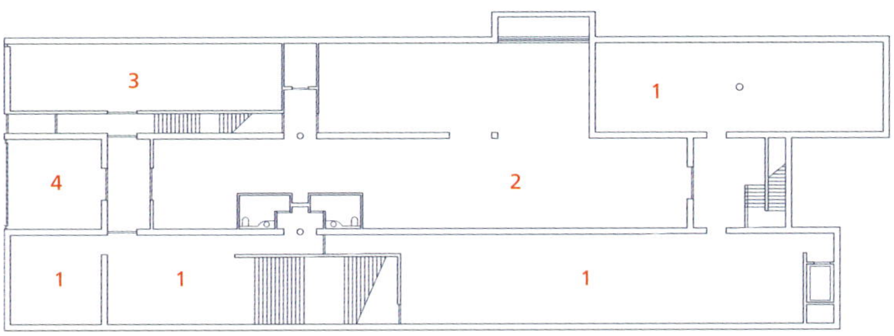

Basement floor plan

1 gallery
2 mechanical
3 storage
4 parking
5 entrance hall
6 lobby
7 terrace
8 office
9 library
10 water garden
11 void
12 lounge
13 roof terrace
14 roof garden

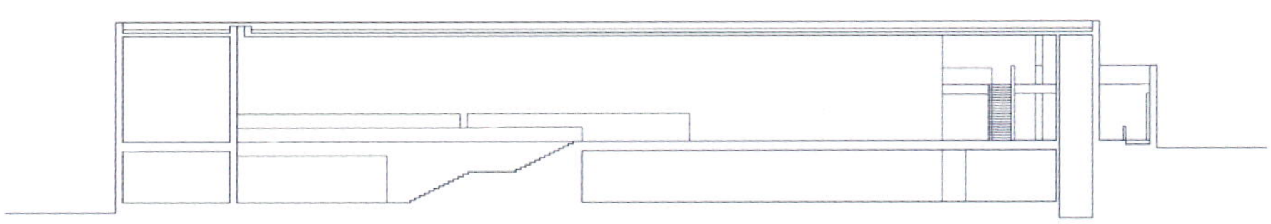

Section 1:700

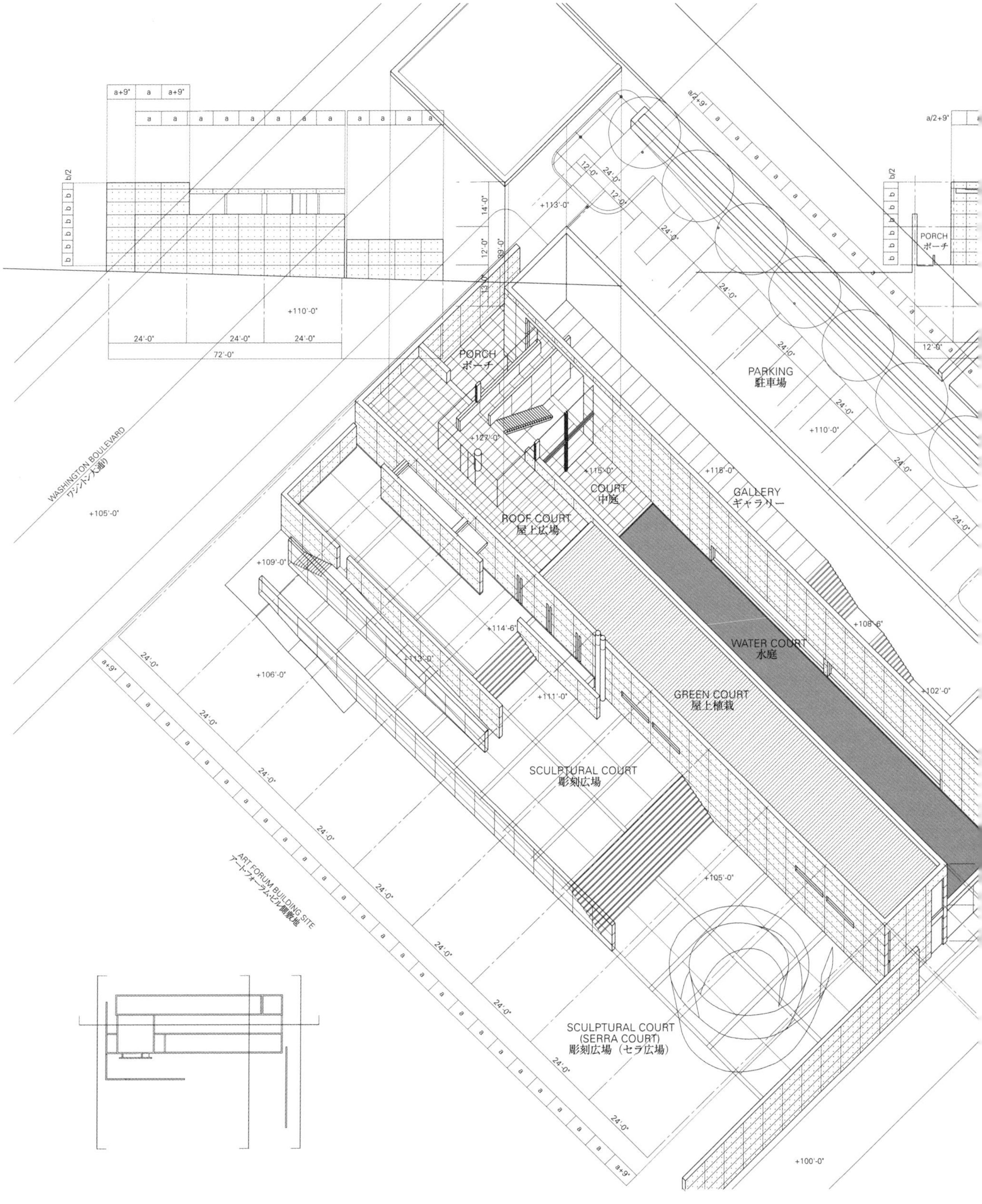

PORCH
ポーチ
ROOF COURT
屋上広場
COURT
中庭
GALLERY
ギャラリー
PARKING
駐車場
WATER COURT
水庭
GREEN COURT
屋上植栽
SCULPTURAL COURT
彫刻広場
SCULPTURAL COURT
(SERRA COURT)
彫刻広場（セラ広場）
WASHINGTON BOULEVARD
ワシントン大通り
ART FORUM BUILDING SITE
アート・フォーラム・ビル建設地
+105'-0"
+109'-0"
+110'-0"
+113'-0"
+114'-6"
+115'-0"
+116'-0"
+127'-0"
+106'-0"
+111'-0"
+108'-6"
+102'-0"
+100'-0"
24'-0"
72'-0"
12'-0"
14'-0"
39'-0"
a+9"
a/2+9"
b/2

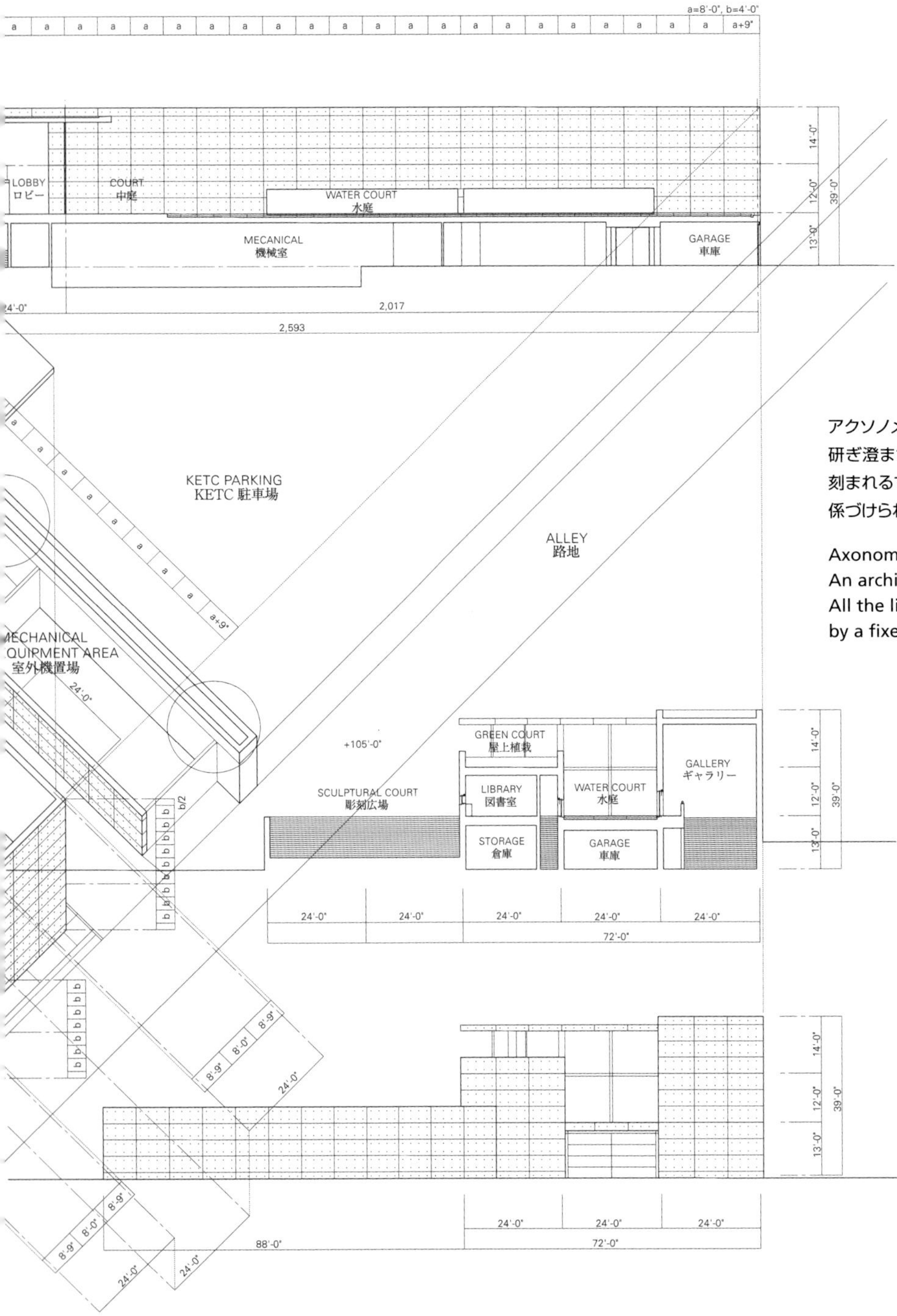

アクソノメトリック・ドローイングと断面図および立面図。
研ぎ澄まされたプロポーションによる箱の建築。建築に刻まれるすべてのラインが一定のモジュールに従い、関係づけられている。

Axonometric, section and elevation.
An architecture of boxes with finely honed proportions.
All the lines inscribed on this building are related by a fixed module.

2階ロビーからガラス越しに水庭を見る。高さの異なる2本のボックスを結びつけ内外空間をつなぐ、建物にとって最も重要な〈余白〉の空間。

Looking at the water garden through the glazing in the lobby on the second floor. Connecting to the interior and exterior space that joins the two boxes with varying heights, this is the most important "blank" space for the building.

メインギャラリーから水庭越しに隣の低層棟を見る。
ミニマルな構成が生み出す空間の無限の奥行き。

Looking across the water garden from the main gallery to the lower building adjacent. Infinite spatial depth produced by a minimal composition.

エッセイ

エミリー・ロウ・ピューリッツァー

建築がそれを収めるために建てられた組織や機関をかたちづくる。このことが、安藤忠雄がピューリッツァー芸術財団のために建てたものほど当てはまるケースはありません。

1980年代後半、リチャード・セラとエルスワース・ケリーが安藤の作品を、私と、今は亡き私の夫に紹介してくれた時点では、安藤忠雄の名前はアメリカではほとんど知られていませんでした。だから私たちがはじめに安藤を選択したのは、純粋に美的な判断に基づいてのことだったのです。元の案では古い自動車工場を改装するつもりだったのですが、その近くの敷地にまったく新しいものを建てるという計画に変更されました。こうして完成した建築は、それ自体が「美」の次元においてというだけではなく、その中で展示されるアート作品の見え方の次元においても、私の大いなる夢を凌駕するものとなったのです。この建物に収められた当財団は、サンクチュアリであると同時にラボでもあるのです。

この素晴らしく機能的な建築は、ピューリッツァー財団のアイデンティティーを特徴づけてくれているだけではありません。アート作品のインスタレーションを建物との対話において行なう、素晴らしい音響効果をもつ空間で室内楽のコンサートを開く、ギャラリースペースでシンポジウムを開く……そうした私達の全行為に規律を与える力として常に働いているのです。多くの美術館においてギャラリーは、アート作品にとっての背景としてのみ存在するだけの、面白みのないニュートラルなものであるか、逆に作品を圧倒してしまう建築的にアグレッシブなものになっています。しかし、ピューリッツァー が内包する複数の空間は微妙な変化に富み、それが互いに関係をもちつつ、広範なアート作品 にとって絶妙ともいえるセッティングを可能としてくれます。

私は建物と並行するかたちで、エルスワース・ケリーとリチャード・セラに彫刻作品の製作を依頼したのですが、安藤忠雄は、このふたりと協同するというチャレンジを受けてくれました。彼ら3人のアーティストは、同じ美の感覚をもち、互いの仕事を尊敬し尊重し合っています。チャンレンジとはアートと建築が互いに高めあうようにするということでしたが、それは見事に達成されました。リチャード・セラがいうには、建物のふたつのウイングの間にある池によって、安藤は空を建物の中に引き下ろしてきている。そしてそのセラが、池に隣接する、捩じれたスパイラル状の作品 Joe によって、同様の経験を生み出しているのです。

安藤忠雄の建築といえば、多くの人の脳裏にはまずコンクリートが浮かびます。安藤の熟達した、エレガントで、詩的でさえあるコンクリートの扱いを考えれば、それも当然のことでしょう。しかし、このピューリッツァー財団の建物で6年間を過ごしてみて、この建築においては自然もまた同様に重要な役割を担っているのだと感じています。風が水面を揺らして池の端から端まで吹き渡り、雨が変化し続ける水玉のパターンをつくり出します。寒い日の朝にはそこから水蒸気が霧のように立ち上り、穏やかな日には鏡の表面のように静まり返っている。こうして、常に自然の力を意識させられるのです。

自然の中でも、最も大きな役割を果たすのは光でしょう。メインギャラリー、ホールウェイ、そしてオフィススペースにおいて、電気照明を使うのは午後も遅くなってからのことです。自然光は、しばしば水面を反射しつつ、天井、壁面、そして床を渡っていく、明るくドラマティックな投影を見せることもあれば、曇った日には静謐で瞑想に誘うような雰囲気を醸し出すこともあり、その質をさまざまに変化させます。こうした自然光の中でアート作品を観ること、それにまさる経験は存在しません。

安藤忠雄の優れた才能のひとつは、彼のサイトの扱いに見ることができます。それが美しいランドスケープであろうと、郊外の匿名地区であろうと、そしてまたこの財団の立地がそうであるように、文化と教育の中心としてのかつての活気を取り戻そうと苦心している都市部のエリアであっても。ここの建物はもともと空き地に囲まれていたのに、安藤の手にかかると、そこに入り、その中を動くという経験が、ひとつのコントロールされた流れとなる。内部、外部両方の眺めが変化することで、見る者は方向感覚を与えられ、経験は満たされたものとなるのです。近くに建つマソニックテンプル・ビル頂部の古典様式の神殿デザイン部分は、素晴らしい「借景」効果を生んでいます。来館者は、建物をゆっくりと通り抜けていくことで、さまざまに質を変化させる光と物理的空間の中においてアート作品を観るという経験を全身で味わいます。それは、美術館での鑑賞ではなく、自宅でアート作品とともに暮らすという特権に近い経験かもしれません。安藤忠雄の並外れた建築においては、美と機能が両立するのです。ここにこそ、マジックとワンダーを感じます。

エミリー・ロウ・ピューリッツァー
ピューリッツァー美術館チェアマン。

Essay

Emily Rauh Pulitzer

Rarely does architecture shape an institution as does Tadao Ando's building for the Pulitzer Foundation for the Arts.

Tadao Ando was little known in the United States in the late 1980s when artists Richard Serra and Ellsworth Kelly introduced my late husband and me to his work. Initially, our choice of Ando was purely an aesthetic one. The original project, remodeling a former automobile factory, was transformed into the construction of an entirely new structure on a nearby site. The finished building has not only surpassed my greatest dreams in terms of aesthetics but also in the way works of art look within it. The institution housed in this building is simultaneously a sanctuary and a laboratory.

The beautifully functioning building not only informs the identity of the Pulitzer Foundation but continually acts as the disciplining agent for all we do, whether it is the installation of works of art in dialogue with the building, chamber music concerts in the acoustically excellent space, or symposia held in the gallery spaces. Unlike many museums where the galleries are either neutral, and as such without much interest except as a background for works of art, or architecturally aggressive, overpowering the art, the Pulitzer spaces vary subtly yet relate to each other and provide exquisite settings for a wide range of art.

Tadao Ando accepted the challenge to work with Ellsworth Kelly and Richard Serra, whom I commissioned to make sculpture in conjunction with the building. All three are artists with a similar aesthetic who respect and honor one another's work. The challenge, successfully met, was for the art and architecture to enhance each other. Richard Serra commented that, in the pool between the two wings of the building, Tadao Ando pulls the sky down into the building. Serra creates a parallel experience with his adjacent torqued spiral Joe.

Concrete comes first to mind when most people think about Tadao Ando's buildings—and with good reason—as he uses the material in a masterful, elegant and even poetic way. However, after six years in the Pulitzer Foundation for the Arts, I feel that the building allows nature to play an equally important role. Wind ruffling the surface of the water pool, moving down its length, raindrops making pebbled ever-changing patterns, steam rising as mist on cold mornings or a mirror surface on quiet days make one constantly aware of the forces of nature.

Perhaps nature's largest role is played by light. In the main gallery, along hallways and in offices, electric light is used only late in the day. The quality of natural light ranges from bright, dramatic projections moving across ceilings, walls and floors, often reflecting the surface of the water, to a calm contemplative atmosphere on grey days. The effect of seeing works of art in natural light provides an unparalleled experience.

One of Tadao Ando's great talents is his use of site, whether it is in a beautiful landscape, an anonymous suburb or, as here, in an urban neighborhood struggling to regain its former liveliness as a cultural and educational center. Tadao Ando made the experience of entering and moving through the building, originally surrounded by vacant land, one of controlled flow. Varying views, both internal and external, orient the viewer and charge the experience. A classical temple atop a nearby Masonic building provides a wonderful "borrowed landscape." The visitor slowly moves through the building absorbing the experience of works of art seen in varying qualities of light and physical spaces. The experience can be related more to the privilege of living with works of art in a home than viewing them in a museum. Aesthetics and function work together in Tadao Ando's extraordinary building. Here, there is the sense of magic and wonder.

Emily Rauh Pulitzer
Chairman of the Board, The Pulitzer Foundation for the Arts.

1997年に行われた国際設計競技により、われわれの案が選ばれた。敷地はテキサス州フォートワースの郊外の都市公園の一部に位置し、隣接してルイス・カーンの傑作キンベル美術館が建っている。現代の古典ともいうべきキンベル美術館と新しい美術館とをどのように関係づけるか、そして広大な敷地をどのように性格づけるかが争点となった。

私もまた、カーンとの対話を試み、そこから抽出される明晰さ、単純性ゆえの強さといった空間のエッセンスを新しい建物に組み込んでいくことを考えた。さらに、与えられた広大な敷地に対しては、内外の区別なくどこにいても芸術を感じることのできる〈芸術の森〉とするコンセプトを構想した。

フォートワースの自然は厳しく、森や池のない、大げさに言えば砂漠のような過酷な土地である。そこに、緑や水の豊かなアートと人間のための空間をつくろうと考えた。

そのようにして導かれたのが、水と緑で囲まれた森の中に、コンクリート打ち放しの箱をガラスで包み込んだ二重構造の直方体を5列に並べる構成である。まず敷地東側に広い水庭をとり、交通量の多い交差点に対しては森を配して、水と緑で囲まれた環境を整えた。そこにコンクリート打ち放しの箱をガラスで包み込んだ、長い2列の公共空間のブロックと、短い3列の展示空間のブロックからなる、二重構造の直方体を平行に並べる。

フォートワース現代美術館
Modern Art Museum of Fort Worth

1997-2002 アメリカ合衆国 フォートワース――Fort Worth, U.S.A.

20世紀を代表する素材であるガラスとコンクリートを用いて、今までにない新しい魅力をもった建築をつくりたかった。ガラスに包み込まれたコンクリートはガラスの透明性を引き立たせ、逆にガラスの被膜は、直方体という強い形態がコンクリートというマッシブな素材のまま露出するのを抑え、周囲に対し、軽く、柔和な印象を与える。コンクリートという安定した素材は、フォートワースの苛烈な気候から、美術品を保護する。コンクリートの箱は構造的な安全性を保証し、その外にさらにガラスの箱を設けることで、展示室内部への外の気候からの直接的な影響を軽減し、美術品の安全性を向上させることができる。二重被膜の間に生まれるスペースは、外部であり内部でもある日本の縁側のような空間であり、内部に水と緑、光を取り込む一方で、外部にもガラス越しに展示室の様子を伝えることができる。二重被膜構造の直方体を連続させ、さらに数種の自然採光システムを導入することで、単純な全体構成でありながら、その中に展示空間として多様な平面、ヴォリュームが用意される。

この美術館は、鑑賞や研究という目的に加え、一般市民に開放されたコミュニティの核となる。屋外の芝の広場と水の庭では、敷地に点在する美術品を常に感じながらコンサートや野外パーティー、フェスティバルなどを楽しむこともできる。この場所が、真の意味で人々に開かれた美術館として、厳しい自然環境のこの地に潤いを与えるオアシスとして、現在と未来の人々の想像力を育むことを願う。

現在、レンゾ・ピアノによるキンベル美術館の増築が計画されており、その完成により、ルイス・カーンのキンベル美術館とフォートワース美術館の関係性はより緊密なものとなり、全体として、フォートワースの人々の文化的な生活の中心としての役割をさらに高めることであろう。

配置ドローイング。アートの空間を水と緑で包み込む、〈芸術の森〉のイメージが描かれている。単純なボックスの反復による構成に、隣接するルイス・カーン設計のキンベル美術館との関係が見てとれる。

Site drawing. Wrapping the spaces for art in water and greenery, the image of an "art forest" is depicted. A relationship with the adjoining Kimbell Museum designed by Louis Kahn can be seen in the composition of repeated simple boxes.

Our proposal was selected as the result of an international design competition held in 1997. The site is located in one part of an urban park in the suburbs of Forth Worth, Texas, adjacent to Louis Kahn's masterpiece, the Kimbell Art Museum. The Kimbell Art Museum should be described as a modern classic, and the points at issue were what kind of relationship could be made with the new art museum, and what kind of character should be given to such a vast site.

I also wished to attempt a dialogue with Kahn, and thereby extract a spatial essence comprising a strong simplicity and clarity with which to imbue the new building. Furthermore, for this large site, I conceived the concept of an "art forest" in which there is no distinction between interior and exterior, so the art may be sensed wherever you are.

The natural environment of Fort Worth is harsh, with no forests or ponds, and with some exaggeration it could be described as having the severity of a desert. Here we wanted to makes spaces with abundant greenery and water for people and art.

This led to a composition of five rectangular solids in a row, each with a double-layer structure of a bare concrete box enclosed by glass, within a forest surrounded by water and greenery. We prepared an environment surrounded by water and greenery by first making a wide water garden in the eastern part of the site, and placing a forest in front of the busy traffic intersection. The double-layer rectangular solids were arrayed parallel, comprising two longer public space blocks and the three shorter exhibition space blocks, each of bare concrete boxes enclosed by glass.

I wished to create an architecture of unprecedented charm using only glass and concrete, two materials that

Modern Art Museum of Fort Worth

represent the 20th century. Wrapping glass around concrete enhances the transparency of the glass. Conversely, the glass shell mitigates the massive materiality of concrete in the strong form of the rectangular solid, giving a light and gentle impression to the surroundings. The stable material of concrete protects the artworks from the harsh climate of Fort Worth. By adding glass boxes, the direct influence of the exterior climate on the exhibition room interiors is reduced, and so the safety of the artworks can be improved. The space created between the glass and concrete shells is outdoor as well as indoor space, similar to a Japanese *engawa* (veranda). Water, greenery, and light are taken into the interiors, whereas from outside the appearance of the exhibition rooms can be followed through the glass. Although the overall composition is simple, diverse plans and volumes have been prepared for the exhibition spaces inside by placing double-layer shell-structure rectangular volumes in a row, and introducing several types of natural lighting systems.

In addition to its purposes of art appreciation and research, this museum will be open to ordinary citizens, becoming a nucleus of the community. While constantly aware of the artworks that dot the site, concerts, outdoor parties, festivals, or similar events may be enjoyed in the outdoor lawn plaza and water garden.

As an art museum open to people in the truest meaning, it is my hope that this place will serve to enhance the imaginative powers of people, both now and in the future, as an oasis that gives moisture to the harsh climate of this environment.

Renzo Piano is now planning an addition to the Kimbell Art Museum, and its completion will further strengthen the relationship between Louis Kahn's Kimbell Art Museum and the Forth Worth Art Museum, and overall it will increasingly take on its role as the heart of the cultural life of the people of Fort Worth.

単純な構成の内に展開する、複雑多様な空間のシークエンス。安藤の建築のテーマが最も端的に現れた作品のひとつが、このフォートワース現代美術館といえる。

A complex and varied spatial sequence expands inside a simple composition. The Modern Art Museum of Fort Worth is a work in which the themes of Ando's architecture appear most plainly.

北東よりギャラリー部分を池越しに見る。さざなむ水面にその身を写す、水上の美術館。

Looking from the northeast across the pond at part of the gallery. The museum above the water is reflected in the rippling water surface.

北側外観。水上に突き出た屋根スラブをＹ字型のコラムが支える、簡潔な構成の反復が紡ぐ"人工"の自然の風景。左手の湾曲した壁面部分には、カフェとレストランが入っている。

Exterior view from the north. A scene of "artificial" nature in the concise repetition of the composition and the Y-shaped columns supporting the roof slabs projecting over the water. The café and restaurant are incorporated in the curved wall on the left.

水上に浮かぶガラスボックスのイメージを損なわぬよう、アルミカーテンウォールの足もとのディテールには細心の注意が払われている。

To avoid losing the image of a glass box floating above the water, careful attention was paid to the details at the base of the aluminum curtain wall.

カーテンウォールのサッシの線の重なりが、光と影の交錯する繊細なギャラリー空間を演出する。内部の彫刻は、ミケランジェロ・ピストレットの作品。

The layering of the curtain wall sash lines produces a delicate gallery space that blends light and shadow. The sculpture inside is a work by Michelangelo Pistoletto.

北側からのパースペクティブ・ドローイングと立面図
およびペリメーター部分のディテール。

Elevation and perspective from the north, detail of the perimeter.

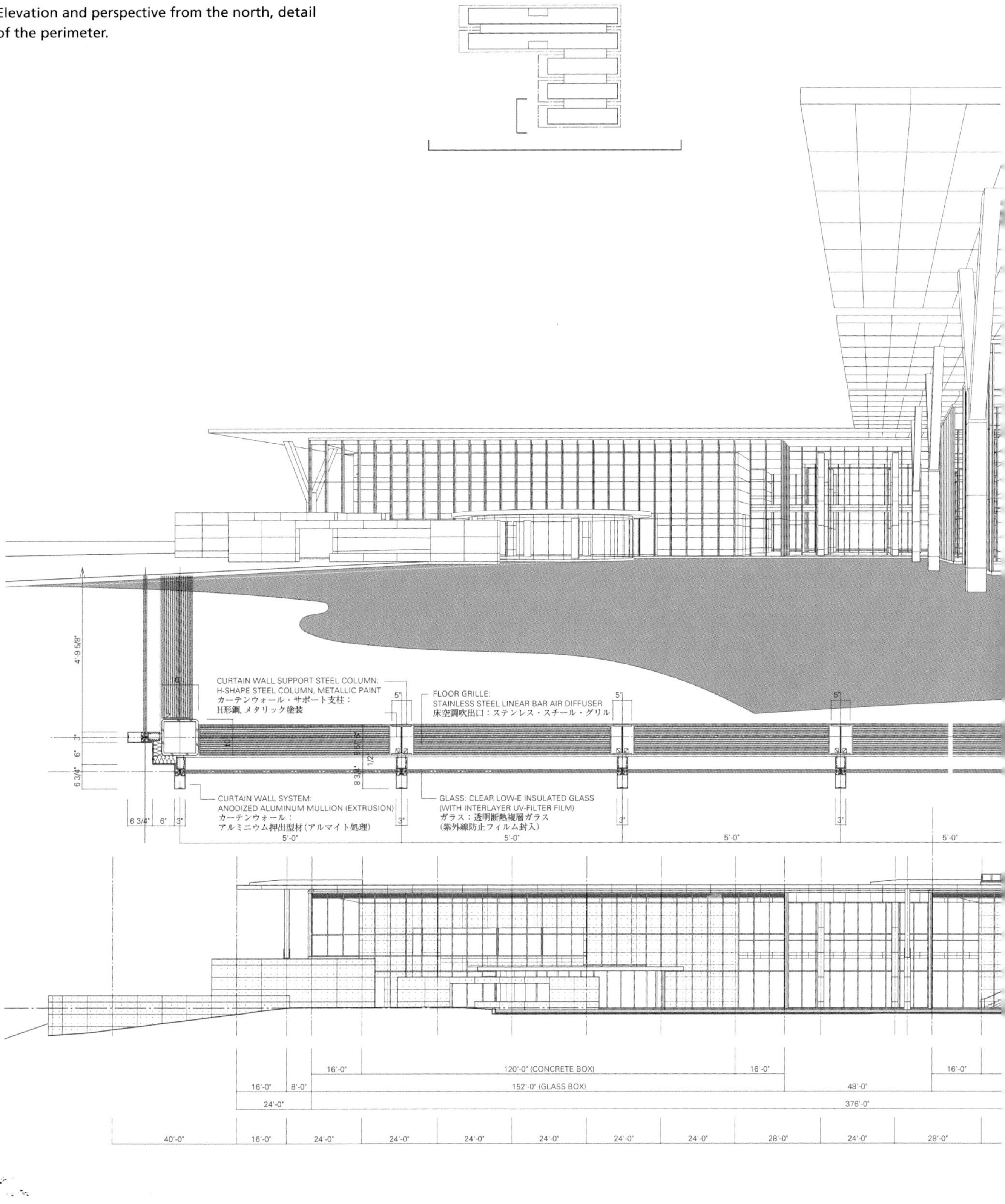

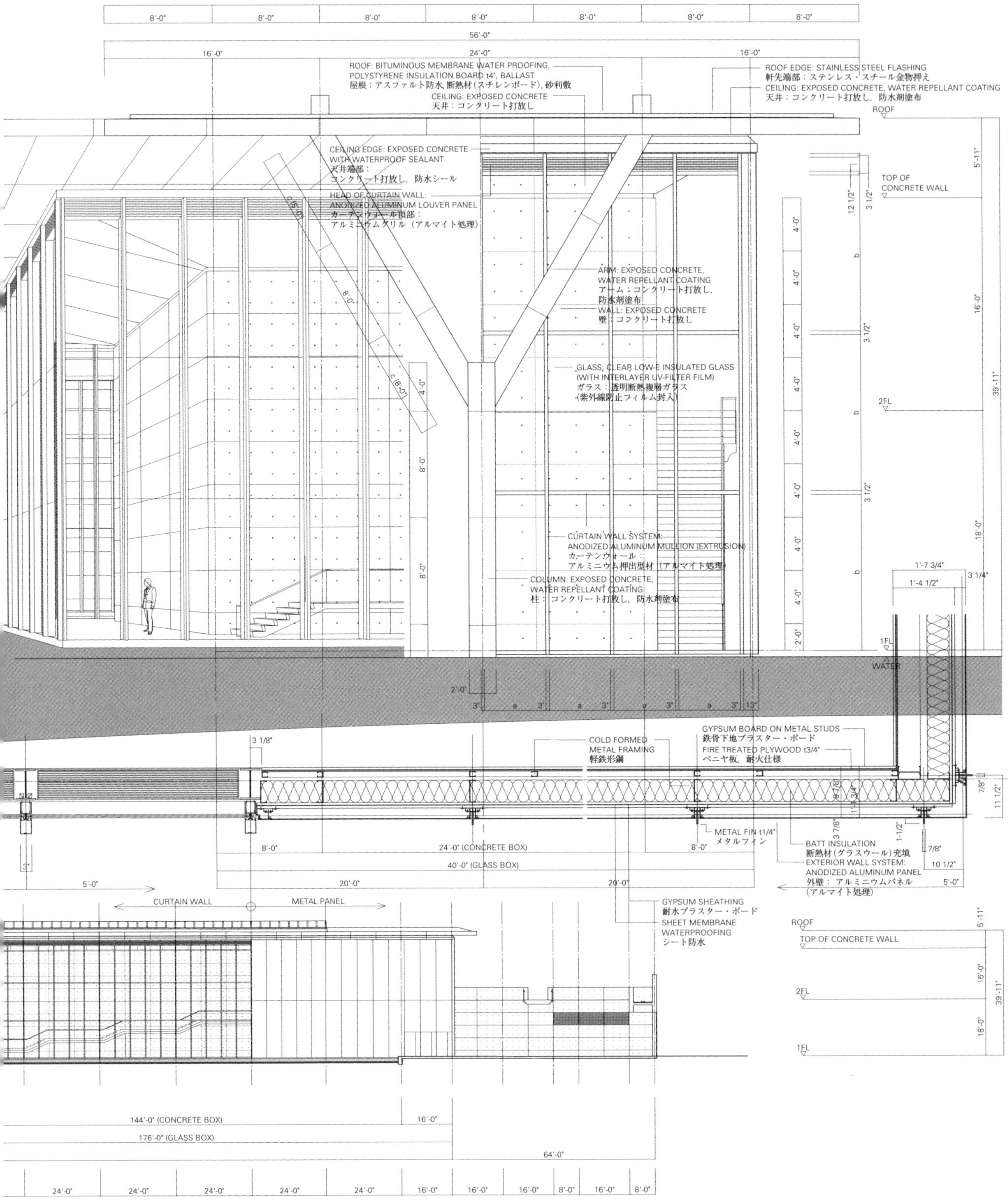
ROOF: BITUMINOUS MEMBRANE WATER PROOFING, POLYSTYRENE INSULATION BOARD t4", BALLAST
屋根：アスファルト防水, 断熱材(スチレンボード), 砂利敷
CEILING: EXPOSED CONCRETE
天井：コンクリート打放し
ROOF EDGE: STAINLESS STEEL FLASHING
軒先端部：ステンレス・スチール金物押え
CEILING: EXPOSED CONCRETE, WATER REPELLANT COATING
天井：コンクリート打放し, 防水剤塗布
CEILING EDGE: EXPOSED CONCRETE WITH WATERPROOF SEALANT
天井端部：コンクリート打放し, 防水シール
HEAD OF CURTAIN WALL: ANODIZED ALUMINUM LOUVER PANEL
カーテンウォール頂部：アルミニウムグリル（アルマイト処理）
ARM: EXPOSED CONCRETE, WATER REPELLANT COATING
アーム：コンクリート打放し, 防水剤塗布
WALL: EXPOSED CONCRETE
壁：コンクリート打放し
GLASS: CLEAR LOW-E INSULATED GLASS (WITH INTERLAYER UV-FILTER FILM)
ガラス：透明断熱複層ガラス（紫外線防止フィルム封入）
CURTAIN WALL SYSTEM: ANODIZED ALUMINUM MULLION (EXTRUSION)
カーテンウォール：アルミニウム押出型材（アルマイト処理）
COLUMN: EXPOSED CONCRETE, WATER REPELLANT COATING
柱：コンクリート打放し, 防水剤塗布
TOP OF CONCRETE WALL
ROOF
2FL
1FL
WATER
COLD FORMED METAL FRAMING
軽鉄形鋼
GYPSUM BOARD ON METAL STUDS
鉄骨下地プラスター・ボード
FIRE TREATED PLYWOOD t3/4"
ベニヤ板, 耐火仕様
METAL FIN t1/4"
メタルフィン
BATT INSULATION
断熱材（グラスウール）充填
EXTERIOR WALL SYSTEM: ANODIZED ALUMINUM PANEL
外壁：アルミニウムパネル（アルマイト処理）
GYPSUM SHEATHING
耐水プラスター・ボード
SHEET MEMBRANE WATERPROOFING
シート防水
24'-0" (CONCRETE BOX)
40'-0" (GLASS BOX)
CURTAIN WALL
METAL PANEL
144'-0" (CONCRETE BOX)
176'-0" (GLASS BOX)
56'-0"
64'-0"

水上に突き出す屋根スラブを支えるコンクリートのＹ字型コラム。

Concrete Y-shaped columns supporting the roof slabs projecting above the water.

Y字コラム越しに見るフォートワースの街の風景。

The townscape of Fort Worth beyond the Y-shaped columns.

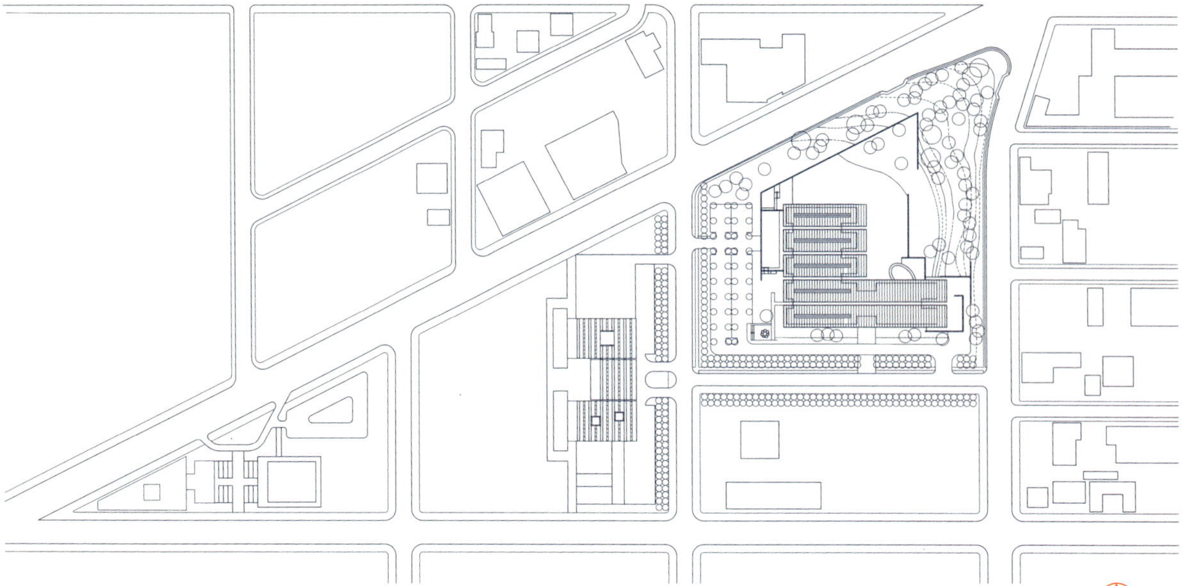

Site plan 1:6,000

建物は同断面の長棟2棟、短棟3棟が並列するシンプルな構成。ボックスはそれぞれコンクリートとガラスの二重皮膜構成による。

The building has a simple composition of two long and three short wings arrayed parallel, all with the same cross-section. The boxes are each composed of a two-layer skin of concrete and glass.

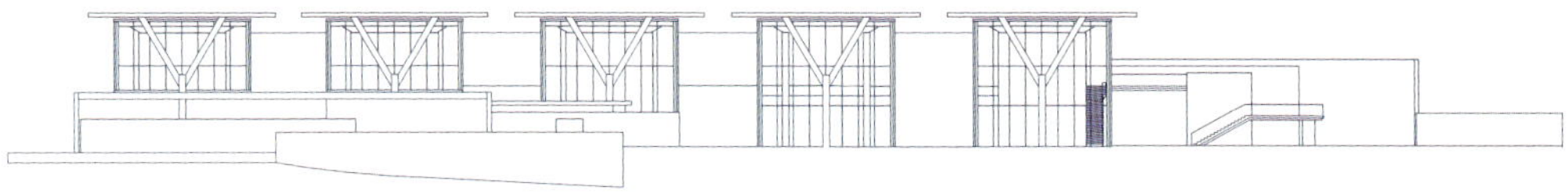

East elevation

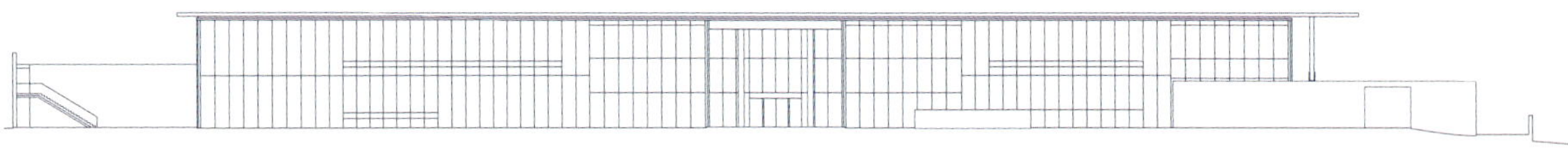

South elevation

Sections 1:1,000

ギャラリーへとアプローチする大階段。キンベル美術館へのオマージュとしてつくられた。
Large staircase leading to the gallery. This was made in homage to the Kimbell Museum.

コンクリートとガラスの隙間の空間が連続する回廊となり、単純な建物構成の中で、回遊性の高い多様な空間体験を可能にしている。

The interstitial spaces between the concrete and glass become a continuous corridor, and this simple building composition enables various spatial experiences with a high feeling of recursion.

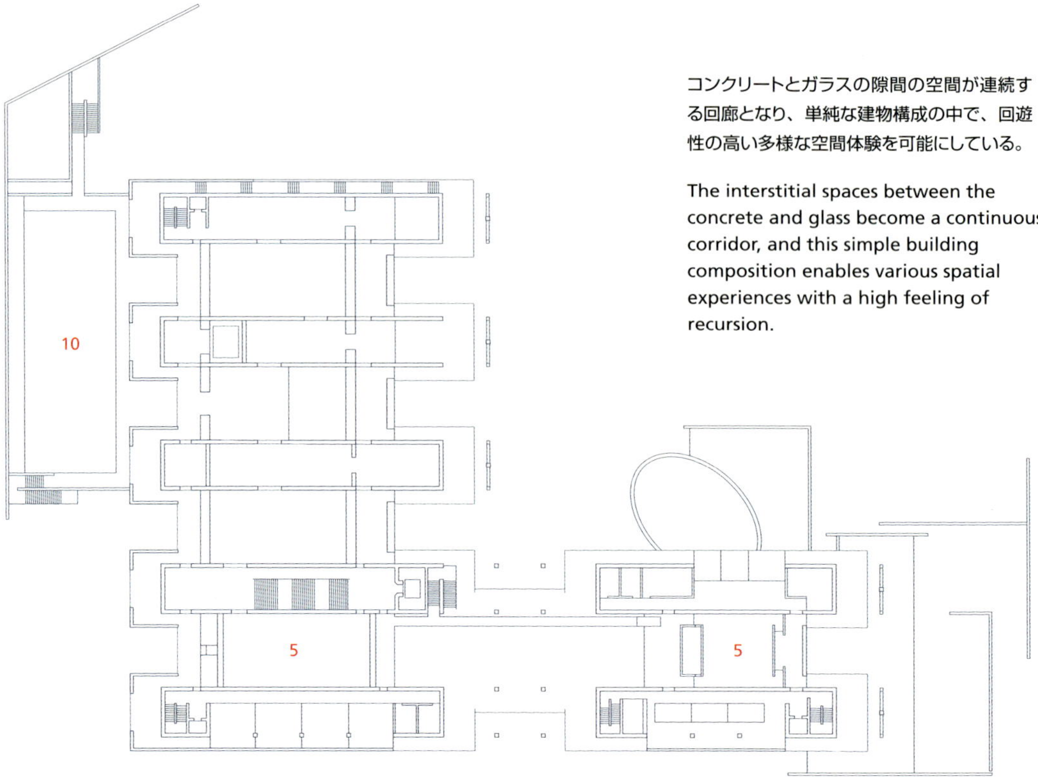

Second floor plan

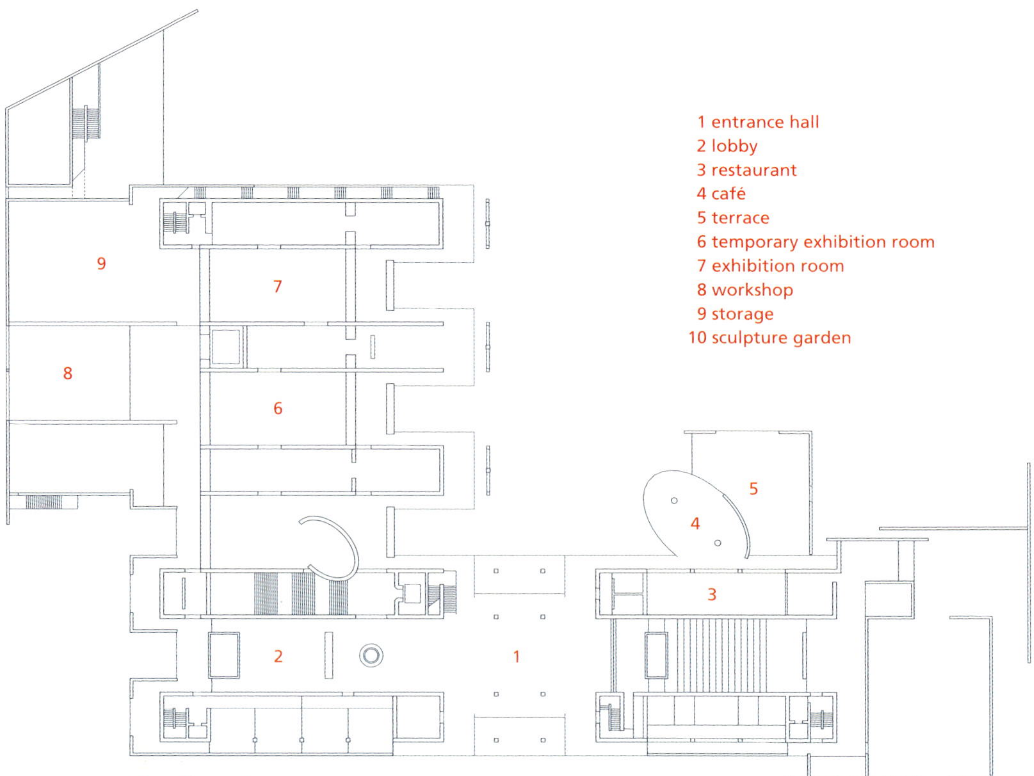

First floor plan 1:1,200

1 entrance hall
2 lobby
3 restaurant
4 café
5 terrace
6 temporary exhibition room
7 exhibition room
8 workshop
9 storage
10 sculpture garden

南側に設けられたエントランスホール。左側を抜けるとガラスボックスの浮かぶ水庭に出る。奥に見えるのは全250席のオーディトリアムへの入口。

Entrance hall established on the south side. Exiting from the left, one emerges at the water garden where the glass box floats. Visible behind is the entrance to the 250-seat auditorium.

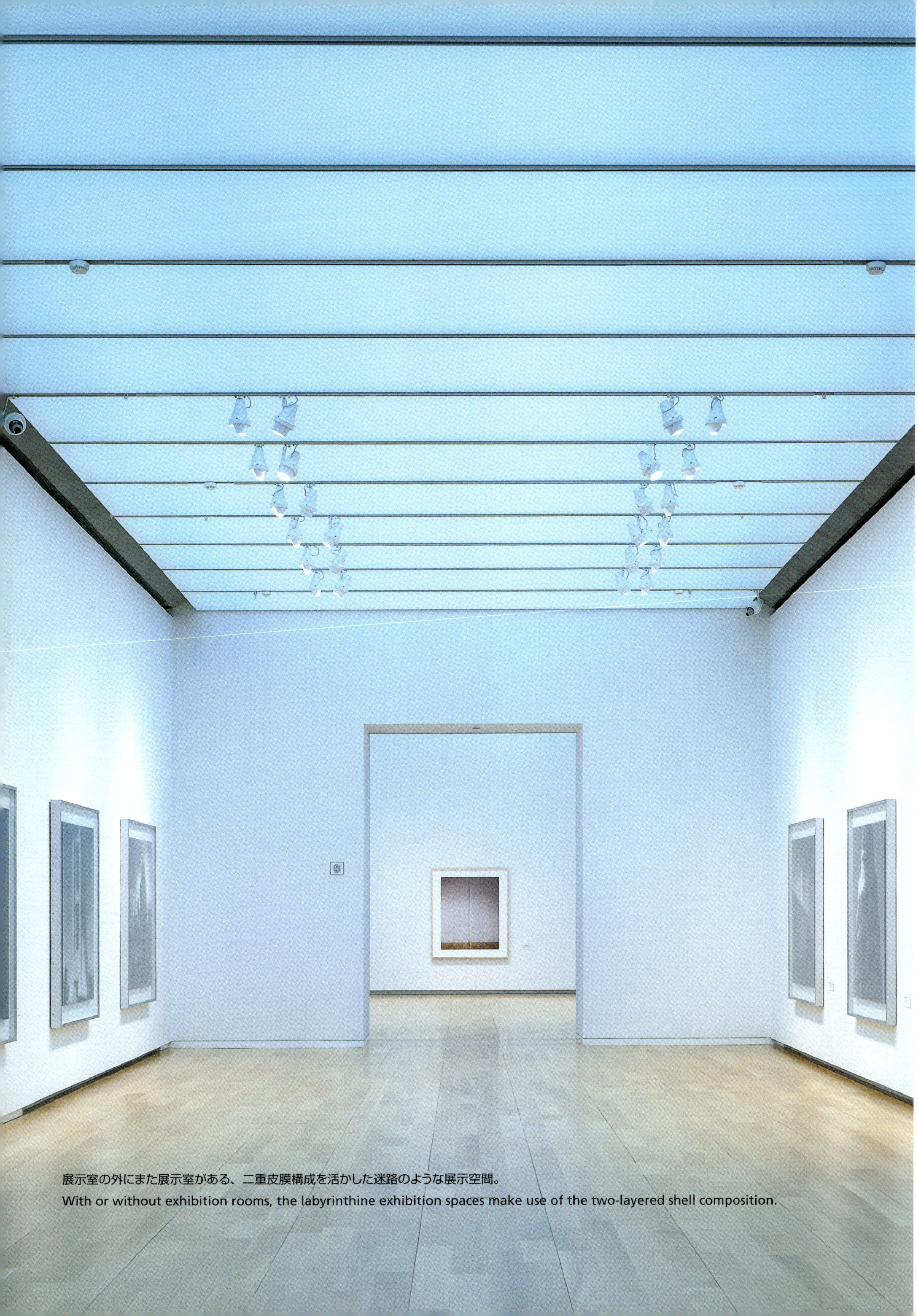

展示室の外にまた展示室がある、二重皮膜構成を活かした迷路のような展示空間。
With or without exhibition rooms, the labyrinthine exhibition spaces make use of the two-layered shell composition.

2階展示室内部から、回廊越しに彫刻テラスを見る。手前に見える作品はリチャード・ロングの彫刻。

Looking from inside the second floor exhibition room across the corridor to the sculpture terrace.
The work visible in front is a sculpture by Richard Long.

左頁：アンゼルム・キーファーの「Book with Wings」の常設展示スペース。
右頁：1階北東端のギャラリー。作品はマーティン・プライヤーの「Ladder for Booker T. Washington」。

Left page: Permanent exhibition space for Anselm Kiefer's artwork "Book with Wings." Right page: Gallery at the northeast end of the first floor. The artwork is Martin Puryear's "Ladder for Booker T. Washington."

展示室の断面図。トップライト、ハイサイドライトなどの自然光の制御方法と人工照明の組み合わせにより、さまざまな質の光の空間が計画されている。

Exhibition rooms connected Cross-section of the exhibition rooms. Through a mixture of artificial light and methods to control natural light from skylights and clerestories, spaces with light of different qualities were designed.

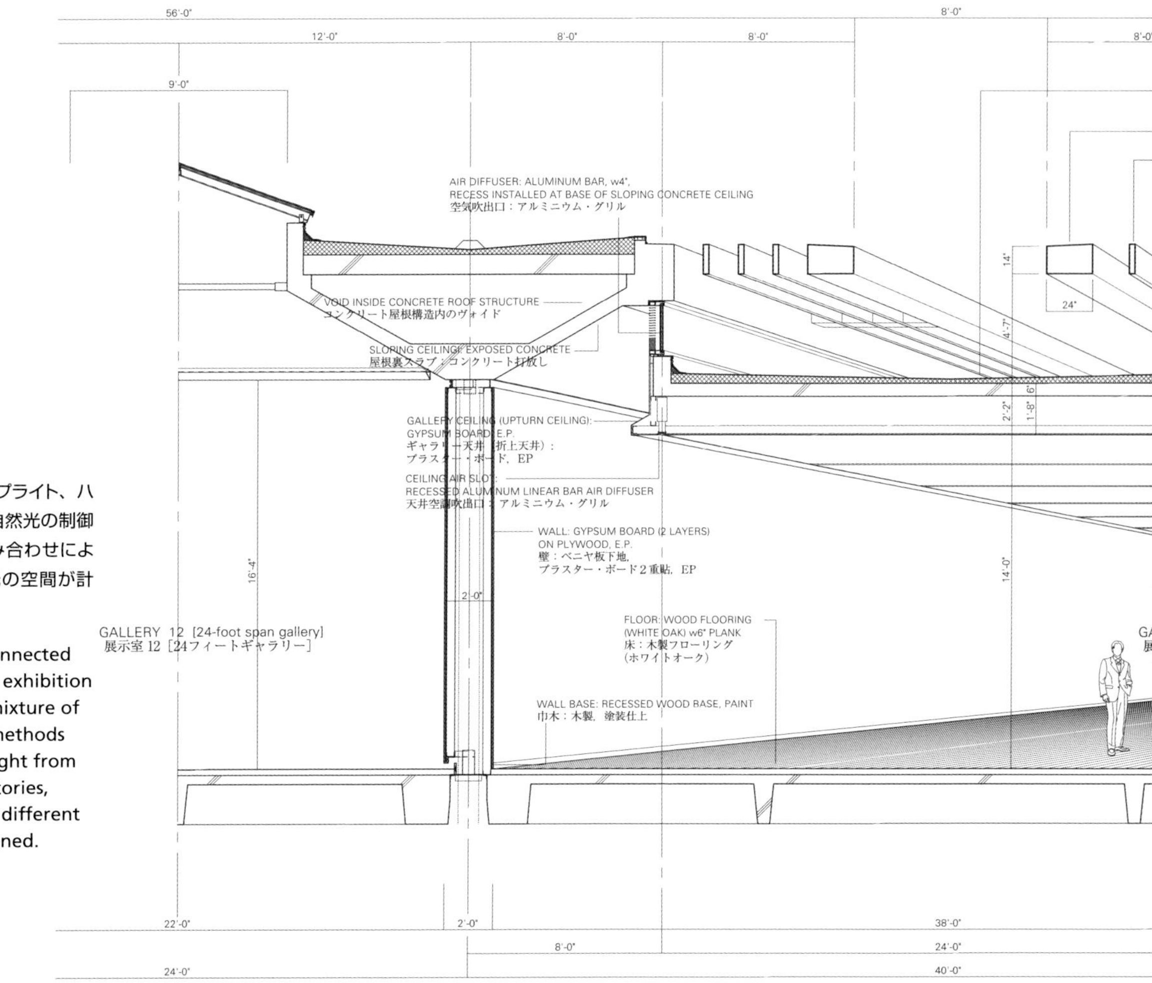

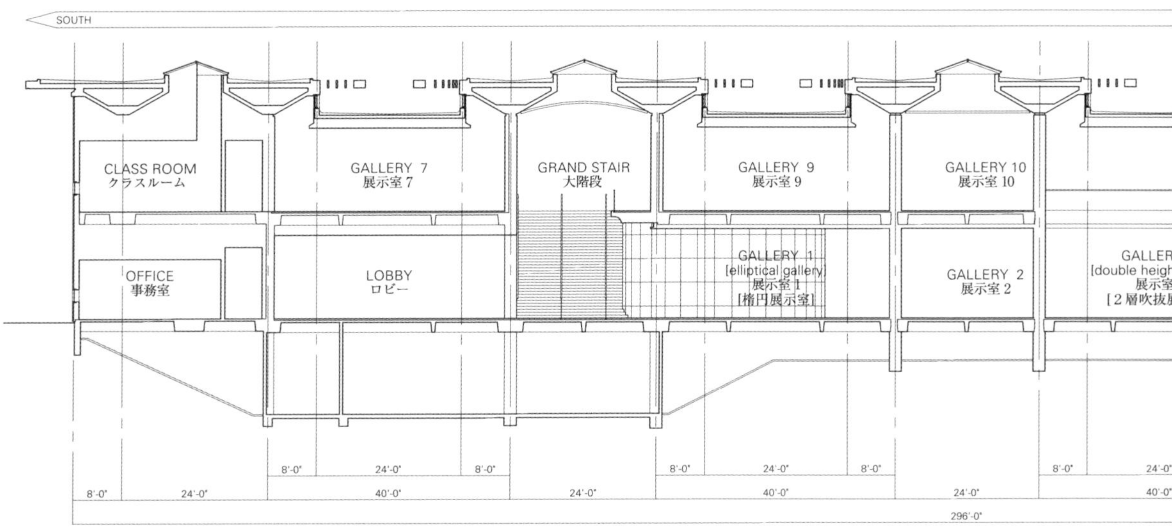

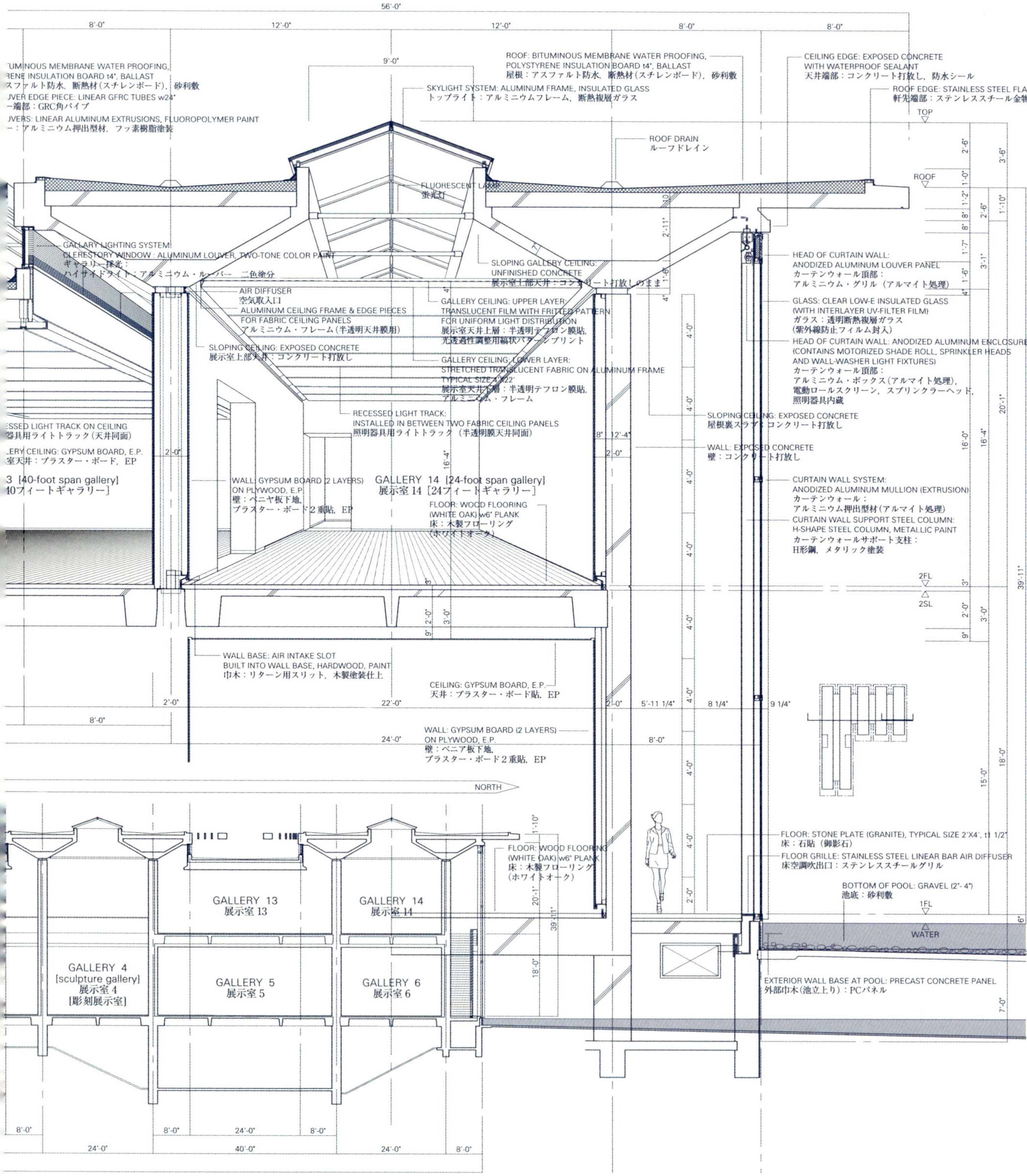
56'-0"
8'-0"
12'-0"
12'-0"
8'-0"
8'-0"
9'-0"
ROOF: BITUMINOUS MEMBRANE WATER PROOFING, POLYSTYRENE INSULATION BOARD t4", BALLAST
屋根：アスファルト防水，断熱材(スチレンボード)，砂利敷
SKYLIGHT SYSTEM: ALUMINUM FRAME, INSULATED GLASS
トップライト：アルミニウムフレーム，断熱複層ガラス
CEILING EDGE: EXPOSED CONCRETE WITH WATERPROOF SEALANT
天井端部：コンクリート打放し，防水シール
ROOF EDGE: STAINLESS STEEL FLASHING
軒先端部：ステンレススチール金物押え
TOP
ROOF DRAIN
ルーフドレイン
ROOF
FLUORESCENT LAMP
蛍光灯
GALLARY LIGHTING SYSTEM:
CLERESTORY WINDOW : ALUMINUM LOUVER, TWO-TONE COLOR PAINT
ギャラリー採光：
ハイサイドライト：アルミニウム・ルーバー　二色塗分
SLOPING GALLERY CEILING: UNFINISHED CONCRETE
展示室上部天井：コンクリート打放しのまま
HEAD OF CURTAIN WALL: ANODIZED ALUMINUM LOUVER PANEL
カーテンウォール頂部：
アルミニウム・グリル（アルマイト処理）
AIR DIFFUSER
空気取入口
ALUMINUM CEILING FRAME & EDGE PIECES FOR FABRIC CEILING PANELS
アルミニウム・フレーム（半透明天井膜用）
GALLERY CEILING: UPPER LAYER: TRANSLUCENT FILM WITH FRITTED PATTERN FOR UNIFORM LIGHT DISTRIBUTION
展示室天井上層：半透明テフロン膜貼，光透過性調整用縞状パターンプリント
GLASS: CLEAR LOW-E INSULATED GLASS (WITH INTERLAYER UV-FILTER FILM)
ガラス：透明断熱複層ガラス（紫外線防止フィルム封入）
HEAD OF CURTAIN WALL: ANODIZED ALUMINUM ENCLOSURE (CONTAINS MOTORIZED SHADE ROLL, SPRINKLER HEADS AND WALL-WASHER LIGHT FIXTURES)
カーテンウォール頂部：
アルミニウム・ボックス（アルマイト処理），電動ロールスクリーン，スプリンクラーヘッド，照明器具内蔵
SLOPING CEILING: EXPOSED CONCRETE
展示室上部天井：コンクリート打放し
GALLERY CEILING: LOWER LAYER: STRETCHED TRANSLUCENT FABRIC ON ALUMINUM FRAME TYPICAL SIZE 4'X22'
展示室天井下層：半透明テフロン膜貼，アルミニウム・フレーム
RECESSED LIGHT TRACK: INSTALLED IN BETWEEN TWO FABRIC CEILING PANELS
照明器具用ライトトラック（半透明膜天井同面）
SLOPING CEILING: EXPOSED CONCRETE
屋根裏スラブ：コンクリート打放し
WALL: EXPOSED CONCRETE
壁：コンクリート打放し
GALLERY 14 [24-foot span gallery]
展示室 14 [24フィートギャラリー]
WALL: GYPSUM BOARD (2 LAYERS) ON PLYWOOD, E.P.
壁：ベニヤ板下地，プラスター・ボード２重貼，EP
FLOOR: WOOD FLOORING (WHITE OAK) w6" PLANK
床：木製フローリング（ホワイトオーク）
CURTAIN WALL SYSTEM: ANODIZED ALUMINUM MULLION (EXTRUSION)
カーテンウォール：
アルミニウム押出型材（アルマイト処理）
CURTAIN WALL SUPPORT STEEL COLUMN: H-SHAPE STEEL COLUMN, METALLIC PAINT
カーテンウォールサポート支柱：
H形鋼，メタリック塗装
2FL
2SL
WALL BASE: AIR INTAKE SLOT BUILT INTO WALL BASE, HARDWOOD, PAINT
巾木：リターン用スリット，木製塗装仕上
CEILING: GYPSUM BOARD, E.P.
天井：プラスター・ボード貼，EP
WALL: GYPSUM BOARD (2 LAYERS) ON PLYWOOD, E.P.
壁：ベニア板下地，プラスター・ボード２重貼，EP
NORTH
FLOOR: WOOD FLOORING (WHITE OAK) w6" PLANK
床：木製フローリング（ホワイトオーク）
FLOOR: STONE PLATE (GRANITE), TYPICAL SIZE 2'X4', t1 1/2"
床：石貼（御影石）
FLOOR GRILLE: STAINLESS STEEL LINEAR BAR AIR DIFFUSER
床空調吹出口：ステンレススチールグリル
BOTTOM OF POOL: GRAVEL (2"- 4")
池底：砂利敷
1FL
WATER
EXTERIOR WALL BASE AT POOL: PRECAST CONCRETE PANEL
外部巾木(池立上り)：PCパネル
GALLERY 13
展示室 13
GALLERY 14
展示室 14
GALLERY 4 [sculpture gallery]
展示室 4
[彫刻展示室]
GALLERY 5
展示室 5
GALLERY 6
展示室 6
3 [40-foot span gallery]
40フィートギャラリー]
LERY CEILING: GYPSUM BOARD, E.P.
室天井：プラスター・ボード，EP
ESSED LIGHT TRACK ON CEILING
器具用ライトトラック（天井同面）
UMINOUS MEMBRANE WATER PROOFING, RENE INSULATION BOARD t4", BALLAST
スファルト防水，断熱材(スチレンボード)，砂利敷
UVER EDGE PIECE: LINEAR GFRC TUBES w24"
一端部：GRC角パイプ
UVERS: LINEAR ALUMINUM EXTRUSIONS, FLUOROPOLYMER PAINT
一：アルミニウム押出型材，フッ素樹脂塗装
24'-0"
40'-0"
24'-0"
8'-0"
39'-11"
20'-1"
18'-0"

吹き抜けを介して結ばれた展示室。展示室相互の空間的なつながりが、来訪者の活発なアクティビティーを誘う。

Exhibition rooms connected through double-height spaces. The mutual spatial connections between the exhibition rooms positively welcome the activities of the visitors.

ハイサイドライトの展示室。展示室は全21室あり、1階と2階で、同じ作品を別々の視点で鑑賞できるユニークな展示もある。

Exhibition room with a clerestory. There are 21 exhibition rooms in total, while on the first and second floor there are also unique exhibitions where the same artwork can be appreciated from different points of view.

棟の狭間から望む西側の彫刻テラス。彫刻はヘンリー・ムーアの「Two-Piece Reclining Figure No.2」。

Looking from the gap between wings at the sculpture terrace to the west. The sculpture is "Two-Piece Reclining Figure No. 2" by Henry Moore.

建物南西端に設置されたリチャード・セラの「Vortex」。

Richard Serra's "Vortex" has been placed at the southwest end of the building.

クラーク美術館はマサチューセッツ州ウィリアムズタウンにあり、ニューヨーク、ボストンそれぞれから車で3時間ほどの豊かな自然に囲まれた伝統のある美術館である。クラーク夫妻により1995年に創設されたこの美術館は、19世紀の印象派絵画を中心としたコレクションを所有し、またアートヒストリーの分野での多くの優秀な美術関係者、学芸員を輩出する美術研究教育施設を併設する。そうしたコレクションや研究機関の拡大に伴う美術館の増築をわれわれは計画することになった。

57ヘクタールの敷地の周りは緩やかな丘陵地で、雑木林やところどころに湿地帯もあり、自然の豊かな場所である。現在そこには、美術館創設以来のネオクラシックスタイルの建物と、1973年に増築された新館とが建っているが、それらと隣接した場所が今回のプロジェクトの敷地となった。

なだらかな丘に囲まれた敷地に計画されるこの建物は、既存の地形の条件を活かしながら地上のボリュームは低く抑え、地下には中庭を通し自然光の入る新しい企画展示室やアトリウムなどが設けられる。ボリュームの過半は地下に沈めるよう配置され、要求される複雑なサーキュレーションを満足させるよう、既存のふたつの建物とも結ばれる。既存の異なったふたつの時代の建築を尊重しつつ、中央に人工の大きな水面を設けることにより、自然景観の中で全体をひとつにまとめるようなあり方が模索された。

訪れる人々が周辺に広がる自然に触れ、旧館のギャラリーや新設されるギャラリー、カフェやホールを行き交いながら、アートと自然環境を同時に楽しみ、また新たな発見ができるような美術館になればと考えている。

クラーク美術館増築計画

Sterling and Francine Clark Art Institute Expansion Project

2001-10 アメリカ合衆国 ウィリアムズタウン
——Williamstown, U.S.A.

The Sterling and Francine Clark Art Institute is an art museum located in a rich natural setting in Williamstown, Massachusetts, about a 3-hour drive from both Boston and New York City. Founded by the Clarks in 1955, the museum has a collection focused on 19th century Impressionist paintings. It also has a center for research and higher education with an active program of visiting fellows, conferences and a graduate program in art history. We were appointed to design a new Exhibition, Visitor and Conference Center.

The existing campus of 140 acres is a place rich in natural beauty, surrounded by gentle hills with copses of trees and wetlands in some places. The project site is adjacent to main museum building designed in a neo-classical style as well as an addition built in 1973.

Working within a setting of such natural beauty, we conceived the building so as to take full advantage of the surrounding landscape. The building footprint above grade was kept to a minimum with the special exhibition galleries located below grade, comprising courtyards and atriums to provide natural light. Most of the volume is submerged and connects with the existing circulation of the two adjacent buildings. By establishing a large reflecting pool, the central entrance, the new building and the existing buildings are integrated into one new garden landscape reflecting the natural beauty that surrounds it.

We have conceived a museum where art and nature can be simultaneously enjoyed with expanses of glass and sweeping views as one moves between the gallery spaces and buildings, enabling new discoveries.

生い茂る木々に囲まれた森の中に佇むクラーク美術館。既存の2棟の建物に対し、増築部分が水庭の一部として控えめなかたちでつくられる。

The Sterling and Francine Clark Art Institute is nestled within a forest of abundant trees. With regard to the two existing buildings, the new addition will be made in a modest shape, as one part of a water garden.

アプローチを描いたイメージパース。低く抑えられた建物が、連山を望む森の町の風景を切り取る。

Perspective image depicting the approach route. The building is kept low, cutting off the scenery of the forest town, and commanding a view of the mountain range.

冬になれば、水面はアイススケート場と化す。
森と一体化した自然のステージとしての美術館。

In winter, the water surface becomes an ice skating rink. Unified with the forest, the museum is a stage for nature.

水面越しに望む増築部分の夜景。　Night view of the new extension across the water surface.

敷地はシアトルの近郊、ベルヴュー市の中心からすぐの鬱蒼とした森の中、北向きに緩やかに下降する斜面に位置する。

教会は頂点を東に向けた二等辺三角形となっており、その頂点に近い位置に祭壇がおかれ、その背後は既存の森の中に樹木を避けるようにつくられる水の庭に面して開かれる。二等辺三角形は、三位一体の象徴であると同時に、祭壇に向かう求心性の高い明確な軸線をもつプランとして提案される。以前、西暦2000年を記念して建てられるローマの教会(1995-96)の国際設計競技応募案でもこの三角形の礼拝堂のプランはスタディされた。

144名収容の礼拝堂は祭壇、そして水庭に向けて緩やかに下降する。三角形のプランの底辺部分の中央にはこのためにデザインされたパイプオルガンが設置され、2隅にはスカイライトからの光が差し込み三角形を強調する。2階にはオルガン奏者の席と聖歌隊のバルコニー席が設けられる。

ここでは、宗派を超えた聖なる空間が求められ、日常の教会サービスの他、講演会、コンサートなどにも使用されることが考慮される。

敷地の東南、水の庭を北に望む部分に森に囲まれるようにひっそりと半円形の墓地がつくられる。生きる人、死せる人、そして自然との共存、建築とランドスケープとの融合がテーマとなった。

森の教会
Chapel in the Woods

2004- アメリカ合衆国 ベルヴュー —— Bellevue, U.S.A.

礼拝堂から祭壇方向を見る。祭壇の背後、二等辺三角形平面の頂部は、水庭に突き出すように壁を取り払い、可動式のガラス建具をはめ込んでいる。

Looking from the worship hall in the direction of the altar. Behind the altar, the tip of the isosceles triangle-shaped plan pierces the wall and projects into the water garden, and is fitted with operable glass fittings.

Gently sloping down to the north, the site is located in the middle of a lush forest close to the center of the city of Bellevue, in the outskirts of Seattle.

The chapel is shaped like an isosceles triangle with its tip facing toward the east. The altar is placed near the tip, which juts into a water garden, as if to ward off the trees in the existing forest. The triangle symbolizes the Trinity, and is simultaneously a proposal for a plan with a clear axis oriented toward the altar. The triangular plan had previously been studied for the international design competition for a church in Rome (Vicariato di Rome, 1995-1996) to be built in commemoration of the year 2000 according the Christian calendar.

The worship hall can accommodate 144 people, and gently slopes toward the altar and the water garden. A custom-designed pipe organ has been installed in the base of the triangular plan, and light comes in from skylights in two corners, emphasizing the triangle. The organist's seat and a balcony for the choir are installed on the second floor.

Here, a holy space was requested that transcends denominations and can accommodate daily church services as well as lectures and concerts.

Surrounded by the quiet forest, a semi-circular cemetery will be made in the southeast with a view of the water garden to the north. The theme became coexistence between living people, dead people, and nature, as well as a fusion between architecture and landscape.

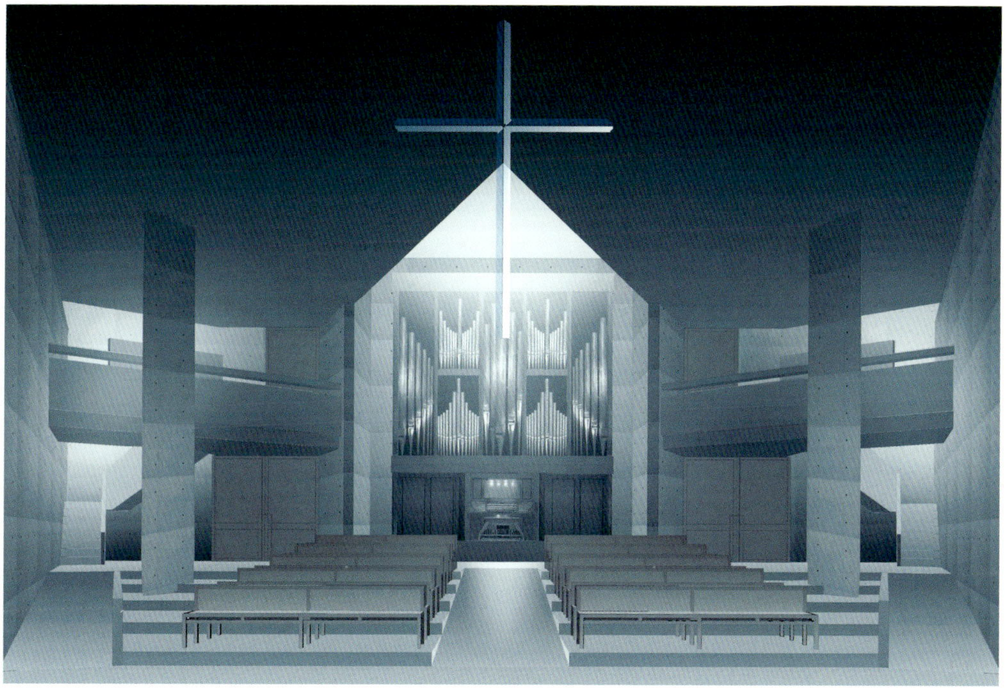

三角形をモチーフに建築と一体にデザインされたパイプオルガン。
Pipe organ designed in unity with the building by means of a triangular motif.

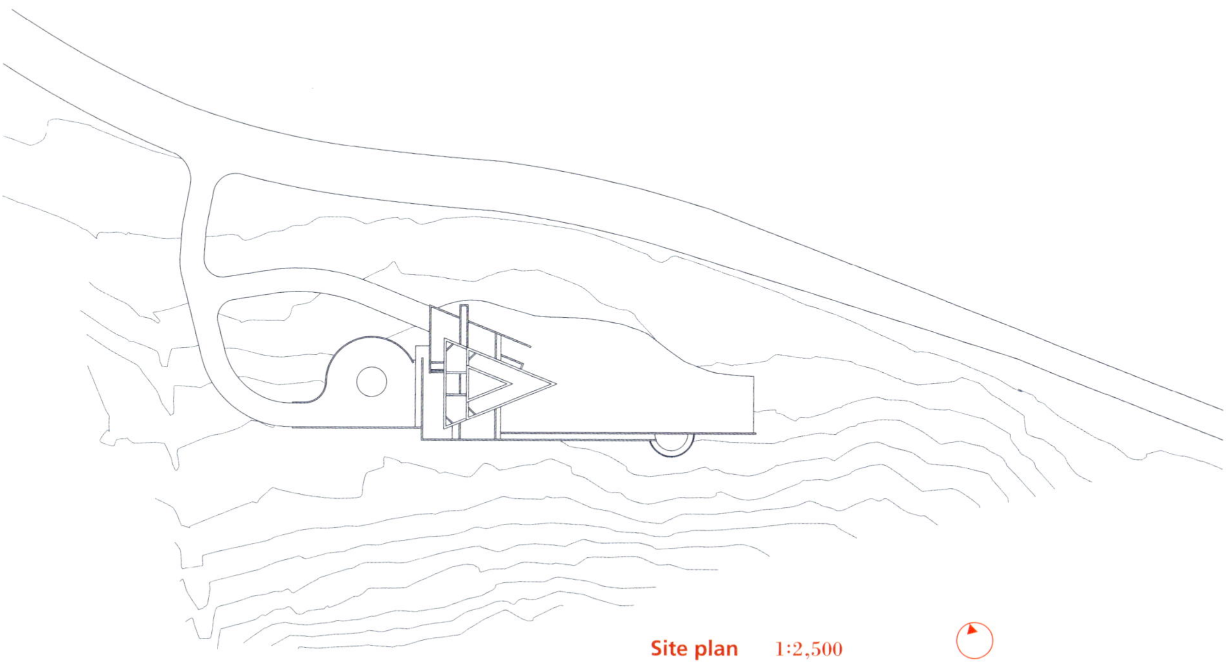

Site plan 1:2,500

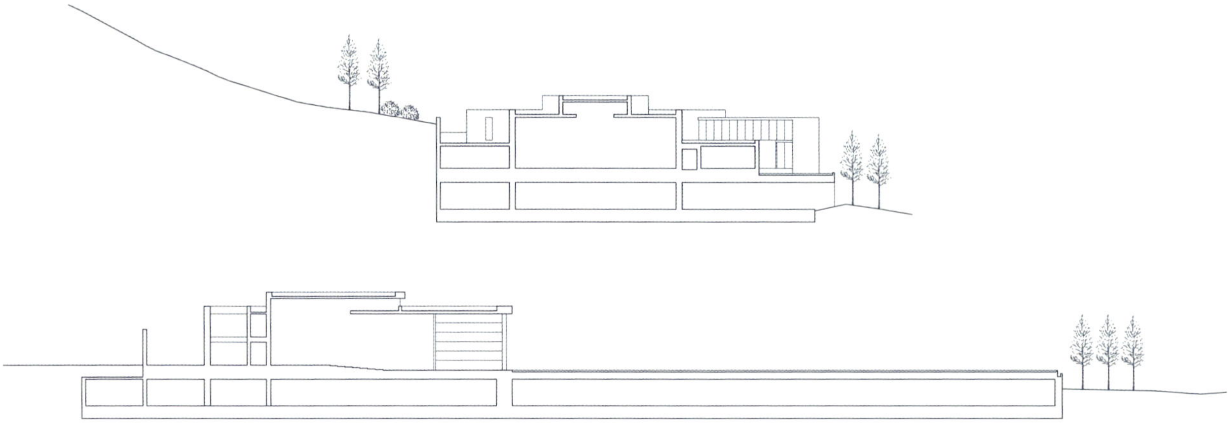

Section

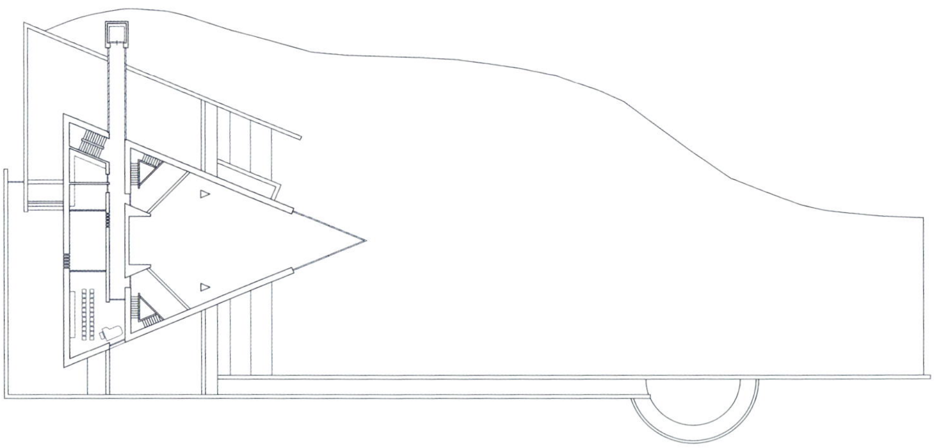

Second floor plan

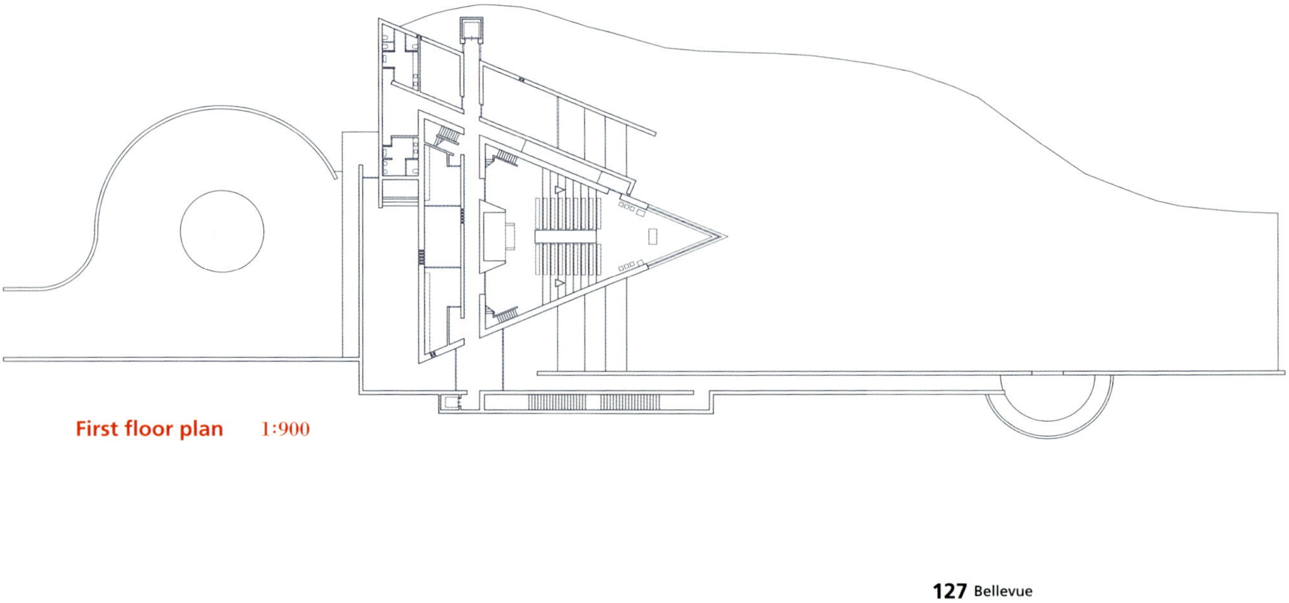

First floor plan 1:900

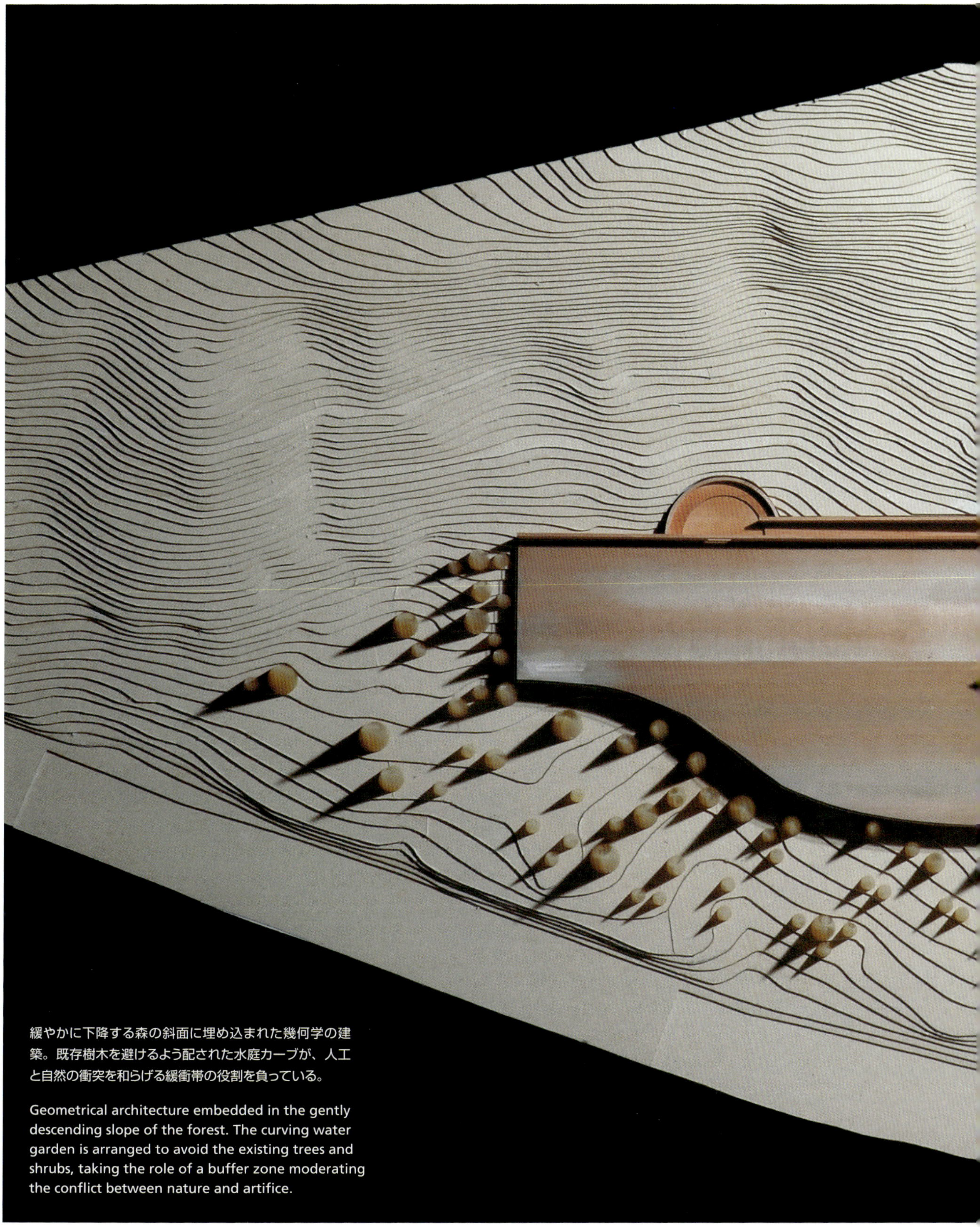

緩やかに下降する森の斜面に埋め込まれた幾何学の建築。既存樹木を避けるよう配された水庭カーブが、人工と自然の衝突を和らげる緩衝帯の役割を負っている。

Geometrical architecture embedded in the gently descending slope of the forest. The curving water garden is arranged to avoid the existing trees and shrubs, taking the role of a buffer zone moderating the conflict between nature and artifice.

パースペクティブ・ドローイング。三角形の幾何学が
人間と自然と建築とを一体に結びつける。

Perspective drawing. The triangular geometry unifies people, nature, and architecture.

エッセイ

レンゾ・ピアノ

Tadao は私にとって、日本の兄弟のようなもの。
われわれは年齢もほぼ同じだし、同じ反アカデミズムを背景としてもっているし、
寿司屋に関するテイストも一緒なのだ。
もちろん、建築家としてのわれわれは大きく異なっているし、
インスピレーションとするものも相異なる。
しかし、ディテールを追求する頑固さは共通している。

シカゴ美術館の日本屏風ギャラリーのマジックが好きだ。
パリにあるユネスコ本部の瞑想空間のサスペンドされた空気が好きだ。
フォートワース現代美術館の穏やかにも力強い静謐さ、
セントルイスのピューリッツァー美術館の美しさ、
そしてヴェネツィアの新しいパラッツォ・グラッシの微妙さが好きだ。

いずれも完璧なプロポーションを備えた珠玉ばかりである。

レンゾ・ピアノ
建築家。1937年イタリア、ジェノバ生まれ。1970年よりリチャード・ロジャースと、
1977年よりピーター・ライスとパートナーシップを組む。1989年 RIBA ゴールドメダル、
1995年高松宮殿下記念世界文化賞、1998年プリツカー賞受賞。

Essay

Renzo Piano

Tadao is a kind of Japanese brother for me.
We have almost the same age, the same anti-academic background
and the same taste for Sushi bars.
Of course, we are very different as architects and we have different inspirations:
but we have the same stubbornness in pursuing details.

I love the magic of the Gallery for Japanese Screen at the Art Institute of Chicago.
I love the suspended atmosphere of the Meditation Space at UNESCO in Paris.
I love the serene and powerful calm of the Mnodern Art Museum of Fort Worth,
the beauty of the Pulitzer Foundation for the Arts in St. Louis and the subtleties
of the new Palazzo Grassi in Venice.

They are all gems of perfect proportion.

Renzo Piano
Architect. Born in Genoa, Italy in 1937. Established a partnership with Richard Rogers from 1970
and with Peter Rice from 1977. Recipient of the RIBA Gold Medal in 1989,
the Praemium Imperiale Award in 1995 and the Pritzker Prize in 1998.

1992年に行われたスペイン・セビリア万国博覧会の日本館として計画された。「新しい時代の発見」をテーマに掲げるこの万博パヴィリオンは、日本の伝統文化と現代の先端テクノロジーが高度に洗練された場所で融合し、しかもそれが国境を超えて交流しうる可能性を提示できるものでなければならないと考えた。間口60m、奥行き40m、最高高さ25mの規模をもつパヴィリオンは、フロアを地上階から3階までの4層で構成し、その上部は集成材の柱・梁で支持されるテフロンの半透明膜の屋根が巨大な空間を覆っている。外部はムクの下見板が反りのついた大壁面となってパヴィリオンを包み込む。私はこのパヴィリオンは、日本の心、日本の技術を、一瞬にして人々に対して伝えることのできるものであるべきだと考えた。日本の文化は「生成り」の文化である。そのため、着色しない生成りの木を構造材および仕上げ材として用い、地上25mのワンルームの迫力ある空間をつくった。また技術、素材の扱いを通して日本人のもつこまやかな自然観を全体で強く表現した。

この世界最大級の木造建築は、日本の建築技術をもとにして、材料調達、その加工、金物等の製作、現場での建設作業とそれぞれの段階で、世界各国の技術者が参加して完成された。つまり、この建設の過程で交わされる各国の技術者の激しい対話によって、木造建築の新しい考え方が発見されることを期待したからだ。この建設の過程自体も大きなイベントであり文化交流であったと思う。

パヴィリオン中央にそびえる11mの太鼓橋が、観客を最上階に導く。この巨大な太鼓橋を渡るという身体的、精神的刺激は、すでに世界のさまざまな歴史と文化を横断する体験でもある。そして橋を昇りきった人々は、そこに立ち現れてくる広大な吹き抜け開放空間のエントランスギャラリーで、更なる新しい世界を思い描くことができるだろう。

1992年セビリア万国博覧会日本館
Japan Pavilion, Expo'92/Sevilla

1989-92 スペイン セビリア —— Sevilla, Spain

This was designed as the Japanese pavilion for the 1992 Expo held in Seville, Spain. Following the given theme of "The Age of Discovery," we thought this Expo Pavilion must be a highly refined place that unifies the traditional culture of Japan and modern advanced technology, and furthermore, presents the possibility of interactions that exceed national borders. The pavilion has a width of 60m, a depth of 40m, and a maximum height of 25m, with four layers of floors from the ground level to the third level, above which is a vast space covered with a huge, translucent teflon membrane roof supported by glue-laminated timber columns and beams. The exterior comprises large walls of solid timber panels wrapping the pavilion. I considered it necessary for this pavilion to be something that could instantly convey to people Japanese spirit and Japanese technology. The culture of Japan is a culture of "raw nature." Therefore, uncolored natural wood was used for the structure and the surface finishes, in order to make a single, compelling space 25m above the ground. Moreover, through the techniques and treatments of materials, it all expresses the sensitive Japanese view of nature.

Based on Japanese architectural techniques, this world-class wooden architecture was completed with the participation of artisans from countries all over the world at every stage—material supply and processing, manufacture of hardware, on-site construction work. In other words, we hoped that a new way of thinking about wooden architecture would be discovered through the heated dialogue between artisans from different countries, exchanged during this construction process. I think that this construction process itself was a big event for cultural exchange.

The 11m-long arched bridge that dominates the center of the Pavilion guides spectators to the top floor. The physical and mental stimulation of crossing this huge arched bridge is the experience of crossing the various histories and cultures already present in the world. The people who ascend the bridge and appear standing there in the vast open void space of the entrance gallery are perhaps able to imagine an even newer world.

反りをもつ外壁と雨樋のデイテール、アプローチのブリッジなど、
ほぼすべてのイメージがこの段階で描かれている。

The curved outer walls, the drainspout details, the approach bridge—almost the entire image had been depicted at this stage.

正面外観。「世界最大級の木の建築」を目標につくられた、間口60m、奥行き40m、軒高さ24mのパヴィリオン。屋根を支える組柱と反りをもつ下見板張りの巨大壁面が、静けさと力強さを併せもったアルカイックな表情をたたえる。

Front façade. Built with the objective of being "the world's largest wooden building," the pavilion is 60m wide, 40m deep, and has an eaves height of 24m. The columns supporting the roof and the siding attached to the huge curved walls have a unified serenity and strength, giving an archaic expression.

左頁：北側外観。右頁：アプローチの太鼓橋を昇ると、巨大な吹き抜けのエントランスギャラリー。巨大な木組の架構がテフロン幕による軽快な屋根を支える。

Left page: North façade. Right page: Ascending the arched bridge of the approach to the huge void or the entrance gallery. The huge wooden assembly supports a light roof made of teflon membrance.

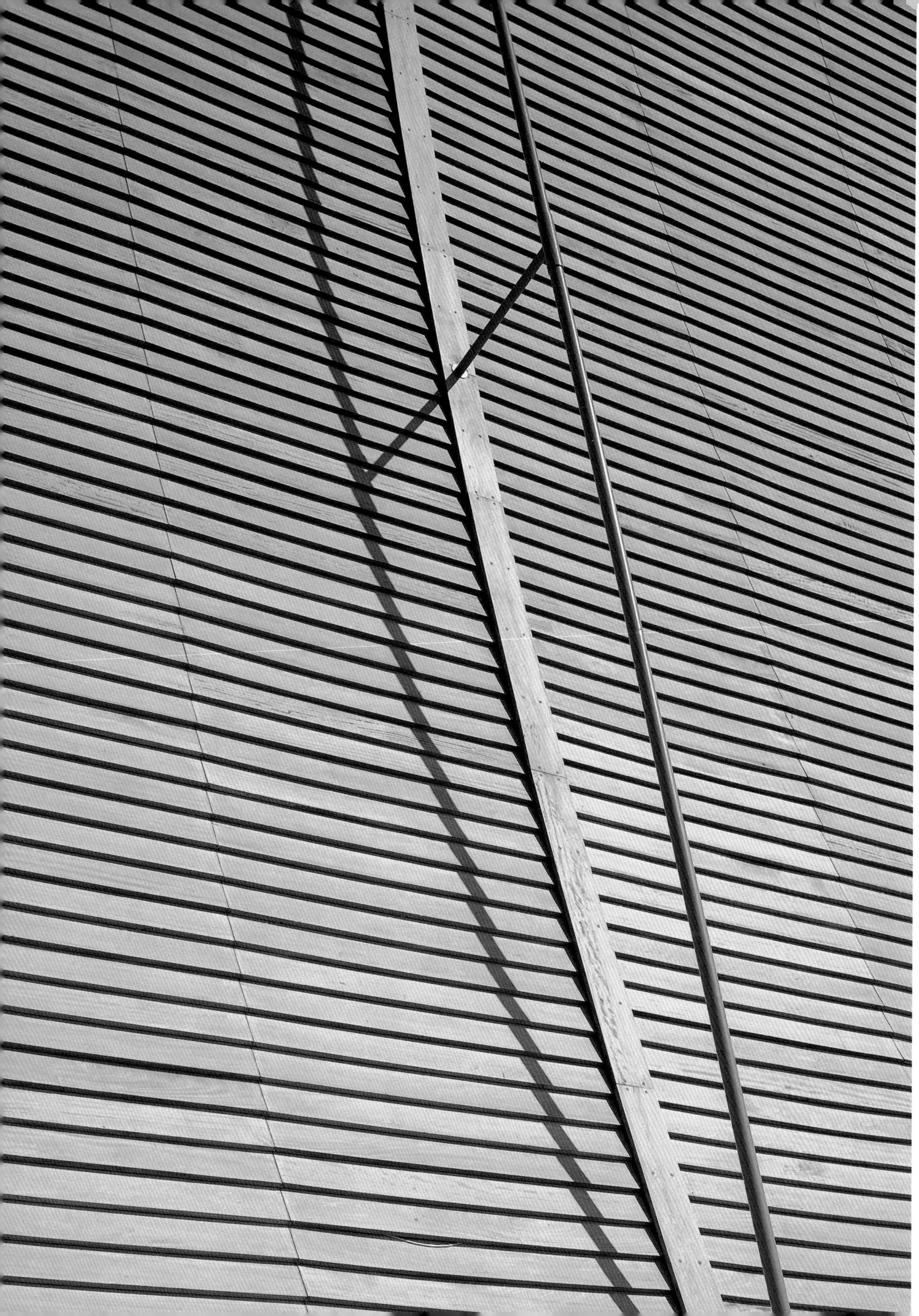

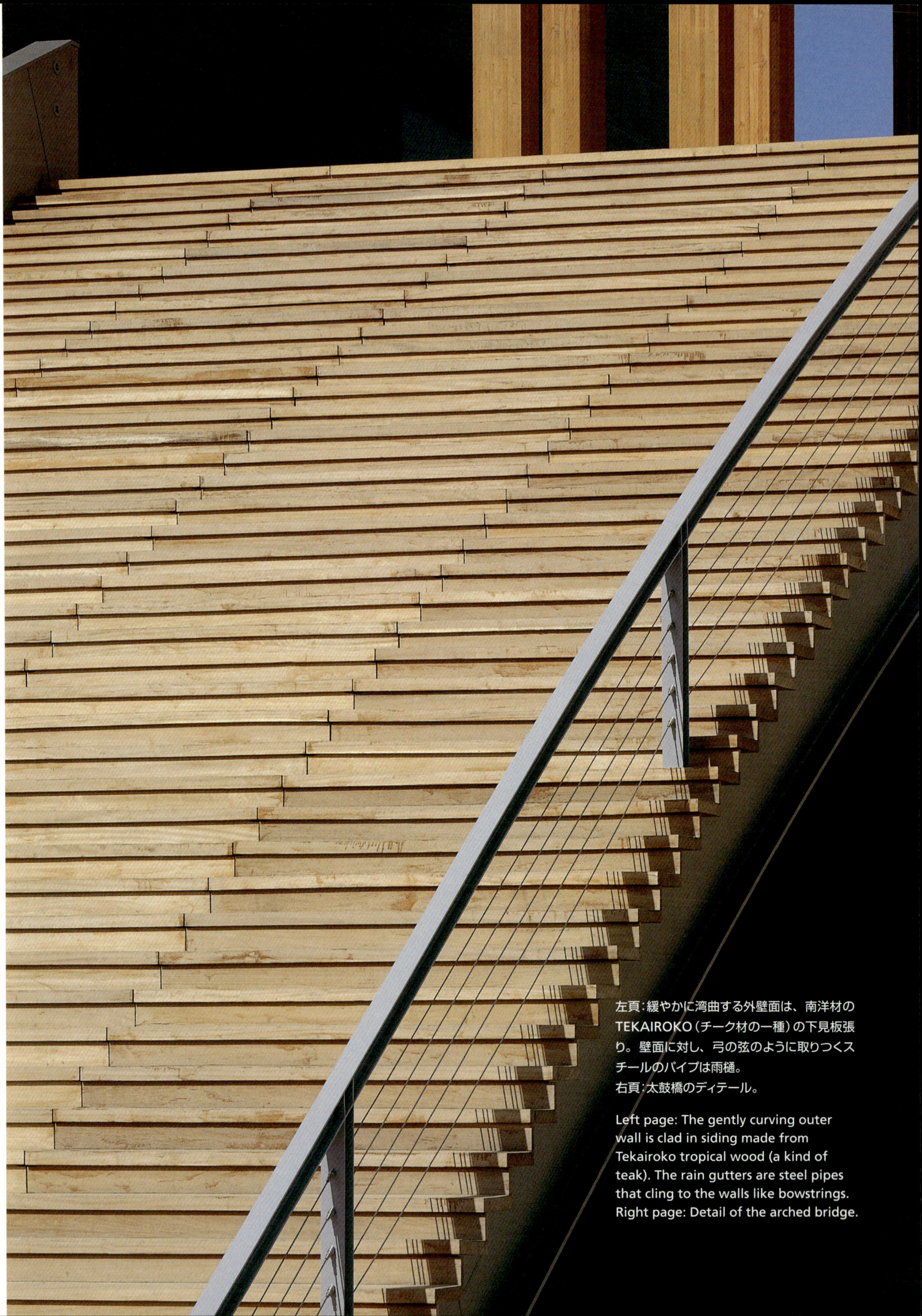

左頁：緩やかに湾曲する外壁面は、南洋材のTEKAIROKO（チーク材の一種）の下見板張り。壁面に対し、弓の弦のように取りつくスチールのパイプは雨樋。
右頁：太鼓橋のディテール。

Left page: The gently curving outer wall is clad in siding made from Tekairoko tropical wood (a kind of teak). The rain gutters are steel pipes that cling to the walls like bowstrings.
Right page: Detail of the arched bridge.

左頁：パヴィリオンは、まず太鼓橋で4階のエントランスギャラリーに昇り、そこから5つの展示室を巡りながらフロアを降りていく構成となっている。
右頁：建物背後からエントランスギャラリーを見る。

Left page: The pavilion composition involves first ascending to the fourth floor entrance gallery via the arched bridge, and from there descending through the floors while walking across the five exhibition spaces.
Right page: Looking at the entrance gallery from behind the building.

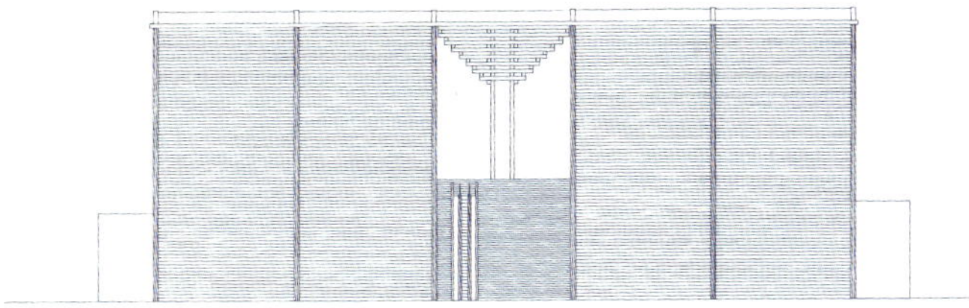

Elevation 1:1,000

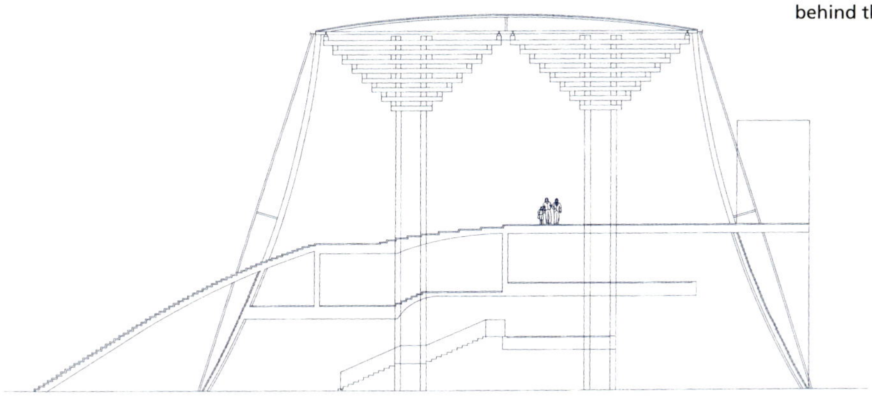

Section 1:500

1 gallery
2 exhibition room
3 auditorium
4 foyer
5 lounge
6 restaurant
7 shop
8 office
9 staff
10 mechanical
11 void

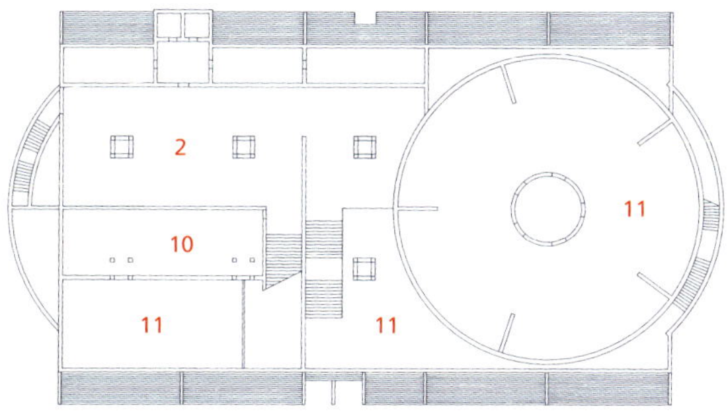

Second floor plan

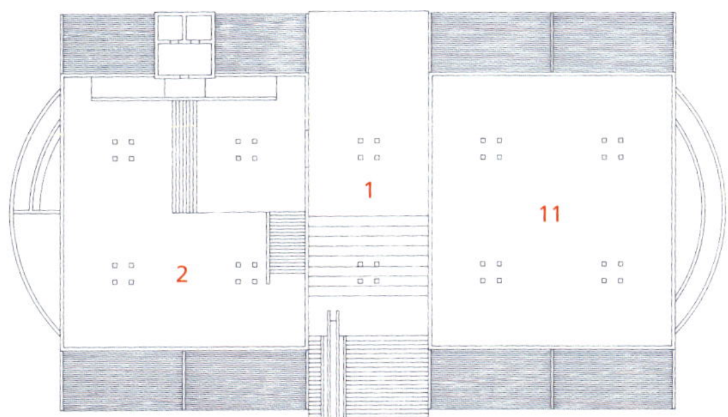

Fourth floor plan

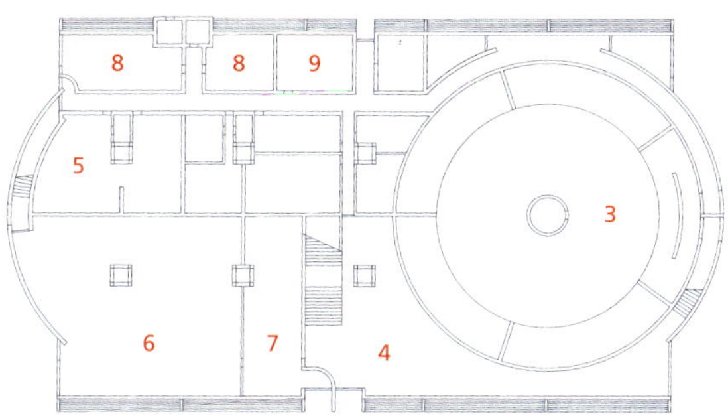

First floor plan

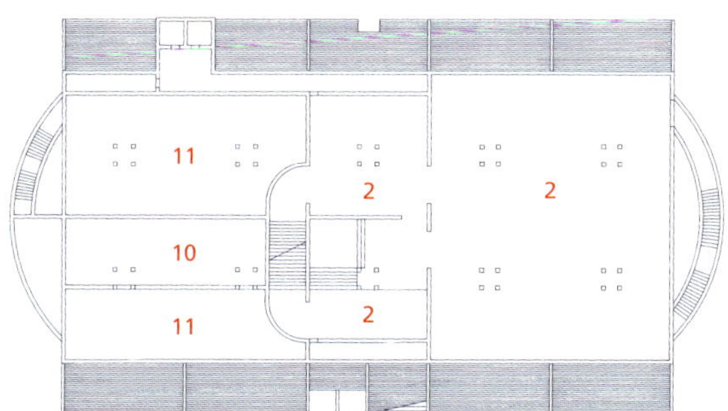

Third floor plan 1:1,000

3階の展示室。木造の架構による空間に、天井のテフロン膜を通した柔らかな光が満ちている。

The exhibition room on the third floor. The space created by the wood framework is suffused with soft light through the teflon membrane of the ceiling.

集成材を組み合わせた柱のディテール。
Detail of the glue-laminated timber columns.

伝統的な日本木造建築の斗供(ときょう)を思わせる集成材の架構。

A glue-laminated timber framework reminiscent of the brackets of traditional Japanese wooden architecture.

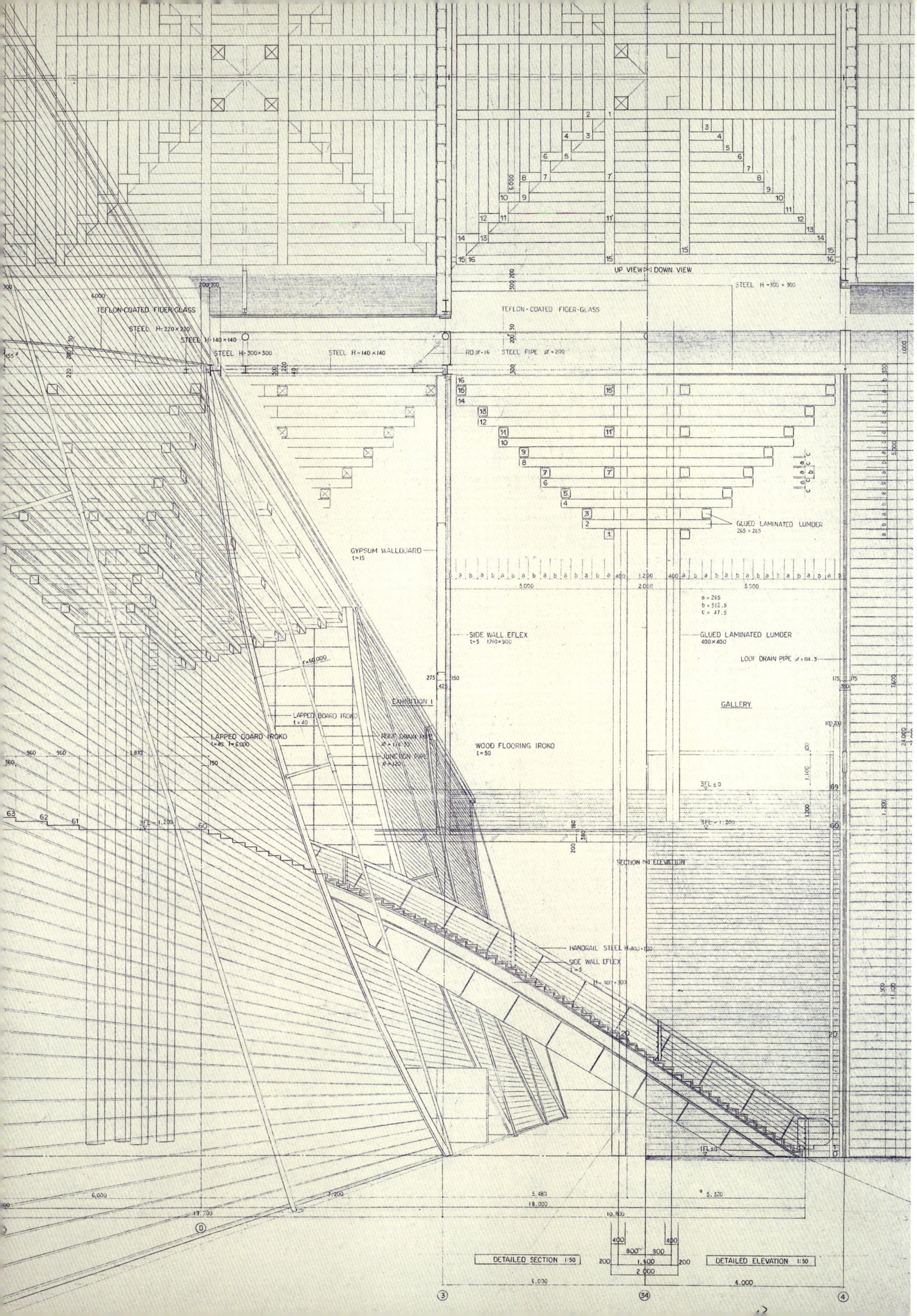

UP VIEW
DOWN VIEW
TEFLON-COATED FIDER-GLASS
STEEL H-220×220
STEEL H-140×140
STEEL H-300×300
STEEL PIPE
STEEL H-300×300
GYPSUM WALLBOARD
t=15
GLUED LAMINATED LUMDER
265×265
SIDE WALL EFLEX
t=5
GLUED LAMINATED LUMDER
400×400
LOOF DRAIN PIPE
EXHIBITION I
GALLERY
LAPPED BOARD IROKO
t=40
LAPPED BOARD IROKO
ROOF DRAIN PIPE
JUNCTION PIPE
WOOD FLOORING IROKO
t=50
SECTION
ELEVATION
HANDRAIL STEEL
SIDE WALL EFLEX
t=5
a=265
b=312.5
c=47.5
DETAILED SECTION 1:50
DETAILED ELEVATION 1:50

エントランスギャラリーより、夕暮れの万博会場を見る。

Looking at the Expo grounds by twilight from the entrance gallery.

1987年の夏、ヴィトラの社長ロルフ・フェルバウムから、1991年に迎える自らの50歳の誕生日の記念に、瞑想のための建築を建てたいのだが、設計を依頼できないかといわれたことから始まった。

ヴィトラ社は新旧の作家の家具を広く制作している家具会社である。設計依頼を受けた建物の用途は最終的に役員用のセミナーハウスに落ち着いた。

敷地はスイス、ドイツ国境近くにある、この会社の工場に隣接している。敷地が平板であるため、建物へのアプローチを含めて、いかに建物を配置するかが問題となった。われわれは、まず建物をできるだけ低く抑え、平坦な敷地に沈みこませたようなかたちを考えた。さらに正方形、円といった純粋な幾何学的形態によってヴォリュームとヴォイドを構成し、そこでの空間の緊張と解放によって、内部に人々の意識深くに訴えかける豊かな空間を孕ませようとした。

建物は2層からなり、大小の会議室、図書室、講義室、およびロビーから構成される。それらは正方形の壁で囲い取られたサンクンコートに開放されている。平板な敷地に穿たれた正方形のサンクンコートは、建物全体に自然を導き入れる装置であり、光や風という自然を建物内部に引き込み、留めようとする。それらは建物に彩りを与え、人々の活動を演出してゆく。

フランク・O・ゲーリーによる自由奔放な形態操作に基づくヴィトラ・デザイン・ミュージアムと、われわれの計画した抑制的ともいえる建物とが、その中間にクレス・オルデンバーグの彫刻を挟んで対峙する。ふたつの対照的な建築表現が、互いに刺激し合うような関係をつくり出すことができればと考えた。

ヴィトラ・セミナーハウス
Vitra Seminar House

1987-93 ドイツ ヴァイルアムライン —— Weil am Rhein, Germany

デザイン家具で知られるヴィトラ社の工場に隣接する広大な野原の中央に、クレス・オルデンバーグの巨大な彫刻が置かれ、それを挟んで、フランク・O・ゲーリー設計のヴィトラ・デザイン・ミュージアムと、安藤によるセミナーハウスが向かい合う。

In the middle of a large open field adjoining the site of the Vitra factory, known for designer furniture, is a huge sculpture by Claes Oldenburg interposed between the Vitra Design Museum, designed by Frank O. Gehry, and Ando's Seminar House.

In the summer of 1987 Rolf Fehlbaum, the president of Vitra, asked me about the possibility of designing a building for meditation as a commemoration of his own fiftieth birthday in 1991.

Vitra is a furniture company with an extensive range of furniture by old and new designers. The function of the building he commissioned me to design was finally settled as a seminar house for the executives.

The site is in Switzerland, in the vicinity of the German border, and is adjacent to the company factory. The site is very flat, so our concern was how to arrange the building, including its approach route. We first thought about keeping the building form as low as possible, sunk into the flat site. We then thought about a composition of volumes and voids in pure, geometrical forms such as squares and circles, in which spatial tension and release would produce rich spaces with a deep appeal to the consciousness of people inside them.

The building has two levels, and is composed of large and small conference rooms, a library, a lecture room, and a lobby. These open onto a sunken court enclosed with square walls. This square sunken court penetrating the flat surface of the site is a device to guide nature throughout the building, drawing natural wind and light into the interior. This gives color to the building, and sets the stage for human activities.

The building we designed, which might be described as introverted, confronts The Vitra Design Museum designed by Frank O. Gehry, which is based on the free manipulation of form, and a sculpture by Claes Oldenburg has been placed between them. We though these two contrasting architectural expressions could produce a mutually stimulating relationship.

オルデンバーグの彫刻越しに描かれた建物全景のイメージスケッチ。

Image sketch showing a panoramic view of the building, depicted beyond the Claes Oldenburg sculpture.

オルデンバーグの彫刻越しに見る建物全景。
Panoramic view of the building looking across Oldenburg's sculpture.

コンクリートの長い壁がエントランスへと人々を導く。
エントランス脇の樹木は既存のもの。敷地内にあった樹木はすべてそのまま残すよう計画されている。

A long concrete wall guides people to the entrance. The trees and shrubs beside the entrance were already there. It was designed in order to leave the trees and shrubs of the site unaffected.

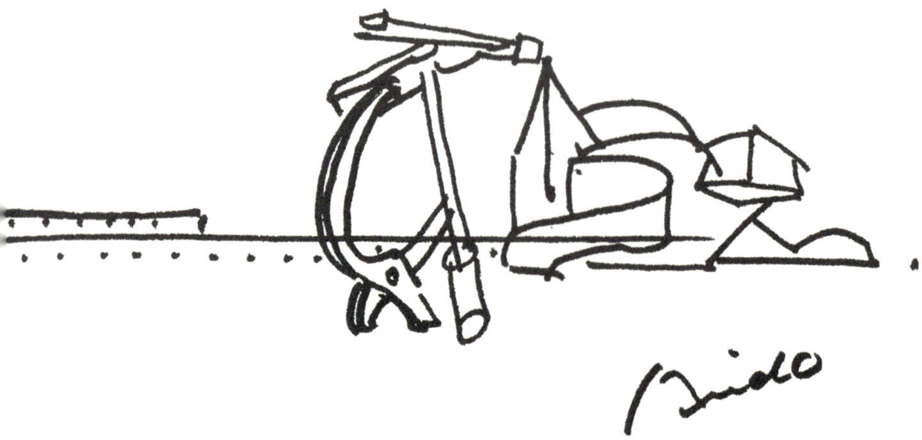

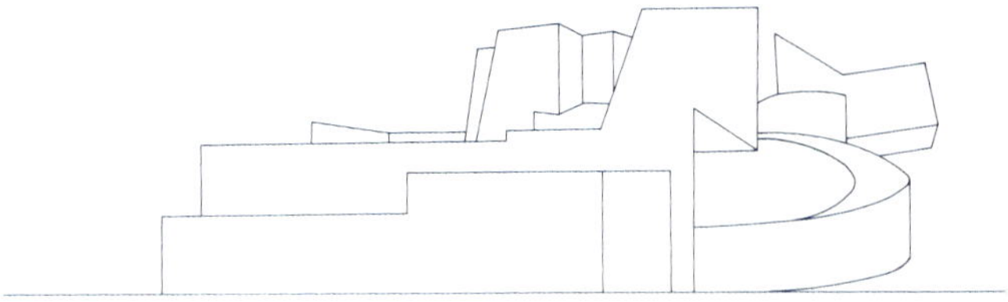

Section 1:600

南側から見る建物全景。緑のなだらかな風景を損なわぬよう、建物のヴォリュームは地下に埋め込み、高さを低く抑えている。

Panoramic view of the building from the south. In order not to damage the gently sloping green scenery, the building volume was buried underground, and its height kept low.

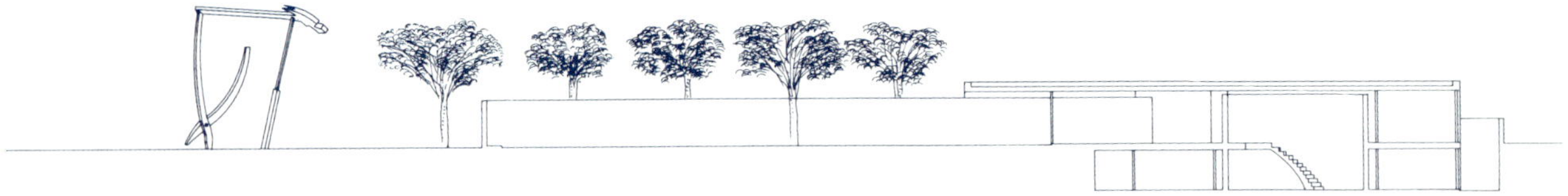

ゲーリー設計のヴィトラ・デザイン・ミュージアムから
セミナーハウスを見る。躍動感溢れるミュージアム
の造形と好対照をなす、静謐なコンクリートの空間。

Looking at the Seminar House from the Vitra Design Museum designed by Gehry. The sculptural forms of the museum brim with a sense of vitality, and the tranquil concrete space achieves a good contrast.

エントランスからアプローチを見る。ストイックなコンクリートの壁面に、生い茂った木の影が映える。
Looking at the approach from the entrance. Shadows from the dense trees are projected on the stoic concrete wall surface.

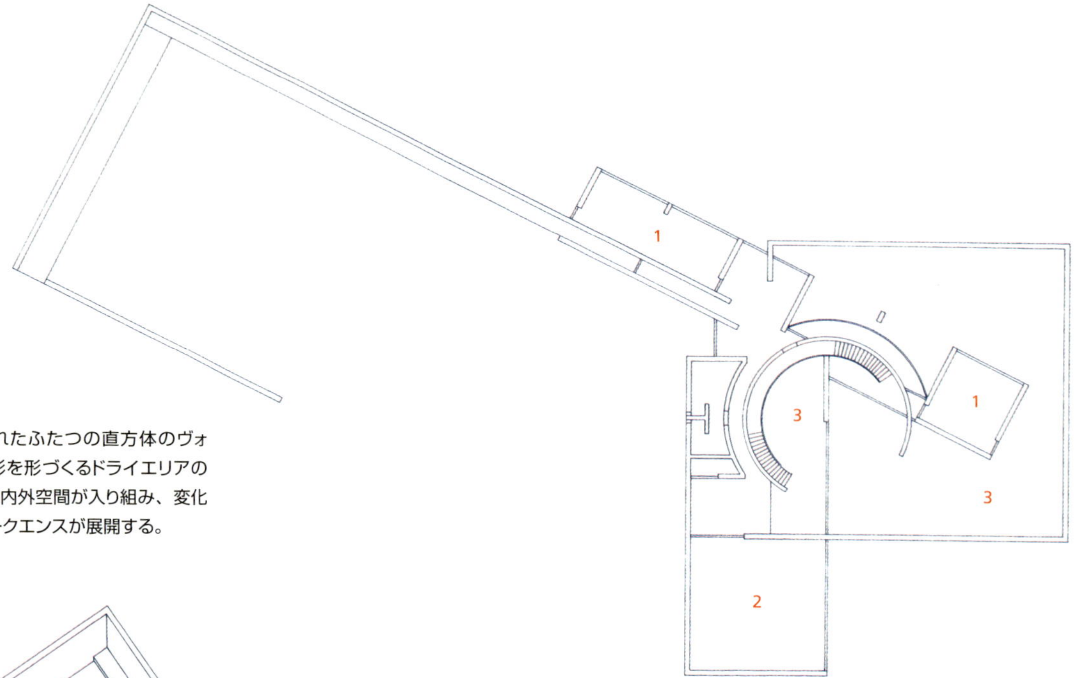

First floor plan

角度を振って配されたふたつの直方体のヴォリュームに、正方形を形づくるドライエリアの壁が重なることで、内外空間が入り組み、変化に富んだ空間のシークエンスが展開する。

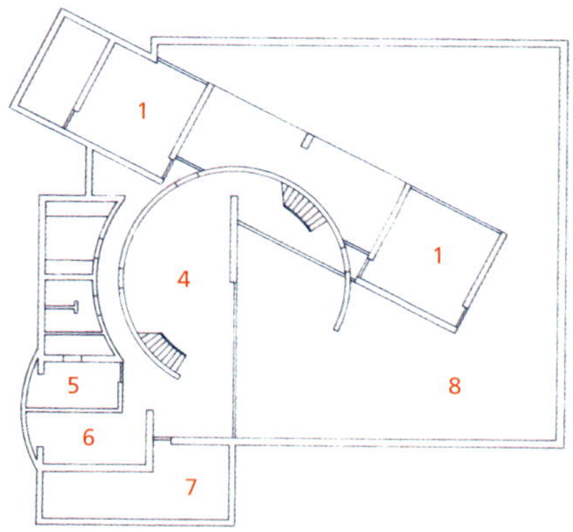

Basement floor plan 1:500

1 seminar room
2 AV room
3 void
4 hall
5 guest room
6 library
7 mechanical
8 court

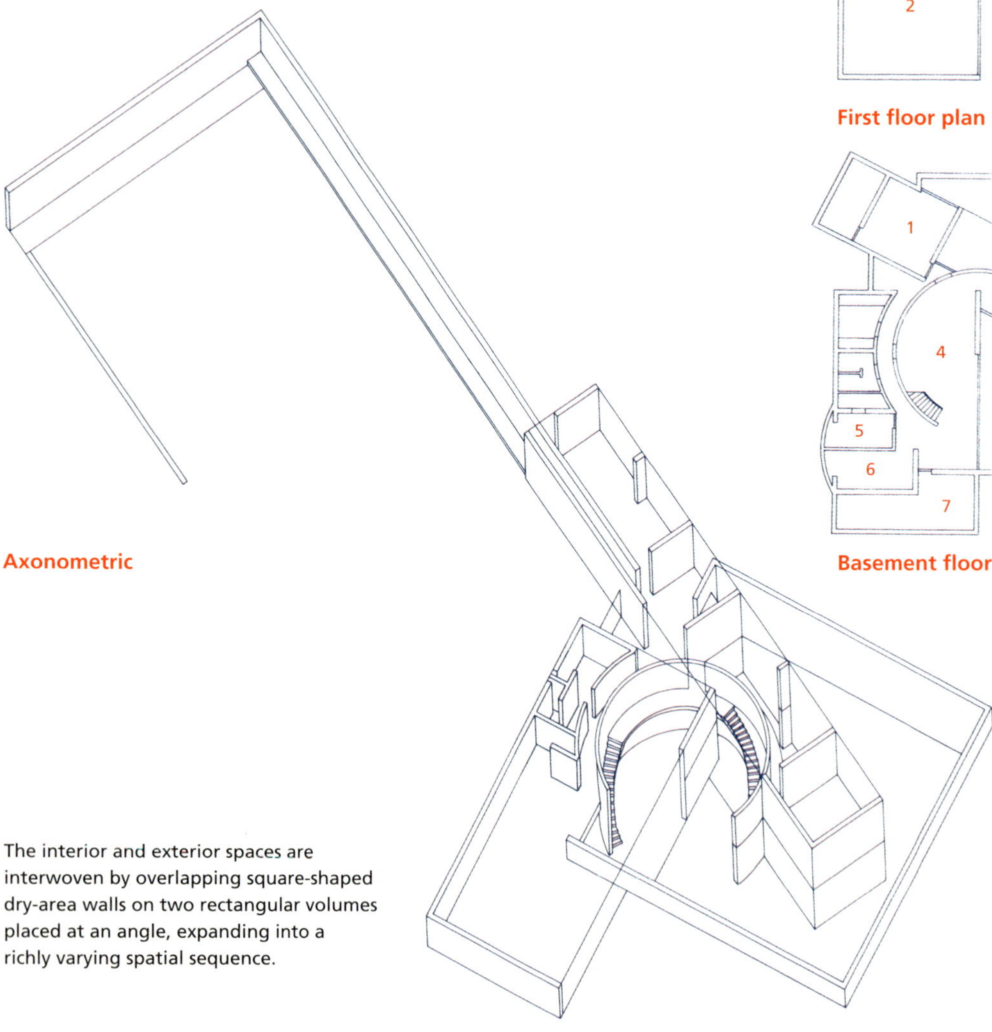

Axonometric

The interior and exterior spaces are interwoven by overlapping square-shaped dry-area walls on two rectangular volumes placed at an angle, expanding into a richly varying spatial sequence.

ドライエリア夜景。壁に囲われた静謐な空間。
Night view of the dry area. A serene space enclosed by walls.

1階から円形の壁が囲いとる吹き抜けのホールを見る。

Looking from the first floor toward the double-height hall enclosed by a circular wall.

単純な構成の内に展開する、変化に富んだ空間のシークエンス。

A richly varying spatial sequence expands within the simple composition.

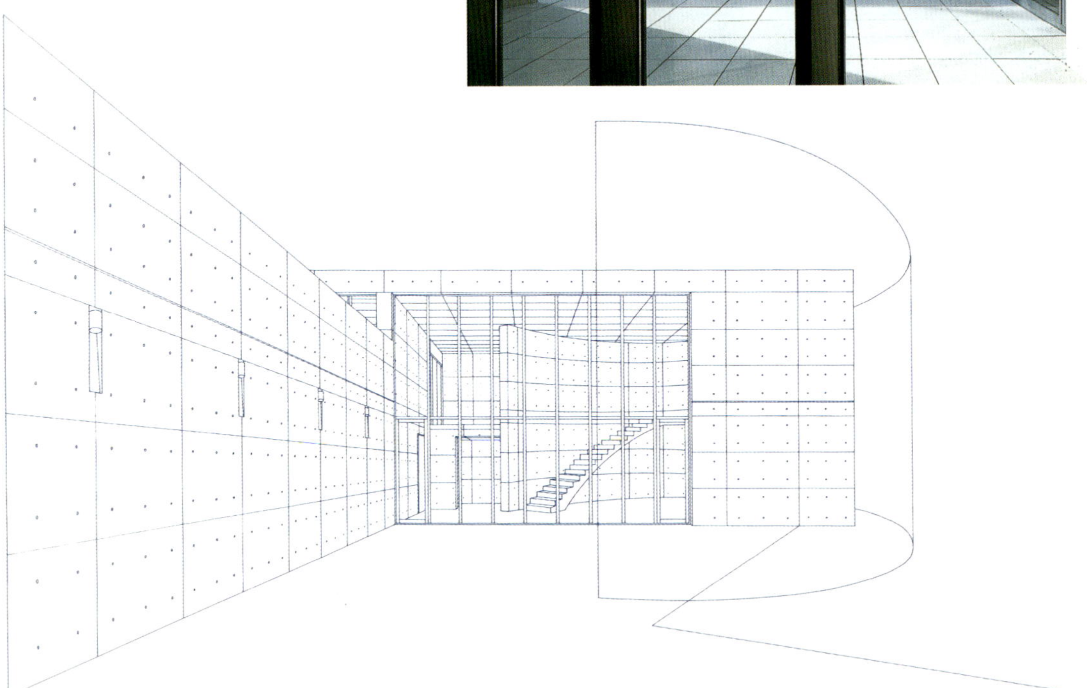

Perspective

ドライエリア北側を見る。
Looking at the north side of the dry area.

内向きの空間構成の中で、唯一全面ガラス開口として外部に開かれた AVルーム。左手に見えるのはドライエリアを囲いとる壁。

Within the introverted spatial composition, the audiovisual room opens toward the exterior through a single opening made entirely from glass. The wall enclosing the dry area is visible to the right.

1995年に設立50周年を迎えたユネスコの、その記念事業として計画されたものである。ユネスコから直接依頼を受けた。求められたのは、あらゆる宗教、宗派を超えた世界平和のための〈祈りの空間〉であった。ユネスコ本部は、マルセル・ブロイヤーらによる近代建築の代表作である。また敷地内には、建物の内外を問わず、ピカソやジャコメッティ、イサム・ノグチらをはじめとするさまざまな作家の芸術作品が点在している。

敷地は、四方をブロイヤー設計の建物に囲まれ、イサム・ノグチの日本庭園に隣接してあった。そのような既存環境に敬意を払いつつ、いかに自立した、強い意志を発する〈祈りの空間〉を表現するかが課題となった。

まず、荒廃していたイサム・ノグチの庭を修復することから始めた。その次に、周囲の空間から切り離された領域を囲いとるために2枚の壁を立て、敷地いっぱいに広がる水面をつくり出した。水面は地形に沿って段状にならされ、その最下段に祈りの空間本体を浮かべる。さらにアプローチとして、水段に沿うように下降して〈祈りの空間〉へと至るスロープを設ける。

〈祈りの空間〉に、空間として根源的な強さをもたせたかったので、建築を構成する要素を徹底して削ぎ落とそうと考えた。その結果、建具も仕上げも一切を排除した、光とコンクリートのみの建物が生まれた。

形態的には、直径、高さともに6.3mのシリンダーとなっている。このスケールは、周囲との景観上の関係性から導かれた。開口部は前後の出入口と、天井に円筒形に沿って穿たれたスリット状のトップライトのみである。要素を限定することで、より劇的な多様さを孕む光の効果を期待した。

床面、池の底には、広島市から寄贈された被爆石が貼られている。その表面に清らかな水を流すことで世界で初めて使用された核兵器のために尊い命を失った人々の鎮魂とすると同時に、ヒロシマの被爆石を前にして、ここを訪れた人々に、人類の平和について深く考えてほしいと思った。この場所が、文字通り〈祈りの空間〉として機能していくことを期待している。

ユネスコ瞑想空間
Meditation Space, UNESCO

1994-95 フランス パリ —— Paris, France

This was designed as a commemorative project for the fiftieth anniversary of the establishment of UNESCO, which occurred in 1995. We were commissioned directly by UNESCO. They requested a "space of meditation" for global peace, transcending all religions and sects. The UNESCO headquarters is a very important work of modern architecture by Marcel Breuer. Moreover, artworks by various artists including Picasso, Giacometti, and Isamu Noguchi are scattered across the premises, both inside and outside the buildings.

The site is enclosed on all sides by the buildings designed by Breuer, and is adjacent to Isamu Noguchi's Japanese garden. While showing deference to this existing environment, our theme was how this "space of meditation" could express a strong, independent will.

We began by restoring Isamu Noguchi's garden, which was in a state of disrepair. Next, two walls were put up to enclose an area separated from the surrounding spaces, and a body of water was created across the entire site. The water steps along the topography, and the main volume of the meditation space floats on the lowest step. We also installed an approach route that descends along the water steps to arrive at the "space of meditation."

Because I had wanted to endow this "space of meditation" with strength, I completely reduced the number of compositional elements in the architecture. As a result, fittings and finishes are entirely excluded, producing a building comprising only light and concrete.

Formally, it is a cylinder of 6.3m in diameter, as well as in height. This scale was determined by the relationship with the surrounding scenery. The only apertures are the front and rear entrances, and a slit-shaped skylight in the ceiling that follows the shape of the cylinder. By limiting the elements, we hoped for more dramatic variety in the effects of the light.

Stone exposed to radiation was donated by the city of Hiroshima, and has been applied to the floor surface and the bottom of the pond. By flowing pure water across this surface, I want the people visiting here, standing before the irradiated stone from Hiroshima, to think deeply about the repose of the souls of those people who lost their precious lives in the world's first use of nuclear weapons, and at the same time, about peace for all humanity. I hope this place will literally function as a "space of meditation."

瞑想空間のイメージスケッチ。　Image sketch of the meditation space.

水上に浮かぶスロープが導く、瞑想空間へのアプローチ。清らかな水の流れる池の底には、広島から寄贈された被爆石が散りばめられている。

The approach to the meditation space, guided by the ramp floating above the water. The bottom of the pond flowing with pure water is lined with irradiated stone donated by the city of Hiroshima.

敷地はマルセル·ブロイヤー設計のユネスコ本部ビルとイサム·ノグチによる日本庭園に挟まれた一段低い位置にある。

The site is located interposed between, and one step below, the UNESCO headquarters designed by Marcel Breuer, and the Japanese garden designed by Isamu Noguchi.

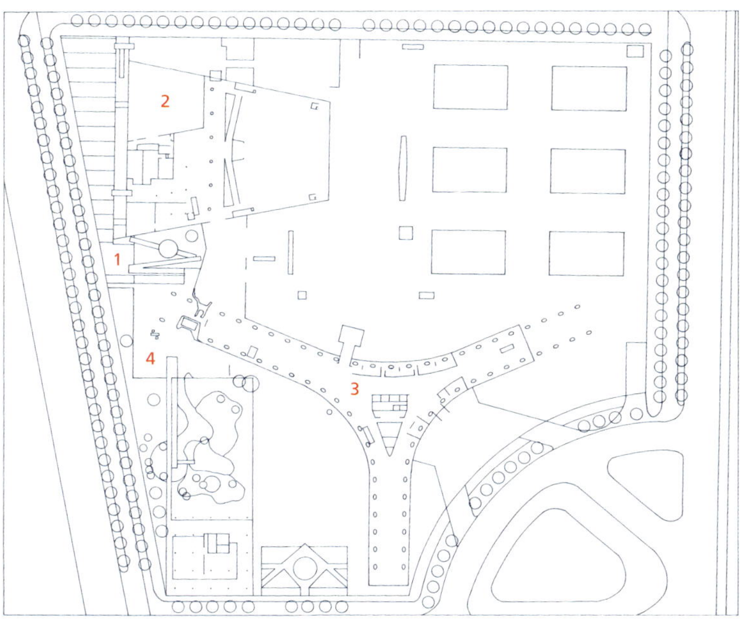

Site plan

1 meditation space
2 office
3 conference building
4 japanese garden

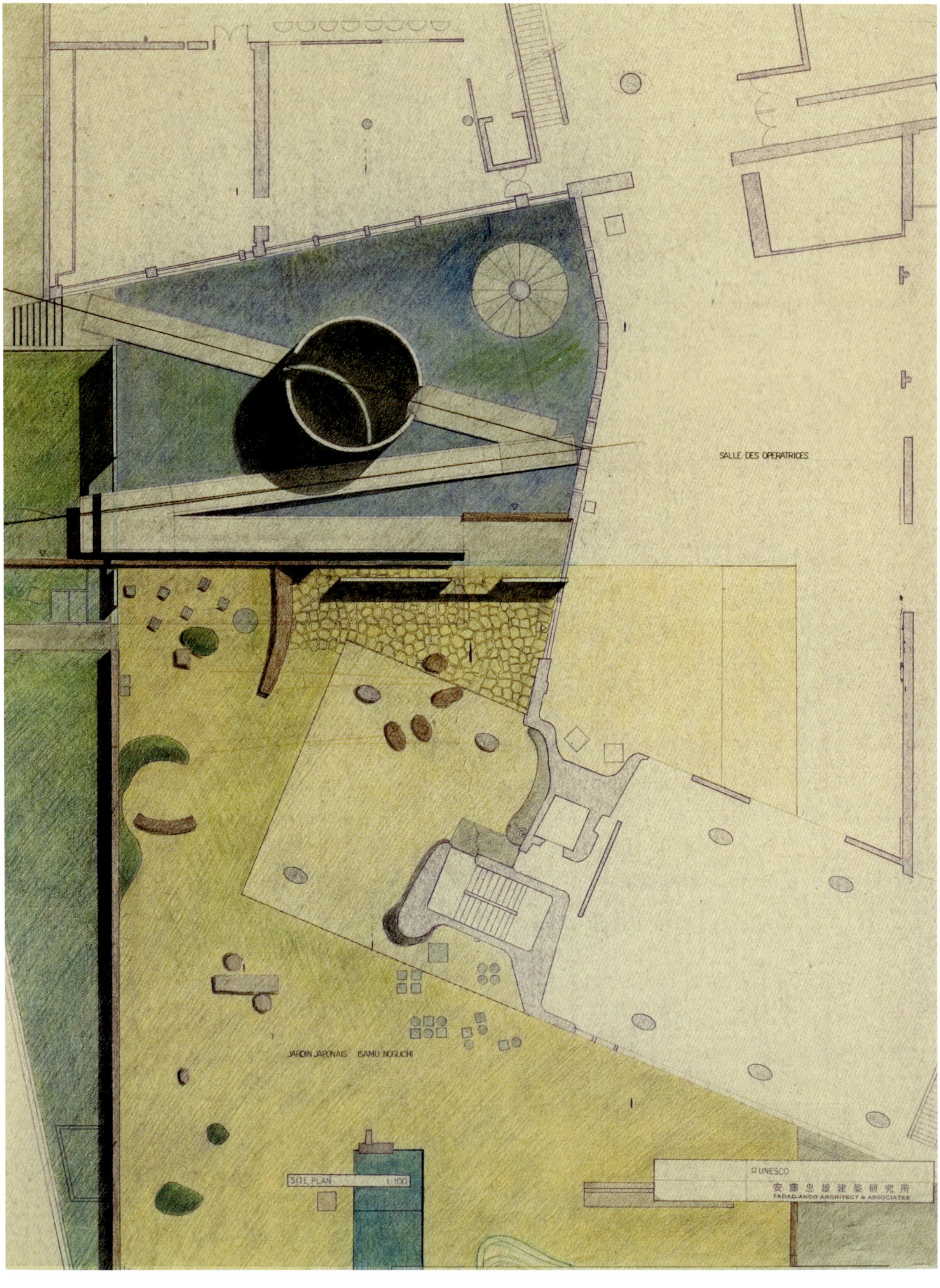
SALLE DES OPERATRICES
JARDIN JAPONAIS ISAMU NOGUCHI
SITE PLAN 1:100
UNESCO
安藤忠雄建築研究所
TADAO ANDO ARCHITECT & ASSOCIATES

左頁：直径と高さが等しい6.3mのコンクリートのシリンダーと、
折れ重なり下降していくアプローチのスロープによる構成。
右頁：シリンダー内部、天井を見上げる。

Left page: The composition comprises a concrete cylinder, 6.3m in diameter as well as height, and a descending approach ramp that folds back.
Right page: Looking up at the ceiling inside the cylinder.

シリンダーの開口部は、スロープが突き抜ける前後の出入口と、天井に穿たれた円形のスリットのみ。素材も要素も削ぎ落とされた、純粋な空間。

The only apertures in the cylinder are the entrance and exit pierced by the ramp at the front and rear, and the circular slits piercing the ceiling. The materials and elements are reduced, leaving a purified space.

2000年にオープンする現代美術館の国際設計競技応募案である。
　敷地はテムズ川を挟んでセント・ポール寺院と向かい合う南岸にあり、ロンドンでも特に重要な位置を占める。要求されたプログラムは、煉瓦づくりの元火力発電所を現代美術館として生まれ変わらせるというものであった。
　計画にあたり、われわれが考え方の基本としたのは、「衝突」である。ロンドンという歴史を背負った街に対し、建築で融和を図るのではなく、裸形の概念をそのまま衝突させ、その対立と緊張のエネルギーの中から新しい創造の可能性を生み出したいと考えた。旧い煉瓦の壁体の内側は、40mの高さをもつワンルームの大空間である。そこに、ギャラリーを内包するふたつのコンクリートの直方体が浮かび、さらにそれらを貫いて２本のガラスのシャフトがテムズ川に向かって飛び出す。採光は天井に穿たれたトップライトからの自然光により、その光は吹き抜けを通じて最下層のパブリックスペースにまで到達する。
　煉瓦とガラスという対照的な素材の衝突によって生まれる力が、創造的な場のエネルギーへと転化されることを期待した。さらにガラスのシャフトが対岸のセント・ポール寺院へと向かう、象徴的な方向性を与えられることで、ロンドンの歴史的景観の中で、新旧の対話の場をつくれるのではないかと考えた。足もとのテムズ川に至る階段状の親水広場、水面に浮かぶガラスのギャラリー、さらに水面と対岸のセント・ポール寺院までを一体に捉え、新たな都市環境創出のひとつの拠点づくりとして本計画に臨んだ。

テート・ギャラリー現代美術館国際設計競技案
Tate Gallery of Modern Art (International Design Competition)

1994-95 イギリス ロンドン —— London, U.K.

This proposal was submitted to an international design competition for a contemporary art museum that opened in 2000.
　The site is on the south bank of the River Thames opposite St Paul's Cathedral, a particularly important location in London. The requested program was the conversion of a disused brick power station into a museum.
　The notion of "collision" was the basis of our design approach. Rather than attempting architectural harmony with the historical weight of London, we instead used the concept of a vital clash of "raw forms" in the existing context, in the hope that a new creativity might emerge from the resulting energy and tension. One large 40m-high space is enclosed within the old brick walls. Two concrete boxes containing the galleries float within it, and the boxes are further pierced by two glass shafts that extend toward the Thames. Natural light enters the building through glazed penetrations in the ceiling, and this light is able to reach as far as the public spaces on the lowest level.
　We expected that the extreme contrast between brick and glass would generate a creative energy in this location. Within London's important historical context, I also thought that the glass shafts pointing across towards St Paul's would create a symbolic dialogue between old and new. The Thames may be reached by the stair-shaped main plaza below the building, and the glass galleries appear to float on the water's surface, combining with St Paul's Cathedral and the water's surface into a single entity, resulting in a design intended to form the basis of an innovative urban environment.

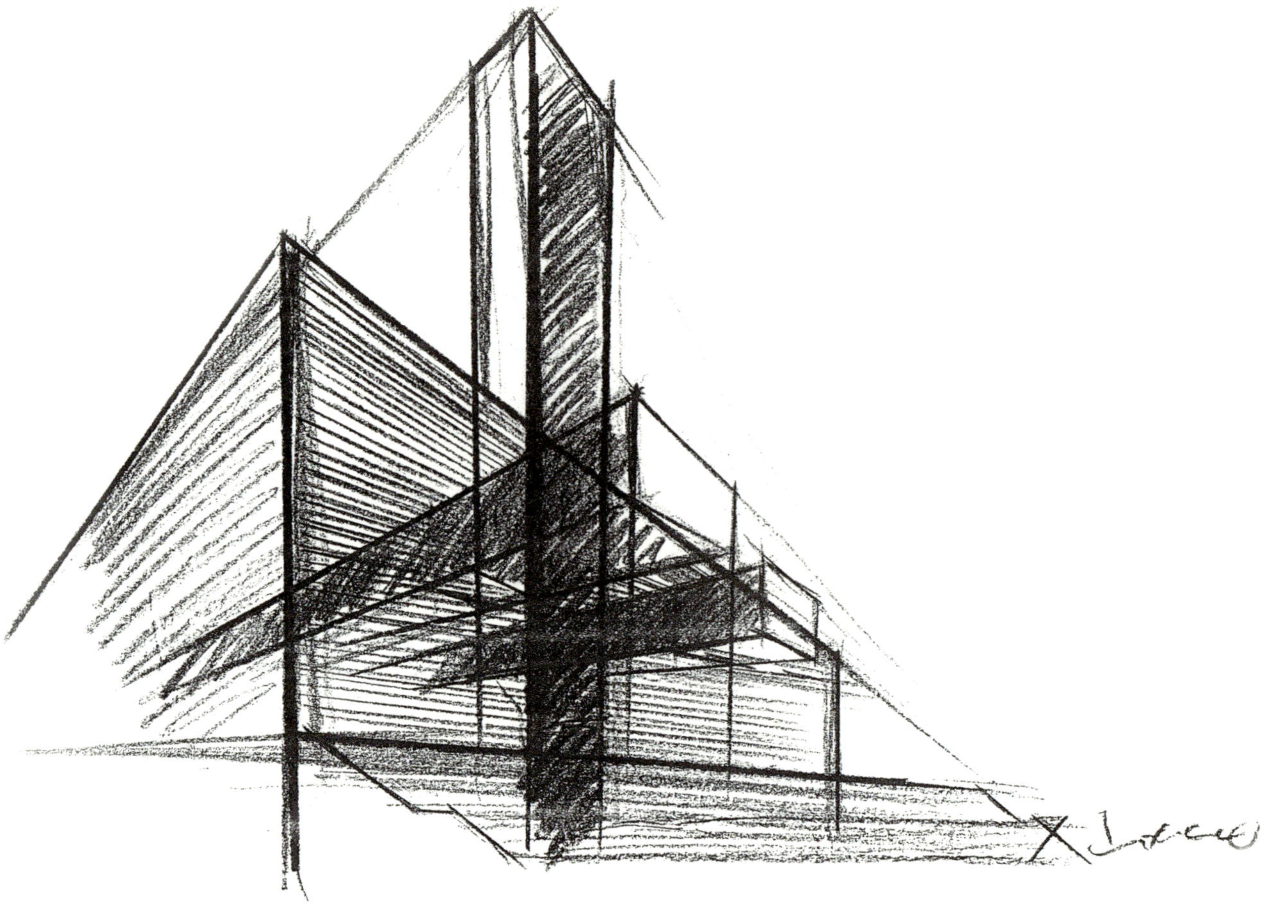

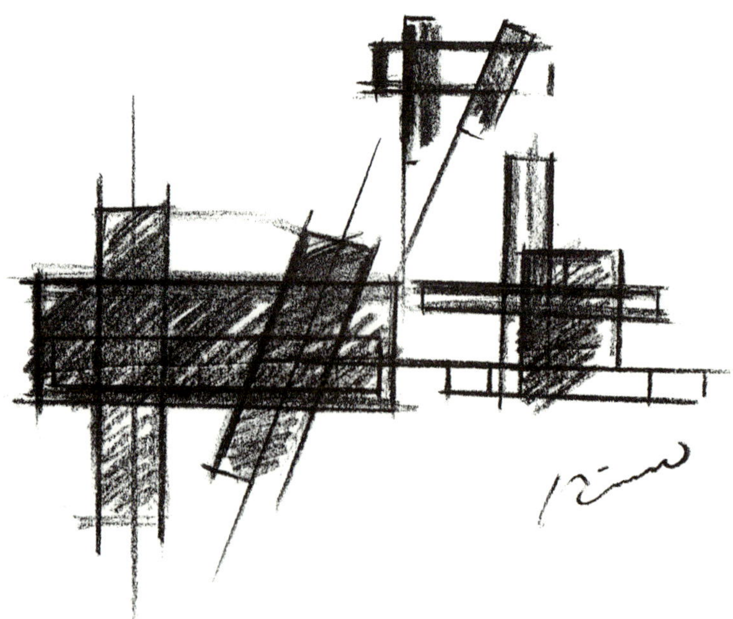

初期イメージスケッチ。既存の火力発電所に、角度を振った2本のガラスのシャフトが突き刺さるイメージが力強く描かれている。

Initial image sketch. A strongly depicted image showing the existing power station pierced at an angle by two glass shafts.

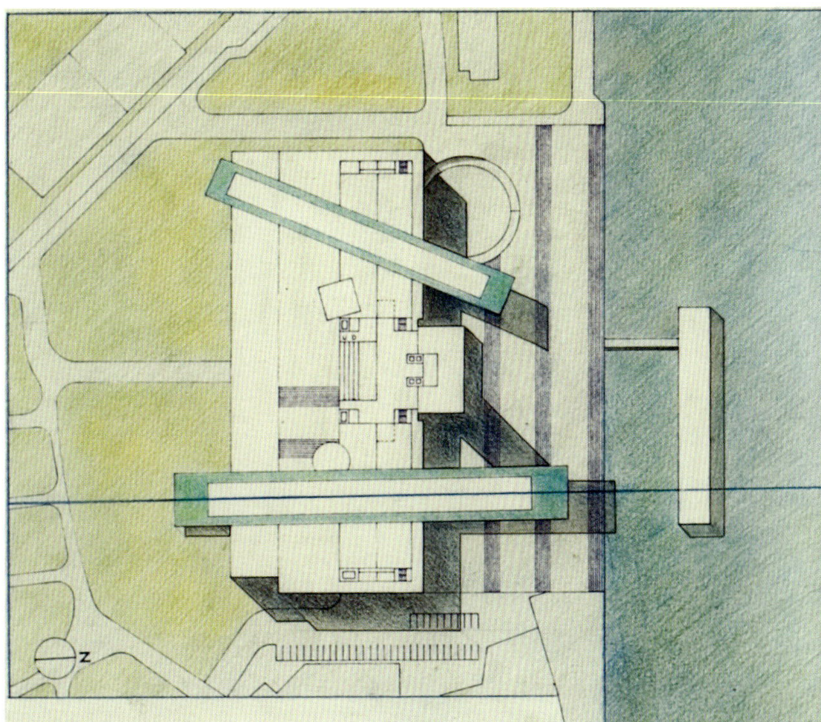

水彩ドローイング。意図的に角度を振ったガラスシャフトの方向性により、セント・ポール寺院に向かう都市軸が、強く意識されている。

Watercolor drawing. There is a strong awareness of the urban axis toward Saint Paul's Cathedral, due to the deliberate directionality of the angles of the glass shafts.

模型写真。テムズ川のほとりで、過去と現代が激しく衝突する。

Photograph of the model. Past and present violently collide in the vicinity of the Thames.

旧火力発電所の外壁に突き刺さる2本のガラスシャフトとセント・ポール寺院との緊張感ある関係が、ロンドンの都市空間に新たな刺激をもたらす。

The tense relationship between Saint Paul's Cathedral and the two shafts piercing the exterior walls of the old power plant gives a new stimulus to the urban spaces of London.

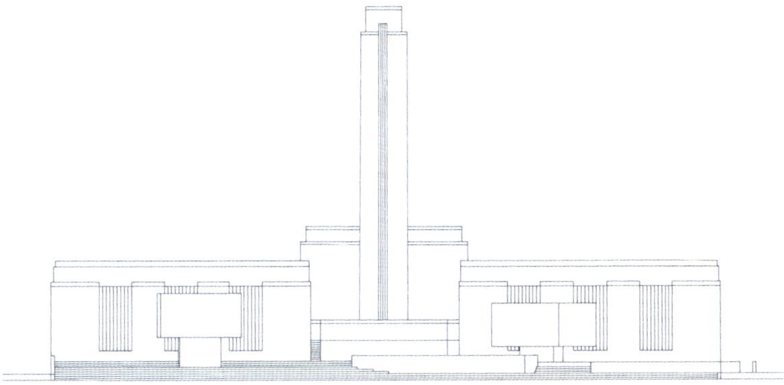

Elevation

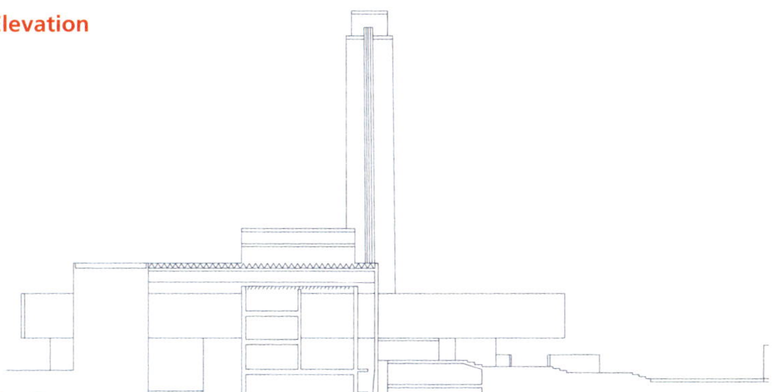

Section

1:2,000

テムズ川の護岸は、水面ぎりぎりまで降りていく階段状の親水広場とする計画。その川沿いのアクティビティーをさらに拡張する仕掛けとして、水上にもガラスのギャラリーが浮かべられる。

The design includes a stepping water plaza that descends to just above the water level at the edge of the Thames. As a device to further expand the activities along the river, a glass gallery also floats above the water.

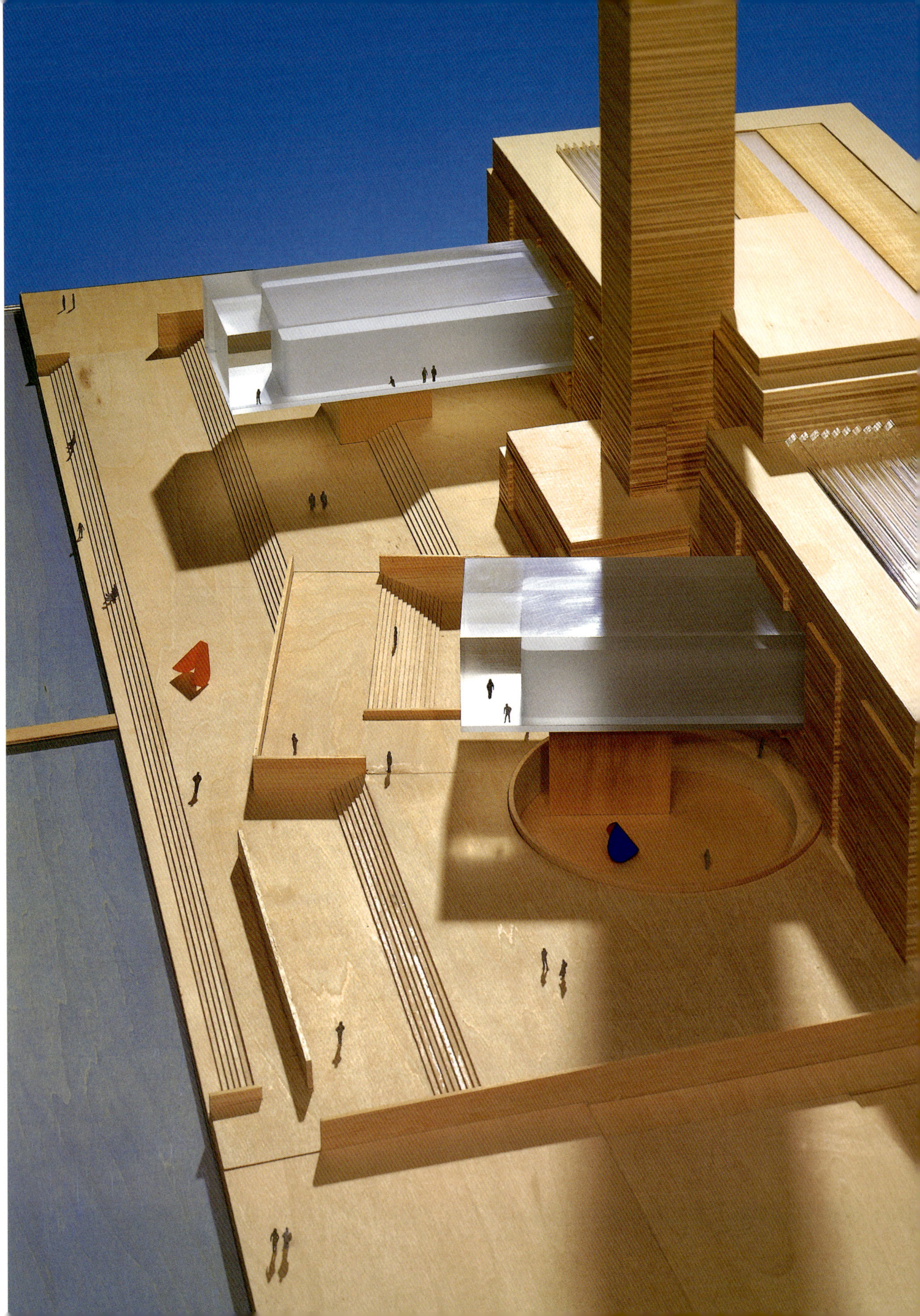

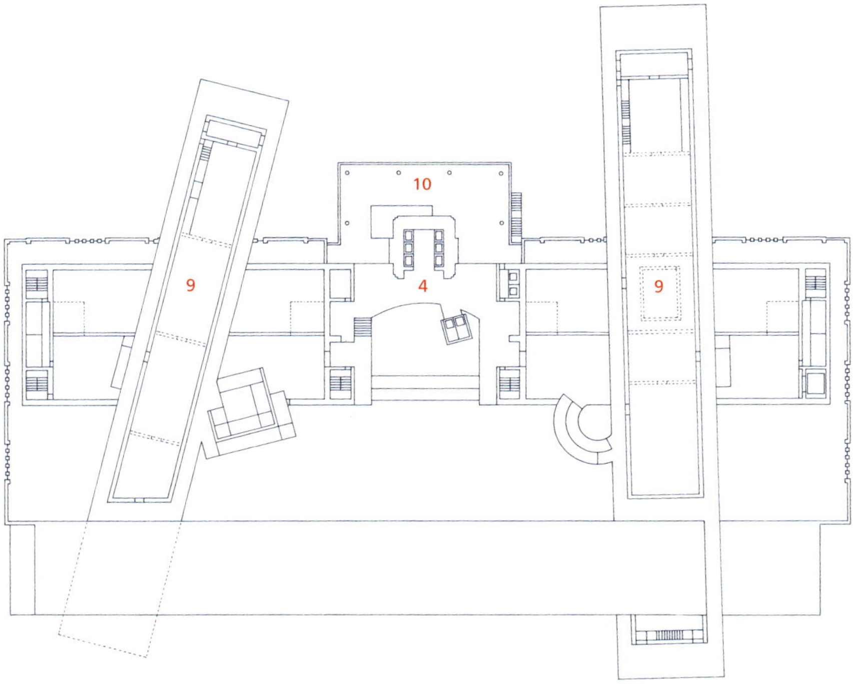

Second floor plan

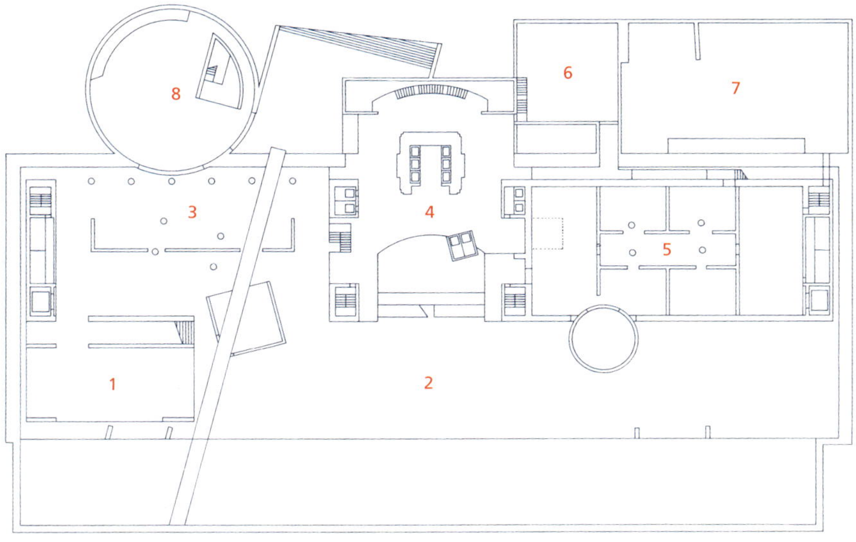

1 library
2 hall
3 museum shop
4 foyer
5 permanent exhibition room
6 multi-purpose studio
7 office
8 sunken court
9 temporary exhibition room
10 cafeteria

First floor plan 1:1,500

ベネトンの会長であるルチアーノ・ベネトンより突然の依頼を受け、初めて敷地を訪れたのは1992年だった。当初は日本とイタリアの距離を思い、若干の戸惑いを感じたが、ヴェネト地方の建築を学ぶよい機会かもしれないと思ったのと、何より世界中の若者にアートを学ぶ機会を与えたいという施主の高い志に共感を覚え、引き受けることを決意した。

敷地は、ヴェニスから車で1時間ほどの所にある小さな街トレヴィソに位置する。イタリア北東部に位置するこの街を発祥の地とし、現在も本社を置く世界的なファッションメーカーの企画による、工芸やデザインを学ぶ若者のためのアートスクールである。

トレヴィソは、マニエリスムの巨匠パッラーディオが数多くの作品を残した、豊かな建築的遺産を有する土地として知られているが、イタリアでは、それらの歴史的建造物の保存・再生が法律によって奨励されている。また修復に必要とされる材料、技術(=職人)が社会の中にシステムとして確立されているため、後期ルネッサンス期に花開いた西洋古典主義建築、特にパッラーディオ風のヴィラ建築などが、トレヴィソを含むヴェネト地方の田園風景の中で、変わらぬ姿で保たれている。

FABRICAの敷地にも、そうした旧いヴィラ建築が残っており、施主はそれらの修復・再生を強く望んでいた。われわれとしても

FABRICA(ベネトン・アートスクール)
FABRICA(Benetton Communication Research Center)

1992-2000 イタリア トレヴィソ —— Treviso, Italy

FABRICAの新設部分を描いた配置ドローイング。地下に切り取られた空間の連なり。
Site drawing depicting the new section of FABRICA. A series of spaces carved underground.

無論、異存があるわけはなく、むしろ既存の旧い部分と、新たに付加する新しい部分との新たな関係性創出を主題として捉え、旧い部分をより活性化することを目標として、計画を進めていった。

既存部分の修復、再生に関しては現地の職人と対話を積み重ねながら時間をかけて進め、新たに付加する新築部分については、そのほとんどを地下に埋設するよう考えた。特に図書室は、地下深く螺旋状に下降する書庫を備えている。新旧の建物を、ただいたずらに対立させるのではなく、既存の田園風景を含めて、旧いものは旧いなりにその内包する歴史を自立的に保存し、新しい部分がさらに旧いものの魅力を増幅させるような、新旧が共振、共鳴し合うような建築を目論んだ。新旧の建物の時間を越えた対話が、場に常に刺激を与え、新たな創造へとつながっていくことを期待している。

海外での仕事ゆえの監理の難しさ、施工者の建築に対する姿勢の違い、そして法的な問題などから、工事はなかなか進まず、着工から完成まで実に10年近くの年月が経ってしまったが、費やした労力に相応しいだけの質を備えた建築ができ上がったように思う。

Having unexpectedly been commissioned by Luciano Benneton, the president of Benneton, we first visited the site in 1992. Thinking about the distance between Japan and Italy, I initially had some misgivings, but I decided to accept, as I thought it would be a good chance to study the architecture of the Veneto region, and above all I remember feeling empathy with the client's motivation to give opportunities for young people from around the world to study art.

The site is located in Treviso, a small town about one hour by car from Venice. The head office of this international fashion maker is still located here at its original location in this town in northeast Italy, and they have planned an art school for young people to study manufacturing and design. Many works by the brilliant Mannerist architect Palladio remain in Treviso, which is known as a district with a rich architectural heritage. In Italy, the preservation and restoration of historical structures is promoted by law.

The necessary materials and techniques (= artisans) for restoration work have been established within the social system, so the Western classical architecture that flowered during the latter part of the Renaissance, particularly Palladian villa architecture, is preserved unchanged throughout the rural landscape of the Veneto region, which includes Treviso. This kind of villa architecture also remains on the Fabrica site, and the client strongly desired its repair and restoration.

FABRICA
(Benetton Communication Research Center)

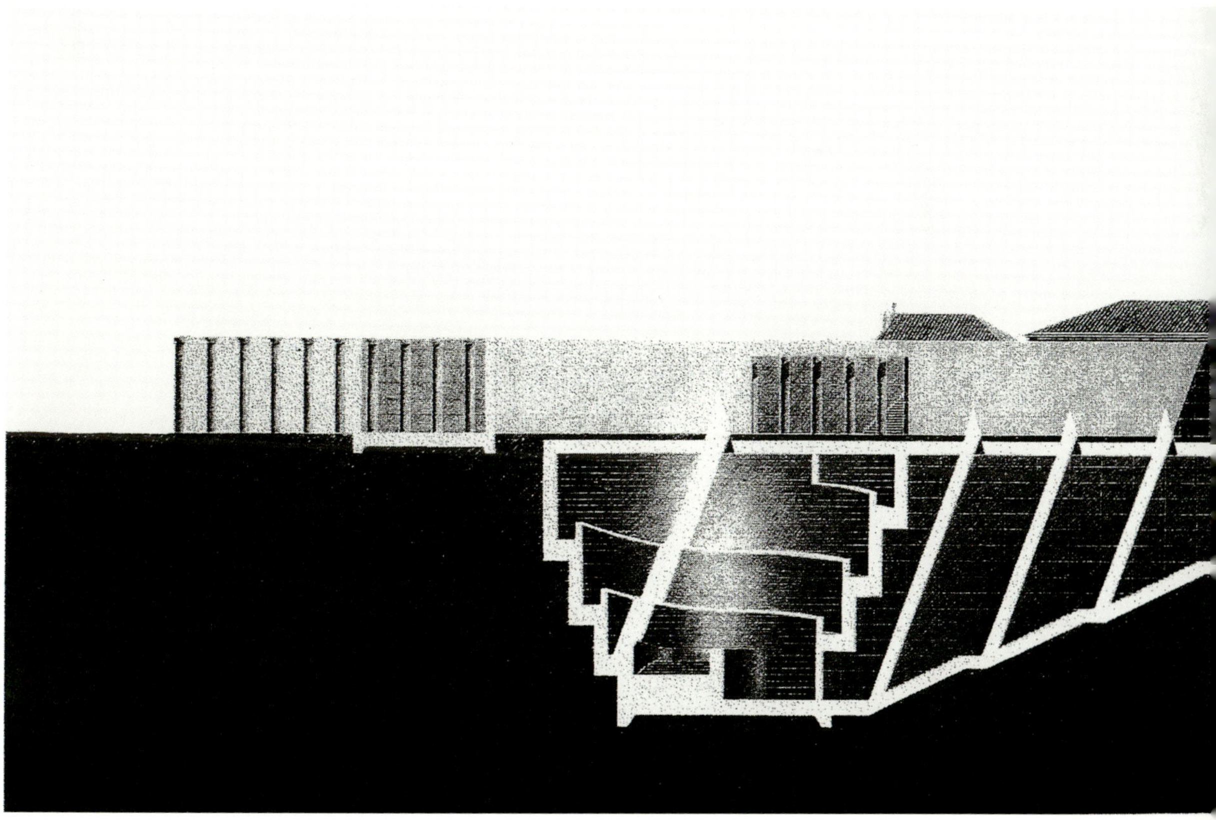

Naturally, we had no objections, but rather we perceived our theme as the creation of new relationships between the preserved old parts and the incorporated new parts, and the design progressed with the aim of further invigorating the old parts.

With regard to the repair and restoration of the existing parts, we spent a great deal of time in dialogue with local artisans, and for incorporating the newly constructed parts, we decided to install most of it underground. The library in particular is furnished with a helical archive that descends deep underground.

This new/old building is not conceived merely as a confrontational collision. We envisioned an architecture with a sympathetic resonance between old and new, in which old things are independently preserved by being enclosed with old history, and the new parts are intended to further enhance the charm of the old things, including the existing rural landscape. We expect that the dialogue across time of this new/old building will give constant stimulus to this place, and will be connected to new creativity.

Due to the difficulty of supervising work in foreign countries, the different attitudes of the contractors toward architecture, and legal problems, the progress of construction work was slow. Close to ten years elapsed from the start of construction to completion, but I think that the architecture has a quality fully appropriate to the energy we expended.

断面ドローイング。トレヴィソの田園風景をそのままに、地下へと展開する空間のイメージ。地下深く差し込む光が象徴的に描かれている。

Section drawing. An image of spaces expanding underground within the unchanging rural scenery of Treviso. A symbolic depiction of light penetrating deep underground.

水庭の上に浮くアプローチのギャラリー（柱廊）から、
既存建物のポーティコを見る。

Looking at the portico of the existing building from the approach gallery (collonade) floating above the water garden.

既存建物のポーティコから水庭越しにギャラリーを見る。

Looking over the water garden at the gallery from the portico of the existing building.

アーチの重なりが、美しい空間のリズムを刻む。

The layering of the row of concrete columns of the gallery and the arches of the portico inscribes a beautiful spatial rhythm.

ギャラリーに並ぶコンクリート柱。控えめな柱頭のデザインが、コンクリートのストイックな表情を和らげ、穏やかなアプローチの空間を演出する。

Concrete columns aligned in the gallery. The restrained design of the capitals mitigates the stoic expression of the concrete, producing a quiet approach space.

南側から見た建物全景。新築部分のヴォリュームはすべて地下に沈められ、地上部のヴィラはほぼ既存のかたちのままで改修されている。受け継がれた風景の記憶。

Panoramic view of the building from the south. The volume of the new section is entirely submerged underground, and the villa above ground has been repaired to almost its original form. Inheriting the memories of the scenery.

ポーティコに面して設けられた講堂。

The auditorium has been established facing the portico.

17世紀につくられた既存建物（Villa Pastega）の傷みは激しく、構造体以外、仕上げは全面改修されることとなった。

There was severe damage to the existing building (Villa Pastega), built in the 17th century, and the finishes were entirely repaired, aside from the structure.

既存建物１階につくられたスタジオの小屋組みと、
既存建物を貫いて連続するギャラリーの列柱との
取り合い。

Combination of the roof assembly on the first floor of the existing building, and the row of columns of the gallery passing through the existing building.

既存の田園風景を損なわぬよう、地上部の建築は既存建物の改修にとどまり、必要なヴォリュームはすべて地下に設けている。角度を振って配された楕円形のコート、階段状に下がっていくサンクンコートが地下に光と風を引き込み、変化に富んだ空間のシークエンスをつくり出す。

1 office
2 reception
3 auditorium
4 studio
5 lobby
6 gallery
7 court
8 archive
9 library
10 pool
11 theater
12 church
13 portico

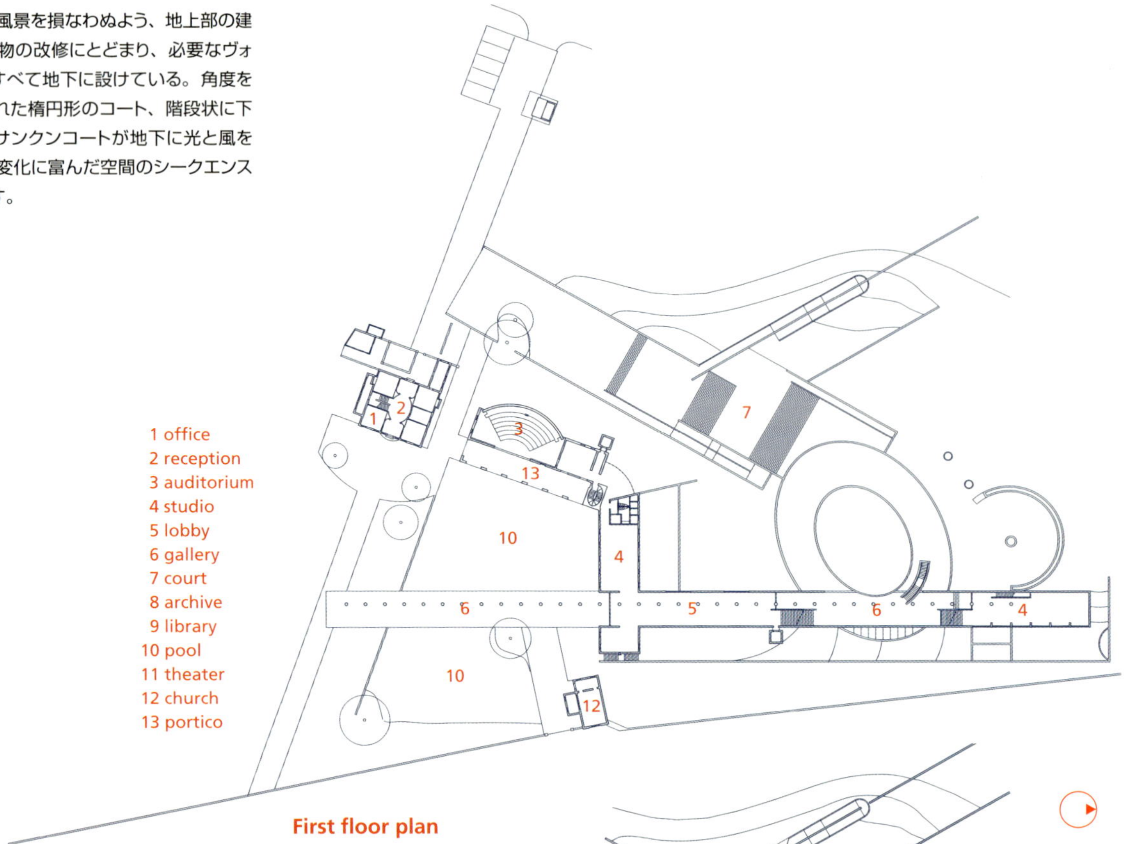

First floor plan

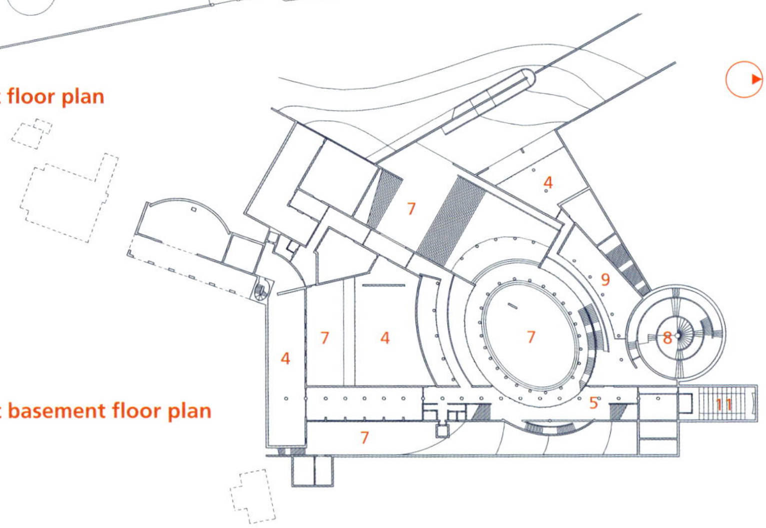

First basement floor plan

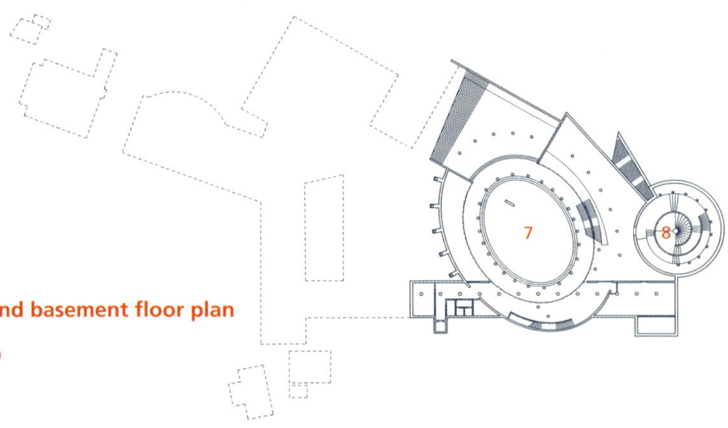

Second basement floor plan

1:500

In order to avoid loss of the existing rural scenery, the above-ground architecture was restricted to repairing the existing building, and the necessary volumes were all established underground. The elliptical court placed at an angle, and the stair-shaped sunken court draw light and air underground, producing a spatial sequence full of variation.

南西から階段状のサンクンコート、楕円形のコートを見る。地面に穿たれたヴォイドの連なりが生み出す空間。

Looking at the elliptical court and the stair-shaped sunken court from the southwest. Spaces produced by a sequence of voids piercing the ground surface.

アクソノメトリックとパースペクティブ・ドローイング。
列柱のかたどる幾何学の重なりが、陰影深い空間のシークエンスを生み出す。

Axonometric and perspective. The geometric layering of the rows of columns produces a spatial sequence full of shadows.

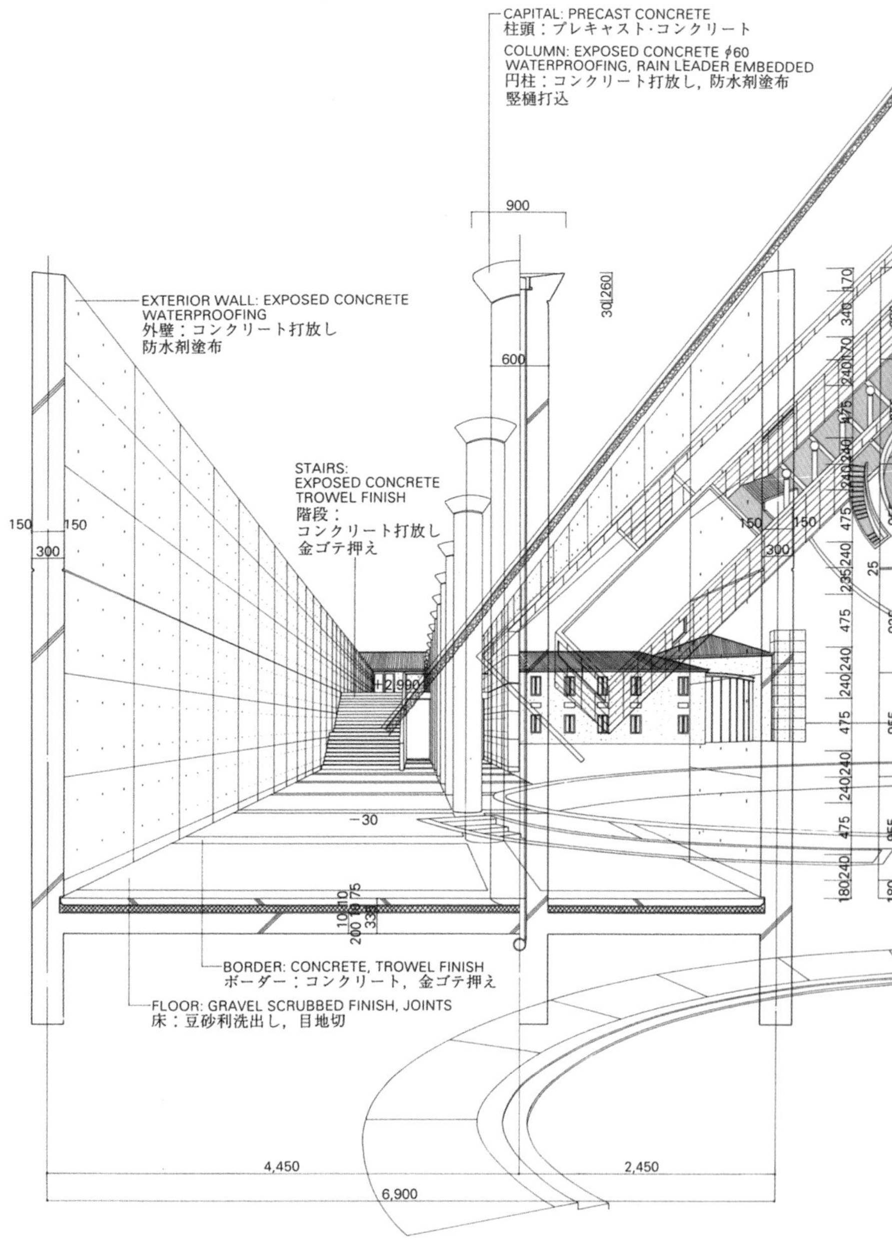

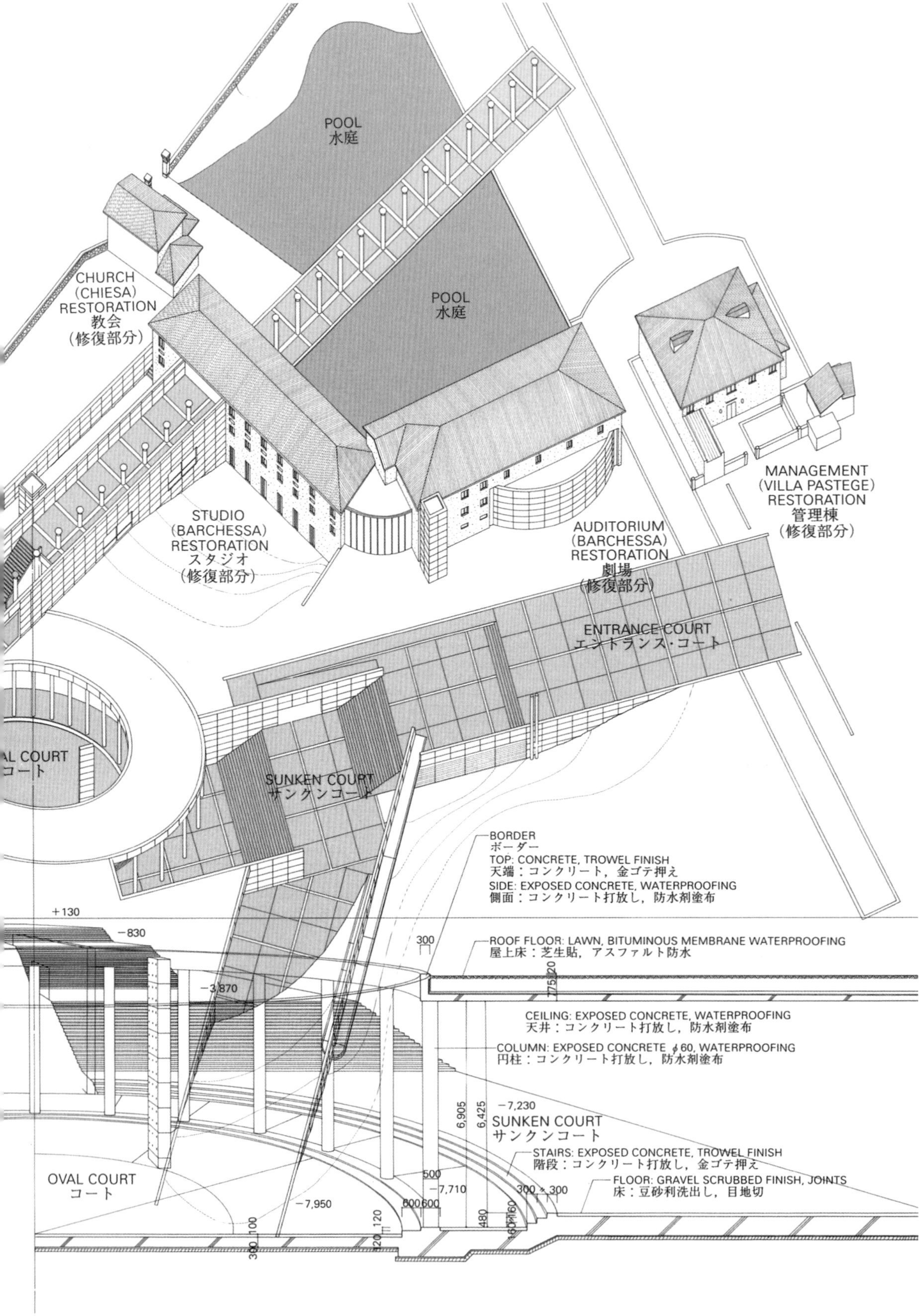
POOL
水庭
CHURCH
(CHIESA)
RESTORATION
教会
(修復部分)
POOL
水庭
MANAGEMENT
(VILLA PASTEGE)
RESTORATION
管理棟
(修復部分)
STUDIO
(BARCHESSA)
RESTORATION
スタジオ
(修復部分)
AUDITORIUM
(BARCHESSA)
RESTORATION
劇場
(修復部分)
ENTRANCE COURT
エントランス・コート
AL COURT
コート
SUNKEN COURT
サンクンコート
BORDER
ボーダー
TOP: CONCRETE, TROWEL FINISH
天端：コンクリート，金ゴテ押え
SIDE: EXPOSED CONCRETE, WATERPROOFING
側面：コンクリート打放し，防水剤塗布
+130
−830
300
ROOF FLOOR: LAWN, BITUMINOUS MEMBRANE WATERPROOFING
屋上床：芝生貼，アスファルト防水
−3,870
CEILING: EXPOSED CONCRETE, WATERPROOFING
天井：コンクリート打放し，防水剤塗布
COLUMN: EXPOSED CONCRETE φ60, WATERPROOFING
円柱：コンクリート打放し，防水剤塗布
6,905
6,425
−7,230
SUNKEN COURT
サンクンコート
STAIRS: EXPOSED CONCRETE, TROWEL FINISH
階段：コンクリート打放し，金ゴテ押え
OVAL COURT
コート
500
−7,710
300 × 300
FLOOR: GRAVEL SCRUBBED FINISH, JOINTS
床：豆砂利洗出し，目地切
−7,950
600 600
480
300 100
120 120

穏やかなトレヴィソの田園風景の下に展開する、地下建築の造形。

The form of the underground architecture expanding below the gentle rural scenery of Treviso.

左:楕円形の中央コートを見下ろす。
右:既存建物を貫き、楕円形の中央コートと重なるギャラリー。

Left: Looking down on the elliptical central court.
Right: Gallery overlapping with the elliptical central court and piercing the existing building.

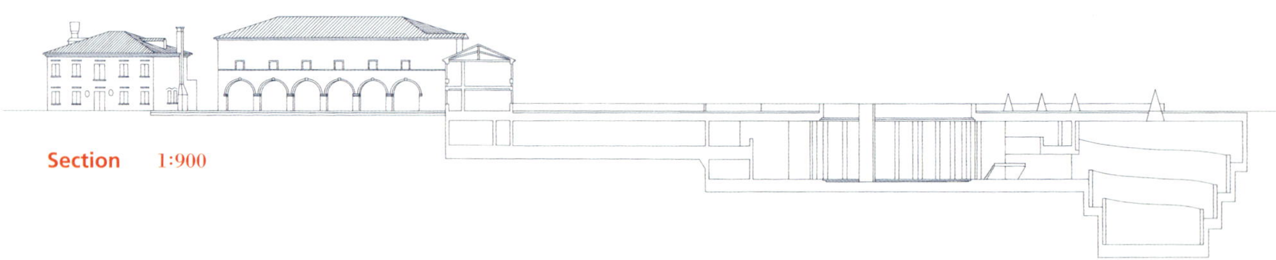

Section 1:900

列柱に囲われた楕円形のコート。
Elliptical court surrounded by a row of columns.

地下に埋め込まれた楕円形コートの夜景。
Night view of the elliptical court embedded underground.

楕円形コートの平面図とパースペクティブ・ドローイング。
地下に埋め込まれたヴォイドを中心に展開する空間構成。

Plan and perspective of the elliptical court.
A spatial composition that expands around voids
embedded underground.

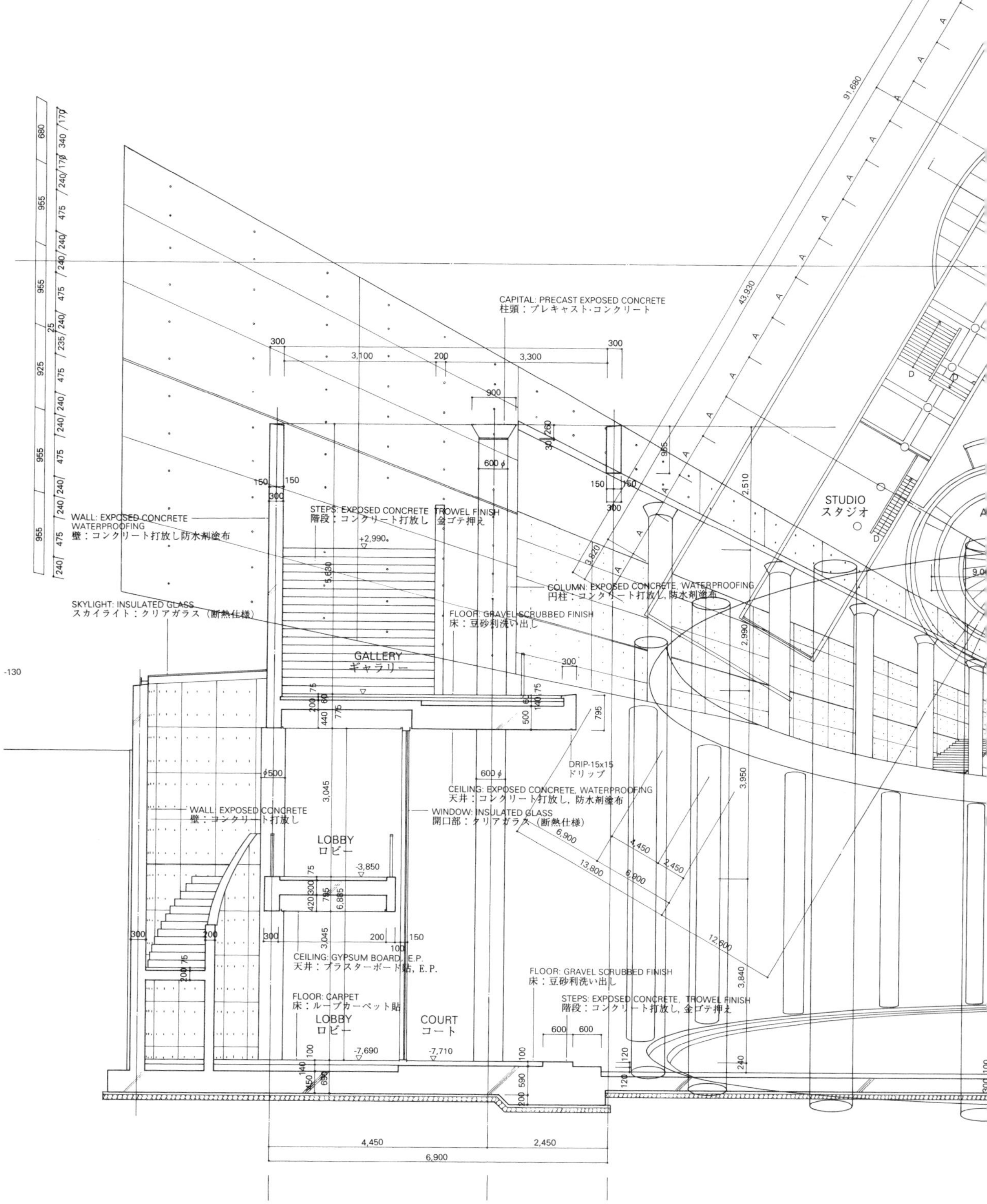

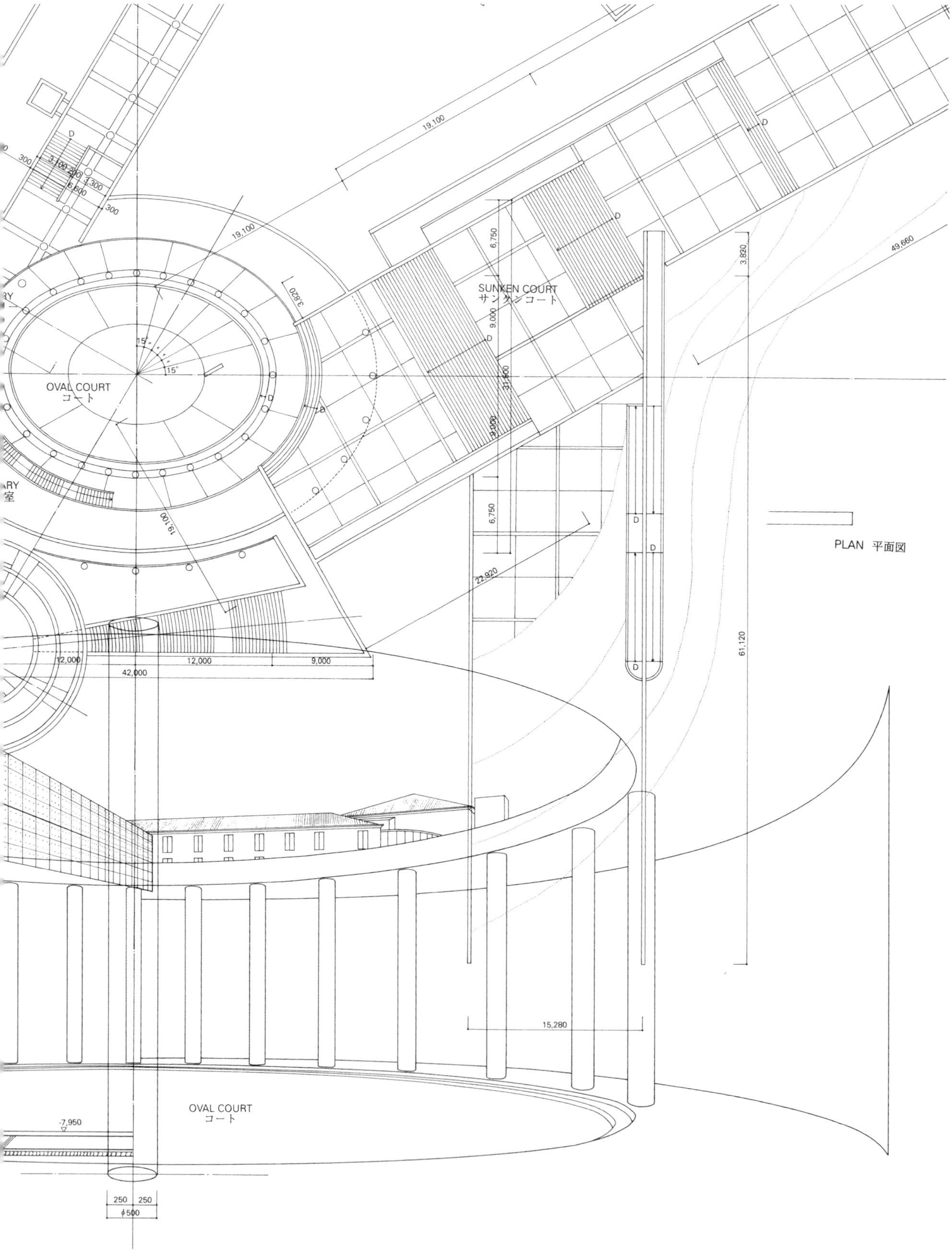
SUNKEN COURT
サンクンコート
OVAL COURT
コート
PLAN 平面図
OVAL COURT
コート

地下アーカイブへと続く階段。円形のトップライトから
差し込む光が、地下へと潜る空間を劇的に演出する。

Stair leading to the underground archive.
The light penetrating through the circular skylight
makes a dramatic production of the spaces
hiding underground.

円形のトップライトを中心に、最下階から最上階まで、らせん状のスロープが巡る。

From the lowest level to the highest level, the spiral slope centers on the circular skylight.

2000年に行われたセント・ポール寺院に置かれるフォント（洗礼盤）デザインコンペの提出案である。

セント・ポール寺院はテート・ギャラリーに近い。テート・ギャラリーのコンペを闘ったわれわれにとってテムズ川を挟んで対峙するその歴史的遺産には深い思い入れがあり、ガラスを用いて新旧の衝突をテーマにしたコンペが思い出された。そこで、単純で限定された要素を用い、複雑な視覚的効果を実現させたいと考え、具体的に現れるかたちを、正方形や円といった原初的な幾何学に限定した。中央よりやや偏心した位置に円形の穴のあいた厚さ5mm、1m四方の正方形の板ガラスを積み重ね、捻りを加えたものである。中心の穴は捻りながら上昇しており、これが水を溜める聖杯の受け皿となる。その結果、ガラスの素材特性、積層と偏心、捻りといった変形操作を際立たせ、水と光の戯れとなって現れ出ることを期待した。

セント・ポール寺院聖台 国際設計競技案

A New Font for St. Paul's Cathedral (International Design Competition)

1999-2000 イギリス ロンドン——London, U.K.

This proposal was submitted to a design competition held in 2000, for a font to be placed in St. Paul's Cathedral.

St. Paul's Cathedral is located near the Tate Gallery. Having taken part in the competition for the Tate Gallery, we had given deep thought to the confrontation with the historical heritage beside the Thames River. I was reminded of the competition, in which my theme was the collision of old and new by using glass. Accordingly, I wanted to achieve complex visual effects using simple, limited elements, and the shape that materialized was limited to primary geometric forms such as squares and circles. Stacked 5mm-thick, one-meter-square glass plates with slightly off-center circular holes are given a twist. Rising while rotating the holes at the center, it becomes a font for holding water. As a result, through the material characteristics of glass, the eccentricity of the layering, and the conspicuous rotation, we expect it to manifest the play of water and light.

セント・ポール寺院内に置かれる新しい洗礼盤のフォトコラージュ。
Photo collage of the new font for St. Paul's Cathedral

ガラスの透明な素材感と、その積層が
生み出す幻想的な光のオブジェ。

An object combining the transparent materiality of glass and the light produced by its layering.

アントワープ市に建つ海洋歴史博物館の国際設計コンペの応募案である。

敷地はアントワープ中心部近くのドックランドに位置する。要求されたのは、単なる展示施設ではない、アントワープ北部を文化的、経済的に活性化させ、街の中心部から都市の活動を滑らかに引き込み、発展させる文化拠点としての建築であった。それに対し、われわれが考えたのは、モニュメントとしての建物ではない、さまざまな可能性を喚起するヴォイドの建築、広場の建築である。それは、この場所にしかできない価値、この場所のもつ力を最大限引き出すことであり、同時に、境界を超えて、周囲との関わりの中で建築を組み立てることである。スタディを重ねた末、われわれが到達したのは、逆円錐の柱によって美術館機能を収めた1枚のスラブを宙に掲げ、敷地いっぱいの広場をつくり出すというアイディアである。この広場は、四周の水面から、既存の都市空間までを一体のものとして体感させる装置であり、同時に都市を行き交うさまざまな情報を受け止め、結びつけ、再び都市に向けて発信する文化のドックでもある。人々は広場の賑わいに引き寄せられ、この場所に集い、またその活動が活気を生み、都市に刺激を与えていく。森の木々の重なり合いの中で、さまざまな生き物のさまざまな営みが行われる様子になぞらえ、われわれはこのアイディアを〈水上の森〉と名づけた。

結果としては落選となったが、都市におけるパブリックの文化施設のあり方を考える上で、非常に有意義な思考の時をもてたように思う。ここで温められたコンセプトは、ピノー現代美術館のコンペへと引き継がれ、浮遊したガラスのヴォリュームの下に設けられた、セーヌ川と連続した「広場」として昇華された。この計画も、もう少しのところで実現には至らなかったが、いつかどこかでこのコンセプトを生かす機会があると信じている。

アントワープ市立博物館国際設計競技案

Museum Aan de Stroom, Antwerp (International Design Competition)

1999-2000 ベルギー アントワープ—— Antwerp, Belgium

海に開かれた美術館の広場を描いたパースペクティブ・ドローイング。階段状の広場に林立する逆円錐型の巨大な柱が美術館の諸機能を収めたフラットなヴォリュームを支える。

Perspective drawing depicting the museum plaza open to the sea. The closely spaced, huge inverted conical columns on the stepping plaza support the flat volume housing the various museum functions.

This proposal was submitted to an international design competition for a museum of maritime history to be built in Antwerp.

The site is located among the docklands close to the heart of Antwerp. The requirements were not merely for an exhibition facility, but for a work of architecture that would become a cultural focus in the cultural and economic reinvigoration of northern Antwerp, smoothly integrated with the urban activities of the city center. Our ambition was therefore not to create a building as a monument, but to induce various possibilities with an architecture of voids, an architecture of plazas. We wished to maximize the value unique to this place, the power possessed by this place, yet at the same time make an architecture that exceeds the site boundaries and generates relationships with its wider context. Having made a series of study models, we arrived at the idea of containing all the museum functions in a single floating slab supported by inverted cone-shaped columns, while turning the entire site into a plaza. This plaza is a device that physically links the surrounding water surface and the existing urban spaces into a continuum, and at the same time it is a "culture dock" that absorbs a variety of information from the city, which it then reconfigures and returns. People gather in this place, attracted by the bustle of activity in the plaza, and their activities here create additional vigor, giving a energy to the city. We have named this idea "forest on the water," because it resembles the intermingling of various creatures and modes of life that may be found among the overlapping trees of a forest.

Although the project failed to win, it provided us with time for extremely meaningful contemplation of the notion of public cultural facilities in the city. The concept that we initiated here was taken up in the competition for the Foundation François Pinault pour L'Art Contemporain, sublimated as a "plaza" continuous with the River Seine, established under a floating glass volume. That design will not be realized either, but we believe that someday, somewhere, we will have the opportunity to revive this concept.

広場から海側を見る。美術館の下に広がるピロティの大空間が市民の多様な活動を誘発する文化のドックとなる。

Looking at the seaside from the plaza. The vast space of pilotis extending under the museum is expected to be a culture dock inducing various citizen activities.

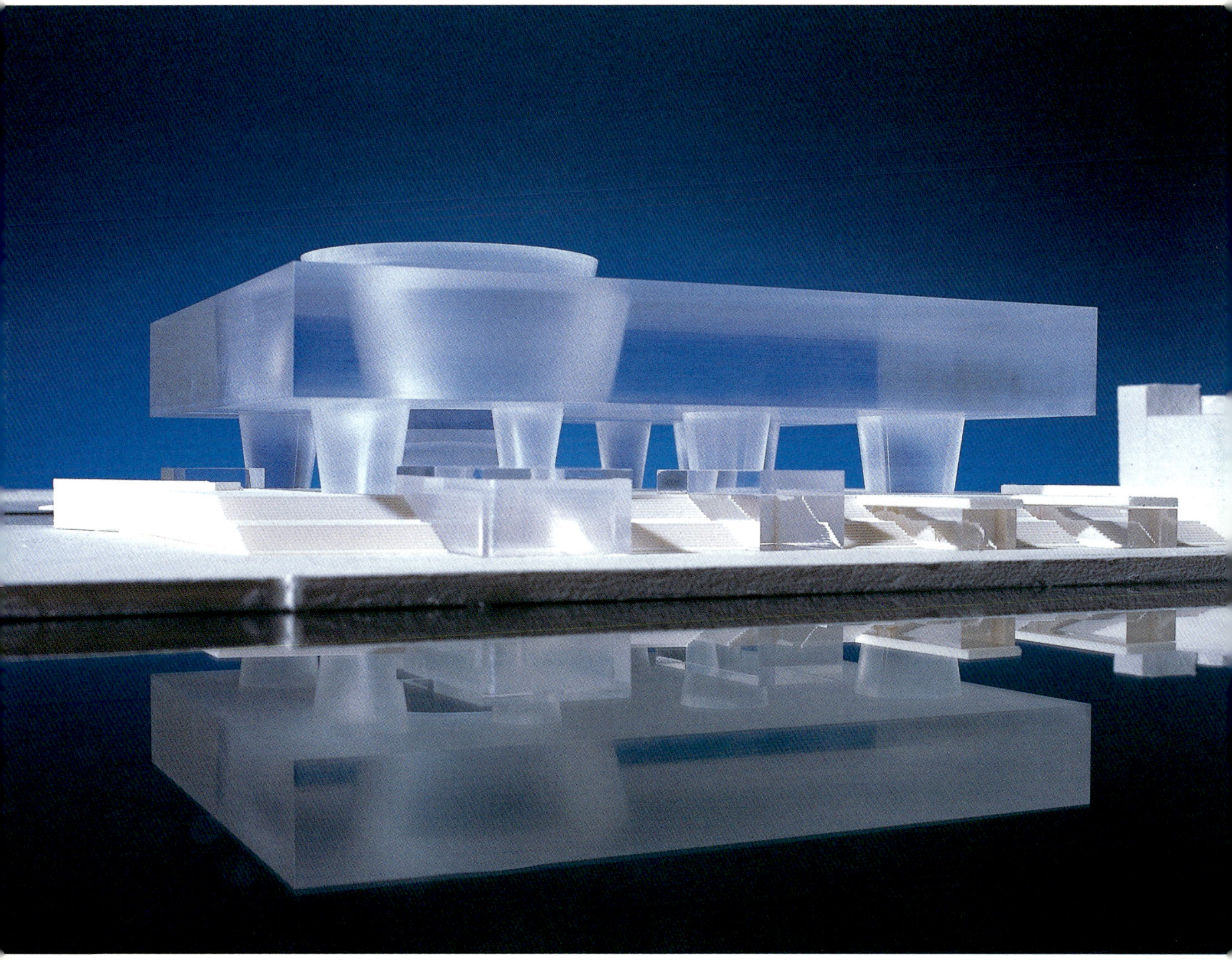

アクリルによるコンセプト模型。マッシブな形態の柱が、軽やかな光の空間を支えるイメージ。柱はコンクリート、上部ヴォリュームは軽やかなガラスによるファサードで計画されている。

Acrylic concept model. Image of massively shaped columns supporting a space of soft light. The columns are concrete, whereas the top volume is designed with a façade of soft glass.

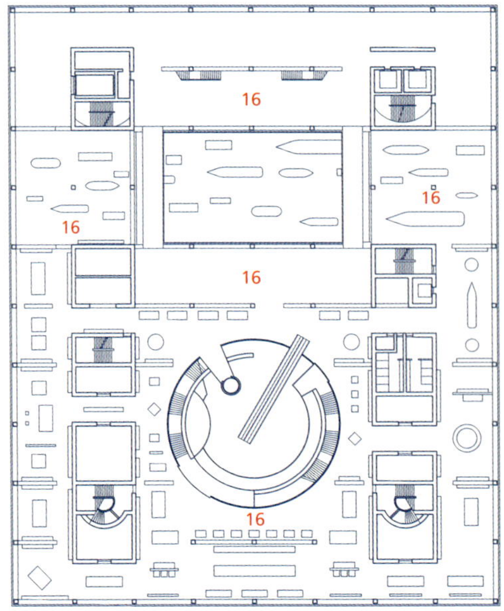

Third floor plan

1. passage
2. court
3. library
4. foyer
5. hall
6. mechanical
7. shop
8. kitchen
9. café
10. parking
11. storage
12. reception
13. office
14. workshop
15. education center
16. exhibition space

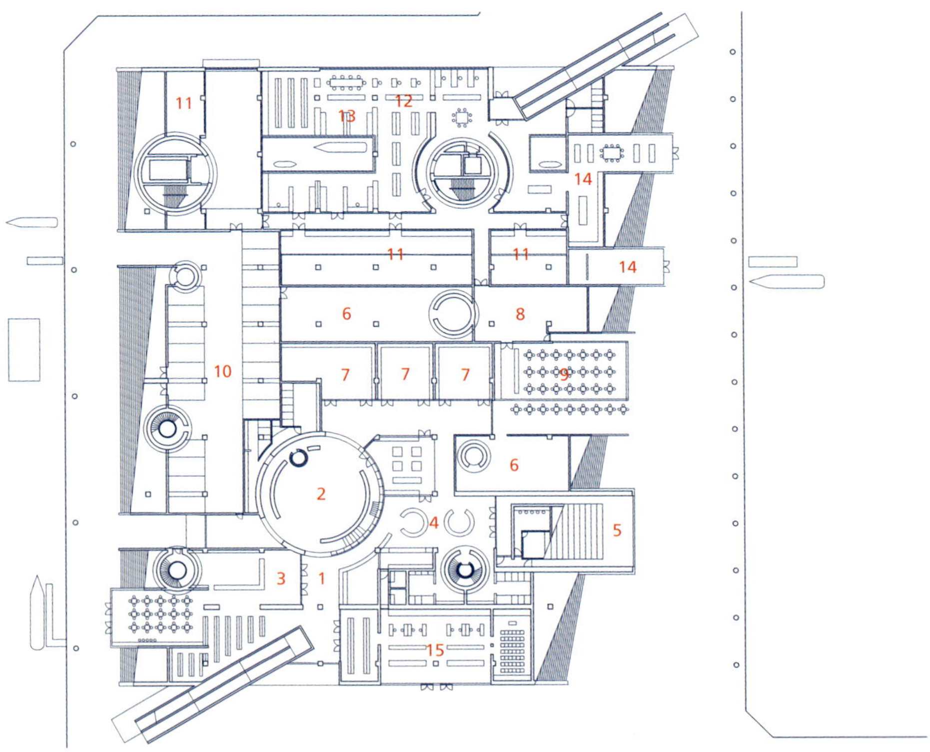

First floor plan 1:1,200

CGによる夜景。海上に浮かぶ光に包まれた博物館建築。

Section

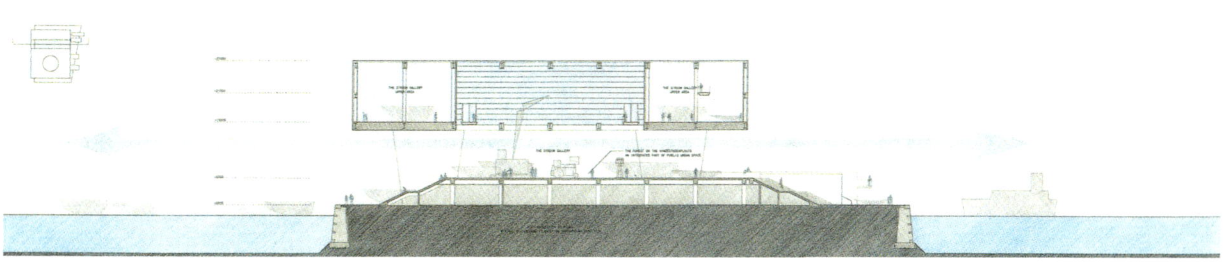

Computer graphic night view. The museum architecture clad in light floats above the sea.

Section

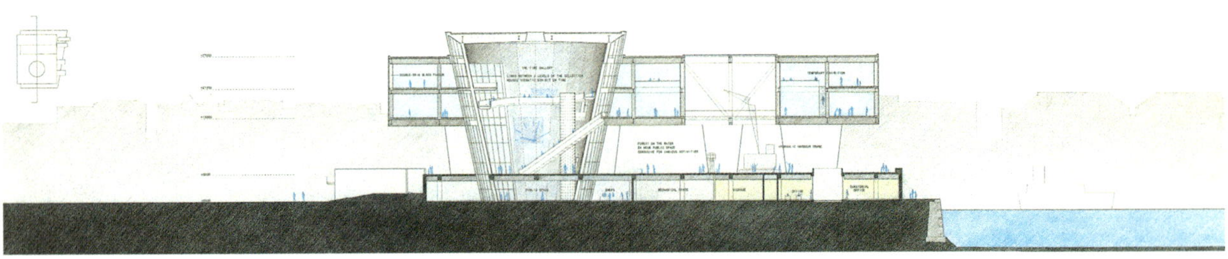

1998年の初頭、ジョルジオ・アルマーニ本人が、私に国際電話をかけてきた。「ミラノ郊外の古い工場を改造して、1000人収容の劇場をつくりたいのだが、その設計を頼めないか」という内容だった。それから1週間後、現地を本人に案内してもらった。半世紀前の工場が廃屋となって残っていた。アルマーニの提示したプログラムは、工場をそのままに、一部改修を加えることで、新たな劇場として再生させるというものだった。旧い建物自体に残すべき価値があるとは思われなかったが、アルマーニの人間性と、「建築にeternityを期待する」という彼の言葉に共鳴して引き受けることにした。ファッションという人間の最も原初的な自己表現のための場として、美術、音楽といった他分野との融合、共同を可能とする"フレキシブルな"空間の創造を主題とした。

イタリアは、常より旧い建物の保存・修復を積極的に推し進めている国である。が、旧いものに新たに手を加えて甦らせた事例はあまり多くない。その意味で、産業施設から文化施設への転用を図ったこのプロジェクトは、この国の都市再生という主題に対して真剣に向き合おうとする先駆的な試みであったといえる。この主題に対し、既存の建物をひとつの敷地とみなし、旧いものの中に、新しい空間を自立した存在として挿入するという応えを返した。これは、これまで関わってきたいくつかの増築、改築の仕事でも一貫して保持してきた考え方である。新築部分は、列柱が立ち並ぶコロネード状のアプローチ空間と、それを受け止める円弧状の壁で囲われたホワイエ空間、そこに1000人収容の劇場とギャラリースペースが接続するという構成からなる。劇場部分は、既存部に対して完全な入れ子構造になっているため、既存工場の旧い内壁と劇場ホール部分の外壁、そこに新旧に挟まれた余白の空間ができる。この隙間が劇場空間の四周に配されていることで、劇場内における客席とステージの関係性の設定、即ち空間のドラマの演出に無限の可能性が生まれる。

アルマーニ・テアトロ
Armani/Teatro

2000-01 イタリア ミラノ——Milan, Italy

In early 1998, I received an international phone call from Giorgio Armani himself. He said, "I want to remodel an old factory on the outskirts of Milan into a theater to hold about a thousand people. Can I commission you to design the project?" One week later, he personally showed me around the site. There was a ruined factory remaining from half a century ago. The program as presented by Armani was to renovate one section of the factory by adding a new theater, while leaving the rest as it is. I did not think it was worth preserving the old building itself, but I undertook the job out of empathy with the humanity of Armani, and his phrase "hoping for eternity in architecture." As a place for the most primal self-expression of people in the fashion world, our theme was the creation of a "flexible" space that enables the fusion and collaboration of art, music, and other fields.

Italy is a country that is exceptionally active in promoting the preservation and restoration of all old buildings. However, there are very few cases where an old structure may be reinvigorated by a new addition. In this sense, as a project intended to adapt an industrial institution into a cultural institution, it may be considered a pioneering experiment that contradicts this nation's theme for urban regeneration. With respect to this theme, our response was to regard the existing building as the site, and insert new, independent spaces within it. This is consistent with our way of thinking in a number of addition and renovation jobs with which we have previously been involved. The newly constructed part is a sequential composition comprising an approach space in the form of a colonnade ending at an arc-shaped wall that encloses the foyer space, and a gallery space and a theater that may accommodate one thousand people. The theater part is a structure entirely nested within the existing part, giving rise to a margin interposed between old and new, between the old interior walls of the existing factory and the outer walls of the theater hall. By arranging this gap around the periphery of the theater space, infinite possibilities are created for establishing the relationship between the audience seating and the stage in the theater, that is, for the production of drama in the space.

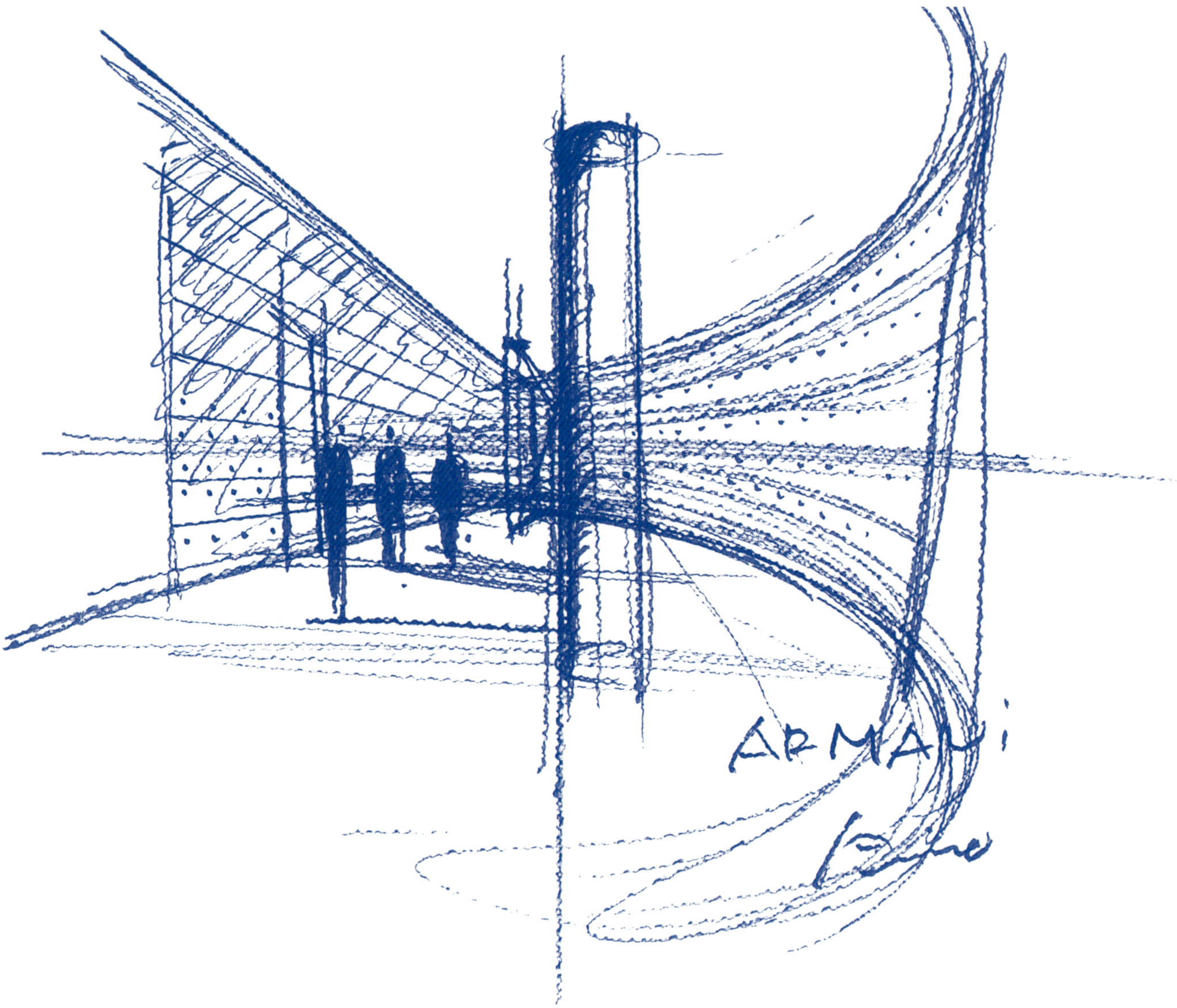

円弧状の壁の囲いとるホールの空間を描いたイメージスケッチ。
Image sketch depicting the hall space enclosed by an arc-shaped wall.

北西側に設けられたテアトロのエントランス。1950年代に建設され、廃屋となっていた工場を改修し、入れ子状に内部にテアトロを設けている。

The entrance to the Teatro, established on the northwest side. An abandoned factory built in the 1950s has been renovated, and the Teatro established inside like a nested box.

エントランスからホールへと導くパッサージュ。意図的に低く抑えられた天井の下、コンクリートの列柱がアプローチを演出する。

Passage leading from the entrance to the hall. The row of concrete columns produces the approach route below a ceiling that has been intentionally kept low.

壁が傾斜しながら緩やかな円弧を描くホール。約100mにおよぶアプローチの天井高さ3.75mに対し、ホールの天井高さは6.2m。

Hall with a sloping wall that delineates a gentle arc. In contrast to the 3.75m-high ceiling of the 100m-long approach, the hall has a ceiling height of 6.2m.

テアトロのパースペクティブ・ドローイングと客席のバリエーション。1000人収容可能。可動客席の仕掛けにより、ファッションショー、コンサート、演劇、イベント、展覧会などフレキシブルに対応できる。

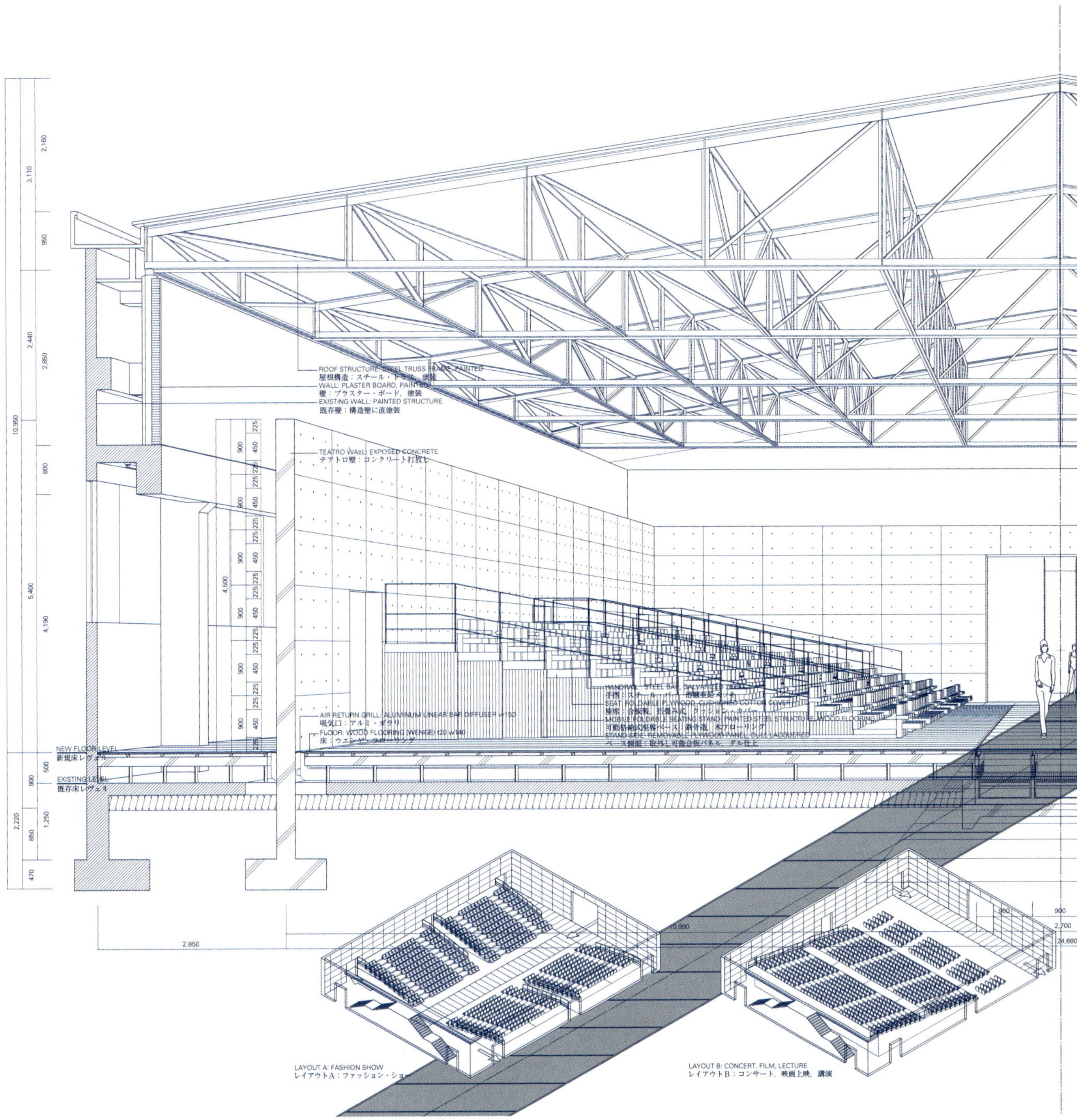

Perspective and diagram of variations. The Teatro can accommodate one thousand people. By means of movable guest seating, it can flexibly accommodate fashion shows, concerts, plays, events, exhibitions, etc.

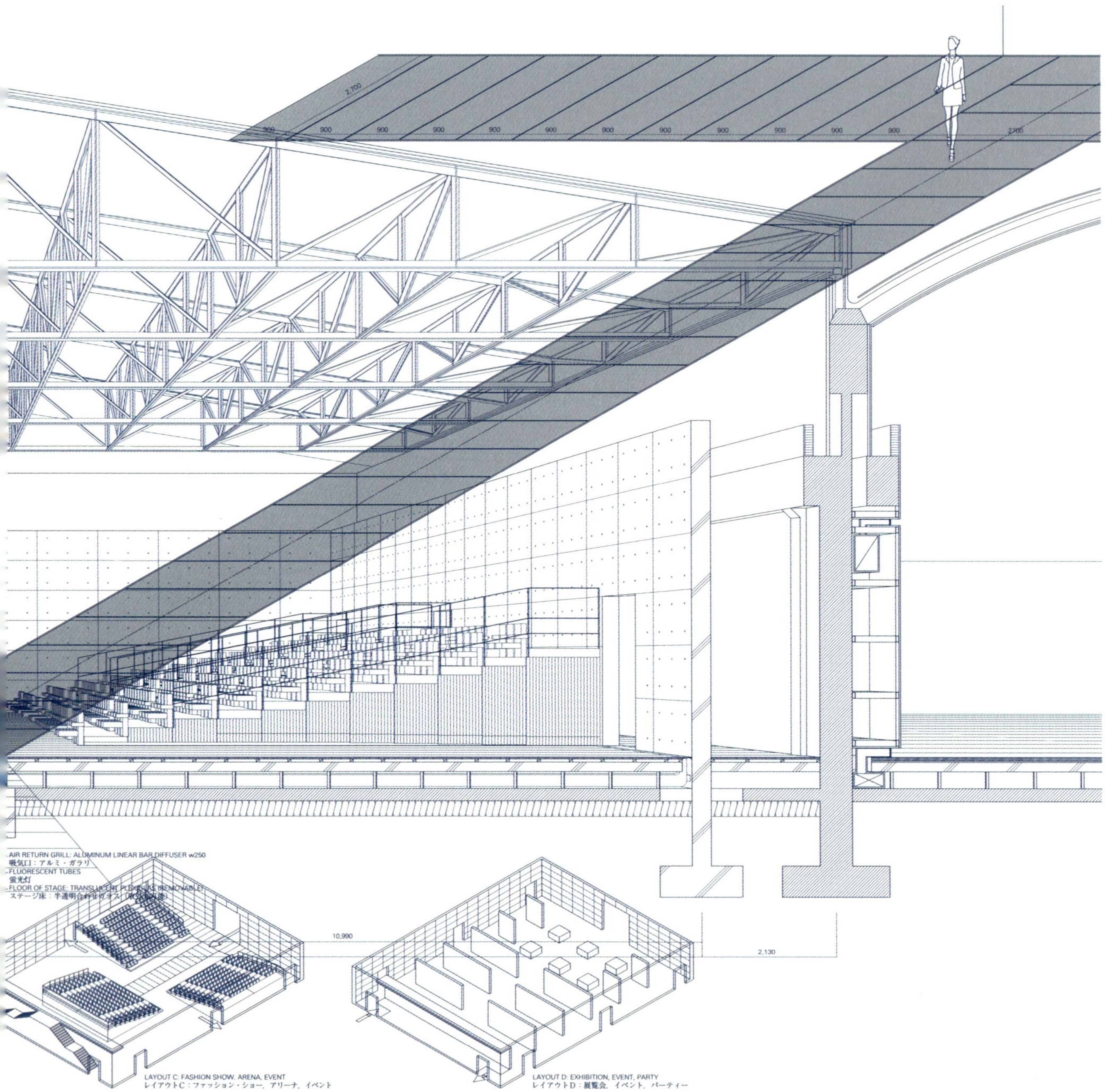

ギャラリー部分の断面図。既存工場のヴォールト天井を活かした改修計画。棟の隙間には、水庭が設けられている。

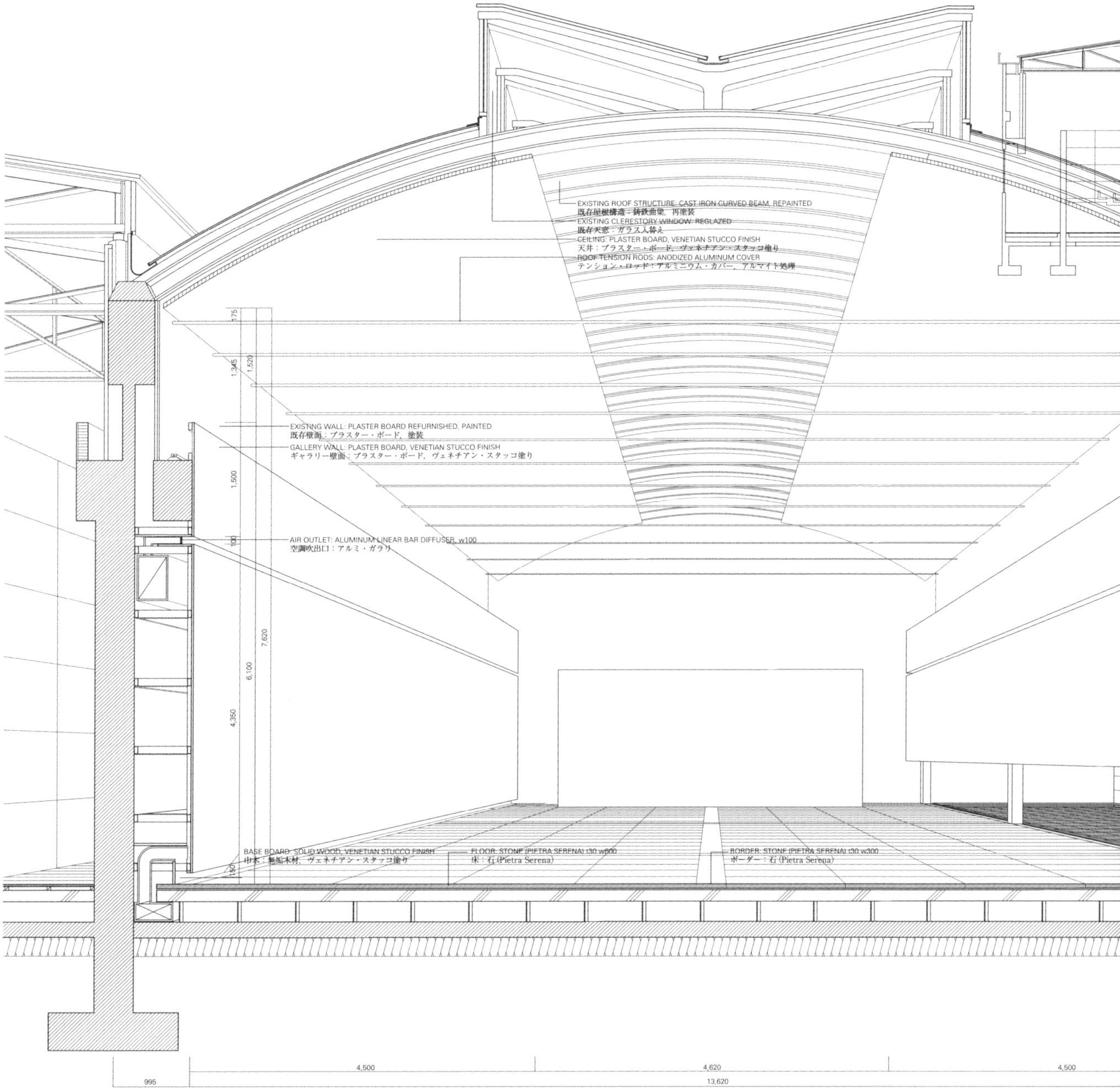

Cross-section of the gallery. The renovation makes use of the vault ceiling of the existing factory. A water garden has been created in the gap between the wings.

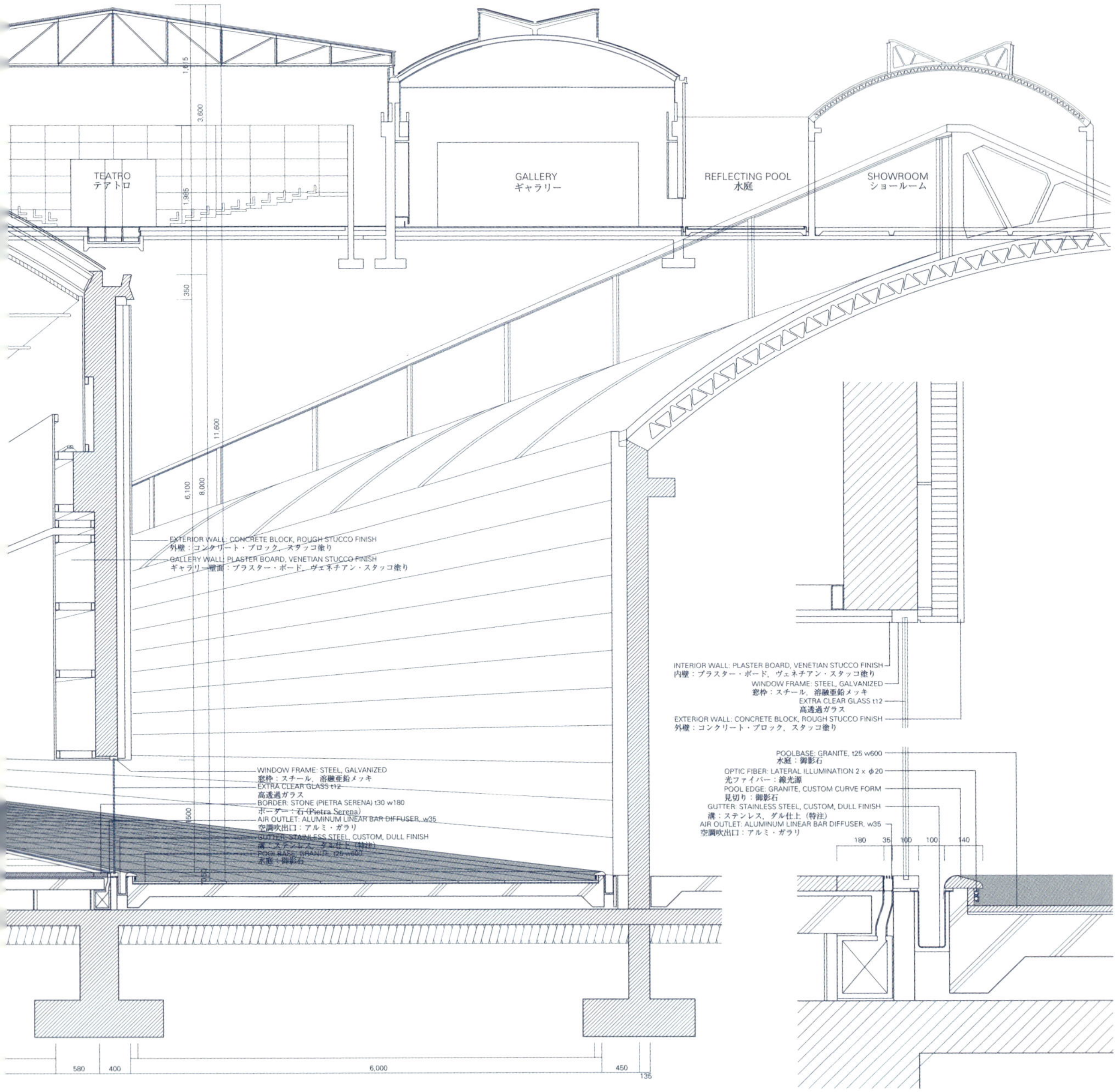

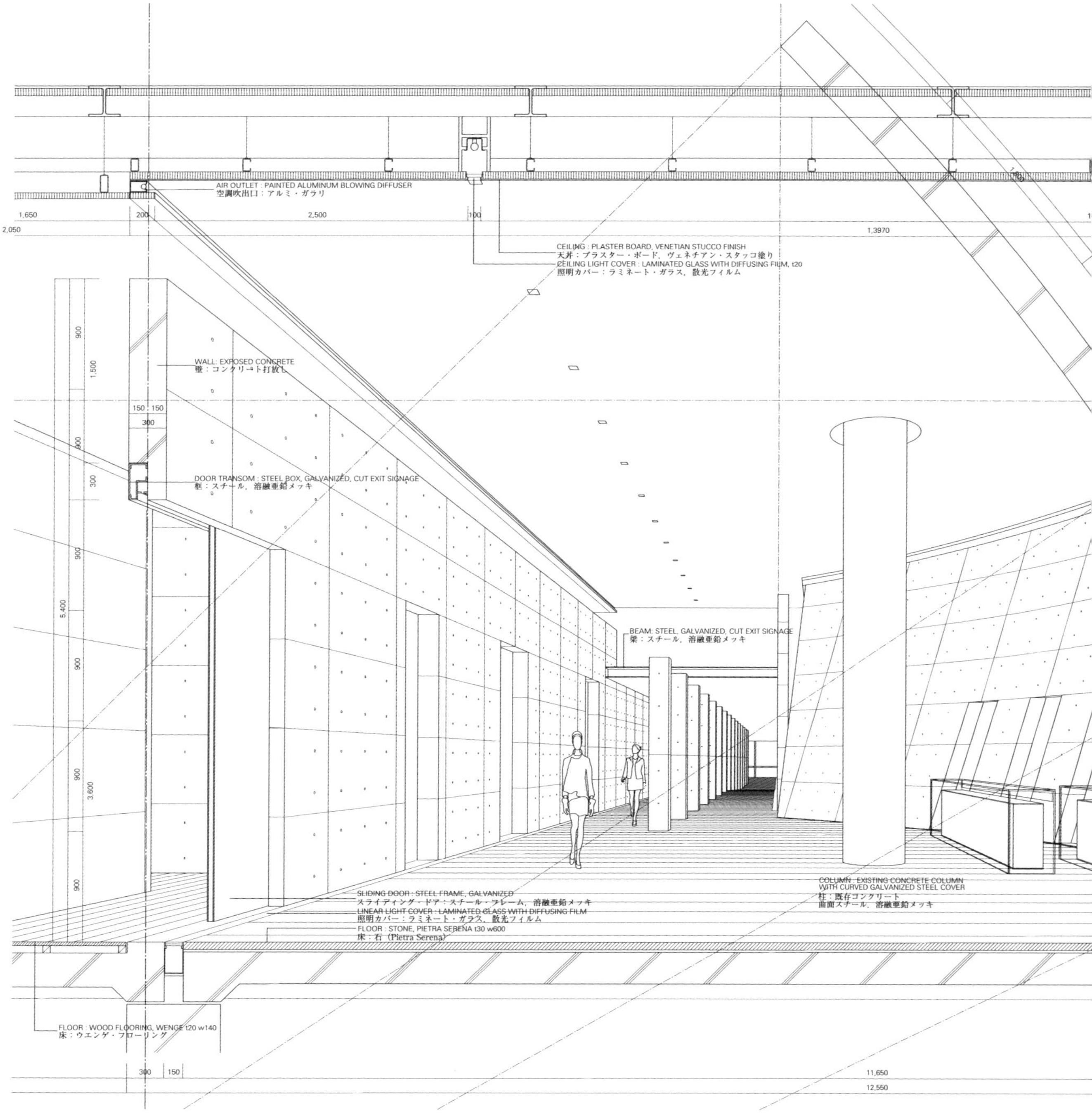

ホールのパースペクティブ・ドローイングと平面図。

Perspective of the hall and plan.

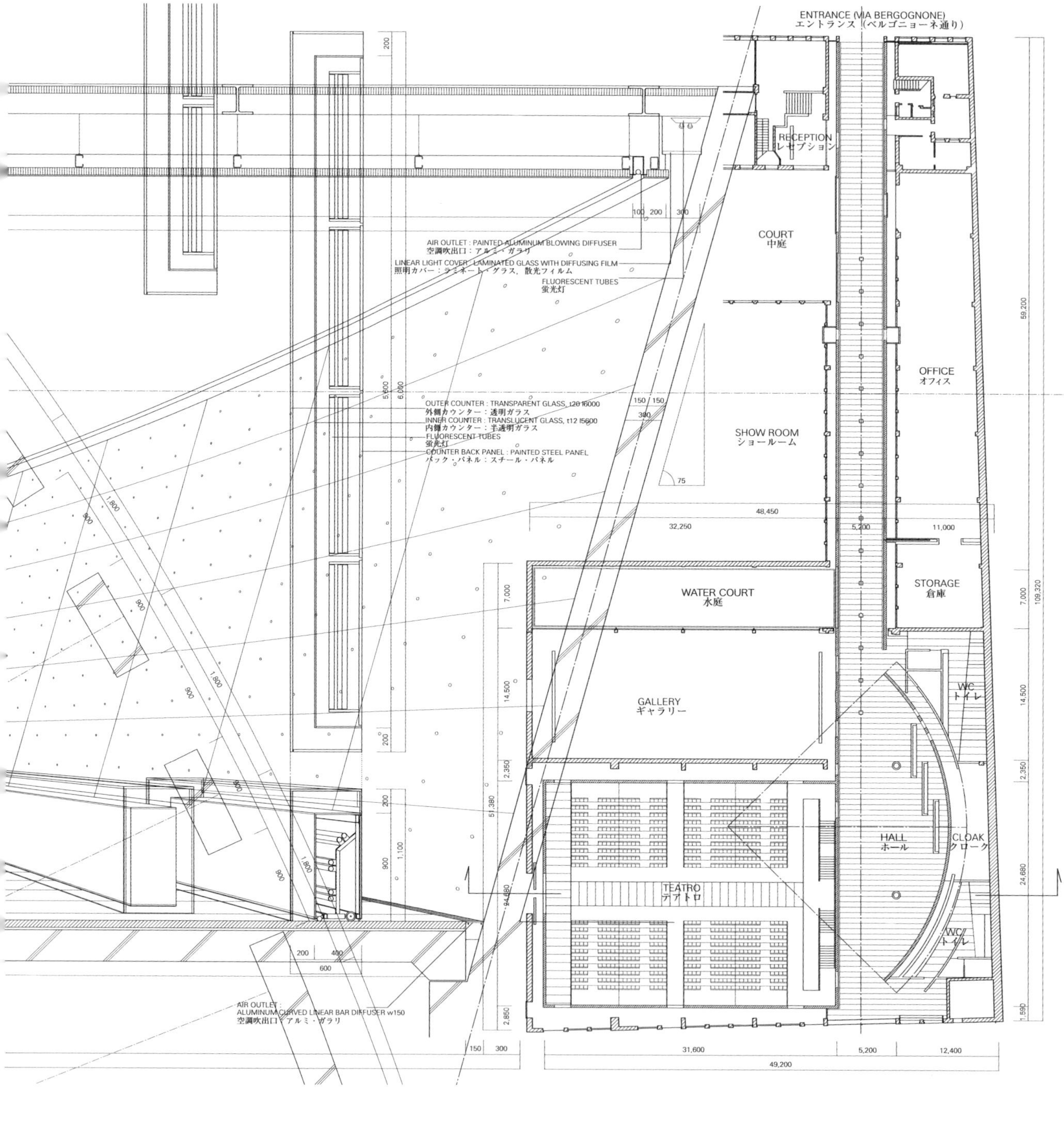
ENTRANCE (VIA BERGOGNONE)
エントランス（ベルゴニョーネ通り）
RECEPTION
レセプション
COURT
中庭
OFFICE
オフィス
SHOW ROOM
ショールーム
STORAGE
倉庫
WATER COURT
水庭
GALLERY
ギャラリー
WC
トイレ
HALL
ホール
CLOAK
クローク
TEATRO
テアトロ
AIR OUTLET : PAINTED ALUMINUM BLOWING DIFFUSER
空調吹出口：アルミ・ガラリ
LINEAR LIGHT COVER : LAMINATED GLASS WITH DIFFUSING FILM
照明カバー：ラミネート・グラス，散光フィルム
FLUORESCENT TUBES
蛍光灯
OUTER COUNTER : TRANSPARENT GLASS, t20 l6000
外側カウンター：透明ガラス
INNER COUNTER : TRANSLUCENT GLASS, t12 l5600
内側カウンター：半透明ガラス
FLUORESCENT TUBES
蛍光灯
COUNTER BACK PANEL : PAINTED STEEL PANEL
バック・パネル：スチール・パネル
AIR OUTLET :
ALUMINUM CURVED LINEAR BAR DIFFUSER w150
空調吹出口：アルミ・ガラリ
48,450
32,250
5,200
11,000
31,600
5,200
12,400
49,200
59,200
109,320
7,000
14,500
2,350
24,680
1,590
51,380
94,480
2,850

テアトロの新たな機能が、既存建築内部に入れ子状に挿入されている。新旧の壁で挟まれる隙間の空間は、設備やサービスのためのスペース。

The new function of the Teatro has been inserted like a nested box in the existing building. The interstitial gaps between the old and new walls are spaces for equipment and other servicing.

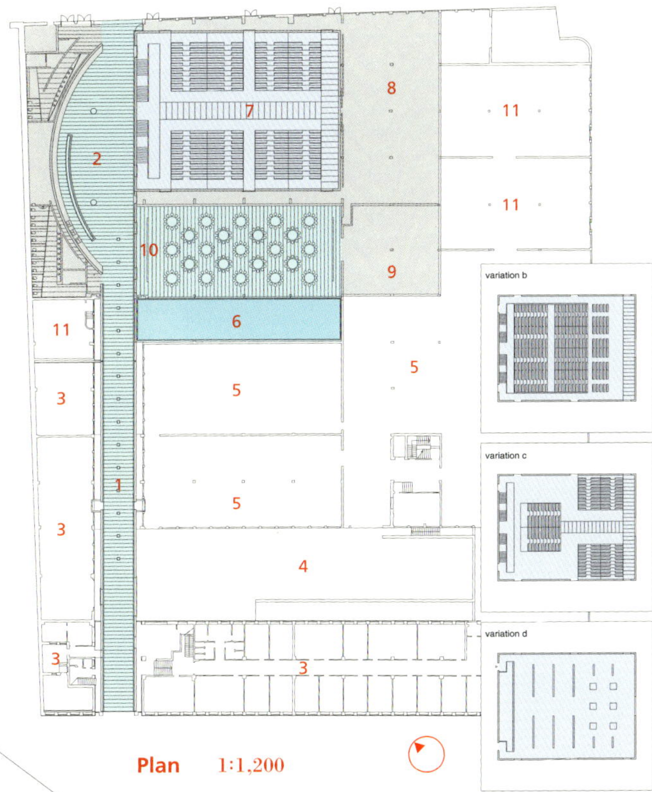

Plan 1:1,200

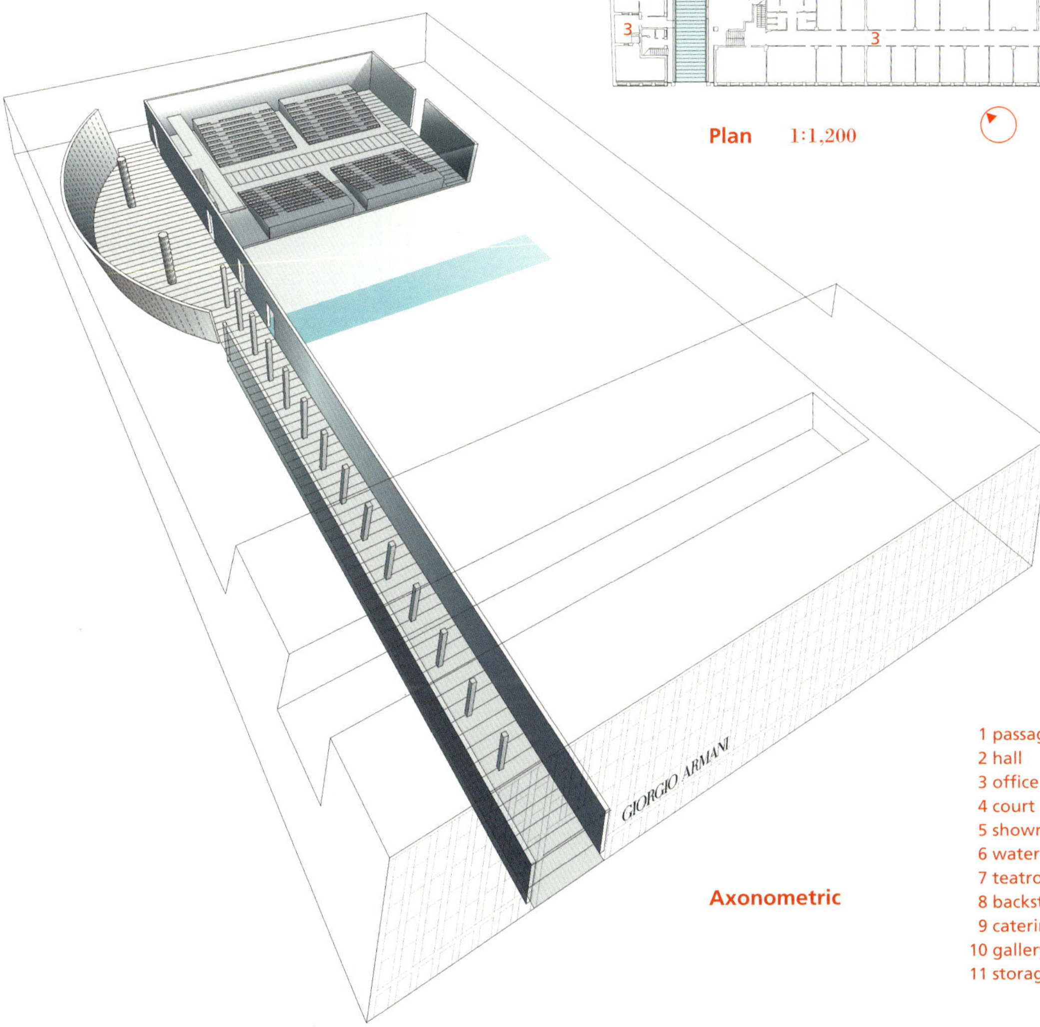

Axonometric

1 passage
2 hall
3 office
4 court
5 showroom
6 water court
7 teatro
8 backstage
9 catering kitchen
10 gallery
11 storage

ギャラリー内観。ウォーターコートからの光が旧い建物に新たな息吹を吹き込んでいる。
Interior of the gallery. The light from the water court breathes new life into the old building.

エッセイ

ジョルジオ・アルマーニ

完成した建物の素晴らしいクオリティに、私は感銘を受けました。

経済的な負担だけでなく、心理的な負担の面からいっても、われわれのプロジェクトは相当の重みをもつものでした。私ははじめ、シアターをファッションショーのためにのみ使うつもりだったのです。しかし、安藤と仕事を進めていく中で、もっと大きなポテンシャル、つまり、パブリックイベントも開ける真のシアターとしてのポテンシャルをもつことに気づいたのです。安藤はサイトに既存の建物をわざと残し、そこに新たな要素を巧みに組み入れることで、「創造」にとって最も相応しい場所を用意してくれました。結果として、私は極めて重要な意義をもつパブリックスペースをミラノに提供することができたのです。未来にわたって価値を保ち続けるものを創造することができたという意味で、私は本当に恵まれました。

安藤には直接電話でこの仕事を依頼したのです。幸いにも、その1週間後にミラノで会うことができて、われわれは互いにはじめからよい感触を受けました。そして10日後、安藤は早くもデザインのフレームワークを用意してくれたのです。何もかもが、信じられないスピードで進行しました。安藤レベルの世界的に著名な建築家から、予想外にもこんなに素早く、しかも共感に根ざした反応を得ることができて、私は驚きと喜びで満たされました。私が安藤に頼もうと思ったのは、安藤が流行に左右されない建築家だからです。安藤は時代を超越する作品をつくるマエストロ。そのことを、彼の作品集を初めて見たときから私は理解していました。安藤こそ、私のテイストを建築文化に移すことのできる人だったのです。

安藤が生み出したシアターは、永遠の時間のためにつくられた場所であるに違いありません。それはニュートラルで匿名の場所、プレタポルテの世界とは異なった次元に存するものです。私は最高のパートナーを得て、最高の建築作品の創出に成功したのです。

ジョルジオ・アルマーニ
1934年イタリア、ピアツェンツァ生まれ。医学を学んだ後、ファッション界に入る。
1975年セルジオ・ガレオッティとともにジョルジオ・アルマーニ社を設立。

Essay

Giorgio Armani

I am impressed by the superb quality of the completed building.

This was a major project, both financially and psychologically. I originally thought of using the theater only for fashion shows but realized it had much greater potential as work with Ando progressed, that is, the potential to be used as a true theater, where public events can also be held. Ando deliberately retained an existing structure on the site, and by skillfully inserting a new element he prepared a most appropriate place for creation. As a consequence, I was able to provide Milan with a public space of extremely important significance. I was quite fortunate in being able to create a thing that will endure and be of value in the future.

I asked Ando directly by telephone to take on this job. Happily, he was able to meet me a week later in Milan. We had good feelings from the start, and ten days later Ando had already prepared the framework of the design. Everything proceeded at an unbelievable speed. I was astounded and gratified by this unexpectedly swift and sympathetic response from an internationally-known architect of Ando's caliber. I thought of asking Ando because he is not an architect swayed by fashion. He is a *maestro* who builds for the ages. I knew this from the first time I saw a collection of his works. He was indeed the person to translate my tastes into the culture of architecture.

The theater Ando has created is indisputably a place designed for eternity. It is a neutral and anonymous place, in a different dimension from the world of *prêt-a-porter*. I have succeeded in creating a supreme work of architecture with a supreme partner.

Giorgio Armani

Born in Piacenza, Italy in 1934. After studying medical science, started fashion work. Together with Sergio Galeotti, he founded GIORGIO ARMANI S.p.A. in 1975.

マンチェスター市中心部に位置するピカデリー公園と、その周辺地域の地区再生プロジェクトである。1996年の爆弾テロをきっかけに始まった都市再興の機運の中で企画され、99年の国際コンペにより、われわれとオヴ・アラップ&パートナーズ、EDAWの共同チームの参加が決まった。

産業革命以降、イングランド最大の商工業都市として栄えたマンチェスターは、近代黎明期の中心都市としてありながら、次第に輝きを失っていった。観光地としての魅力が乏しかったのが衰退の大きな理由であるが、〈近代文明発祥の地〉として町の風景を見つめ直してみると、何気ない街の風景に栄光の歴史の痕跡が刻まれていることに気づく。それを都市の記憶として顕在化することが、再興の鍵になるのではないかと考えた。

荒廃して都市公園としての機能を失いつつあったピカデリー公園であったが、〈時を超えたモニュメント〉となるべき、重要な意味をもつ場所のひとつだった。われわれは、失われた〈市民生活の場〉を取り戻すために、白紙の状態から〈新たにつくり直す〉のではなく、あくまでその場所の記憶を継承しながら新たな生命を吹き込む、〈再生〉を計画の主題として強く意識した。

生まれ変わったピカデリー公園は、改修前と変わらずヴィクトリア女王の記念碑を中心とする構成をもつ。周囲の都市インフラを含めての計画であったが、公園のヒューマンスケールを確保するために、交通量の激しいターミナル側と確かな境界を設ける必要があった。その結界の役目を負う要素として、まず計画されたのが、弧を描くコンクリートの壁である。

その壁の囲いとるスペースを活用した市民情報センターと、楕円形の噴水広場と、多目的な利用を想定された芝生広場、この3つの主要な要素によって、公園は再構成される。構成要素の限定されたランドスケープであるが、敷地全体に敷かれたグリッドに従わせることで、恣意性を排しながら、その一見単純な構成の中に、人々の生活に豊かさをもたらす、多様性を秘めたものにしたいと考えた。全体に空間の秩序感とリズム感を強く意識した。

この公園が、鉄道やバスのターミナルを結ぶ交通の要衝としてのみならず、人々の集まる中心として、将来のマンチェスターの市民活動の拠点として息づいていくことを期待している。

マンチェスター市
ピカデリー公園再生計画

Piccadilly Gardens Regeneration, Manchester

1999-2002 イギリス マンチェスター —— Manchester, U.K.

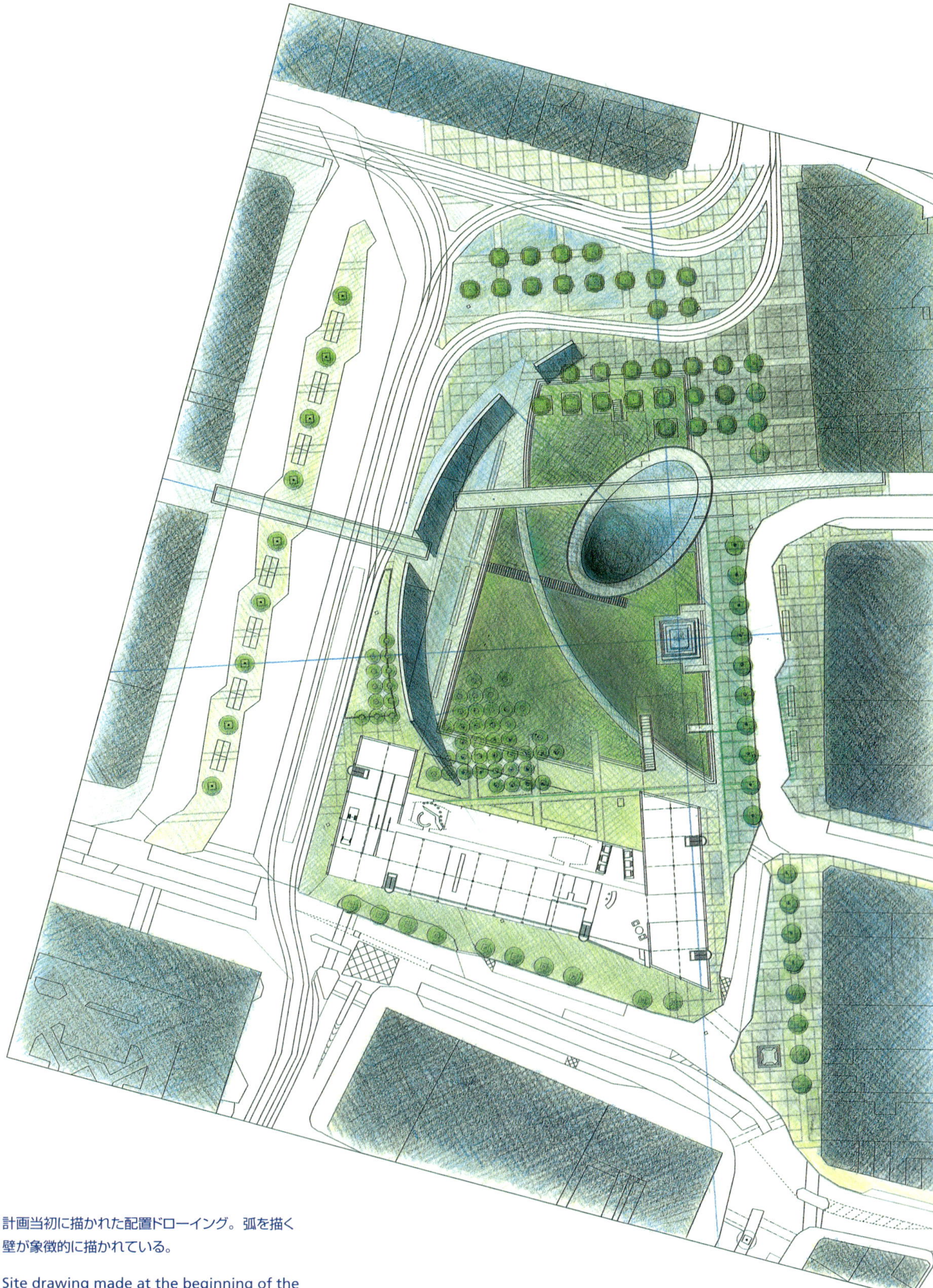

計画当初に描かれた配置ドローイング。弧を描く
壁が象徴的に描かれている。

Site drawing made at the beginning of the design. A symbolic depiction of the arc wall.

This is a regional regeneration project for Piccadilly Gardens, located in the center of Manchester, and the surrounding area. As part of the urban regeneration opportunity triggered by the terrorist bombing in 1996, we were selected to participate in a team together with Ove Arup & Partners and EDAW as the result of an international competition held in 1999.

From the Industrial Revolution onward, Manchester flourished as the greatest commercial and industrial city in England. Although a significant city at the dawn of modern period, it has gradually lost its luster. A big reason for the decay is its meager charm as a sightseeing area, but by gazing at the city scenery as "a portent of modern civilization," traces of its glorious history may be noticed inscribed in the casual townscape. I thought that actualizing these city memories might be the key to regeneration. Although Piccadilly Gardens was a ruin that had lost its function as a city park, it could become a "monument that transcends time," a place with important meaning.

To regain a place lost to "civic life," rather than a "new creation" on a blank slate, with a strong awareness of "regeneration" as the theme of the design, we instilled new life while determinedly holding on to the memory of this place.

The composition of the reborn Piccadilly Gardens is focused on a monument to Queen Victoria that remains unchanged from prior to the renovation. The plan includes the surrounding urban infrastructure, but to ensure the human scale of the park, it was necessary to establish a definite boundary with the fierce traffic on the terminal side. As an element taking the role of the barrier, we first planned a concrete wall that delineates an arc.

The space enclosed by this wall is utilized for a citizen information center, an oval-shaped fountain plaza, and a multipurpose lawn plaza. The park is recomposed by these three major elements. Although a landscape comprising limited compositional elements, while avoiding arbitrariness by following a grid across the entire site, there is a hidden diversity that enriches human life within this seemingly simple composition. Overall, there is a strong awareness of a sense of order and rhythm in the spaces.

As well as being connected to the railway and the bus terminal as a strategic traffic location, this park is also a focus for people to gather, and we expect it to be a future hub for the activities of the citizens of Manchester.

Piccadilly Gardens Regeneration, Manchester

広場鳥瞰。弧を描く壁が都市の喧騒を遮り、穏やかな公園の空間をつくり出している。

Bird's eye view of the plaza. The arc wall blocks the tumult of the city, producing a tranquil park space.

楕円平面の噴水広場。コンピューター制御によりさまざまな水の表情が楽しめる。

Elliptical water fountain plaza. Through computer control, various expressions of water may be enjoyed.

噴水広場を貫くキャットウォーク。
Catwalk going through the water fountain plaza.

グリッドに沿って樹木が配された、公園の東側スペース。
Space on the east side of the park where trees and shrubs are distributed along a grid.

長さ90mにおよぶ円弧状の壁には屋根スラブが架けられ、解放されたピロティ空間をつくり出す。ガラスのカーテンウォールで覆われた部分は、市民のための情報センター。

A roof slab is suspended across the 90m-long arc-shaped wall, producing a space free from pilotis. The section covered with a glass curtain wall is a citizen information center.

2002
Manchester
THE XVII COMMONWEALTH GAMES
mass communication
management ltd
CONCEPT
OUTDOOR
C3imaging Mcr

広場全景。蘇った市民の憩いの場。左手に見えるのは、保存されたヴィクトリア女王像。

Panoramic view of the plaza. A relaxation place restored for citizens. The preserved statue of Queen Victoria is visible on the left.

広場夜景。穏やかなランドスケープの背後にある、
構成の幾何学が浮かび上がる。

Night view of the plaza. The geometrical composition rises behind the quiet landscape.

デュッセルドルフ郊外のエルフト川のほとりに、インゼル・ホンブロイッヒと呼ばれる美術館がある。インゼル（島）の名の通り、広大な沼地に浮かぶ島全体を敷地とした、世界でも稀有の〈公園〉美術館だ。20数万m^2もの鬱蒼とした森に、彫刻家エルヴィン・ヘーリッヒの手による端正な〈展示室〉パヴィリオンが10数棟、野外彫刻とともに、それ自体彫刻として、木々に溶け込むように分散して配置されている。

オーナーのカール・ハインリヒ・ミュラー氏は、敷地周辺の土地を入手後、膨大な労力を費やして、大地のかたちを変え、木々を植え替えて、数世紀前のあるべき自然の姿を取り戻した。

そのミュラー氏が、インゼル・ホンブロイッヒから北西に1kmほどのところにあるNATOのロケット発射基地の跡に、新たな美術館を企画した。より建築的な施設からなる構想で、その中のギャラリーのひとつが、われわれに依頼された。それがホンブロイッヒ／ランゲン美術館計画の始まりだった。

ミュラー氏より依頼を受け、初めて敷地を訪れたのが1994年。資金繰りの問題などから、アイディアを提出してから実際につくり出すまでに、随分時間が空いた。日本とドイツの距離の問題を含め、国内の仕事に比べて、非常に遅々としたプロセスであった。

ホンブロイッヒ／ランゲン美術館
Langen Foundation/Hombroich

1994-2004 ドイツ ノイス —— Neuss, Germany

2000年、ミュラー氏の構想に賛同された90歳になるマリアン・ランゲン夫人が美術館建設への出資を申し出られ、ようやく2002年末に工事再開したが、それまでにもアイディアは日々深度を深め、強度を増していった。これほどの長期間、ひとつの建築を考え続ける機会が得られたことは、仕事としては苦しい一方で、ひとりの表現者としては幸運だったのかもしれない。

美術館には、ランゲン夫妻によって収集された東洋美術と現代美術のコレクションが収蔵される。このプログラムを受け、私はふたつの異なる性格のスペースを考えた。ひとつは、東洋美術のための、柔らかな光で充たされた〈静〉の空間。もうひとつは、現代美術のための、光の交錯する躍動的な〈動〉の空間。それらを環境そのものを美術館とするインゼル・ホンブロイッヒのコンセプトのまま、緑の中に控えめに建つ洗練されたアートの器のイメージに重ね合わせていく。

常設展示棟——〈静〉の空間は、コンクリートとガラスの入れ子構造により、日本建築の〈縁側〉のような緩衝領域を巡らしている。美術館内部にいながら森の中を歩いているような、内外空間の流動性を期待した。企画展示棟——〈動〉の空間は、そのヴォリュームをすべて地中に埋め込み、その閉ざされた箱にスカイライトなどにより劇的に光を採り込む、というストーリーで考えた。

美しい自然の中に、優れた芸術作品が、何の隔たりなしに、手に触れられる距離に置かれている。初めてインゼル・ホンブロイッヒを訪れたとき、「ここにアートの楽園がある」と思った。その感動のまま、ランゲン美術館もまた、自然に溶け込んで一体化するようにつくろうと思った。森の中にひっそりと息づくその佇まいの内に、ミュラー氏、ランゲン夫人の生涯をかけた夢が込められている。芸術を愛するふたりの強い想い、その重なり合いが美術館を生み出した。ランゲン夫人は残念ながら美術館のオープンを待たずに亡くなられたが、その魂はこの美術館とともに生き続けるだろう。

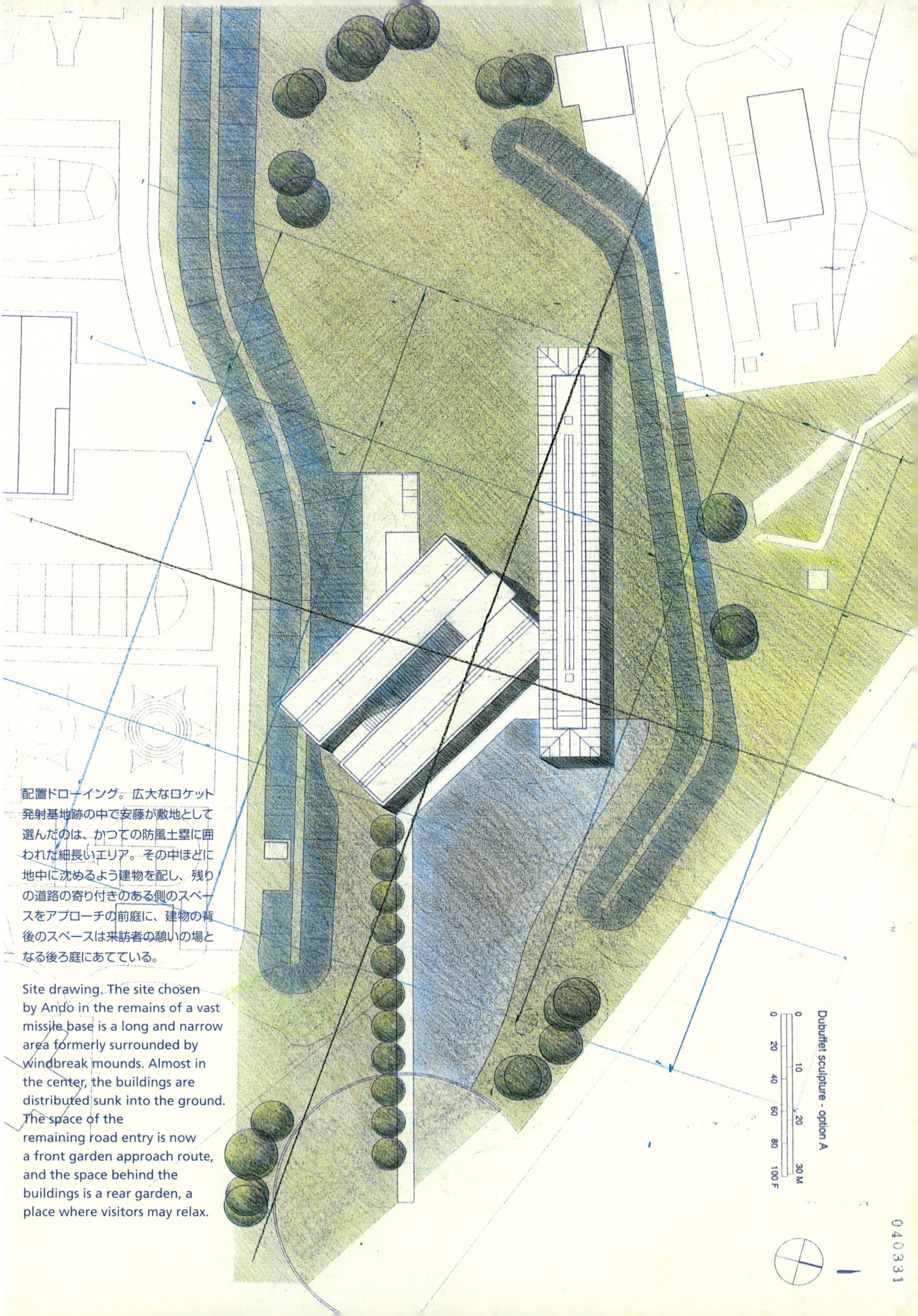

配置ドローイング。広大なロケット発射基地跡の中で安藤が敷地として選んだのは、かつての防風土塁に囲われた細長いエリア。その中ほどに地中に沈めるよう建物を配し、残りの道路の寄り付きのある側のスペースをアプローチの前庭に、建物の背後のスペースは来訪者の憩いの場となる後ろ庭にあてている。

Site drawing. The site chosen by Ando in the remains of a vast missile base is a long and narrow area formerly surrounded by windbreak mounds. Almost in the center, the buildings are distributed sunk into the ground. The space of the remaining road entry is now a front garden approach route, and the space behind the buildings is a rear garden, a place where visitors may relax.

Near the Erft River in the suburbs of Dusseldorf, there is an art museum called Insel Hombroich. As indicated by the name *Insel* (island), the entire site is an island floating in a vast marshland, a "park" museum rarely seen anywhere in the world. Outdoor sculptures are distributed across 200,000m^2 of luxuriant forest, together with many handsome "exhibition room" pavilions made by sculptor Erwin Heerich that are themselves sculptures, all in a dispersed layout that allows them to merge with the trees.

Having obtained the land around the site, the owner Karl-Heinrich Müller devoted a huge amount of effort to changing the topography and transplanting trees in order to regain the appearance of the natural environment as it would have been several centuries ago.

Mr Müller planned a new museum on the remains of a NATO missile base about 1km northwest of Insel Hombroich. We were commissioned to design one of the galleries, comprising more architectural facilities. This was the beginning of the plan for the Langen Foundation / Hombroich.

Having received the commission from Mr Müller, we visited the site for the first time in 1994. Due to financing problems, there was a fairly long interval between presenting our idea and actually building it. Given the problem of the distance between Japan and Germany, it was a very slow process compared with our local work.

In 2000, Müller's scheme was approved by the 90-year-old lady, Mrs Marian Langen, who provided financing for the construction of the art museum. Construction work finally resumed at the end of 2002, but until then the idea increased in depth and strength every day. Being given the chance to think about a work of architecture for such an extended period of time was a painful task, but on the other hand, it was perhaps good fortune for me as the

Langen Foundation/ Hombroich

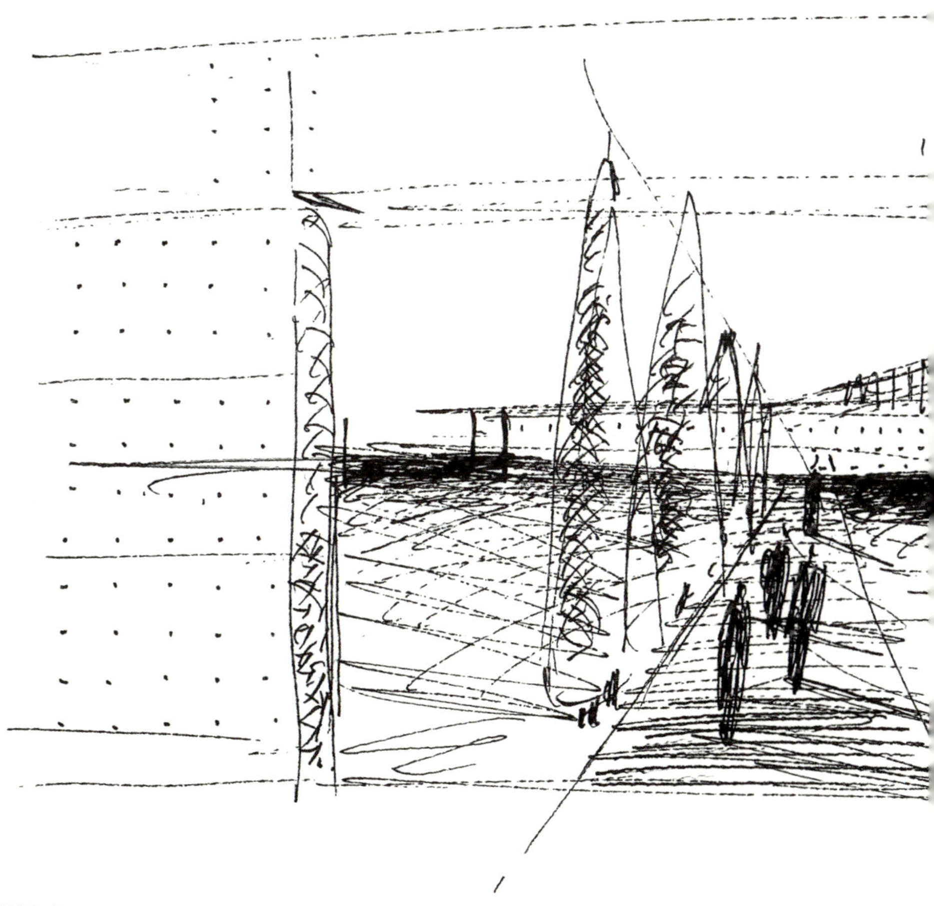

person giving it expression.

The museum contains the collection of Oriental art and modern art accumulated by Mr and Mrs Langen. Having received this program, I conceived spaces with two different characters. One, for the Oriental art, is a space of "quietness" suffused with soft light. The other, for the modern art, is a space of throbbing "movement" with mixed light. Just as the concept of Insel Hombroich is to make the environment itself into the art museum, these are modestly built amid the greenery, superimposed as an image of polished containers for art.

Using a nested structure of concrete and glass, the "quiet" space of the permanent exhibition wing is surrounded with a buffer area like the *engawa* (veranda) of Japanese architecture. As if walking in the forest, we hope for a fluidity of inside and outside space while in the museum. In the "movement" space of the temporary exhibition wing, I conceived the story of a volume entirely embedded underground, with dramatic light brought into this sealed box by means of skylights.

Within a beautiful natural environment, these superlative artworks are placed within range of being touched by the hand, without any intervening distance. When visiting Insel Hombroich for the first time, I thought, "here is a paradise of art." These deep impressions made me want to merge and integrate the Langen Museum with nature. Gently breathing within the forest, the lifelong dream of Mr Müller and Mrs Langen is contained within this figure. The overlapping of the strong desires of these two art lovers has produced this art museum. While it is a tragedy that Mrs Langen passed away before the opening of the museum, perhaps her soul may continue to live here.

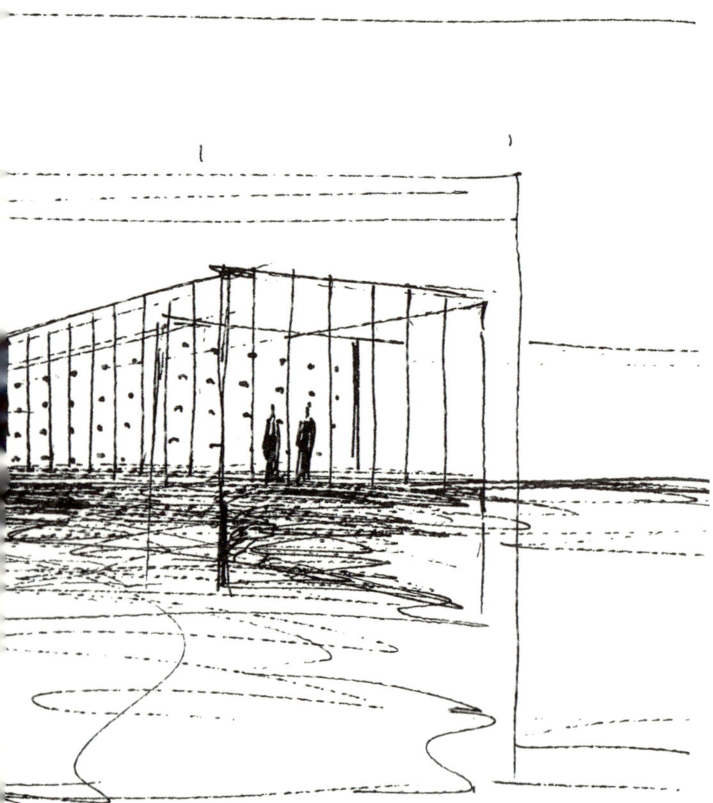

アプローチのイメージスケッチ。アプローチで人々を迎える円弧状の壁、そこに穿たれたゲートから望む建物と水庭の風景。

Image sketch of the approach route. People are welcomed by the arc-shaped wall, and scenes of the water garden and the buildings are visible through the gate that pierces it.

美術館を背に入口ゲートを見る。ゲートから、水盤を迂回してはしる歩廊の連なりが、雄大な風景に相応しい美術館のアプローチ空間をつくり出している。

Looking at the entrance gate against the museum. From the gate a succession of promenades detouring around the water creates the approach space of the museum, as befits the magnificent scenery.

北西側外観。水盤に沿ったＬ字型のアプローチを抜け、美術館に導かれる。

Exterior view from the northwest. Leaving the L-shaped approach route along the flower basins, one is guided to the museum.

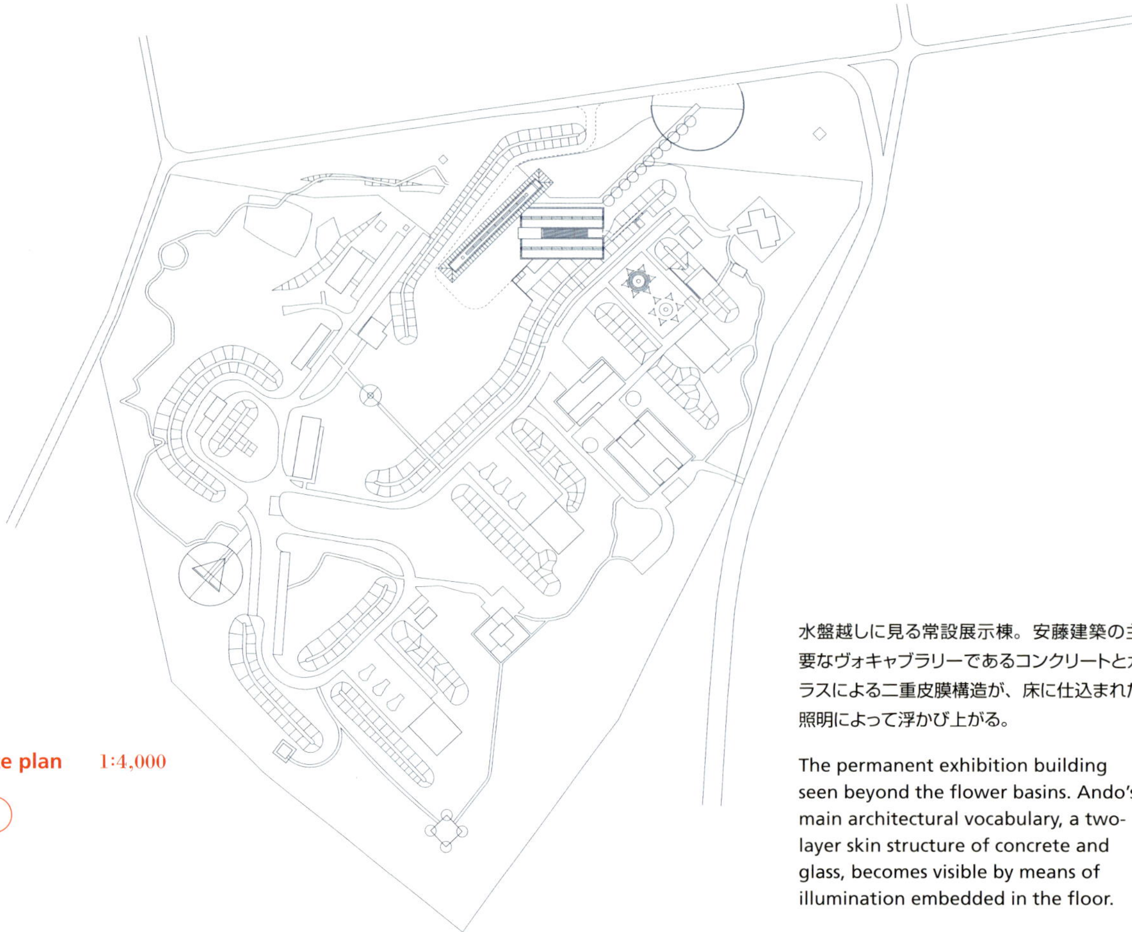

Site plan 1:4,000

水盤越しに見る常設展示棟。安藤建築の主要なヴォキャブラリーであるコンクリートとガラスによる二重皮膜構造が、床に仕込まれた照明によって浮かび上がる。

The permanent exhibition building seen beyond the flower basins. Ando's main architectural vocabulary, a two-layer skin structure of concrete and glass, becomes visible by means of illumination embedded in the floor.

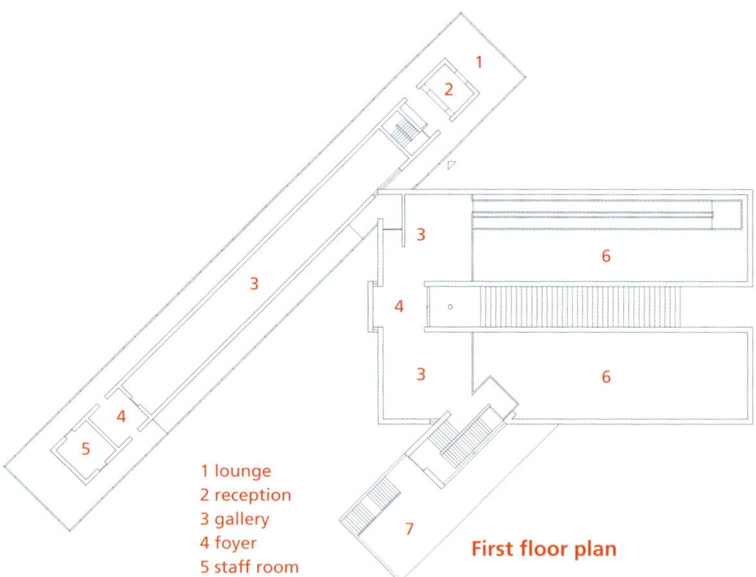

1 lounge
2 reception
3 gallery
4 foyer
5 staff room
6 void
7 sculpture terrace
8 archive
9 storage
10 mechanical

First floor plan

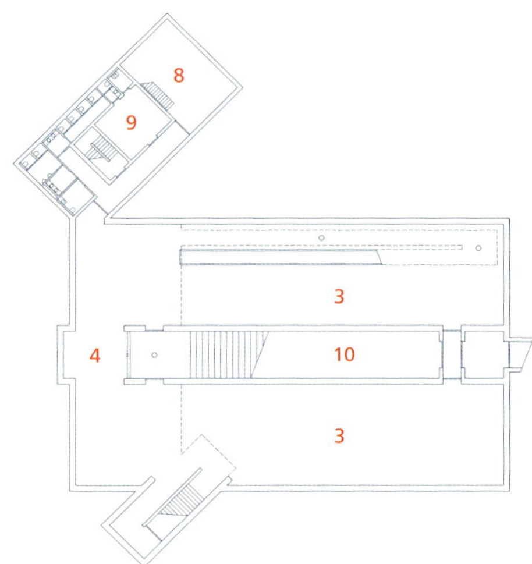

Basement floor plan 1:900

常設展示棟の北側外観。風景を映し出すガラススクリーン越しに見るコンクリートの柔和な表情。

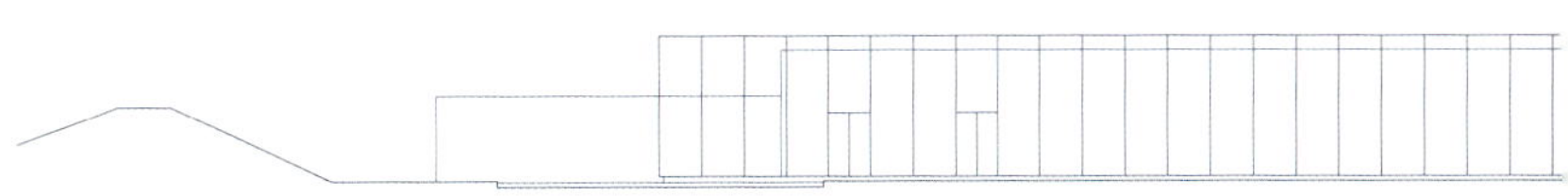

North elevation

Section

Section 1:600

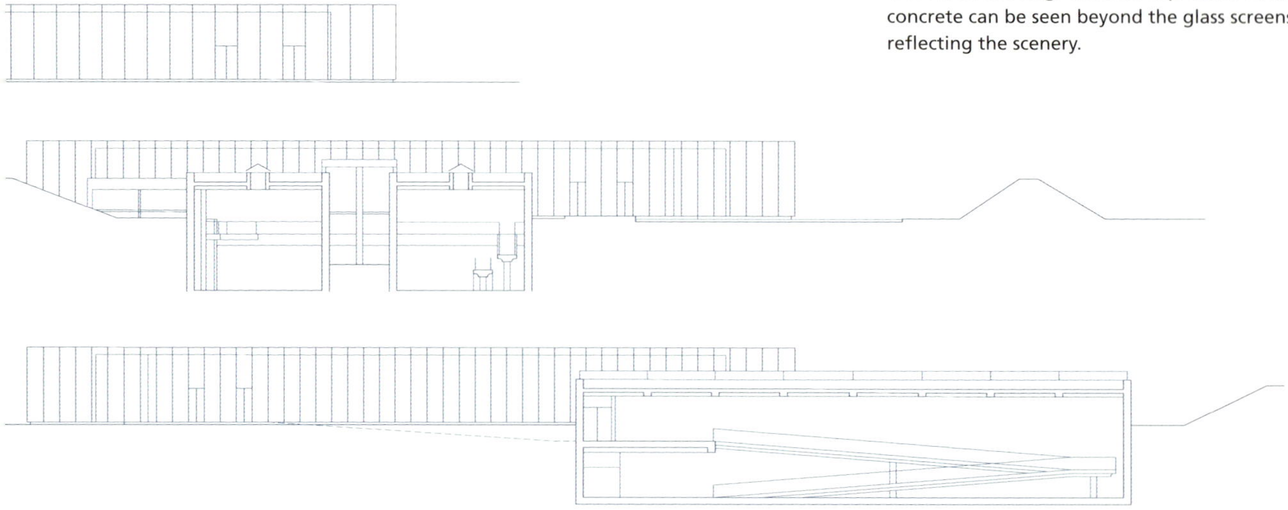

Exterior view of the north side of the permanent exhibition building. The mild expression of the concrete can be seen beyond the glass screens reflecting the scenery.

特別展示棟1階ホワイエより展示室を見る。単純な幾何学的構成に光が切り込み、豊かな空間の表情をつくり出す。

Looking at the exhibition rooms from the foyer on the first floor of the special exhibition building. Light penetrates the simple geometric composition, producing a rich spatial expression.

地下1階吹抜けの展示室。頭上を一直線に走るスカイライトの光。

Exhibition room in the double-height space on the first basement level. Overhead, illumination from a skylight runs in a straight line.

吹き抜けの空間の奥行きいっぱいに斜路が巡る。緩やかな視点の変化が、空間の深さと奥行きを劇的に演出する。

The ramp goes all the way around the deepest part of the double-height space.
The gentle changes of viewpoint dramatically produce spatial profundity and depth.

特別展示室の狭間に設けられた、地上と地下をつなぐ大階段。
大地に埋没する建築へのアプローチ。

A grand staircase connecting underground to above ground has been established in the crevasse of the special exhibition rooms. The approach route toward architecture embedded in the earth.

特別展示棟1階、彫刻テラスを見る。緑の緩やかな傾斜が、周囲の風景との一体感を保ちながら、美術館として必要な静謐な空間をつくり出している。

Looking at the sculpture terrace on the first floor of the special exhibition building. The gentle green slope maintains a sense of unity with the surrounding scenery, while producing the necessary quiet space for a museum.

常設展示棟1階の西側内観。内外の区別なく、緑の大地と一体化する〈縁側〉のような展示空間。球体のオブジェは、イタリア人アーティスト、ミンモ・パラディノの作品。

Interior view of the west side of the first floor permanent exhibition building. Without distinguishing between interior and exterior, the exhibition space is like an "*engawa*" united with the green earth. The spherical object is an artwork by the Italian artist Mimmo Paladino.

西側全景。風景に溶け込むコンクリートとガラスの建築。

Panoramic view of the west side. Architecture of glass and concrete merging into the scenery.

2001年10月、国際コンペにより私が設計者として選ばれた。敷地面積約3.2ヘクタール、総床面積は6万m^2と、民間としては欧州最大規模の美術館の計画であった。

敷地は、パリ南西部の郊外、セーヌ川に浮かぶスガン島の敷地だ。島を中心とした周辺一帯はルノー発祥の地であり、同時に労働運動のメッカである。92年に閉鎖されたが、工場自体はかつての外観を留めたまま、セーヌの中に屹立していた。フランスは歴史を頼りに、都市文化を成熟させてきた都市であるから、当然、開発の議論は保存に集中した。

私自身、計画の最初から〈都市の記憶〉を重要な課題としていた。ただ目に見えるかたちを残していくことだけが必ずしも重要ではない。むしろ、その精神を受け継いで、歴史をひきずりながら新たな価値を築いていくことこそが、本当の意味での再生ではないか。島の外形線と重なる建物の輪郭、全体を覆う林立する柱のグリッドなど、その記憶は抽象化されたイメージとして、必ずどこかに現れるよう考えた。つくりたいのは、過去から現在、未来へと連続する、生きた場所だった。

コンペで私たちが提出したのは、スガン島の水際線そのままに建築化された階段状に隆起する〈広場〉と、同じく島の輪郭をなぞりながら、その上に浮遊するように掲げられたガラスのヴォリュームの、大きくふたつのスペースにより構成される建築である。これは与えられた敷地とプログラムにおいて、私たちが発見したふたつの相反するテーマの葛藤から導かれたものだ。ひとつは、アートと人間との静かな対話に相応しい〈内省の場〉を獲得すること。もうひとつは、人間とアート、人間と自然、人間と社会との豊かな対話を喚起する〈交流の場〉をつくり出すこと。すなわち静と動の両極の性格を併せもった、ひとつの場所の創造である。

さまざまな出会いの可能性に満ちた場所として、人工のNIWAのイメージで計画を進めた。NIWAとは、庭園、広場、中庭、公園、森……といったさまざまな類型の都市空間を束ねる総称である。ヨーロッパの都市の豊かさは、こうした開かれた空白の場が、文化の工房として機能してきたことによる。スガン島には、両側をセーヌの流れに挟まれた、その類稀な立地条件、革命の精神を育んだその歴史的文脈の豊かさにより、かつてない魅力を秘めたNIWAをつくりうる可能性を感じている。

実施設計まで完了し、既存建物も解体され、着工まであと一歩というところで、都市インフラが整備されないという事情で、この計画は中止された。その後、ピノー氏からこれに代わる現代美術のギャラリーとして、ヴェニスのパラッツォ・グラッシの設計依頼を受けることになった。

ピノー現代美術館
François Pinault Foundation for Contemporary Art

2001-05 フランス スガン島——Ile Seguin, France

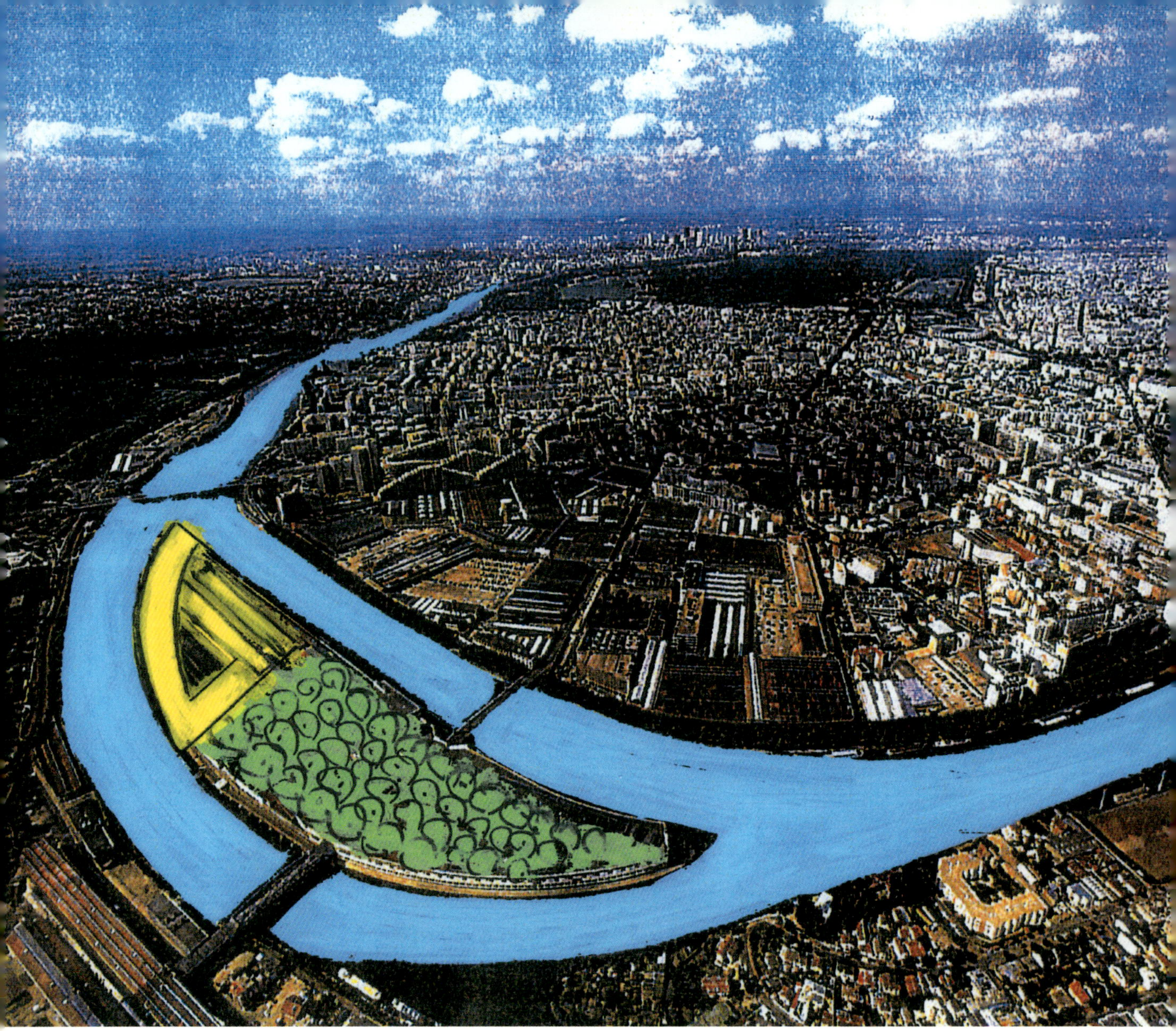

Site plan 1:17,000

パリの航空写真の上に描かれたイメージスケッチ。
Image sketch drawn over an aerial photograph of Paris.

In October 2001, I was selected as the designer through an international competition. The area of the site is approximately 3.2 hectares, and the total floor area is 60000m^2, making this a plan for the largest private art museum in Europe.

The site is located on the Ile Seguin, which floats in the River Seine in the southwest suburbs of Paris. The entire surrounding area centered on the island is the original home of Renault Autumobile, and at the same time it is a Mecca of the labor movement. Although closed in 1992, the factory itself was contained by the outer fortification rising up from the Seine. Because urban culture in France has matured by relying on the history of its cities, naturally the development debate is focused on preservation.

From the outset of the design, I personally made "urban memory" an important task. However, it is not always necessary to just preserve the visible shape. Rather, isn't the real meaning of regeneration to trace history while inheriting its spirit and constructing new values? In the contour of the building overlapping the outline of the island, entirely covered with a grid of closely spaced columns, I was definitely thinking about materializing somewhere an abstract image of these memories. I wanted to make a living place with continuity from the past to the present, and then to the future.

Our submission to the competition was an architecture composed of two large spaces: a stair-shaped extruded "plaza" that was a direct architecturalization of the Ile Seguin waterline, and a glass volume that seemed to float above it while also tracing the contours of the island. This was guided by the conflict of two contradictory themes we had discovered in the given site and program. One was to acquire an "introspective place" appropriate for a quiet dialogue between art and people. The other was to produce a "place of interaction" that would arouse a rich dialogue between people and art, people and nature, people and society. In other words, this was to be the creation of a space that combines the extremes of rest and movement.

As a place full of the possibility of various encounters, the design progressed with the image of an artificial "niwa." Niwa is a general term that includes various typologies of urban space, such as gardens, plazas, courtyards, parks, and forests. The richness of European cities is due the blank spaces opened up this way that function as cultural ateliers. Given the rare site conditions of Ile Seguin, with the Seine flowing either side, amid a rich historical context from which the revolutionary spirit arose, we felt the possibility of creating a niwa that has an unprecedented charm.

Having completed the detailed design, and demolished the existing buildings, we were only one step away from the start of construction, but the plan was cancelled due to a lack of maintenance of the urban infrastructure. Later, Mr Pinault instead offered me a design commission to insert a contemporary art gallery into the Palazzo Grassi in Venice.

François Pinault Foundation for Contemporary Art

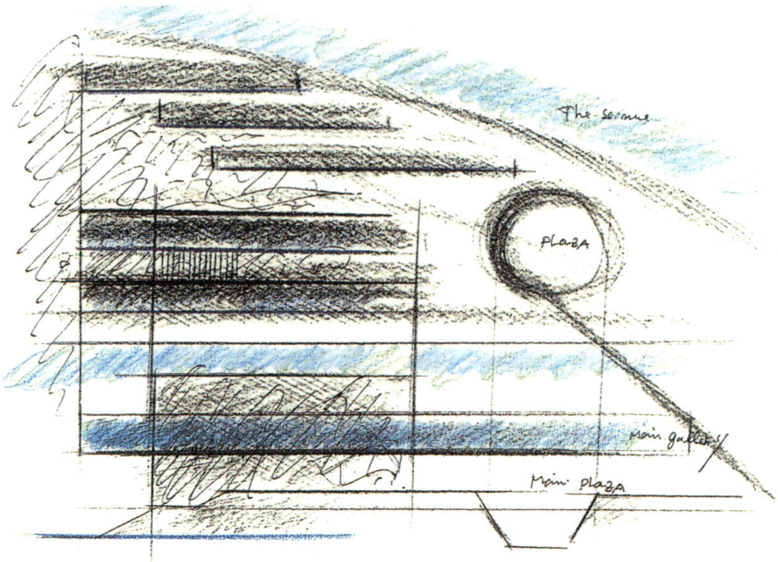

初期イメージスケッチ。美術館のヴォリュームを空中に浮かべ、グラウンドレベルを広場として開放するアイディアが象徴的に描かれている。アントワープ市立博物館設計競技案のアイディアの再登場。

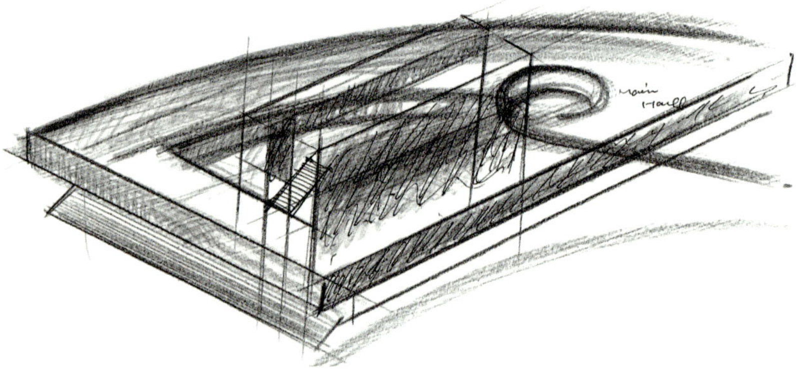

Initial image sketches. A symbolic depiction of the idea of floating the volume of the museum in the air, with the ground level opened as a plaza. A reappearance of the idea from Antwerp's Museum Aan de Stroom.

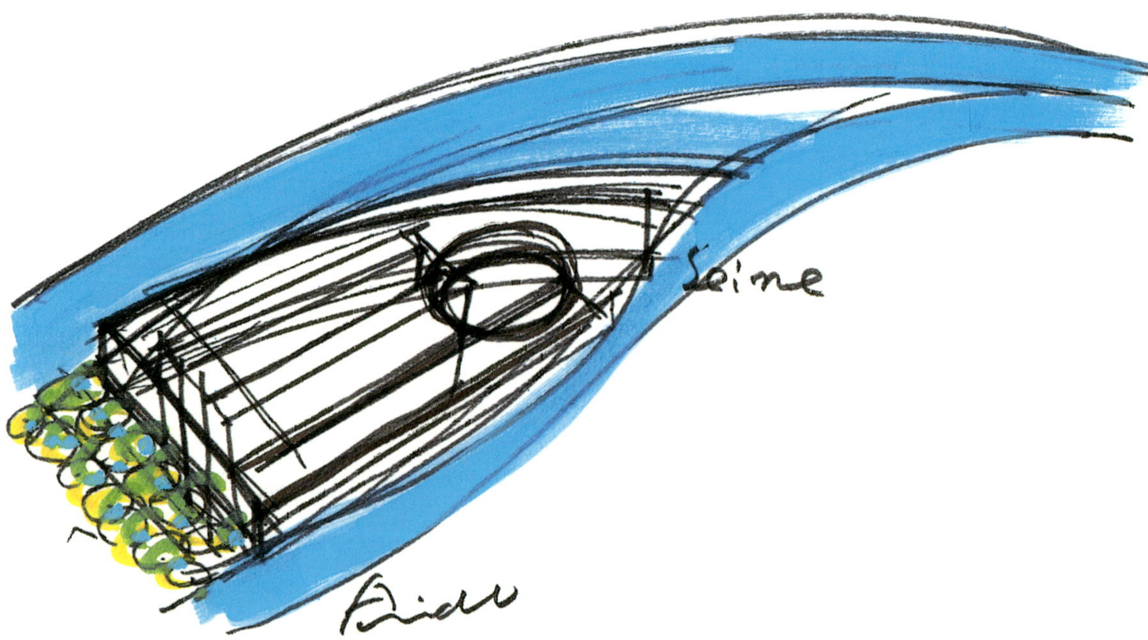

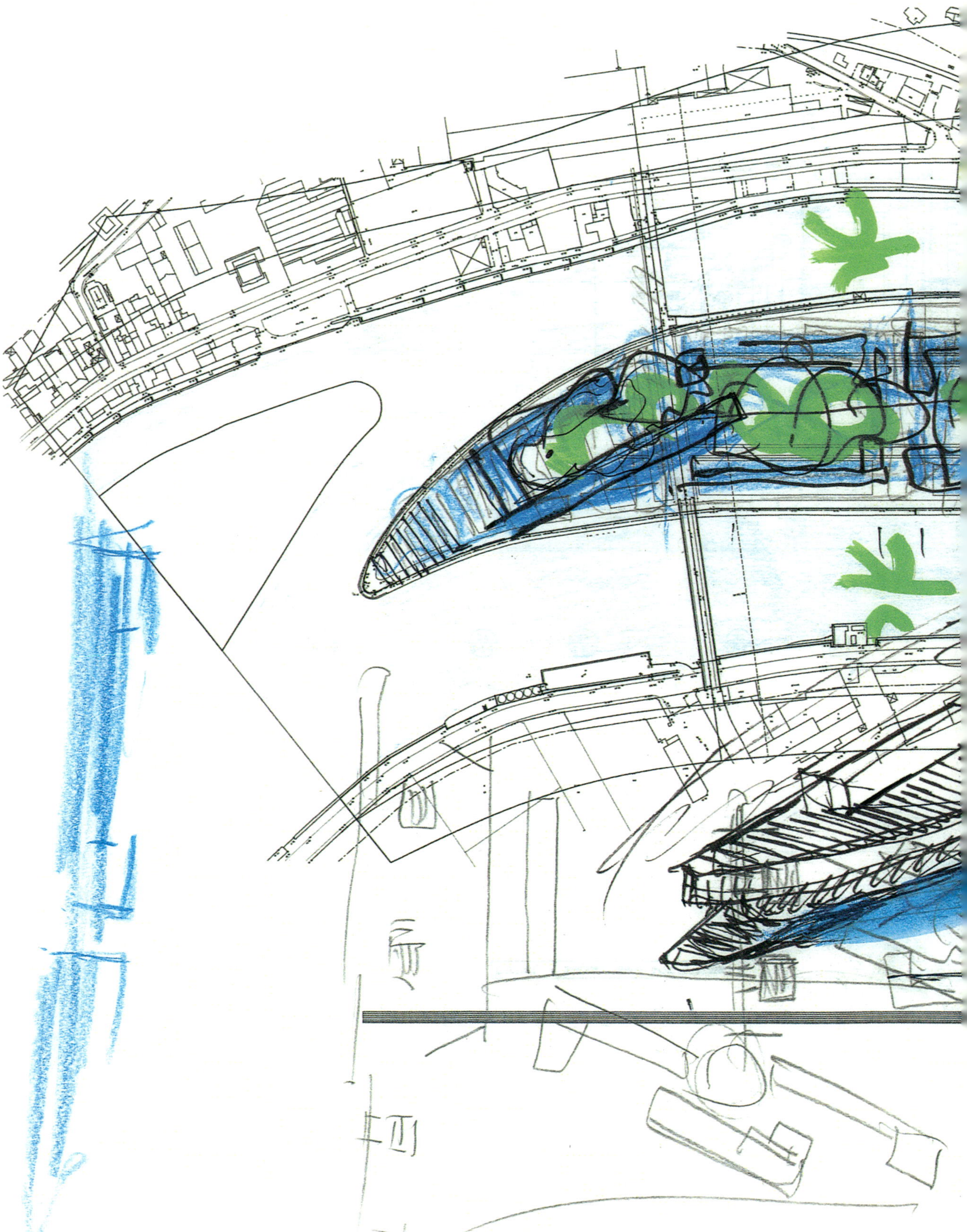

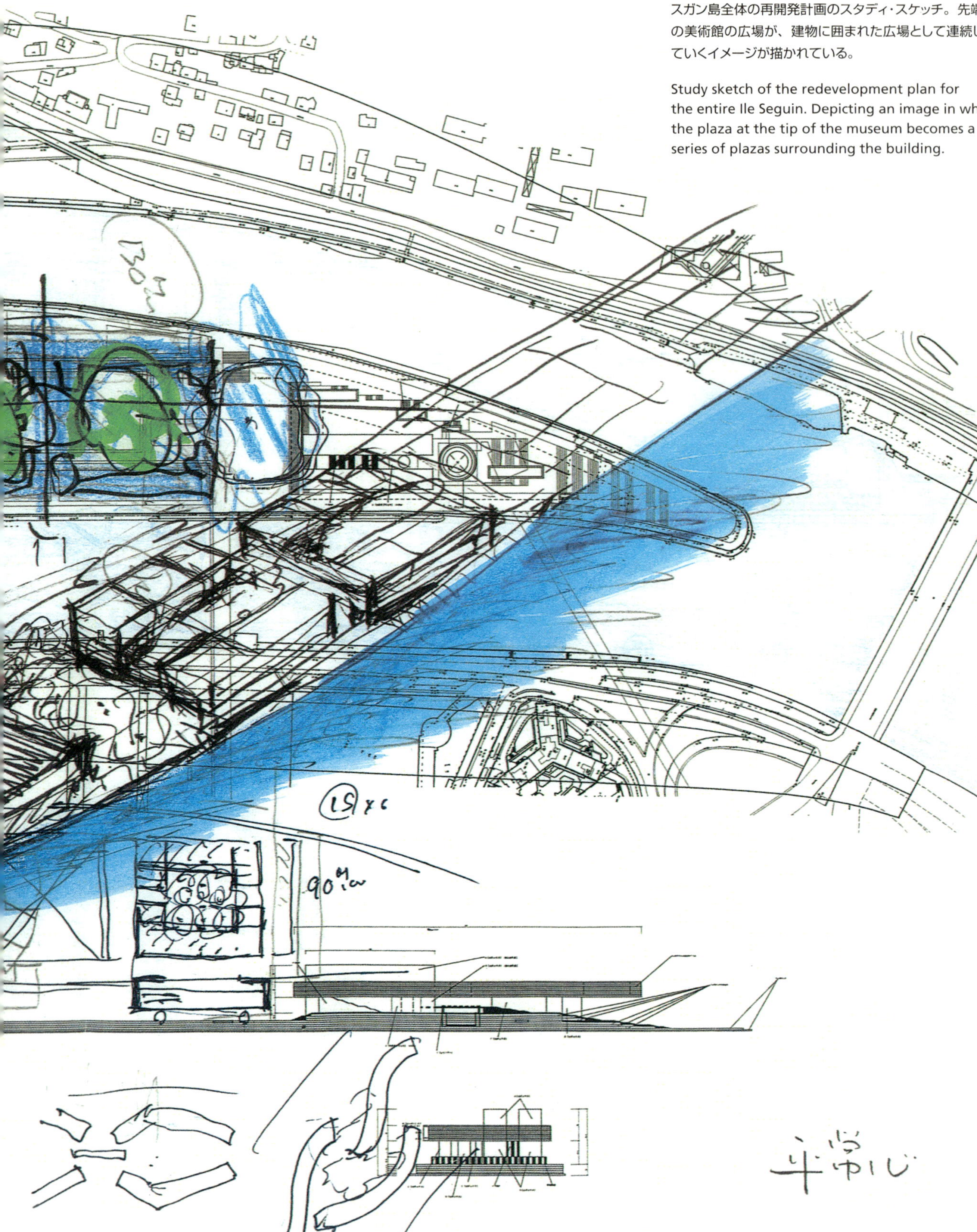

スガン島全体の再開発計画のスタディ・スケッチ。先端の美術館の広場が、建物に囲まれた広場として連続していくイメージが描かれている。

Study sketch of the redevelopment plan for the entire Ile Seguin. Depicting an image in which the plaza at the tip of the museum becomes a series of plazas surrounding the building.

模型写真のコラージュ。背後にはグリッド状に展開する広場のイメージも描かれている。

Model photograph collage. Depicted at the rear is an image of a plaza expanding in a grid formation.

アクソノメトリック・ドローイングと北東側立面およびファサードのディテール。中空に浮かぶ美術館は、曲面ガラスによるファサードで覆われる。

Axonometric, northeast elevation and façade detail. The museum floating in the air is clad with a façade of curved glass.

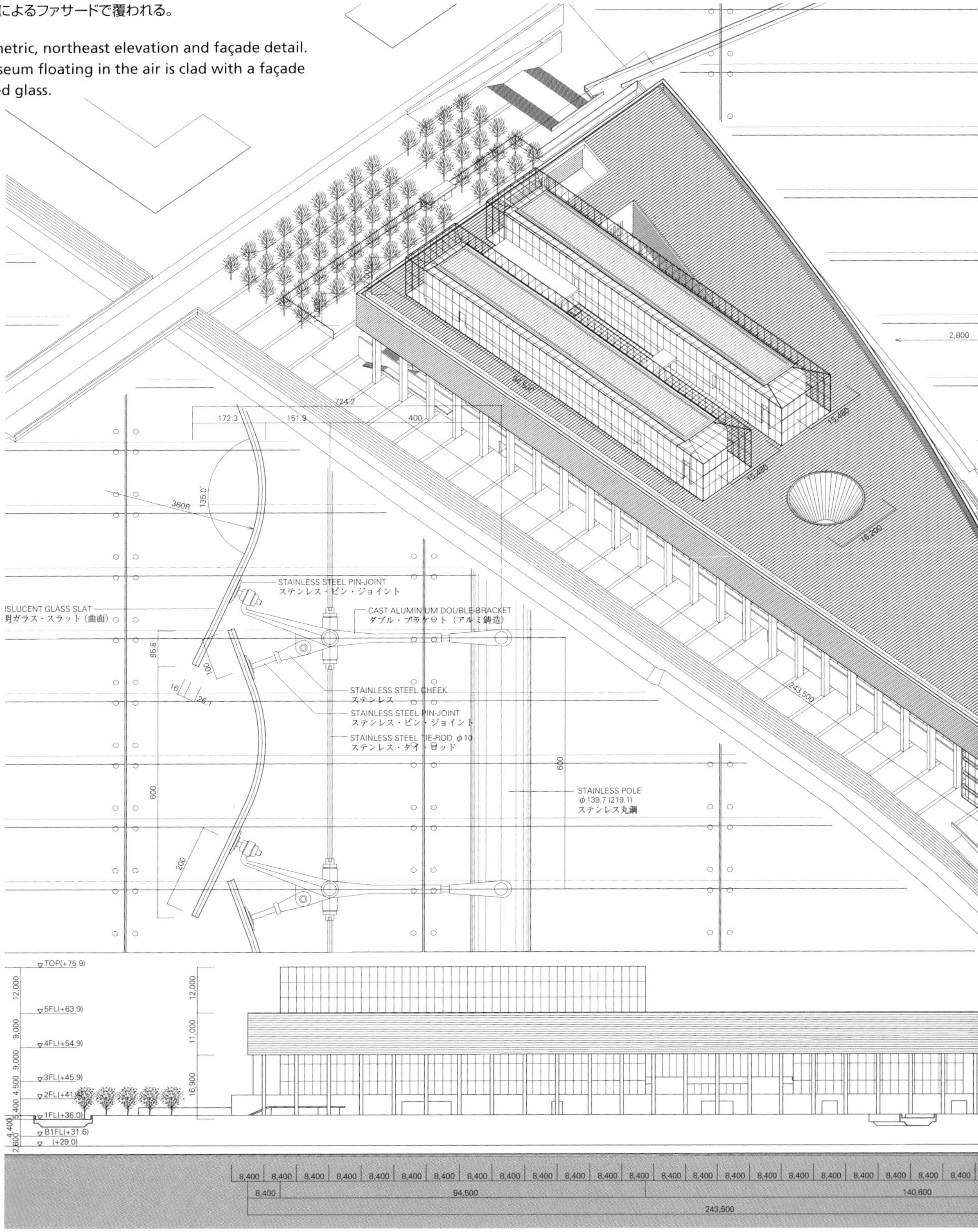

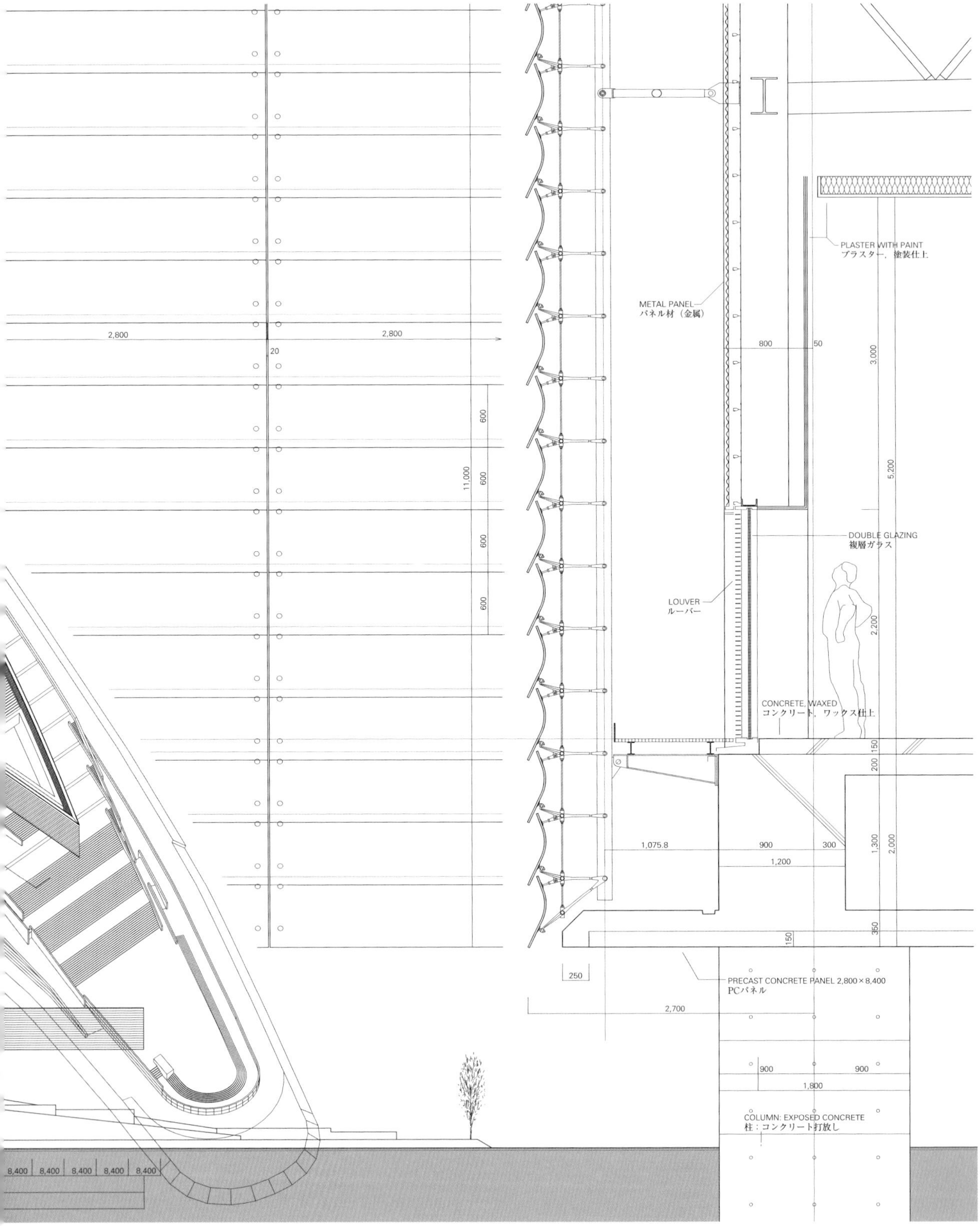

PLASTER WITH PAINT
プラスター，塗装仕上
METAL PANEL
パネル材（金属）
DOUBLE GLAZING
複層ガラス
LOUVER
ルーバー
CONCRETE, WAXED
コンクリート，ワックス仕上
PRECAST CONCRETE PANEL 2,800×8,400
PCパネル
COLUMN: EXPOSED CONCRETE
柱：コンクリート打放し
2,800
2,800
20
800
50
3,000
5,200
2,200
600
600
600
600
11,000
150
200
1,300
2,000
350
150
1,075.8
900
300
1,200
250
2,700
900
900
1,800
8,400
8,400
8,400
8,400
8,400

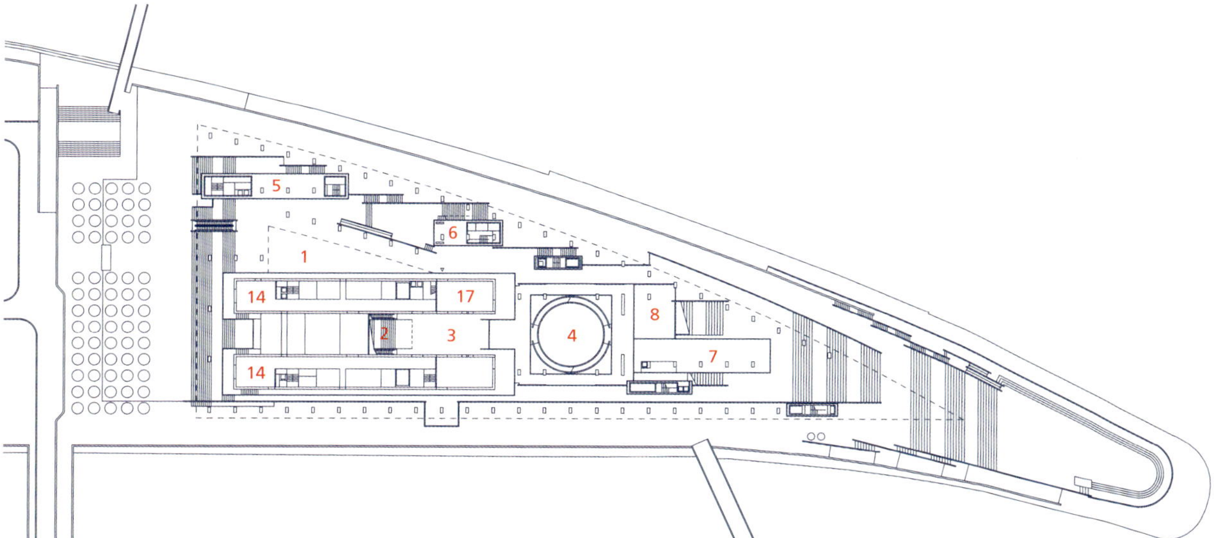

Second floor plan

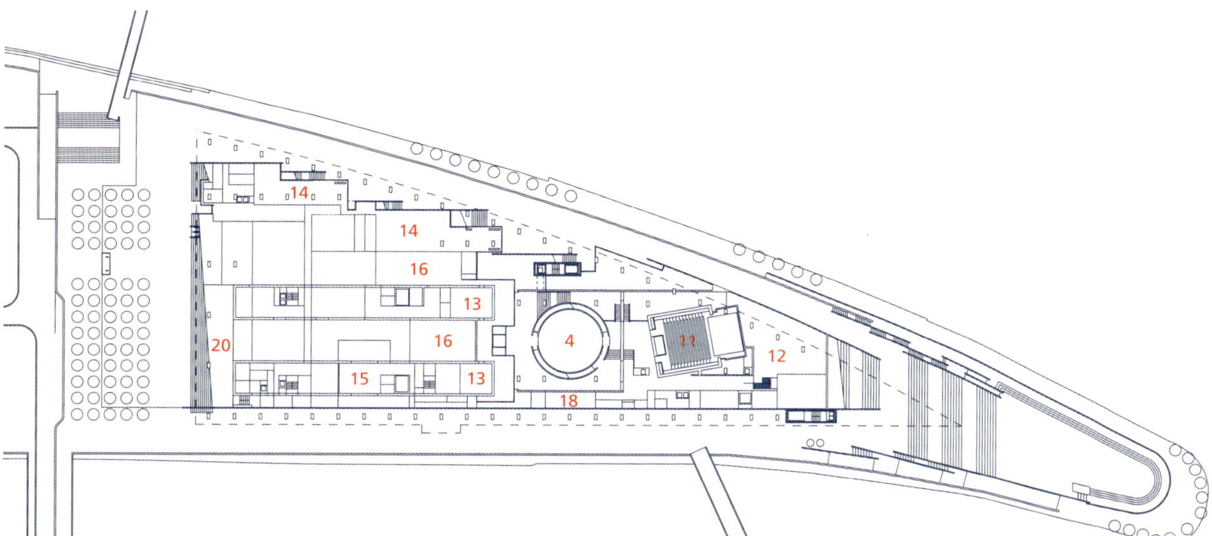

First floor plan 1:2500

ミュージアムへのアプローチに関する施設を中心にオーディトリアムやメディアテックなど、情報発信のための施設や店舗を内包する基壇部分と、静かなアートとの出会いの場を提供する上階の展示室を収めたヴォリューム。人々のアクティビティによる静と動のコントラストが、率直に建築化されている。

Focused on the facilities related to the museum approach route, such as an auditorium and a mediatheque, the base platform includes facilities for information transmission and shops, and the upper level contains exhibition rooms that offer quiet places to encounter art. The contrast between stillness and motion due to human activities is directly converted into architecture.

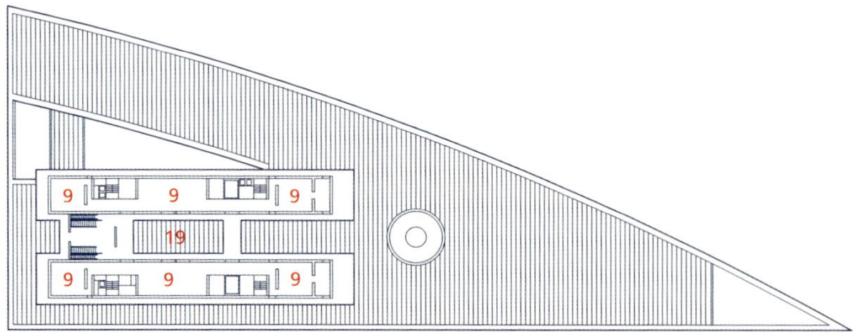

Fifth floor plan

1 entrance court
2 atrium
3 lobby
4 rotunda atrium
5 information center
6 kids workshop
7 café
8 museum shop
9 gallery
10 restaurant

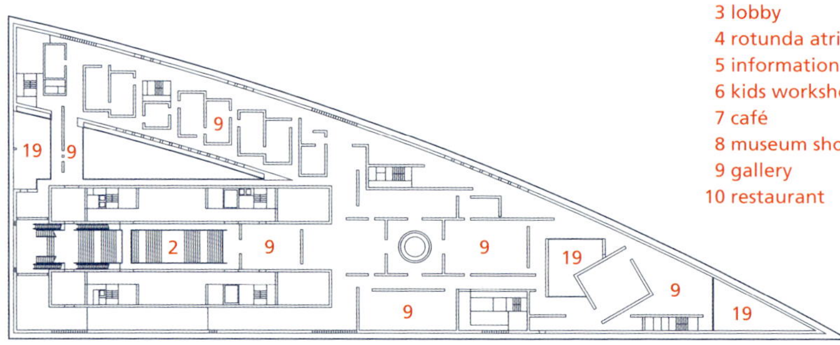

Fourth floor plan

11 auditorium
12 digital gallery
13 media library
14 office
15 conservation workshop
16 storage
17 main entrance
18 auditorium entrance
19 court
20 parking

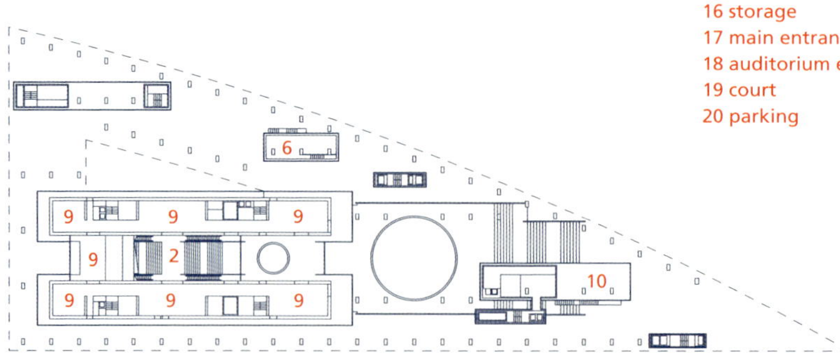

Third floor plan

模型写真。セーヌ川と建物、建物と建物の〈隙間〉のスペースがパリの
この場所でしか得られない劇的な空間のシークエンスを演出する。

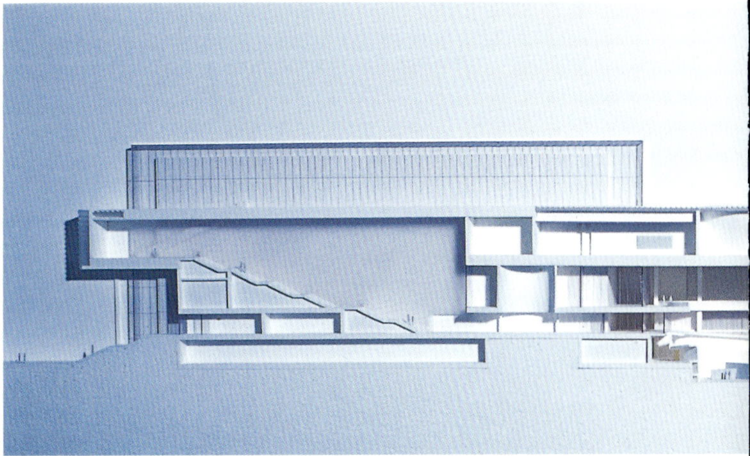

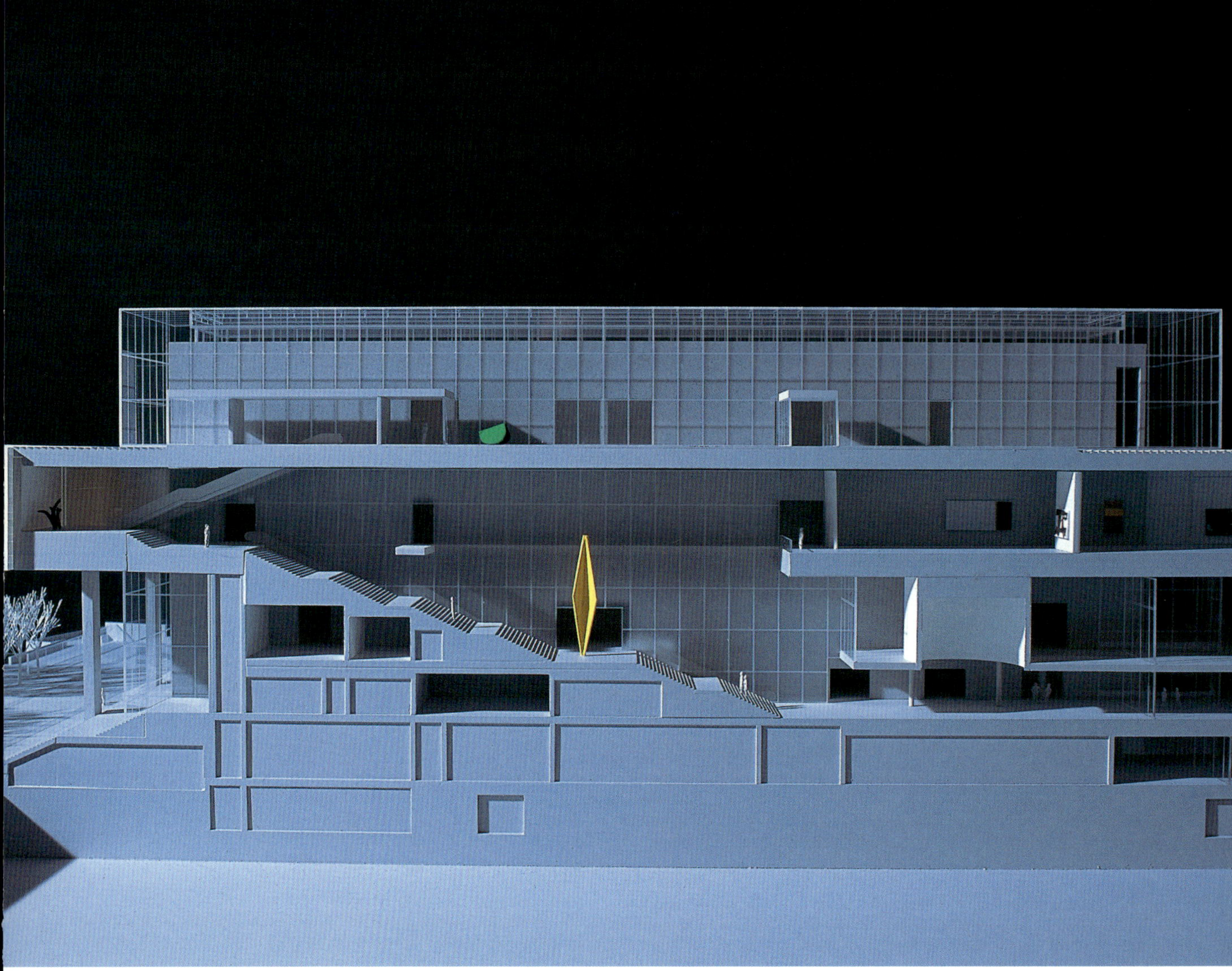

Model photograph. The "gap" spaces between the buildings and the Seine, and between the buildings, produce a dramatic spatial sequence that can only be obtained in this place in Paris.

敷地模型写真。セーヌ川に浮かぶ文化の砦。

Photograph of the site model. A fortress of culture floating in the Seine.

われわれがコンペで設計者に選ばれ実施設計まで終えていた、パリのスガン島に建つピノー現代美術館建設を、インフラ整備などの調整がつかないことなどから断念したという連絡を、クライアントのフランソワ・ピノー氏から受けた。その2週間後、再びピノー氏から思いもよらぬ知らせが届いた。敷地をイタリア、ヴェニスに移しての新たな美術館の計画依頼である。

現代美術館という機能には変わりはなかったが、建築条件はまったく違った。再開発による計画であったピノー現代美術館に対し、今回のプロジェクトはパラッツォ・グラッシという旧い邸館建築の改修利用を前提とした計画だった。

パラッツォ・グラッシは、グランド・キャナル沿いの、サン・マルコ広場にほど近い場所に位置する、ジョルジオ・マッサーリの設計により18世紀後半につくられた新古典主義の建物であり、1983年からは展覧会場として使われていた。

イタリアにおいては歴史的建造物の維持保全については厳しい規制がある。都市景観に関わる外観はもちろんのこと、内部の改修についても、行政による事細かな指導を受ける。このような状況にあって、現代美術のためのホワイトキューブ的空間を既存建物内部につくり出そうという今回の計画は、ある意味、矛盾した計画といえた。しかし、その矛盾から新旧が互いに刺激し合うような活力ある空間が生まれる可能性がある。これまで私が試みてきた〈新旧の対話する空間〉というテーマを、パラッツォ・グラッシ再生計画では、より繊細なディテールの部分で追求することとなった。

まず、建物を竣工当初の姿に復元した。その上で、白い壁に囲われた展示空間を入れ子状に配置する計画をスタディした。その際、展示空間のホワイトキューブとしての完結性にこだわるのでなく、その外側にある既存建物の空間のエッセンスを積極的に活かすようなディテールのスタディに意識を集中した。

白い壁の隙間に垣間見える旧い建物の壁や天井の装飾、フィルターを通して感じる大運河の水面のきらめき、アトリウムの柔らかな光をそのまま活かした中央のギャラリースペース……。新旧の対話するこの空間のシークエンスに、アートが不意に登場するような、驚きと発見に満ちた場所づくりを意図した。

パラッツォ・グラッシ再生計画
Palazzo Grassi Renovation

2005-06 イタリア ヴェニス——Venice, Italy

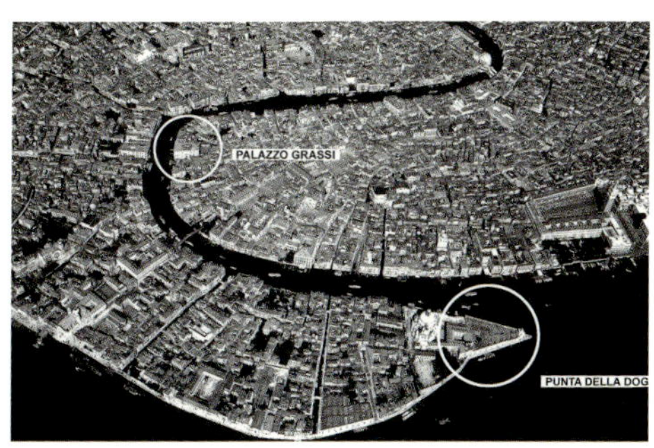

Having been selected by an international competition as the designer of the Foundation François Pinault pour l' Art Contemporain, to be built on the Seguin Island in Paris, we had reached the level of construction documents when we received word from Mr Pinault that the project had been abandoned due to problems with adjusting to infrastructural developments for the project site on the Island. Two weeks later, we again received an unexpected message from Mr Pinault. Shifting the site to Venice, Italy, he commissioned us to design a new modern art museum. Although there was no change in the function as a modern art museum, the architectural conditions were entirely different. As opposed to the redevelopment plan of the Seguin Island for the Foundation François Pinault pour l'Art Contemporain, this project was premised on the renovation and reuse of an old mansion called the Palazzo Grassi. Located along the Grand Canal close to Piazza San Marco, the Palazzo Grassi is a neoclassical building that was designed by Giorgio Massari in the second half of the 18th century, and since 1983 it has been used as an exhibition space.

In Italy, there are stringent regulations about the preservation of historical structures. Naturally, this applies to façades as they affect the urban scenery, but we also received detailed guidance from the public administration about the interior renovations. Given such a situation, our plan to make a white-cube like space for a modern art museum within an existing historical building could be called, in a sense, contradictory. However, it is possible that this contradiction will produce a space with a vitality that mutually enhances old and new. I have previously attempted the theme of "spaces with a dialogue between old and new," but in the renovation scheme for the Palazzo Grassi I focused on more delicate details.

First of all, the building was completely restored to its initial appearance. Having done that, we studied plan layouts with nested exhibition spaces enclosed by white walls. At that point, we were not concerned with creating a self-contained white-cube exhibition space, but focused more on investigating details that would take advantage of the spatial essence of the existing building surrounding them.

The ornamentation on the walls and ceilings of the old building may be glimpsed through gaps in the white walls, the glittering of the water in the Grand Canal may be sensed through a filter, and the central gallery space exploits the unaltered soft light of the atrium. With the intention of making places filled with surprise and discovery, art seems to abruptly appear in this spatial sequence of a dialogue between old and new.

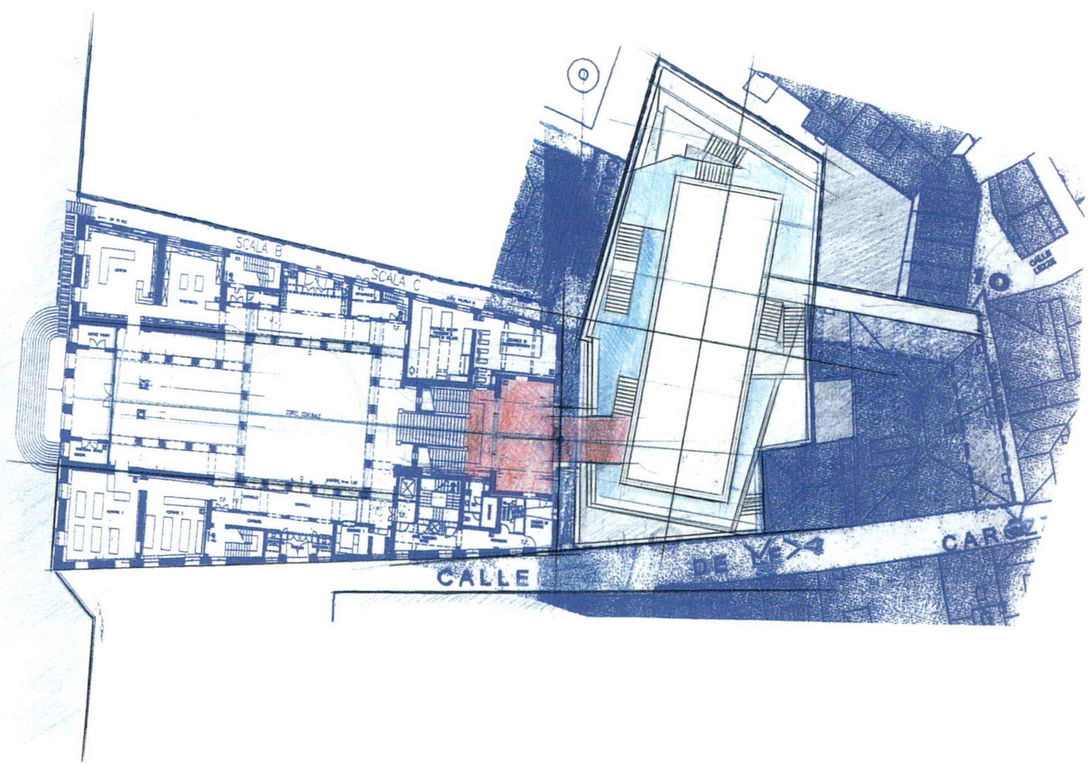

グランド・キャナル対岸からの夜景。ファサードを覆う光のオブジェはオラファー・エリアソンの「Your Wave is」。

Night view from the opposite bank of the Grand Canal. The light artwork covering the façade is Ólafur Elíasson's "Your Wave Is."

1階エントランスに続くアトリウム。建造当初は中庭であった。床面の碁盤目状のパターンは、カール・アンドレの「37th Piece of Work」。

Atrium continuous with the first floor entrance. This was a courtyard of the palazzo when it was originally built. The checkerboard pattern on the floor surface is an artwork by Carl Andre entitled "37th Piece of Work."

2階レベルから見たアトリウム。既存のトップライトの下に新たに設けられた半透明のガラスクロス膜が、吹き抜けの空間に柔らかな光を導く。

Atrium as seen from the second floor level. The translucent glass sheet set under the existing skylight brings soft light into the double-height space.

ウルス・フィッシャーの「Vintage Violence」が天から降り注ぐように展示されたメイン階段。正面の作品はピオトル・ウクランスキの「Untitled (Mousieur François Pinault)」。

Main staircase exhibiting Urs Fischer's artwork "Vintage Violence" as if pouring down from heaven. The artwork in front is Piotr Uklanski's "Untitled (Monsieur François Pinault)."

ジェフ・クーンズの作品が集められた2階展示室。既存の天井装飾を残したまま、白色のドライウォールによる展示スペースが入れ子状に計画されている。

Second-floor exhibition room, in which artworks by Jeff Koons have been collected. The exhibition space is designed as a nested box made of white drywall, preserving the existing ceiling ornamentation unchanged.

天井装飾と新旧の鮮やかな対比をなす、ライティングビームのディテール。

Detail of the lighting beam and the ceiling ornamentation, a vivid contrast of old and new.

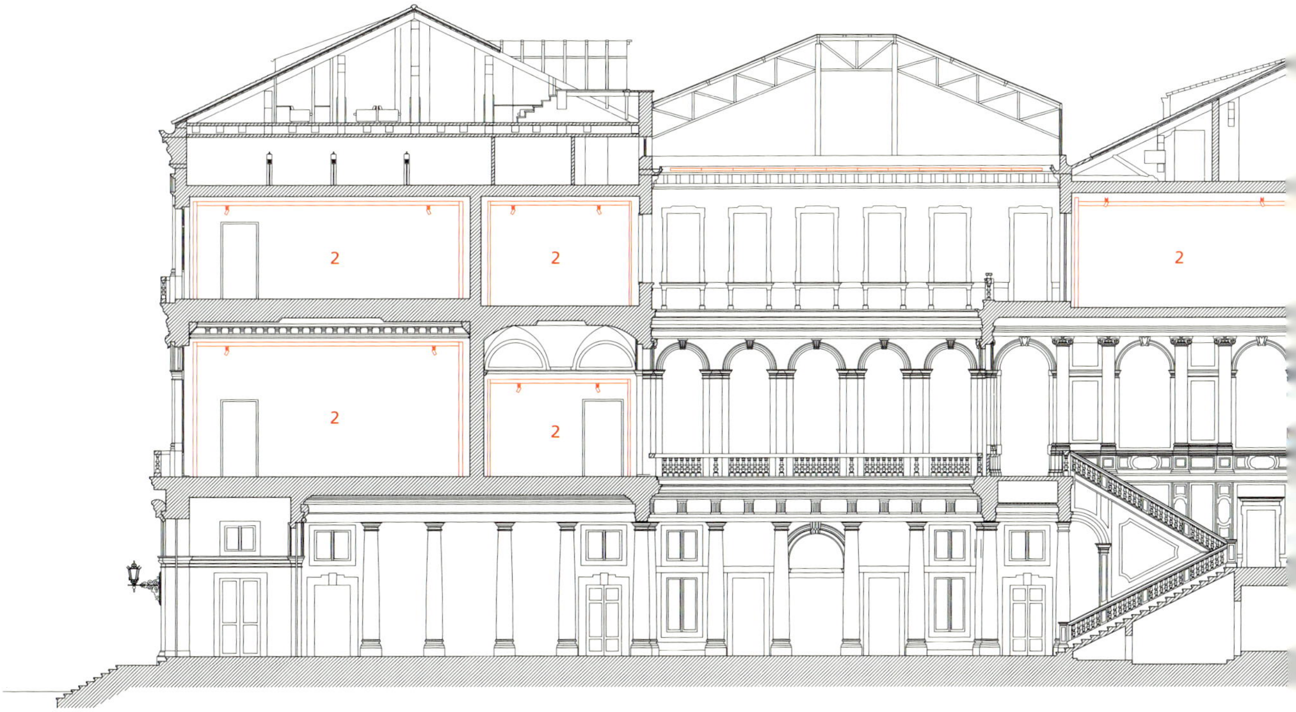

Section

1 atrium
2 gallery
3 void
4 shop
5 cloak

Section 1:300

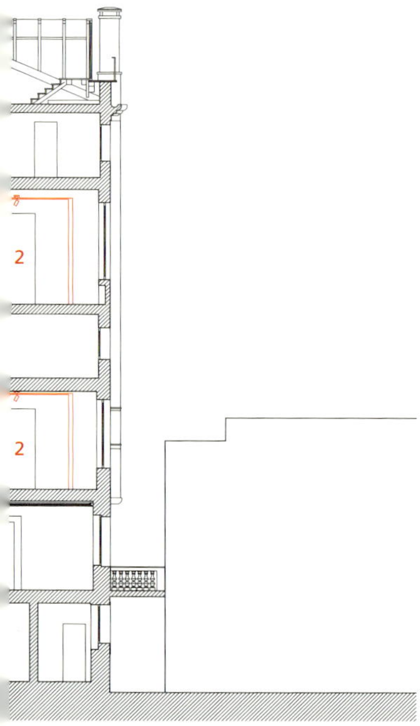

Third floor plan

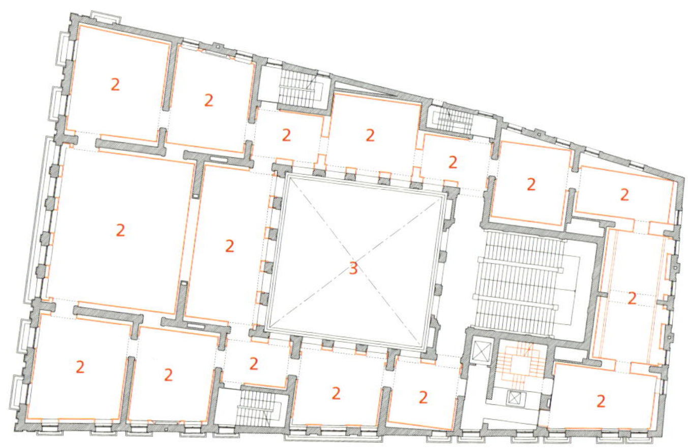

Second floor plan

左：断面図。赤線の部分が新たに付け加えられたドライウォール。
右：平面図。既存の壁面に沿ってドライウォールが設けられ、その隙間が電気配線などのバックスペースにあてられている。中央のアトリウムには自然光が降り注ぐ。

Left: Sections. The red lines indicate the newly added drywall parts.
Right: Plans. The drywall has been installed following the existing wall surfaces and the gaps provide space for electrical wiring, etc. Natural light pours down into the central atrium.

First floor plan　1:600

テアトリーノの敷地は、もともとパラッツォ・グラッシの庭園として使われてきた場所だ。その庭に、1951年のパラッツォ・グラッシ改修の際、設けられた屋外の仮設劇場が、テアトリーノの始まりである。さしたる文化的価値を感じさせる建物ではないが、やはり完全な撤去・新築はヴェニスでは許されない。再生案として現在提案しているのは、旧い外壁を改修し、そのままの姿で残しながら、内部にオーディトリアムを内包するコンクリートボックスを挿入するアイディアだ。

屋根は、この地方で多く用いられる白大理石の段状テラスとして計画している。場所に刻まれた記憶の、現代建築による再構築を主題としている。

テアトリーノ
Teatrino

2005- イタリア ヴェニス——Venice, Italy

The Teatrino site is in a place originally used as the garden of Palazzo Grassi. When Palazzo Grassi was renovated in 1951, the Teatrino was initiated with the establishment of a temporary outdoor theater. This is not a building that has a feeling of particular cultural value, but even so, complete removal and reconstruction are not permitted in Venice.

As a regeneration proposal, the idea is to restore the old exterior walls, leaving their appearance unchanged, and insert within them a concrete box containing an auditorium.

The roof has been designed as a stepped terrace made of a type of white marble often used in this region. The theme is the reconstruction of the memories inscribed in this place by means of contemporary architecture.

パラッツォ・グラッシ側から見るテアトリーノの俯瞰全景。ヴェネチアの街並みと調和しつつ、拮抗する現代建築のイメージ。

Commanding a panoramic view of the Teatrino as seen from the Palazzo Grassi. An image of contemporary architecture in harmony, as well as rivalry, with the townscape of Venice.

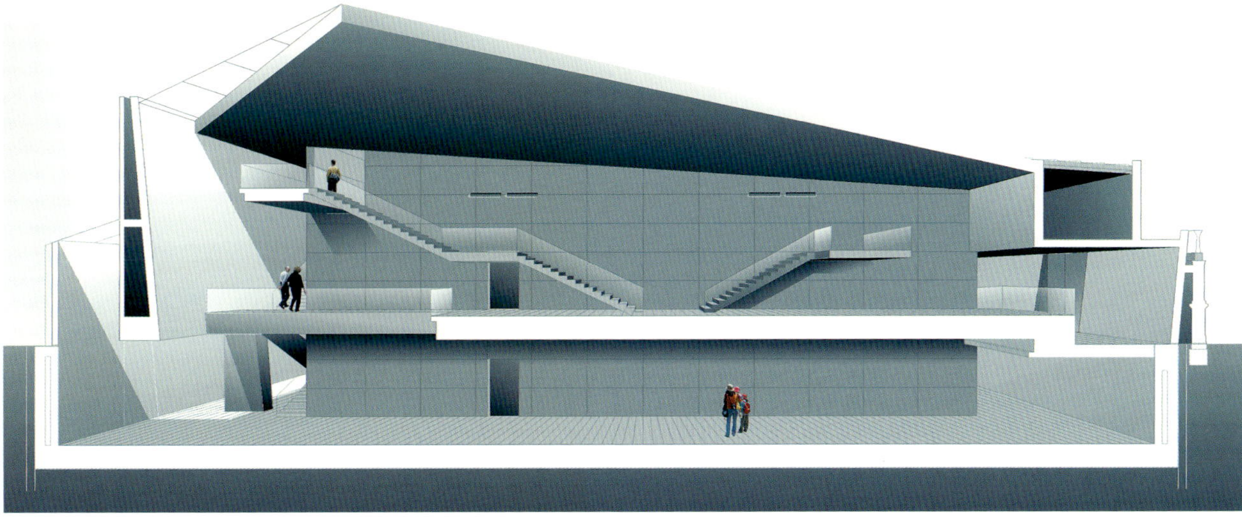

既存外壁に沿って不定形の空間をかたどる控え壁と、その内部に配された矩形平面の空間による入れ子状の構成。矩形平面のニュートラルなボックス空間と、内側に5度傾いた控え壁の隙間のスペースに、立体迷路のように階段が巡り、変化に富んだ空間のシークエンスをつくり出す。

A nested composition, which comprises a rectangular space arranged within buttressed walls that follow the amorphous space of the existing exterior walls. A spatial sequence rich in variety is produced by this rectangular-plan neutral box space, encircled by a three-dimensional labyrinth of stairs in the interstitial spaces contained by the buttressed walls, which incline at five degrees.

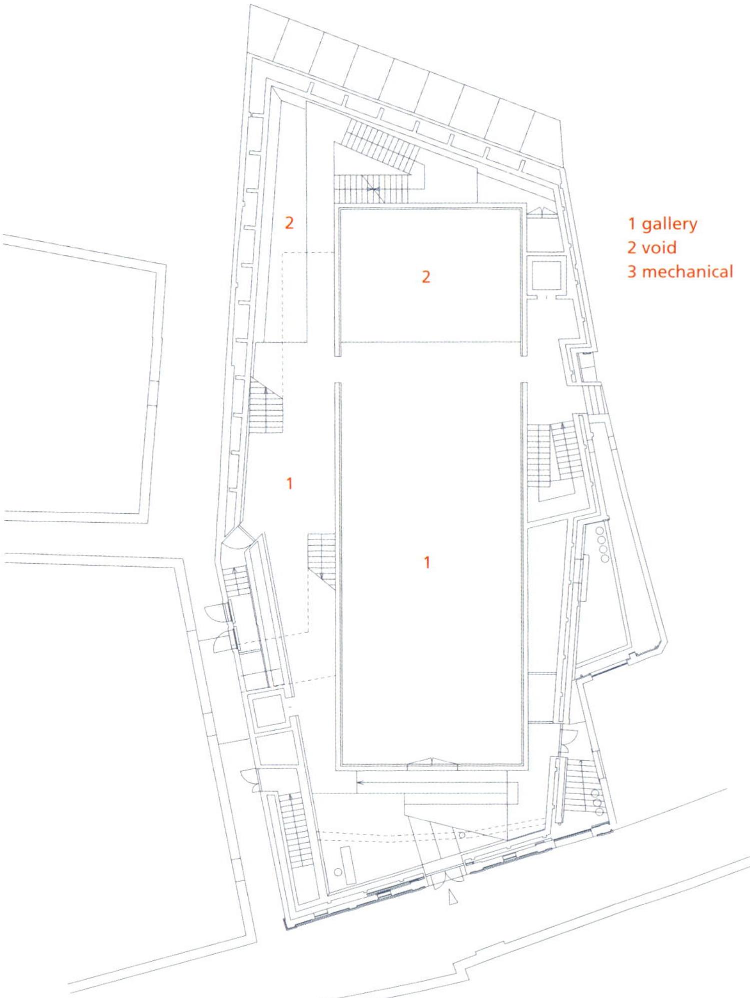

Ground floor plan 1:400

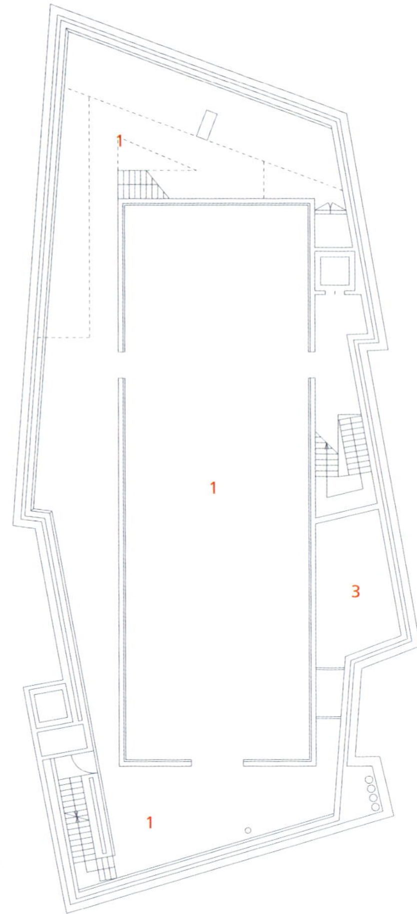

Basement floor plan

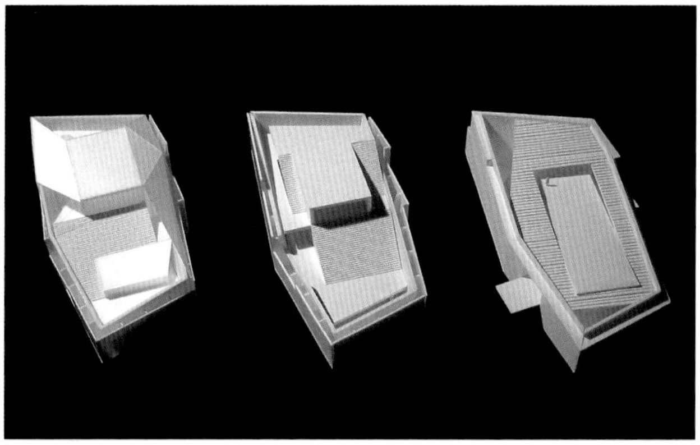

スタディは、ヴェニスの街を見晴らす屋上テラスのイメージからスタートした。歴史を刻む旧い外壁の向こうに潜む、垂直方向に展開する立体的空間。

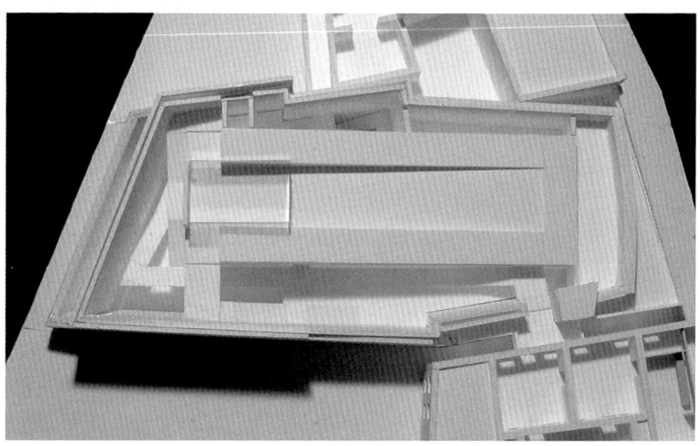

Studies began with the image of a roof terrace that commands a view of the townscape of Venice. The old exterior walls, inscribed with the passing of time, expand vertically into a three-dimensional space.

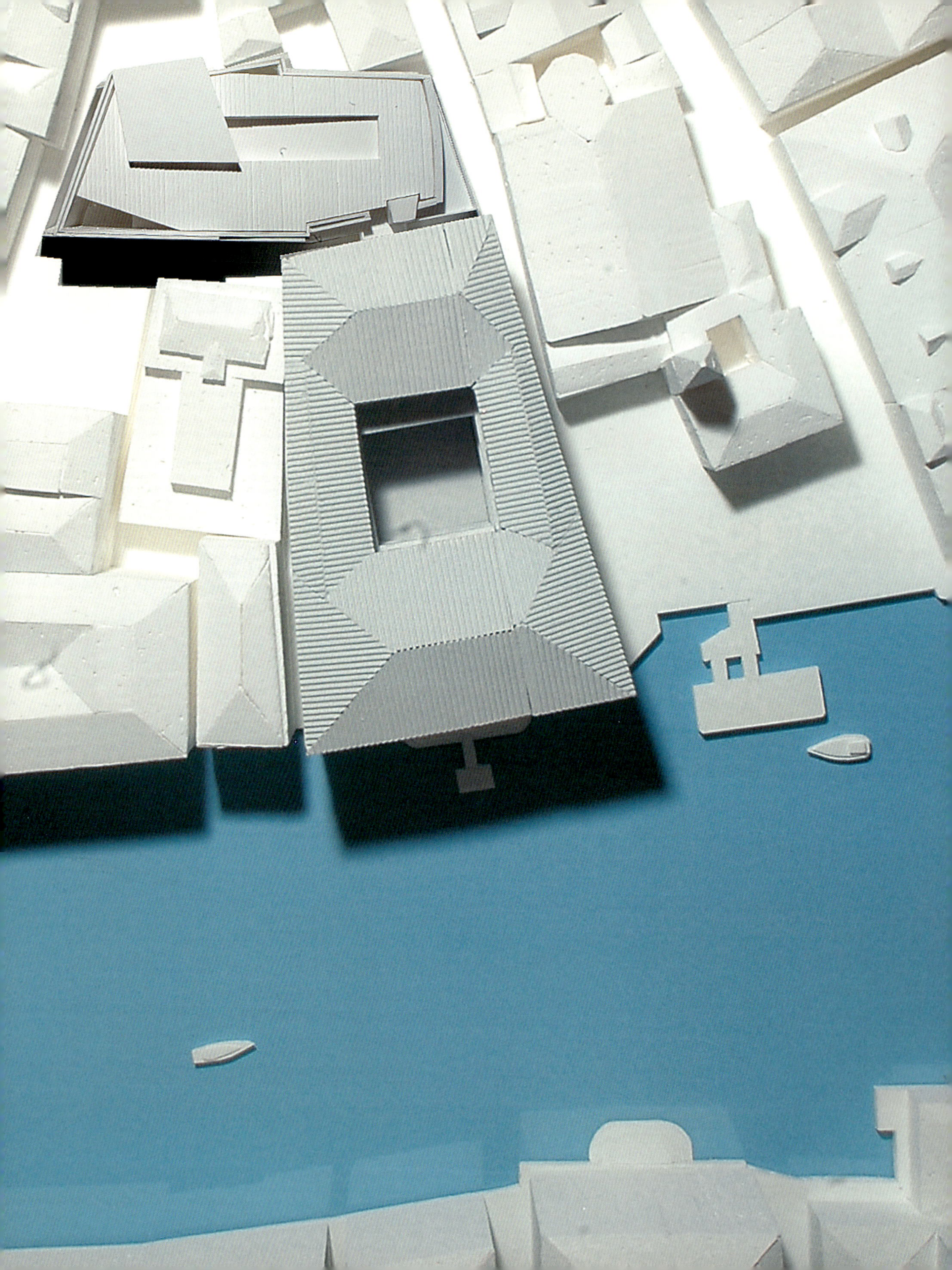

サンマルコ広場の対岸にある15世紀に建てられた国が所有する歴史的建造物「海の税関(Dogana di Mare)」を現代美術館に改造するプロジェクトである。ヴェニス市が行ったコンペで、最終的にザハ・ハディド+グッゲンハイム財団、安藤忠雄+ピノー財団(Palazzo Grassi)の2チームの戦いとなり、われわれのチームが選ばれた。

プンタ・デラ・ドガーナはドルソドーロ島の先端であるこの敷地の名前であり、「海の税関」は15世紀初頭より海運の増加に伴い計画され、幾度かの建て替えを経て、17世紀後半の改修で現在のかたちとなった。今はその一部を事務所や倉庫として利用されるのみであるが、ヴェニス市民にとっては愛着があり象徴的な場所といえる。

建物は、岬の形状に沿って縁取られた三角形平面を、外壁と同じレンガ造の壁で短冊状に分割した構成となっている。

われわれに求められたのは、老朽化したこの建物を、構造的に補強し、増水対策を施した上で、現代美術を展示する美術館として甦らせることであった。

パラッツォ・グラッシの時と同様、外部、内部ともに、歴史的建造物の保存に関する法律で、原型への修復以外の変更は厳しく制限されており、その制約の中で、本来建物のもっていた潜在力を引き出しながら、いかにして、現代性のある空間を生み出すかという課題と再び向き合うことになった。度重なる改造の中で覆われ、隠されていた壁のレンガや屋根の木造トラスを露出させることで、この建物の個性を浮かび上がらせながら、許された数少ない新たな建築的要素が空間の魅力をさらに引き立たせるようにしたいと考えている。

もうひとつのアートの拠点パラッツォ・グラッシと、運河を使って往復する定期船で結ぶことも計画されている。現代アートと都市に堆積された歴史的な魅力が互いに刺激しあうことによって、人々は、ここにしかない特別な経験を味わうことだろう。海運における物流の拠点であったこの場所が、現代美術の新たな発信拠点として生まれ変わるという期待をこめながら、計画を進めている。

プンタ・デラ・ドガーナ再生計画
Punta della Dogana Renovation

2007-09 イタリア ヴェニス——Venice, Italy

今回の計画では、度重なる改造の中で加えられた仕切り壁などをすべて撤去し、建物を15世紀建設当初のかたちに戻すことを原則とした。

In this plan, the main principle was to remove all the partition walls etc. that had accumulated during the frequent renovations, and to return the building to its original shape as built in the 15th century.

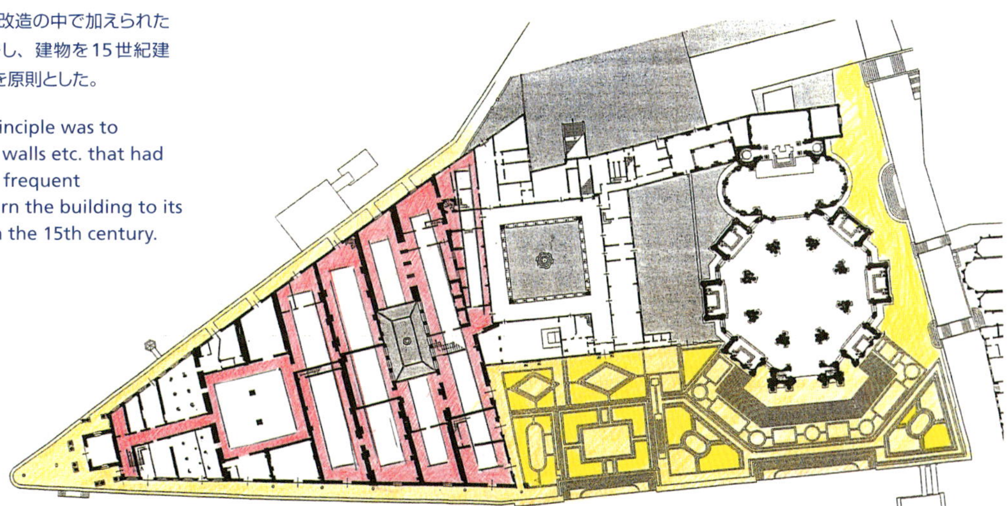

This is a project to remodel into a modern art museum the government-owned historical landmark "Customhouse in the sea" (Dogana di Mare), built in the 15th century on the shore opposite Piazza San Marco. The competition held in Venice finally became a battle between the two teams of Zaha Hadid + Guggenheim Foundation and Tadao Ando + Pinault Foundation (Palazzo Grassi), following which our team was chosen.

Punta della Dogana is the name of this site at the tip of the Dorsoduro district, and Dogana di Mare was designed to accommodate the increase in marine traffic at the beginning of the 15th century. Having been rebuilt many times, its present form dates from a renovation in the latter half of the 17th century. Although now partly used as an office and warehouse, it is a symbolic place beloved by the citizens of Venice.

The composition of the building is a triangular plan with a perimeter that follows the shape of the coastline, and the exterior walls are made of the same red brick with a rectangular articulation.

We were requested to structurally reinforce this dilapidated building, and having incorporated defenses against rising water levels, to renovate it as a museum for displaying contemporary art.

Just as with Palazzo Grassi, for the exterior as well as the interior, alterations other than returning them to their original appearance are severely restricted under the laws concerning the preservation of historical structures. Within these constraints, we were again faced with the theme of how to produce a space possessing modernity while drawing out the latent power of the original building.

By exposing the bricks of hidden walls and the wooden roof trusses that had been concealed during the frequent renovations, I want to further emphasize the charm of the spaces by adding just a few new architectural elements, while manifesting the individuality of the building.

Together with the other art hub of Palazzo Grassi, it is designed to be connected with the boat tours that use the canal. Due to mutual stimulus between the modern art and the historical charms that have accumulated in this city, people will be able savor a special experience available only here. We have been pursuing this project with the expectation that this place, which was once a distribution hub for marine traffic, will be reborn as a new hub for modern art.

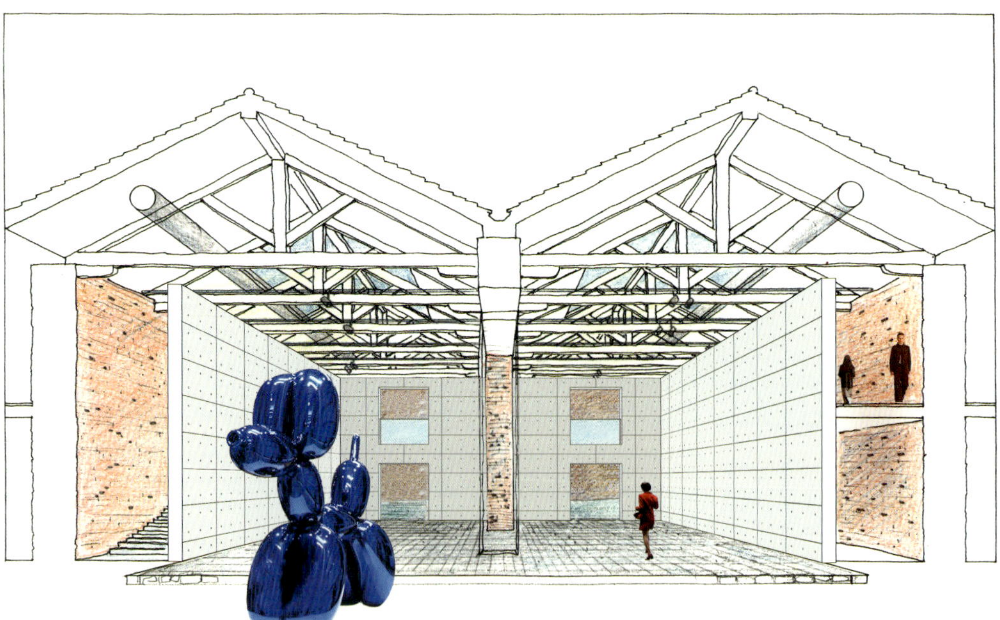

ただし、建物中央にある、後の改造による2列分を1室としたスペースについては、例外的にそのままのかたちに留め、さらにその内にコンクリートボックスを挿入して新たな空間をつくり出している。

However, the exception is the space at the center of the building, which has been left unchanged in the form of one room comprising two spans from a later renovation. Furthermore a concrete box has been inserted within it, to produce a new space.

外観は基本的には現状ファサードの復元となるが、開口部はスチールとガラスによる今回改修のオリジナルデザインに更新される。サルーテ広場に面したエントランス脇には、一対のコンクリート柱のモニュメントが建てられる。

The exterior is basically a restoration of the current façade, although as part of these repairs the openings have been replaced with an original design of steel and glass. A monumental pair of concrete columns will be built at the entrance facing onto Campo della Salute.

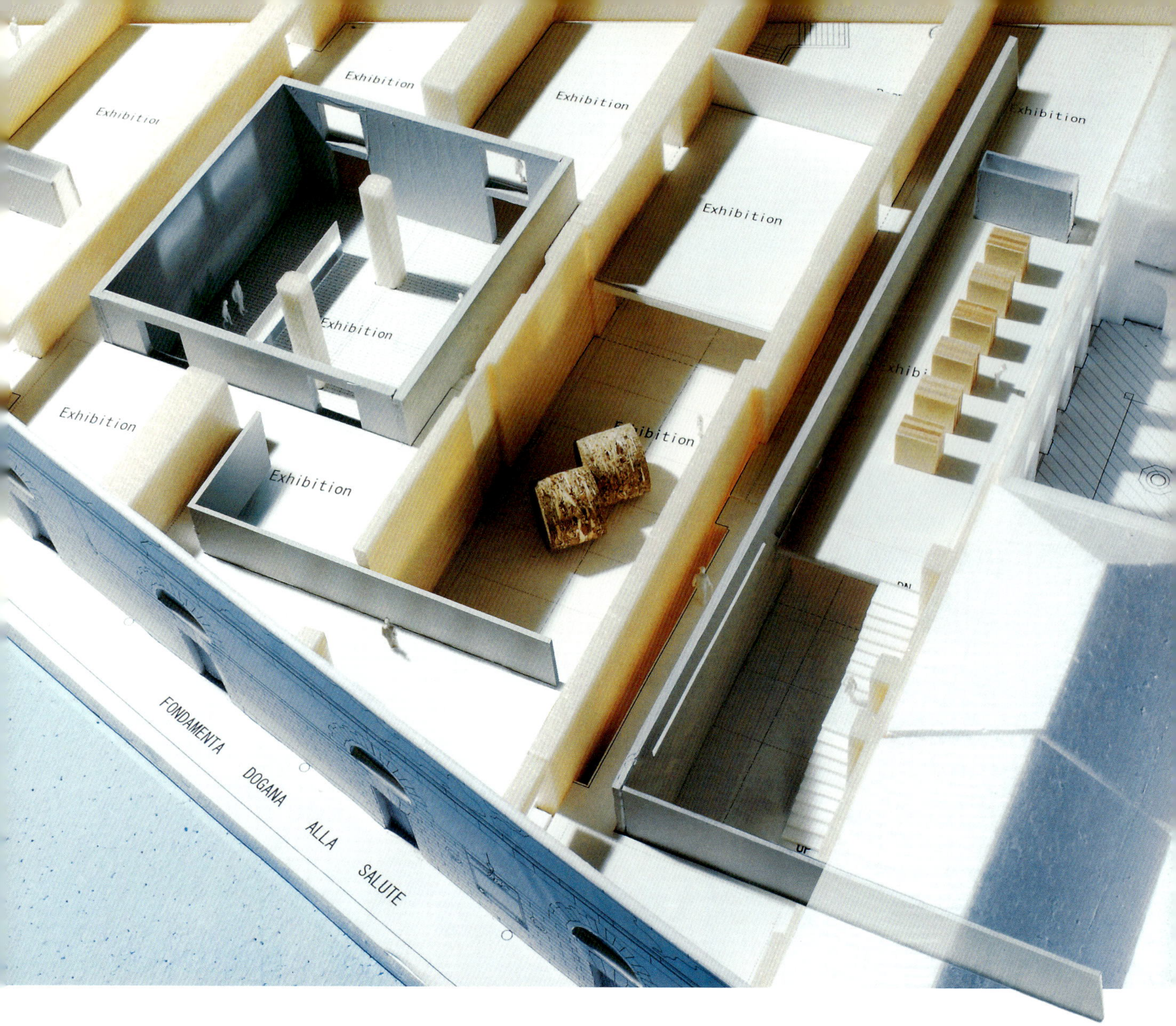

レンガ壁と木造のトラス小屋組による既存の空間に、
コンクリートの壁を入れ子状に挿入することによって、
新旧が対話する新たな場をつくる。

A new place of dialogue between old and new is made by inserting concrete walls in a nested arrangement within the existing spaces of sheds comprising brick walls and wooden trusses.

敷地はドイツ、フランスと国境を接するスイスの都市、バーゼルにある。スイスに本社を置く世界をリードする製薬会社ノバルティス社の動物研究施設棟である。ライン川沿いのキャンパスでは、現在、老朽化した建物の建て替えが順次進められており、この建物もその一環となるものである。ヴィットリオ・ランプヤーニによる厳格な格子状の配置のマスタープランに基づく建て替え計画には、世界中から建築家が招かれ、ディーナー&ディーナー、SANAA(妹島和世+西澤立衛)、ピーター・マクリ、アドルフ・クリスチャニスによる建物はすでに完成。現在、フランク・O・ゲーリー、ラファエル・モネオ、デイヴィッド・チッパーフィールドによる建物なども工事が進められている。さらに、ソウト・デ・モウラ、レンゾ・ピアノ、谷口吉生、槇文彦、レム・コールハース、ジャン・ヌーヴェルなどによる建物が計画中であり、将来はさながら建築博物館のようになると思われる。

建物の計画においては、特に安全、安心を心がけて設計に臨んだ。人の命を扱うというノバルティス社の責任ある使命を考え、スイス独特の清潔さと完璧さに、日本人の繊細さと器用さをもって建築に統合できればと願った。機能的な美しさと、人々に対するやさしさを建築で表現したい、緊張感の中にも、軽やかに、かつ強靭な建物を目指したいと考えた。

スイス特有の厳しい省エネ基準が、南側開口部に設置するルーバー、西側のダブルスキンのファサードなど、新たなデザイン・ヴォキャブラリーを生み出すきっかけとなった。キャンパス全体の北端にある三角形の特長ある敷地で、フランスの国境に面した場所であることを強く意識したデザインとなっている。建物プランも三角形で、その頂部は吹き抜けのアトリウムとなっており、日夜緊張を強いられている研究者たちの新たな刺激と憩いの空間となる。屋上には1年中花の咲き乱れる庭園を計画している。

ノバルティス社の新たな顔になるような、新しい時代を象徴する建築にできればと思う。

ノバルティス研究施設棟
Novartis WSJ-352

2004-09 スイス バーゼル——Basel, Switzerland

楔形の敷地に建つ鋭角三角形の平面形状の建物のイメージ。
与条件により限定されたヴォリュームに対し、40m余りの高さのファサードの表情が計画の主要なテーマとされた。
Image of a building with an acute-angled triangular plan on a wedge-shaped site. Given that this volume is constrained by the given conditions, the major design theme became the expression of the approximately 40m-high façade.

The site is in the Swiss city of Basel, which adjoins the national borders of Germany and France. This is an animal research facility building for Novartis, a leading international pharmaceutical company with headquarters in Switzerland. The building is part of a series of reconstructions of dilapidated buildings underway in the campus along the Rhine River. Architects from all over the world were invited to contribute to the reconstruction plan, based on the strict grid arrangement of Vittorio Magnano Lampgnani's masterplan, and buildings by Diener & Diener, SANAA (Kazuyo Sejima + Ryue Nishizawa), Peter Markli, and Adolf Krischanitz have already been completed. Construction is now underway on buildings by Frank O. Gehry, Rafael Moneo, and David Chipperfield. In addition, buildings by Souto de Moura, Renzo Piano, Yoshio Taniguchi, Fumihiko Maki, Rem Koolhaas, and Jean Nouvel are at the planning stage, and it seems that in future this will be an architectural museum.

The plan of the building was designed with particular regard to safety and security. Keeping in mind Novartis' mission of saving human life, we hope the building will incorporate the unique cleanliness and perfection of Switzerland, as well as the delicacy and dexterity of Japan. We want the architecture to express functional beauty, and gentleness towards people. Even within a sense of tension, we aimed at a tough yet light building.

The strict energy-conservation standards characteristic of Switzerland were a chance to invent a new design vocabulary, such as the louvers installed in the south-facing openings, and double-skin façades on the west side.

On a site in the exceptionally long triangular area at the northern tip of the entire campus, we designed with a strong awareness of the fact that this place faces the national border of France. The building plan is also a triangle, and the tip is a double-height atrium. This acts as a space that gives new stimulation and relaxation to the researchers, who are under stress day and night. On the rooftop, a garden is planned where flowers will bloom throughout the year.

I hope this architecture will become a new face for Novartis, symbolizing a new era.

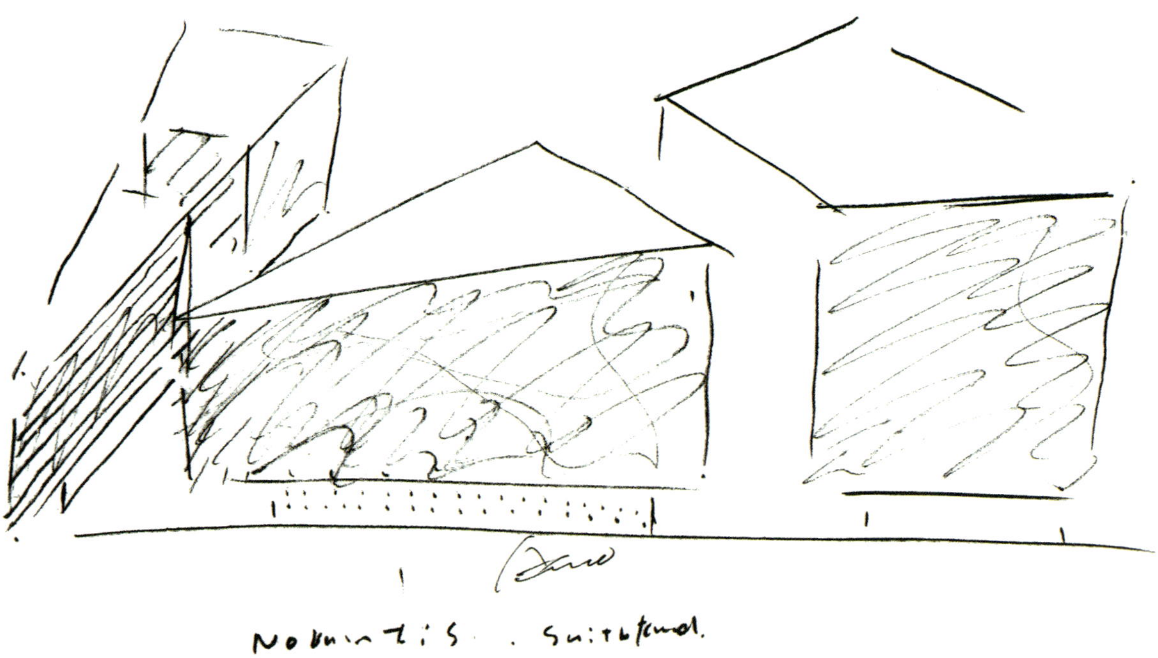

中央のリチャード・セラの彫刻を挟んで、対をなす建物のイメージ。
Image of Richard Serra's sculpture interposed between the two opposing buildings.

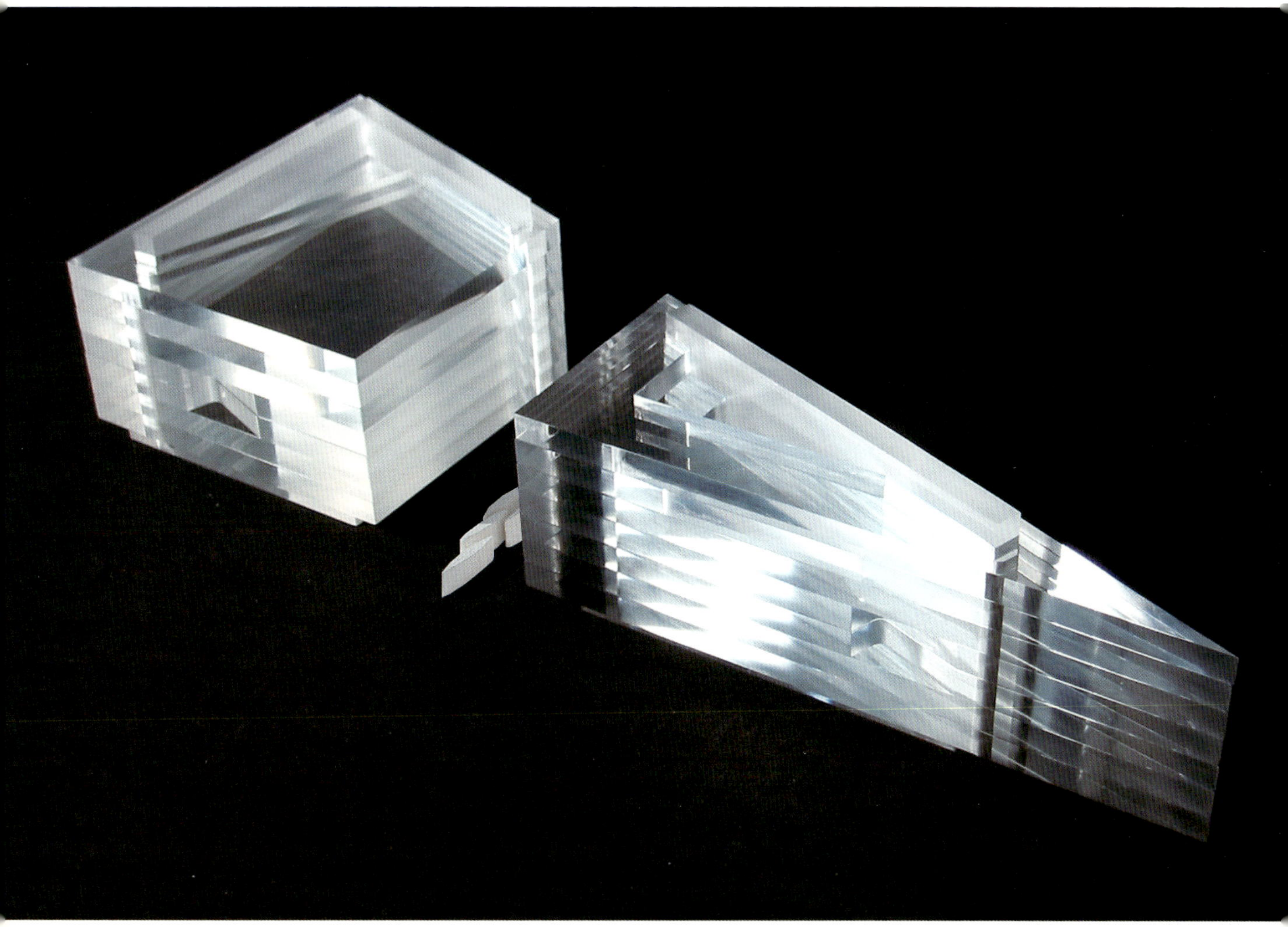

先行して進めているのは、楔形の敷地の建物の計画。特異な敷地形状そのままの鋭角三角形のオープンスペースを随所に設けることで、機能的に必要な方形のスペースを巧みにつくり出している。一定のスペースを要する設備コアは、北側のリニアなソリッドとして集約されている。グラウンドレベルは、広場側を、彫刻を取り込むような奥行きの深いコロネードとしている。

Priority was given to developing the design of the building on the wedge-shaped site. The functionally required rectangular spaces have been skillfully produced by using the unique site shape of an acute-angled triangle to establish open spaces all round. The fixed spaces of the required service cores are condensed as a linear solid toward the north. The ground level on the plaza side is a deep colonnade, as if drawing in the sculptures.

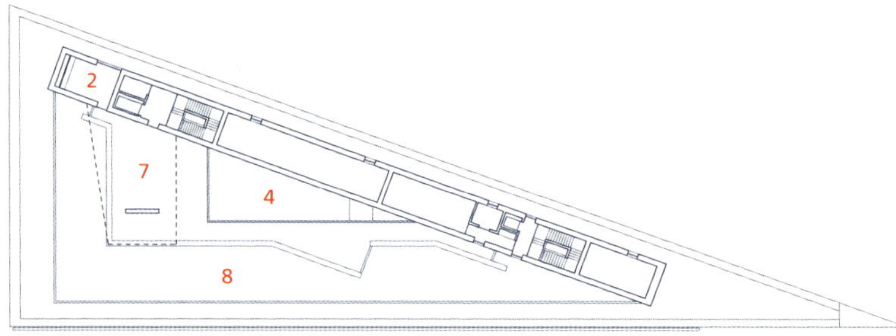

Roof floor plan

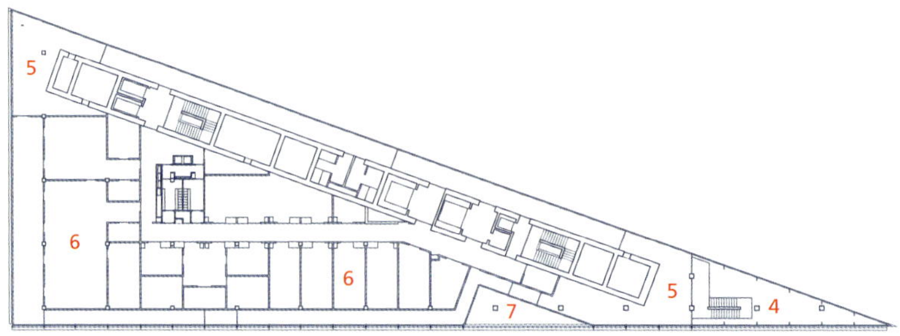

Fourth floor plan

1 entrance
2 lounge
3 seminar / conference
4 void
5 office
6 lab / research
7 terrace
8 planting
9 "Dick's Pod" sculpture (Richard Serra)

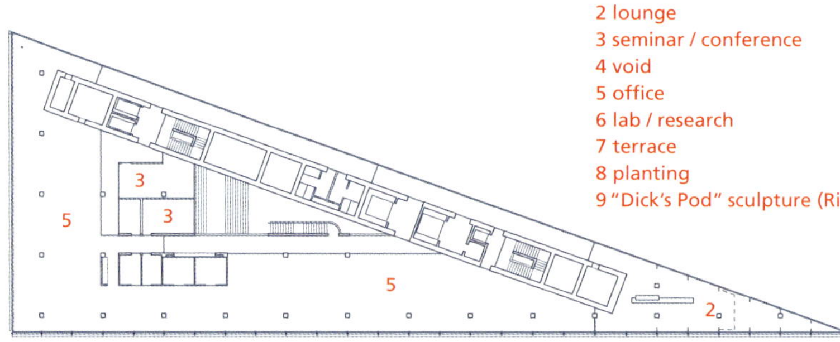

Second floor plan

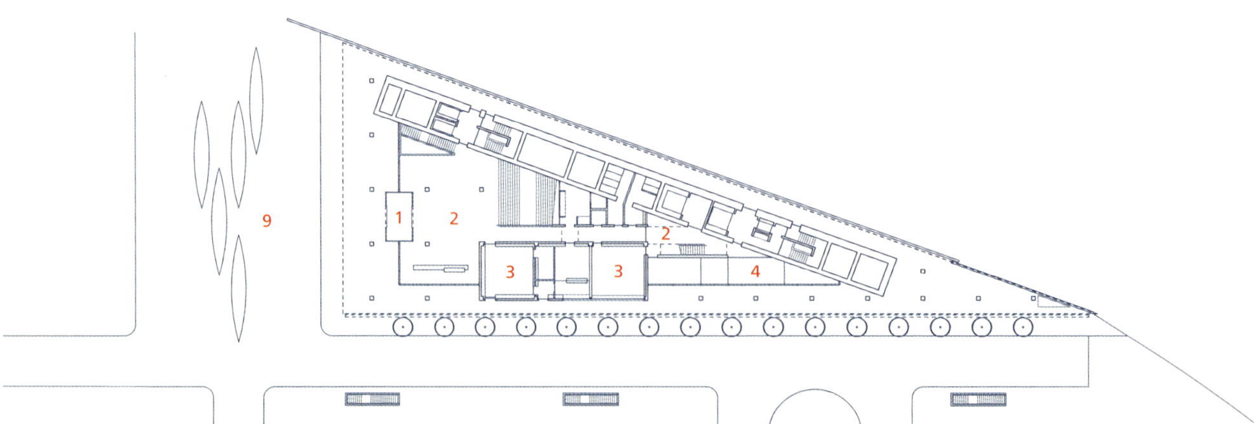

First floor plan 1:1,000

キャンパスの南北軸を受け止めるゲートのような、一対の建物。ガラスカーテンウォール外側を日照調整のための可動式アルミルーバーが覆う。スタティックなルーバー部分の表情と、ペアガラスのみのオープンスペース部分の軽快な表情との対比が、長大なファサードを緊張感あるものに仕立てている。

A pair of buildings, like a gate terminating the north-south axis of the campus. In order to regulate sunlight, the exterior glass curtain wall is covered with moveable aluminum bars. The contrast in expression between the static louver parts and the casual expression of the open space parts with only double-glazing gives the vast façade a feeling of tension.

彫刻家ヴォルガング・クーバッハとその夫人アンナ・マリア・クーバッハ=ヴィルムゼンの作品を展示する小さな美術館である。クーバッハ氏は、1冊の本、あるいは積み重ねられた数冊の本のかたちを、そのまま石で造形した彫刻作品で有名である。

敷地はドイツ、バーデンバーデンに近い緩やかな丘陵地に位置している。18世紀に建てられたこの地方特有の切妻屋根の納屋を、敷地中央に移設・保存修復し、メインの屋内展示施設としている。さらに、自然の地形に沿うように新たに設けられる数枚のコンクリートの壁によって、彫刻を配置するコートや水庭は仕切られ、内外の空間は分節され、それぞれの領域を形成している。旧い納屋の妻面上部は木組みのみを残し、壁は撤去された。その隙間から自然光が吹き抜けに降り注ぎ、そこに設置される彫刻作品に生命を与えるよう改造された。また、下部は土台部分からコンクリートの新しい壁が立ち上がり、既存の屋根の小屋組みと対比をなしている。中央の水庭には旧い納屋の姿が映り、風にゆれ、ここでも新旧の要素が融合する。

2007年春、完成を見ずして、クーバッハ氏は病気で亡くなられたが、クーバッハ=ヴィルムゼン夫人とその財団が彼の遺志を引き継いで、実現を目指している。

ストーン・スカルプチュア・ミュージアム
Stone Sculpture Museum

1996- ドイツ バード・クライツナッハ——Bad Kreuznach, Germany

This is a small museum for exhibiting the work of sculptor Wolfgang Kubach and his wife Anna Maria Kubach-Wilmsen. Kubach is famous for his sculptures in the shape of a single book, or the shape of a pile of books, carved directly in stone.

The site is located in a region of gentle hills near Baden-Baden, Germany. A gabled-roof barn, built in the 18th century and characteristic of this area, was moved to the middle of the site, restored, and converted into the main indoor exhibition facility. In addition, by means of several new concrete walls that follow the natural topography, courtyards and water gardens for sculptures have been partitioned, interior and exterior spaces divided, and various areas given form. The old walls were removed, leaving only the timberwork from the upper gables of the old barn. This was remodeled so that natural light pours down through these gaps into the double-height space, a remodeling that animates the sculptures arranged there. Moreover, in the lower part, new concrete walls project from the foundations, in contrast with the trusses of the existing roof. The figure of the old barn is reflected in the central water garden, moving with the wind. Here too, old and new elements are fused.

In Spring 2007, Kubach died of an illness without seeing the building's completion, but his wife Kubach-Wilmsen took up this foundation as his dying wish, aiming at its realization.

展示室の断面パースペクティブ。地方特有の切妻屋根の納屋を移設・修復してつくられる。石貼りの外壁の内部は、外構同様の打ち放しコンクリート。既存の木組みを活かした妻面上部のスカイライトからの光が、吹き抜けの壁に美しい光と影のパターンを映す。

Perspective cross-section of the exhibition rooms. Relocation and renovation of a gable-roofed barn characteristic of the region. Within the stone-clad exterior walls is exposed concrete similar to outside. The light from the skylight in the upper part of the gable surface revitalizes the existing timber structure, which projects a beautiful pattern of light and shade on the double-height walls.

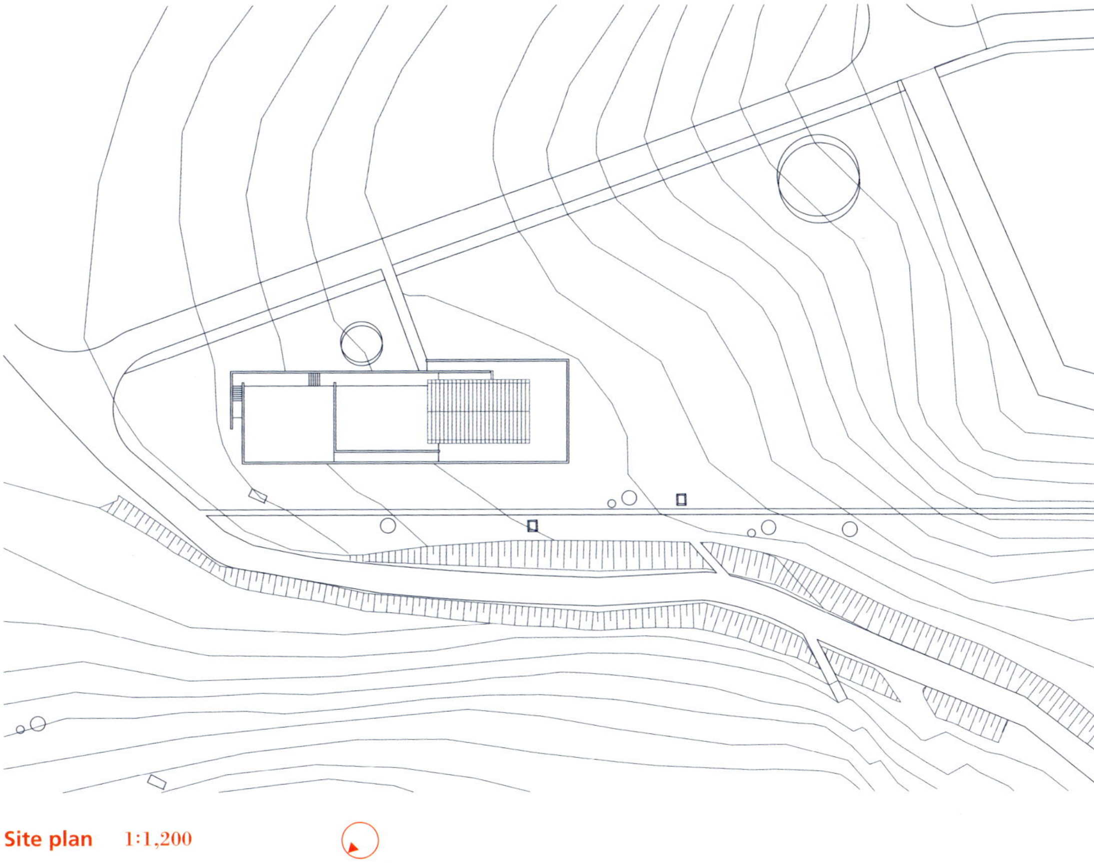

Site plan 1:1,200

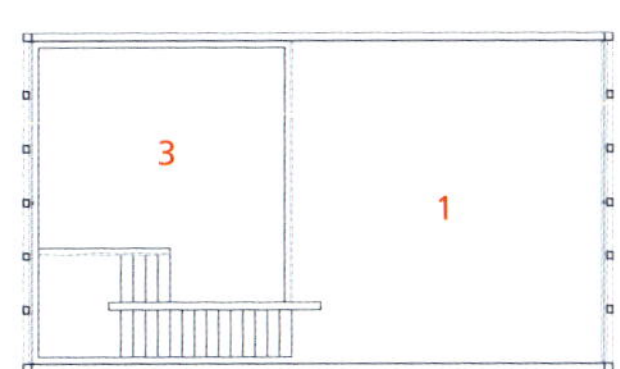

Second floor plan

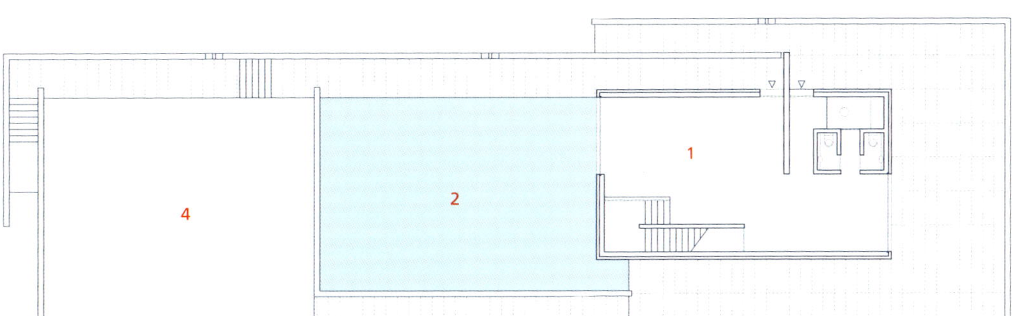

First floor plan 1:400

1 exhibition room
2 water garden
3 void
4 outdoor exhibition space
5 reception

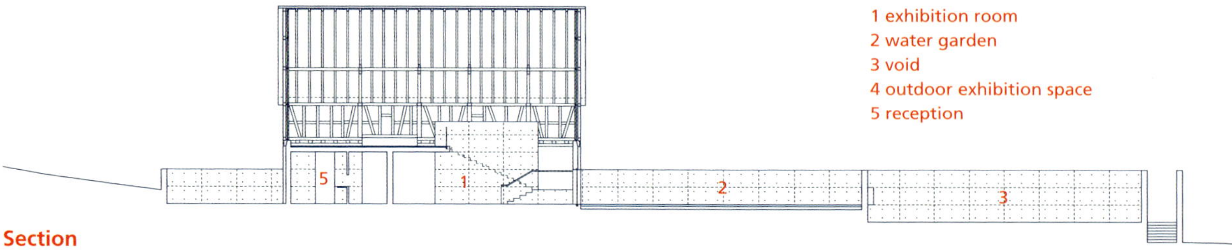

Section

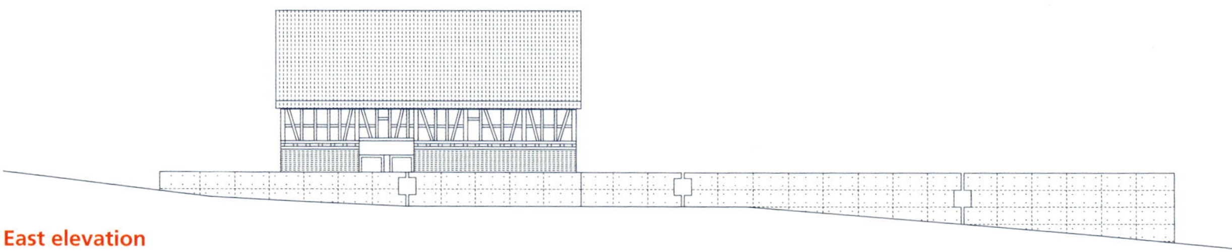

East elevation

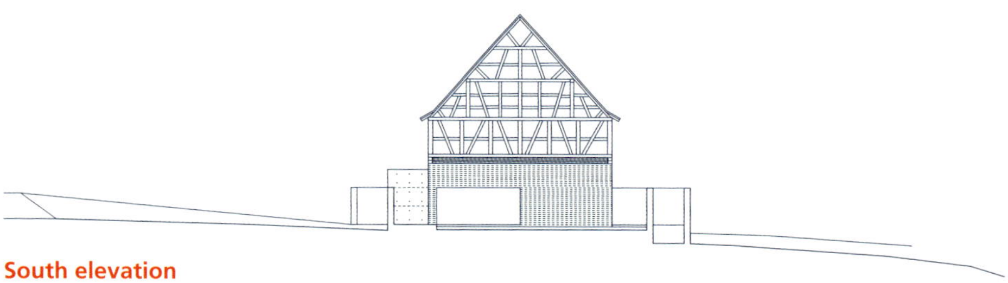

South elevation

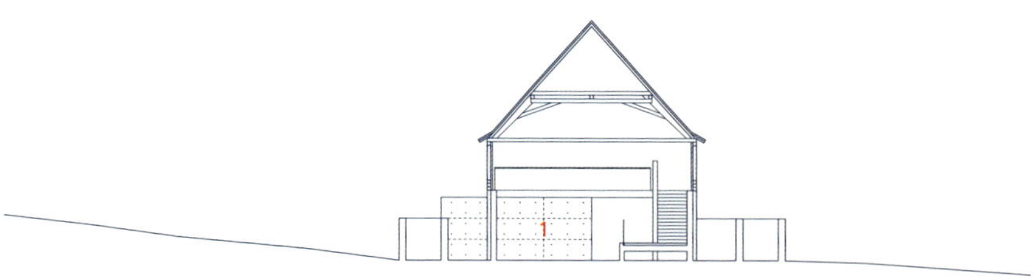

Section

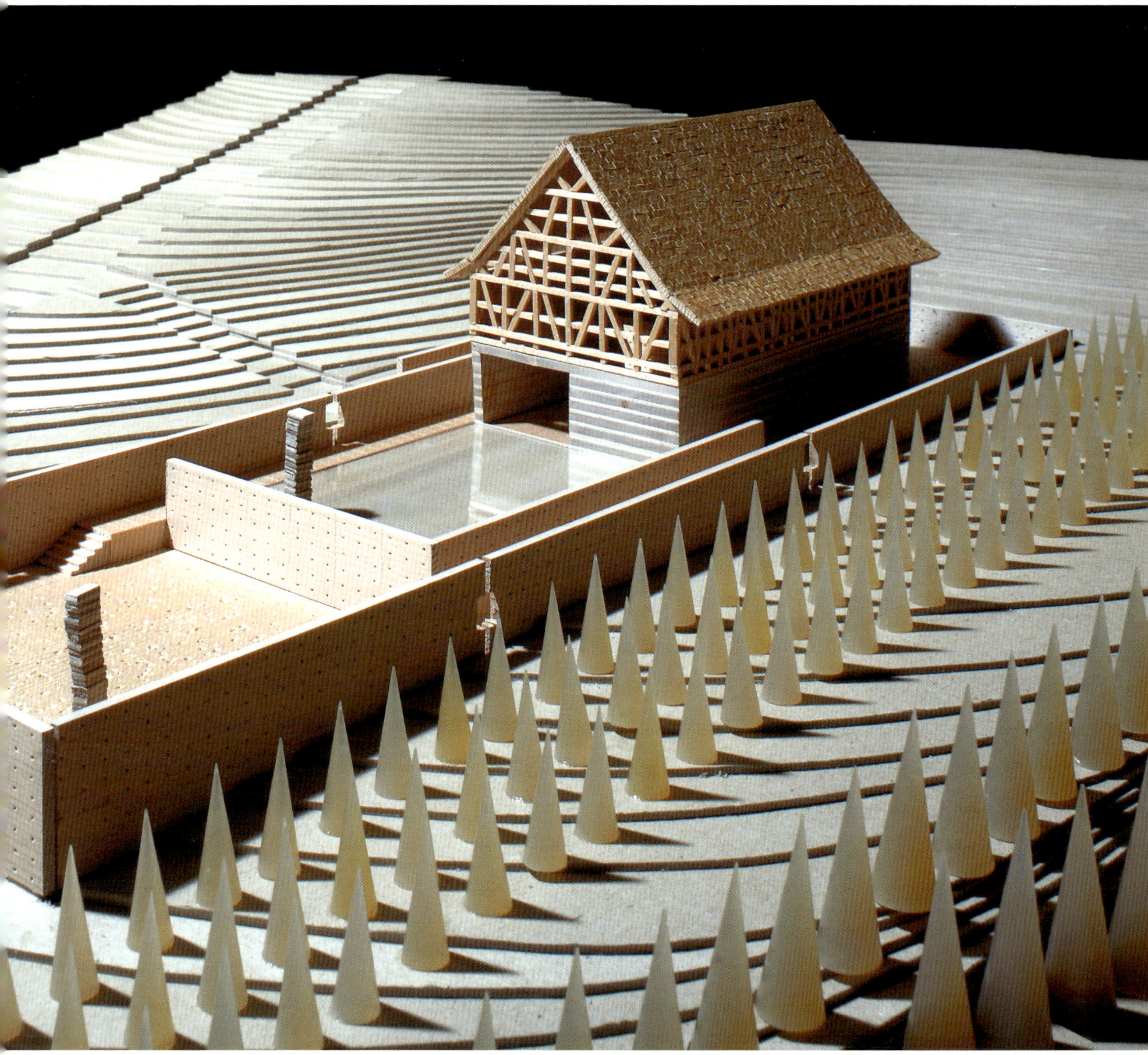

敷地形状を活かした展示室と彫刻庭園の配置。
傾斜にあわせ展開する壁に囲われた中庭が、流れるような空間のシークエンスをつくり出す。

Layout of the sculpture garden and the exhibition room, making use of the shape of the site. The walls enclosing the courtyard were developed in response to the slope, and produce a flowing spatial sequence.

エッセイ

ジャン・ヌーヴェル

永遠の感覚

その昔、原初の建築者はおそらく、石を完璧に切り出して直方体を得ようと考えついたに違いない。そして同時に、切り出した石を空積みして、精度の高い組積壁をつくり上げようと考えたはずだ。やがて建築者は、必然的に、繰り返し積み重ねた直方体の部材のひとつひとつが、その集合である壁体のうちに融け入っていることに驚きをもって気づく。次に、建築者は、石の部材に曲面加工をほどこし、円筒形をつくろうと試みる。時を経て、また別の建築者が、今度は、四角錘台、あるいは螺旋をつくろうとする。これらの建築エレメントは、今なお時の流れに耐え、数千年もの歳月に対して頑なに闘いながら、その静謐さでわれわれを圧倒し続けている。建築技術は文明とともに進化した。だが一方で、時の流れにいかに抗するかの希求は絶えることがない。基礎的な工法は、今もってその戦略の一端を担い続けている。

鉄筋コンクリートの世紀である20世紀に、私はある建築家を知った。彼は母国の建築の伝統や、石、木、瓦などの素材に眼差しを向け、それらの組み合わせの明瞭な技法を精察していた。また、その地の建物と岩や、木々の葉の動きや色が四季を通じて織りなす光景に心打たれた経験をもっていた。さらに、祖国の住まいと水——凪いだ海や湖、あるいは小川や渓流、滝のほとばしり——との調和に心を動かされたこともあった。そして、この建築家は、同じような精妙な感覚を、彼の時代の最も親しみある素材、コンクリートを用いて探求していこうと決意したのだ。そう、あの灰色で平板なありきたりの素材——馴染みの施工法、つまり規則正しいピッチでセパレーターを配置し、規格のベニヤ板で型枠を組んで打設し、型枠を外すと、Pコンの丸い穴が句読点のように残る——あのコンクリートだ。この建築者は、そのコンクリートの表面にベニヤ板の長方形の刻印を完璧に繰り返し、これを空積みし、そこにセパレーターの名残である丸い穴を厳密に配列した最初の人物であった。やがて彼は、必然的に、6つの点をもつドミノ牌のような繰り返し重ねた長方形の部材のひとつひとつが、面としての表現のうちに融け入っていることに、喜びをもって気づく。そこで彼は次に、円筒形の壁や螺旋をつくろうと試みる。そして、彼の作品の基本となる幾何図形を空や水や樹木と取り合わせ、生地で父祖より伝わる建築に抱いたものと同じ静けさや、喜びを覚えるのである。彼は光を自在に操る。日中の光を壁のマチエールをかすめるように採り込み、その光によって壁面の完璧さを的確に問い、乱し、あるいは揺さぶる。日の光線で太陽の幾何図形をつくり出し、空で真っ青な正方形を描き出す。つまり、陰影と風景の奥行きとを操っていたのだ。彼がつくり出した静けさを最初に認識するのが彼自身であることは間違いない。その平静を、彼はまず、住まいやアトリエに取り入れる。そして、内省や潜心熟慮、瞑想や精神生活に適したその平安を、洗練していく。そうして、彼は巨匠となった。幾十もの住宅、寺院、美術館、セミナーハウスといった設計の依頼が舞い込む。はじめは自国の山々や海岸沿いで、そして、やがては古きヨーロッパから新しきアメリカに至る全世界で、彼は作品を展開していくのである。

日本、それがその静謐の詩人、永遠の感覚を呼び起こす名手の祖国。そして、彼の名は安藤忠雄。

ジャン・ヌーヴェル
建築家。1945年フランス、フェメル生まれ。1984-89年ジャン・ヌーヴェル・エ・アソシエ、1989-94年JNEC、1994年アトリエ・ジャン・ヌーヴェル設立。2001年高松宮殿下記念世界文化賞、RIBAゴールドメダル、2006年アーノルド・ブルンナー記念建築賞受賞。

Essay

Jean Nouvel

Un sentiment d'éternité

Probablement un jour, un bâtisseur a, le premier, eu l'idée de tailler parfaitement une pierre pour en faire un parallélépipède rectangle. Probablement, il a eu l'idée simultanée de les assembler à joint vif pour créer un mur à l'appareil précis. Forcément, il fut surpris de constater que la répétition de l' élément parallélépipèdique disparaissait au bénéfice d'un ensemble: le mur. Alors, ce bâtisseur testa le cylindre en cintrant l'élémentaire pierre, puis, avec le temps, d'autres ont continué, avec le tronc de pyramide ou la spirale… Aujourd'hui ces éléments d'architecture défient le temps et imposent toujours leur silence dans leur lutte obstinée contre les millénaires… Les techniques constructives évoluent au cours des civilisations. L'espoir de défier le temps demeure. L'élémentarité des moyens reste une stratégie.

Au siècle du béton armé, le XXème, je connais un architecte qui a regardé la tradition constructive de son pays, les éléments, pierre, bois, terre cuite, qui a observé les techniques d' assemblages limpides, et qui a été ému par la relation entre l'abri de chez lui avec le roc, le mouvement et la couleur de la feuille de l'arbre en toutes saisons, touché par l'harmonie de sa maison avec l'eau plane de la mer et du lac, ou l'eau en mouvement du ruisseau, du torrent et de la cascade. Cet architecte a décidé de chercher des sensations aussi subtiles en utilisant la matière la plus accessible de son temps: le béton. Oui, ce béton banal, gris, plan, mis en œuvre de la manière la plus courante, c'est-à-dire moulé, coffré avec des plaques standards de contreplaqué traversées régulièrement par des barres de serrage qui laissent une trace, une ponctuation dans le mur. Ce bâtisseur a eu le premier l'idée de répéter parfaitement l'empreinte d'un rectangle de bois sur du béton, d'assembler ces empreintes à joint vif, de les ponctuer rigoureusement par le souvenir des tubes de tension. Forcément, il fut ravi de constater que la répétition de l'élément—rectangle, domino avec six points—disparaissait au bénéfice de l'expression du plan. Alors, ce bâtisseur testa le mur cylindrique, la spirale… et mis la géométrie élémentaire de ses constructions en relation avec le ciel, l'eau, l'arbre et ressenti le même calme et le même plaisir qu'il éprouvait devant les architectures ancestrales de sa terre natale. Il apprivoisa la lumière, qu'il fit tomber en jour frisant sur la matière de ses murs pour mieux en questionner, en troubler, en contester la perfection. Il traça des géométries de soleil avec des rais et dessina des carrés bleus avec l'azur. Enfin, il joua avec profondeurs des ombres et des paysages. Et, il fut sûrement le premier à constater le calme qu'il avait instauré. L'apaisement, il l'avait ainsi introduit d'abord dans la maison, dans l'atelier. Puis, cette quiétude propice à la réflexion, au recueillement, à la contemplation et la spiritualité, il la cultiva. Il devint alors un maître. Il fut appelé pour construire des dizaines de maisons, de temples, de musées, de lieux de séminaires. D'abord dans les montagnes et sur les rivages de son pays, puis dans le monde entier, jusqu'à la vieille Europe et la nouvelle Amérique.

Le Japon est la terre de ce poète du silence, de cet évocateur d'éternité qui se nomme Tadao Ando.

Jean Nouvel

Architect. Born in Fumel, France in 1945. Founder of Jean Nouvel et Associés, 1984-89. Founder of JNEC (Jean Nouvel and Emmanuel Cattani), 1989-94. Established Ateliers Jean Nouvel in 1994. Received the Praemium Imperiale Award and the RIBA Gold Medal in 2001, the Arnold Brunner Memorial Prize in 2006.

阪神大震災の際、アジア・アフリカから寄せられた援助への「お返し」として始まった計画である。新聞社の呼びかけで集まった寄付金により、AMDA（Asia Medical Doctor Association）が運営する子どものための病院が建設されることとなった。建設地はインドに近く、釈迦の聖地であるルンビニ近郊のブトワール市に決まった。土地、インフラ設備などは市の提供によるものである。

建設前、ネパールには、カトマンズに子ども病院がひとつあるだけで、また5歳未満の子どもの死亡率は日本と比べると、20倍にも及んでいる。新しい病院の設立は、地元の人々にとって最も期待されるものだった。建設条件は非常に厳しいものであったが、建築と社会との関わりという意味では、大変有意義な仕事であった。

建物自体は単純な矩形によるものである。素材、工法の選択についてはコスト面、技術面の問題から現地で可能な手法を取らざるを得なかった。外壁には現地で生産されている赤レンガを用いた。内部はモルタル塗りの上白ペンキ塗り。明るく清潔なイメージを意図しての仕上げである。

南面には列柱のコロネードを配している。その奥に窓を設けることで強烈な太陽光から内部空間を保護し、穏やかな室内環境を確保できるよう考えた。診察室、病室、ロビーなどの子どものための部屋は、すべてこのコロネードに面して連続するよう考えている。現地の風土に相応しい開放性と明るさの実現が、ひとつの主題だった。

コンクリートの架構を建ち上げ、煉瓦を積み、仕上げを施していく、その建設過程のすべてが、ここでは人間の力によった。完成した病院では現在1日に200人を超える患者を診察している。建物がこの場所に息づいていくことを、強く願っている。

ネパール子ども病院
Shiddhartha Children and Women Hospital

1997-98 ネパール ブトワール——Butwal, Nepal

This plan was initiated as an expression of our gratitude for the help received from countries in Asia and Africa following the Great Hanshin Earthquake. A hospital for children run by AMDA (Asia Medical Doctor Association) was constructed with the donations raised by a Japanese newspaper appeal. The selected site was close to India, in Butwal city on the outskirts of Lambini, the Buddha's holy land. The land and infrastructural installations were contributed by the city.

Prior to this construction, Nepal had only one children's hospital, in Katmandu, and the mortality rate of children less than five years old was up to twenty times higher than in Japan. Mmore than anything else, the local people hoped for the establishment of a new hospital. The construction conditions were harsh, but in terms of the relationship between architecture and society, it was a very meaningful work for us.

The building itself is composed of simple rectangles. With regard to the selection of materials and construction methods, due to issues of cost and technology, we were limited to adopting methods available in the area. Locally manufactured red bricks were used for the exterior walls. Inside, white paint was applied to a mortar finish. This finish was intended to produce a bright, clean image.

A row of columns in the form of a colonnade has been arranged on the south side. By installing windows behind this, we thought that the inner spaces could be protected from severe sunlight, ensuring a calm indoor environment. I thought that the rooms for the children, such as consultation rooms, sickrooms, and the lobby, could form a consecutive sequence facing the colonnade. Implementing an openness and brightness appropriate to the local climate was one of our themes.

From erecting the concrete frame to stacking the bricks and applying the finishes, the entire construction process here relied on human power alone.

Currently, more than two hundred patients per day are being examined in the completed hospital. I strongly hope the building will continue to vividly take root in this place.

配置ドローイング。2棟の建物の主要な室はすべてコロネードを配した南側に沿うよう計画されている。
Site plan drawing. It has been designed by arranging all the main rooms of the two buildings along the colonnade on the south side.

東側全景。現地で生産されている赤レンガを用いたファサード。

Panoramic view from the east. The façade uses red bricks produced locally.

北西から見る建物全景。ソリッドな赤レンガのマッスにL字型のポーチが取りついただけの素朴な造形が、ネパールの荒々しい大地の光景によくマッチしている。

Panoramic view of the building from the northwest. The simple form of an L-shaped porch on a mass of solid red bricks is a scene well matched to the rugged land of Nepal.

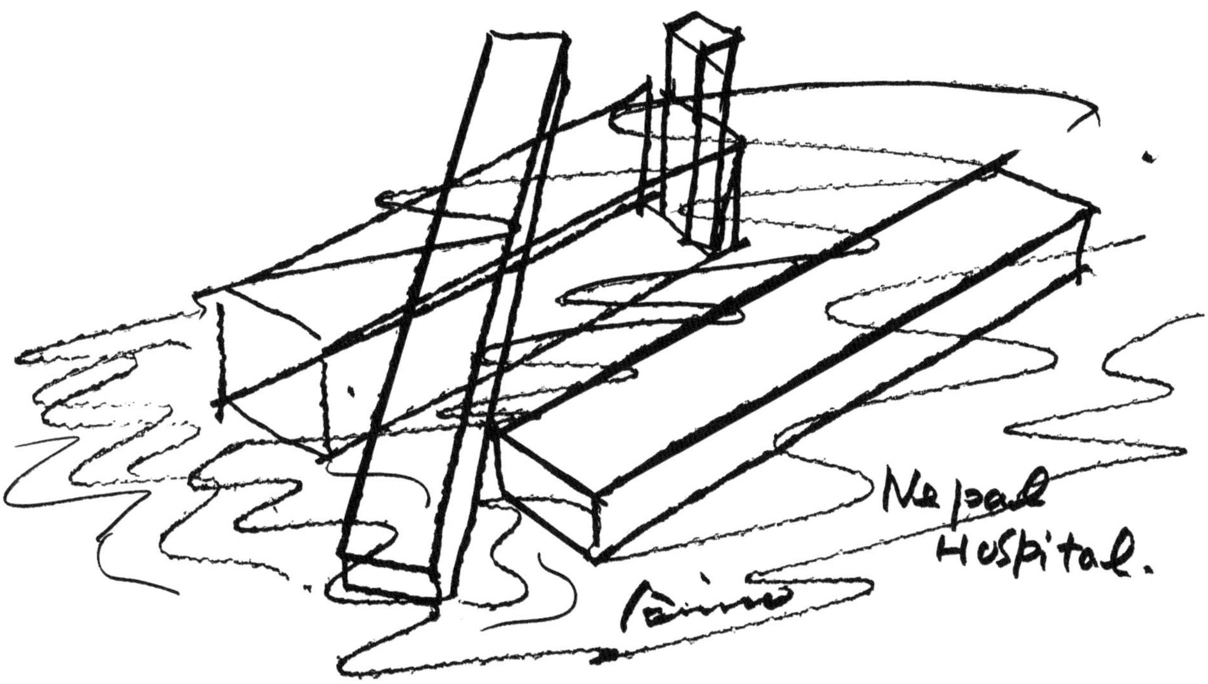

単純な幾何学からなるヴォリューム構成を描いたスケッチ。激しい気候風土ゆえに、ここではより単純で力強い建築が志向された。

Sketch depicting a composition of simple geometric volumes. Because of the harsh climate, the aim was an even simpler and stronger architecture.

ホールの方向に斜路を見返す。
Looking back at the ramp in the direction of the hall.

2階レベルから、斜路を踊場方向に見る。内部仕上げはすべてモルタル塗りの上、白ペンキ仕上げ。
Looking in toward the landing of the ramp from the second floor level. The interior finishes are all white paint on a layer of mortar.

木立越しに見る建物南側全景。コロネードの連続する陰影深いファサード。

Panoramic view of the south side of the building across a grove of trees. The façade has a series of deep shadows from the colonnade.

中国、上海で進められている「The Tongji Science & Technology Zone Project」の一環をなす計画である。敷地は、すでに完成している第1期開発地区の西側、同済大学に隣接する位置にある。デザインに関わる企業、研究機関のためのオフィス、ギャラリー、ホールなどを収める複合文化施設の計画である。

「再開発地区に誕生する、新たな情報発信基地」というテーマに対し、われわれは外部に対しては新しい街の風景の核となるような強いメッセージを発しながら、その内には創造拠点に相応しい、奥行きと広がりをもった空間性を孕むような構成を模索した。

スタディを重ねた結果辿り着いたのが、現在のような異なる幾何学形態の組み合わせからなる構成である。外壁をすべてガラスの皮膜としながら、立体的に絡み合う各ヴォリュームの相互関係により、変化に富んだ場面を、全体に散りばめていく。敷地中央の囲われた中庭空間は、多様な要素からなる施設をひとつにつなぎ留める、緩衝領域の役割を担う。

上海という都市の凄まじいエネルギーに負けないような、スピード感と生命感に溢れた建築にしたいと考えている。

上海デザインセンター
Shanghai Design Center

2004- 中華人民共和国 上海 —— Shanghai, China

This is part of the "Tongji Science & Technology Zone Project" now underway in Shanghai, China. The site is located next to Tongji University, on the west side of the already completed phase one development area. This is a project for a cultural complex that will provide halls, galleries, and offices for design-related businesses and research laboratories.

In response to the given theme of "a new facility for transmitting information produced within the redevelopment district," we began by creating a volumetric composition that externally emanates a strong message as the core of the new development, and that internally offers interior spaces with a feeling of spatial depth, appropriate to a place that will be hub for creativity.

Comprising a combination of various different geometric forms, the current composition was derived through our repeated studies. All the exterior walls are made of glass membranes, and the richly varied scenery is dispersed by the interrelationships of the three-dimensionally interwoven volumes. The enclosed courtyard space at the center of the site will play the role of a buffer area, which connects and integrates the various elements of the facility.

To avoid being overwhelmed by the fierce energy of Shanghai, we wanted to make an architecture that brims over with a sense of speed and vitality.

配置ドローイング。敷地は同済大学に隣接する、再開発地区の西側に位置する。
Site drawing. Adjoining Tongji University, the site is located on the west side of a redevelopment district.

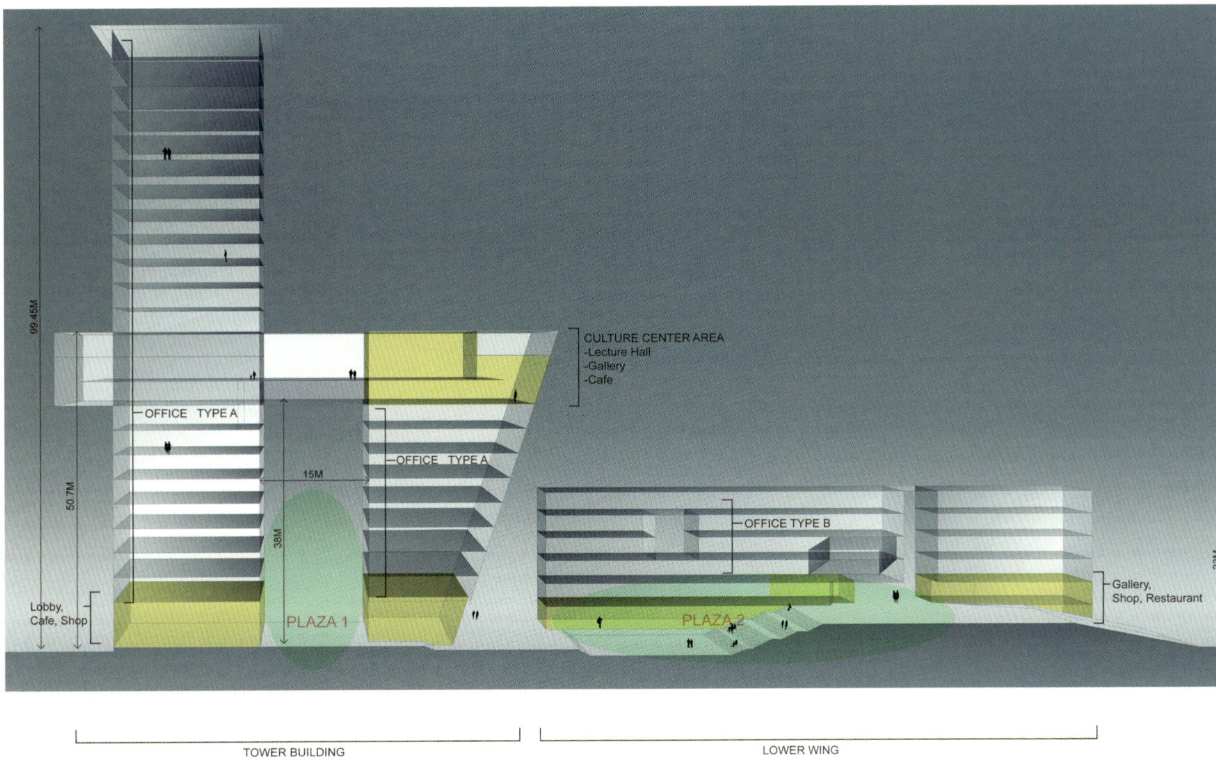
99.45M
CULTURE CENTER AREA
-Lecture Hall
-Gallery
-Cafe
OFFICE TYPE A
OFFICE TYPE A
15M
50.7M
38M
OFFICE TYPE B
23M
Gallery,
Shop, Restaurant
Lobby,
Cafe, Shop
PLAZA 1
PLAZA 2
TOWER BUILDING
LOWER WING

Diagram

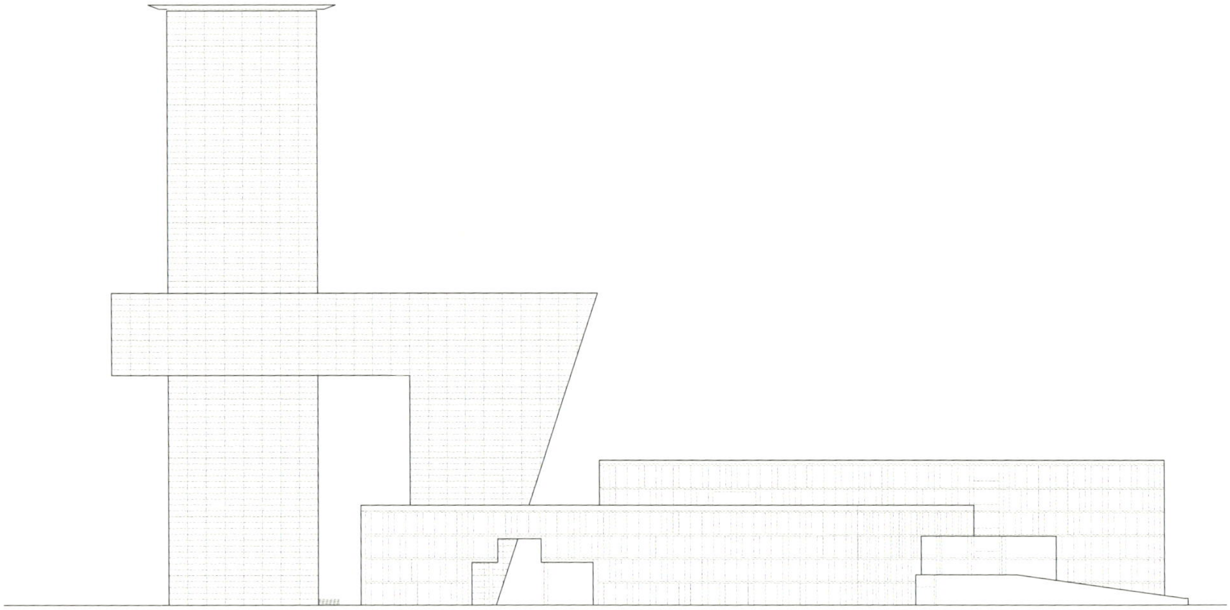

South elevation 1:1,200

ガラス皮膜で覆われたSRC造による空間ヴォリュームが、立体的に絡み合ってひとつの建築をつくり出す。

The spatial volumes made of steel-reinforced concrete covered with a glass membrane are three-dimensionally intertwined to produce one building.

現代的なガラス素材による建築空間の凹凸が、巨大なスケールの建築を適度に分節し、変化に富んだ建築の風景を生み出す。

The indented architectural spaces made from the contemporary material of glass produce a moderately segmented vast building, full of variations in architectural scenery.

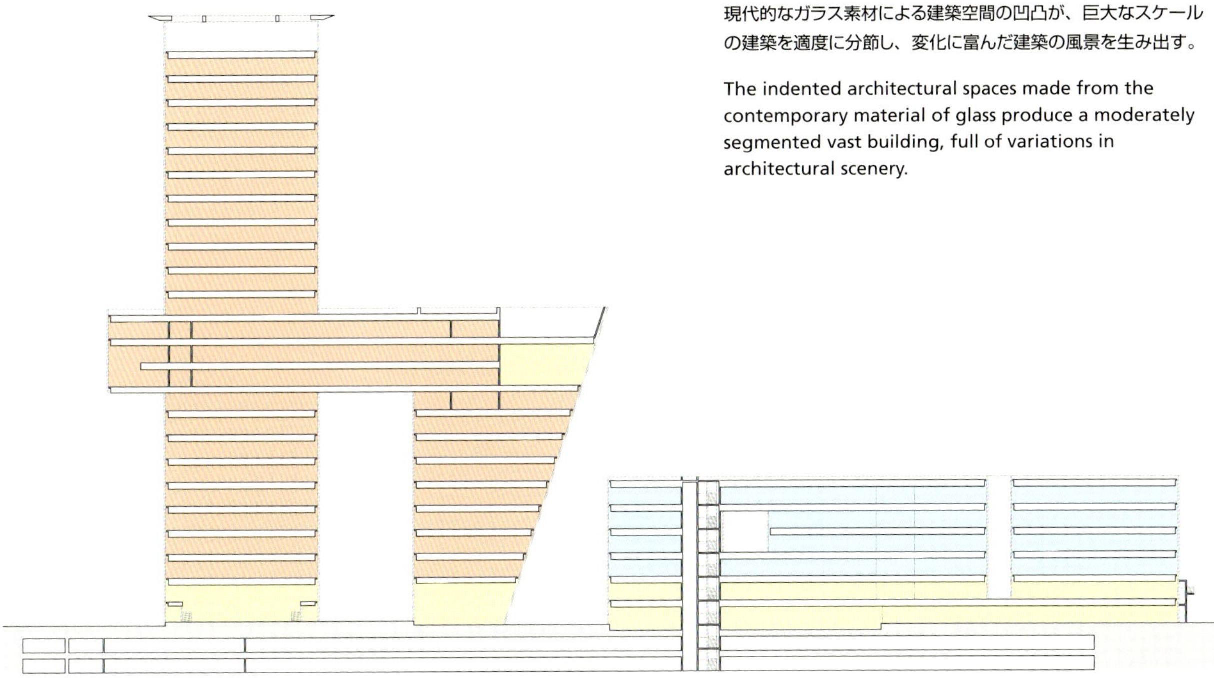

Section 1:1,200

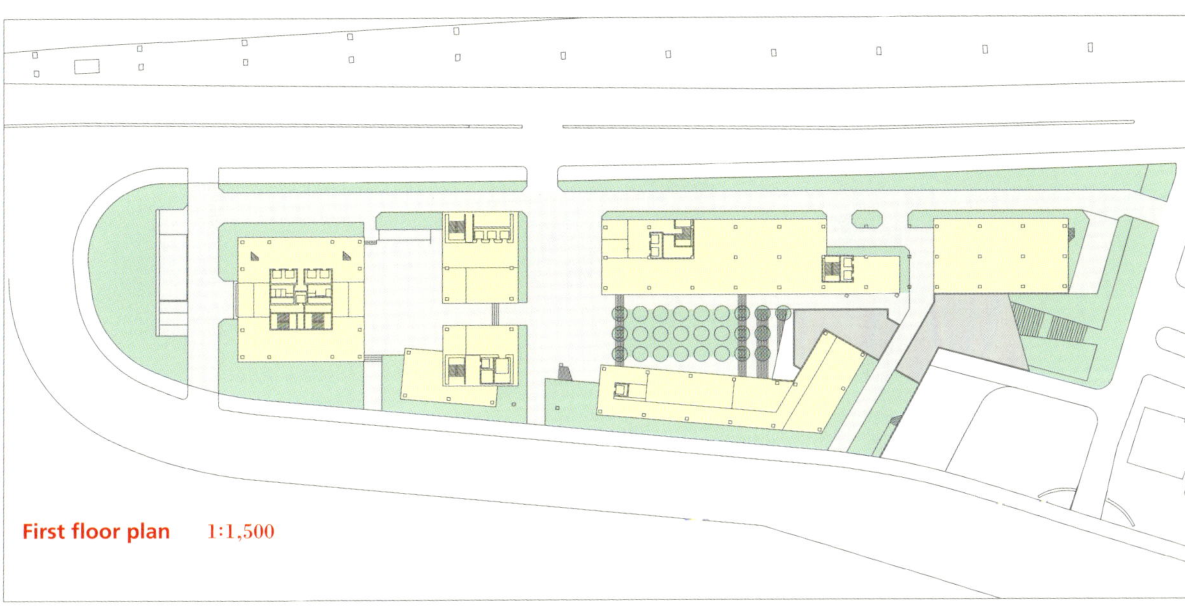

First floor plan 1:1,500

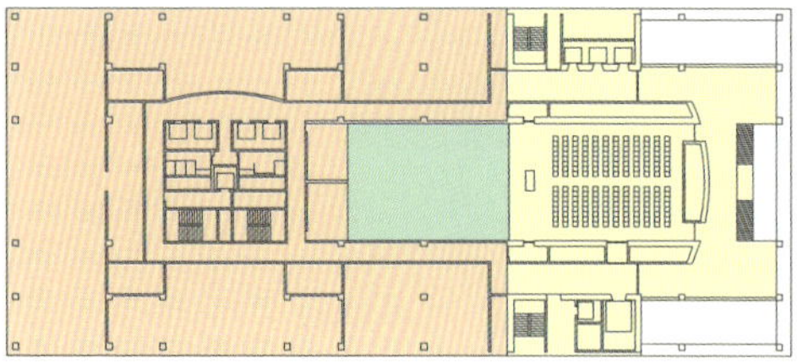

Twelfth floor plan

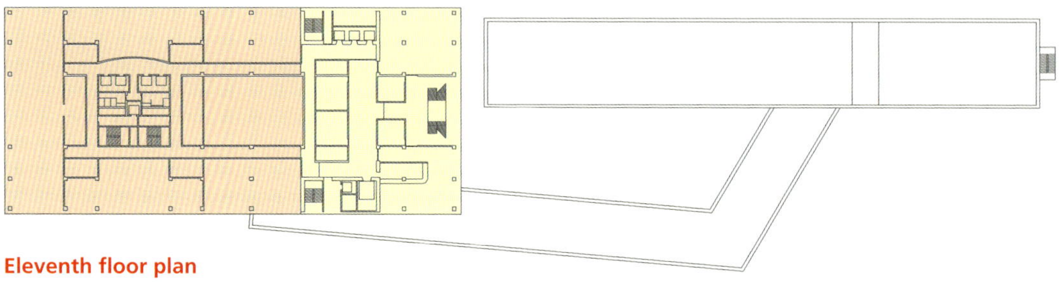

Eleventh floor plan

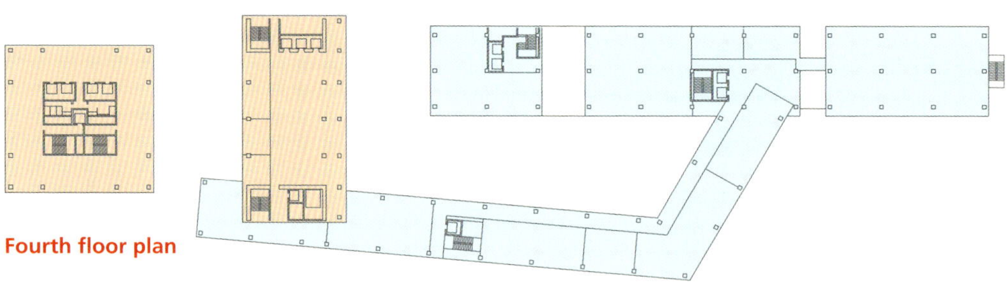

Fourth floor plan

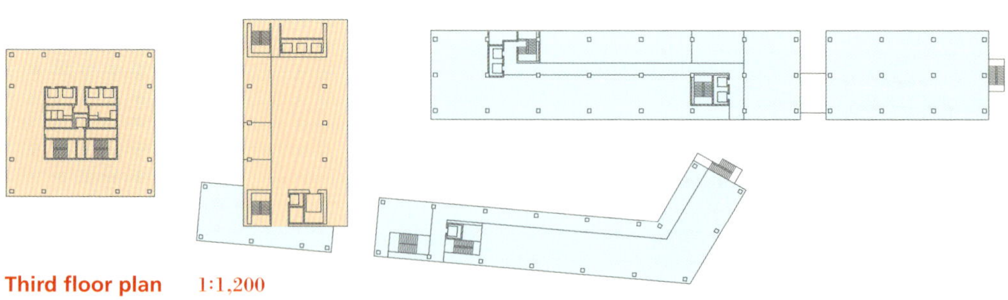

Third floor plan 1:1,200

ダイナミックな建築形態が光の彫刻となり、上海の夜を照らす。

The dynamic architectural form becomes a sculpture of light, illuminating the Shanghai night.

建築を統合する敷地中央の中庭空間。

The architecture is integrated by the courtyard space in the center of the site.

クライアントは韓国のある企業の文化財団である。これまでに収集してきたアートコレクションをより多くの人々に楽しんでもらうための美術館をつくりたいという依頼であった。

広大な総合リゾートの一角の山頂を削り取った細長い土地が美術館の敷地として選ばれた。敷地に足を運んでみると、自然を見渡すことができるすばらしい場所であると同時に、敷地の周りが谷になっているために外界から隔絶された別世界が実現できるのではないかと思った。敷地条件の面白さと、クライアントの熱意に打たれて、引き受けることにした。

敷地は全長約700mある。この長さを活かすために、敷地への導入路から比較的近い位置に駐車場とウェルカム・センターを設け、ここから敷地の中ほどにある美術館のエントランスまで、ランドスケープを楽しみながら移動していくよう計画した。

全体は雁行して配置された4つの棟からなる。それぞれの棟は、外側にある石壁と内側にあるコンクリート打ち放し壁の入れ子の構成をとっている。内側の箱の中が展示空間である。石壁とコンクリート壁の間は回廊になっており、そのところどころに、自然の風景を楽しめる大きな開口部がある。4つの棟の間には3つのヴォイドが置かれる。3つのヴォイドは、それぞれ正方形、三角形、円形である。ヴォイドや回廊は、美術に接するときに、その体験を増幅させてくれる場所であり、展示室と展示室の間にあって、ひと息つける、思索にふけることのできる何もない空間である。

敷地の一番奥には屋外美術館を計画した。慶州の古墳の形態をモチーフにしてつくった地形を現地に産する石で覆うことで、懐かしく、しかし今まで一度も見たことのないランドスケープになっている。敷地のロケーションや形状を最大限に活かし、また、韓国の材料や造形を用いることで、美術品・展示品そのものを最もよい環境で楽しめることはもとより、韓国の自然・風土・文化といったものをここを訪れる人々が再発見できることを願っている。

H ミュージアム
H Museum

2005- 大韓民国——Korea

The client is the cultural foundation of a South Korean corporation. We were commissioned to make an art museum that would allow many more people to appreciate their accumulated art collection.

A long and slender lot made by slicing off the top of a mountain in the corner of a vast resort complex managed by the corporation was chosen as the site for the museum. Having visited the site, I found it to be a fantastic place for looking out over the natural landscape, and at the same time, because the site is surrounded by valleys, I thought it could achieve another world completely isolated from the outside world. I was struck by the site's interesting conditions and the enthusiasm of the client, and I decided to undertake the task.

The entire length of the site is about 700m. In order to make the best use of this length, we planned the parking lot and the welcome center comparatively close to the road leading to the site, and so the landscape may be enjoyed while moving from there to the museum entrance near the center of the site.

Overall, it comprises a staggered array of four blocks. Each block has a nested composition of stone walls outside and exposed concrete walls inside. The exhibition spaces are contained within the inner boxes. There are corridors between the stone walls and the concrete walls, and in some places there are large apertures from which the natural scenery may be enjoyed. Three voids are placed between the four blocks. These three voids are in the shape of a square, a triangle, and a circle respectively. The voids and the corridors are places that amplify the experience for people enjoying the art, and as empty spaces between the exhibition rooms they allow people to pause and mediate.

I planned an outdoor museum in the innermost area of the site. By covering the terrain with locally produced stone using a motif in the form of an old Kyongju tomb, it becomes a landscape that is nostalgic yet never seen before. By making maximum use of the site's location and shape, and by using Korean original materials and forms, I want to enable visitors to rediscover South Korean nature, climate, and culture, offering the best possible environment for enjoying the artworks and exhibits themselves.

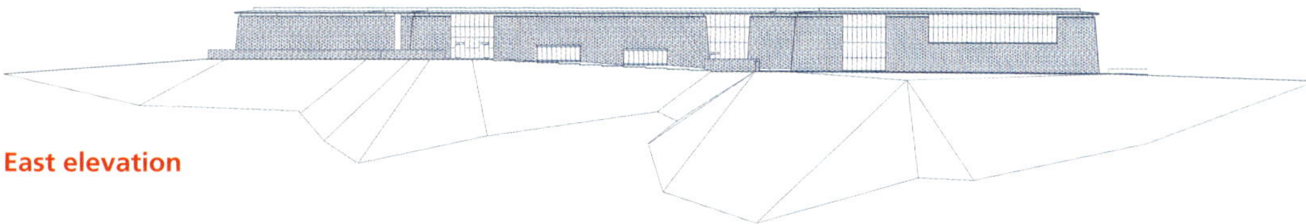

East elevation

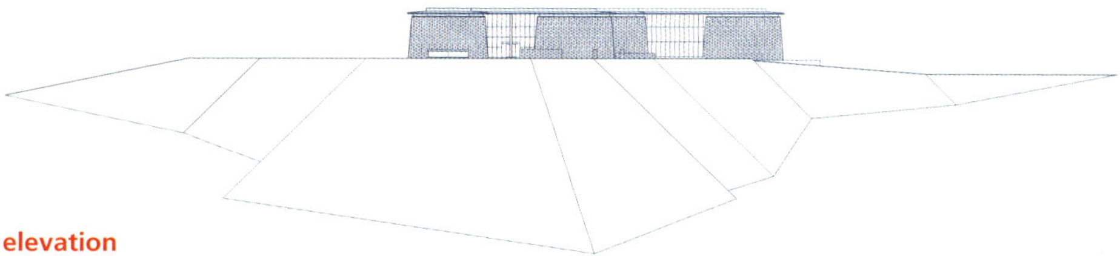

South elevation

雁行するボックスと、それを結ぶ原初的な幾何学形態をなぞるヴォイドによる単純明快な構成の中に、明と闇、動と静のコントラストが鮮やかな空間のシークエンスが展開する。

A spatial sequence comprising vivid contrasts between light and dark, movement and rest, expands within the simple, lucid composition of stepping boxes linked by voids tracing primary geometrical forms.

1 entrance hall
2 gallery
3 guest room
4 void
5 café
6 shop
7 seminar room
8 works
9 terrace
10 lounge
11 court
12 storage

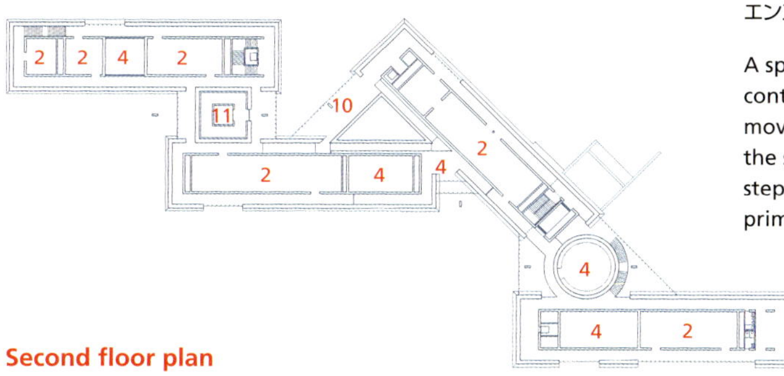

Second floor plan

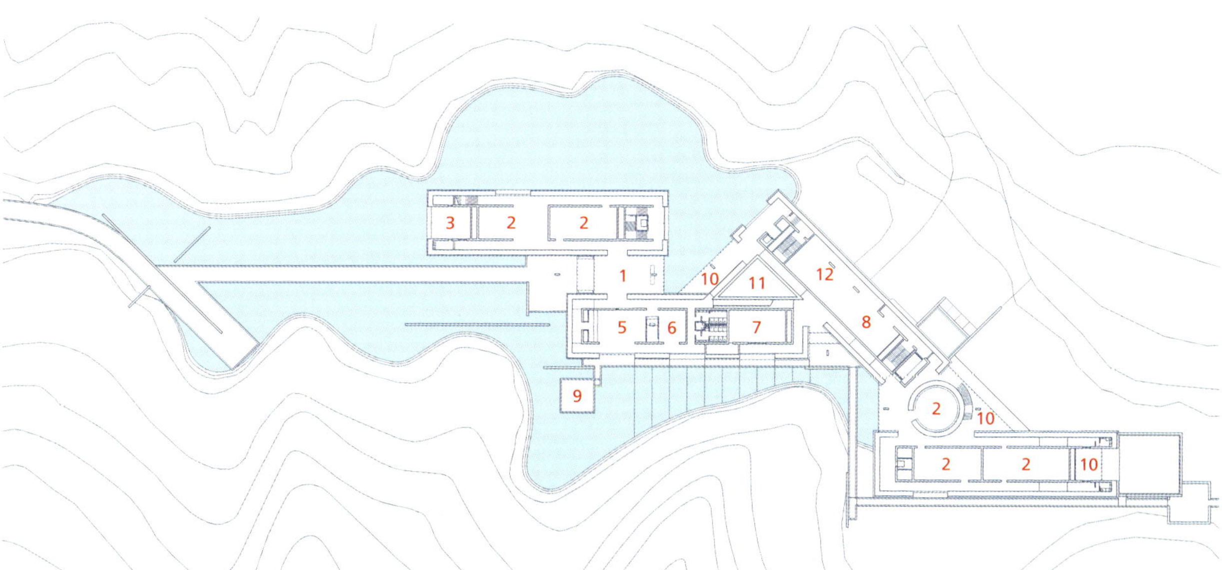

First floor plan 1:1,800

石壁で囲われた円筒形のヴォイドの空間。円形のスカイライトからのダイナミックな光が、原初的な幾何学の空間を浮かび上がらせる。

A cylindrical void space enclosed by a stone wall. The dynamic light from the circular skylight reveals the primary geometry of the space.

水、石、空と限定された要素に囲まれた建物エントランス部分の空間。水庭によるパースペクティブの強調が、静なる空間への荘厳なアプローチを演出する。

The space of the building entrance is enclosed by elements limited to water, stone, and sky. The emphasized perspective due to the water garden produces a solemn approach toward a quiet space.

石壁に閉ざされた展示棟の隙間のブリージングスペース。天井いっぱいに穿たれた大開口からの風景が、閉ざされた箱の隙間に自然の息吹を吹き込む。

A breathing space between the exhibition wings enclosed by stone walls. From the scenery visible through large openings that go right up to the ceiling, the breath of nature blows into the interstitial spaces between the closed boxes.

2007年1月、アラブ首長国連邦（UAE）の首都アブダビが、沖合の島サアディヤット島の開発プロジェクトを正式に発表した。自然環境と文化を同時に楽しめる「文化島」を目指すプロジェクトで、その中核となる文化地区はミュージアム、シアターなど5つの文化施設を中心に構成される。その設計者として、フランク・O・ゲーリー、ジャン・ヌーヴェル、ザハ・ハディドとともに、われわれが参加することになった。

われわれが担当するのは地元アブダビの文化を紹介する海洋博物館である。プロジェクトの性格上、新たに生まれる建築には、場所に根差したある種のシンボリズムが期待された。それに対し、われわれは矩形平面のヴォリュームから、海風を受けた船の帆のふくらみをなぞるようにシェル状のヴォイドをくり抜いたかたちの建築を提案した。

造形をそれ単体として見たならば、単純な幾何学によるオブジェでしかない。しかし、それがサアディヤット島の海際で、海を取り込むようにつくられた水庭の上に浮かべられたとき、なだらかな曲面に覆われたヴォイドの空間は雄大な海景を身近に引寄せる装置となる。

建物内部は、外観のイメージそのままの、船の底のような動的な空間となっている。その巨大な吹き抜け空間の中にはさまざまなレベルのフロアが浮かべられ、その間をスロープが巡り、立体的な空間構成をつくり出す。

建物の浮かぶ水庭の底は、ちょうど水面を境に鉛直方向に地上部のヴォリュームを反転したかたちに掘り下げられており、その巨大な展示水槽を、訪問者は地階のロビーから眺めることができる。

アブダビ政府は、このかたちのない自然の営みをモチーフとする建築のコンセプトを受け入れ、プロジェクトは2012年竣工を目標に、実現へと向けて動き出した。新しい時代へ向けた、中東からの文化発信に建築家として関われることを幸運に思う。

アブダビ海洋博物館
Abu Dhabi Maritime Museum

2006- アラブ首長国連邦 アブダビ —— Abu Dhabi, UAE

海へと連続するシェルの下に設けられた水庭。

In January 2007, Abu Dhabi, one of the United Arab Emirates (UAE), officially announced a development project for an offshore island called Saadiyat Island. The project aims to create a "Culture Island" wherein culture and the natural environment may be simultaneously appreciated. The cultural district as its core is composed of five cultural facilities, including museums and a theater. We are participating as designers together with Frank O. Gehry, Jean Nouvel, and Zaha Hadid.

We are in charge of a maritime museum that will showcase the local culture of Abu Dhabi. Due to the nature of this project, the newly created architecture is expected to have a kind of symbolism that is rooted in its locality. Our response was a proposal for a building in which an upside-down shell-shaped void, tracing the swelling of a boat's sail inflated by sea breezes, is excavated from a rectangular volume.

Looked at as an independent sculpture, it is merely an object with a simple geometry. However, floating on the water court made as if framing the sea of the Saadiyat Island coast, this void space covered with a gently curved surface is a device for drawing one closer to the magnificent seascape.

Exactly as with the exterior image, the inside of the building is a dynamic space like the underside of a boat. Within the huge void space, floors float at various levels and slopes run between them, creating a three-dimensional spatial composition.

The base of the water court in which the building floats is excavated in a inverted shape of the vertical aboveground volume exactly at the edge of the water, and visitors can see this huge exhibition water tank from the lobby in the basement.

The Abu Dhabi government has accepted this architectural concept using the motif of the amorphous workings of nature, and the project is moving toward implementation, aiming at completion in 2012. Turning toward a new era, I consider myself fortunate to be an architect involved in conveying culture from the Middle East.

Water court created under the shell, continuous with the sea.

南西から見る全景。北側に向かって数百mおきに、フランク・O・ゲーリー、ジャン・ヌーヴェル、ザハ・ハディドの建築が並ぶ。

Panoramic view from the southwest. Toward the north are buildings by Frank O. Gehry, Jean Nouvel, and Zaha Hadid, lined up at intervals of a few hundred meters.

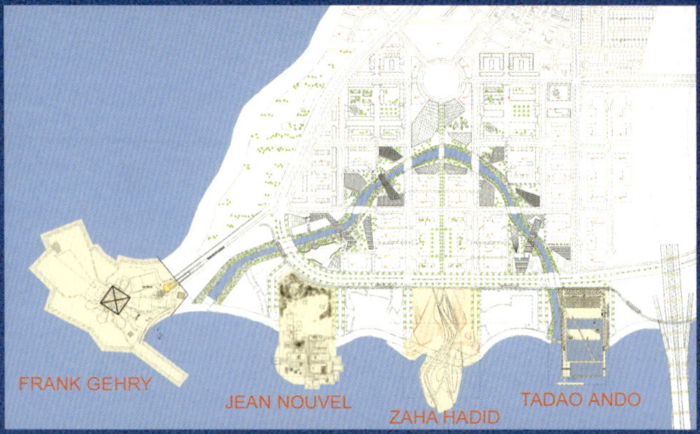
FRANK GEHRY
JEAN NOUVEL
ZAHA HADID
TADAO ANDO

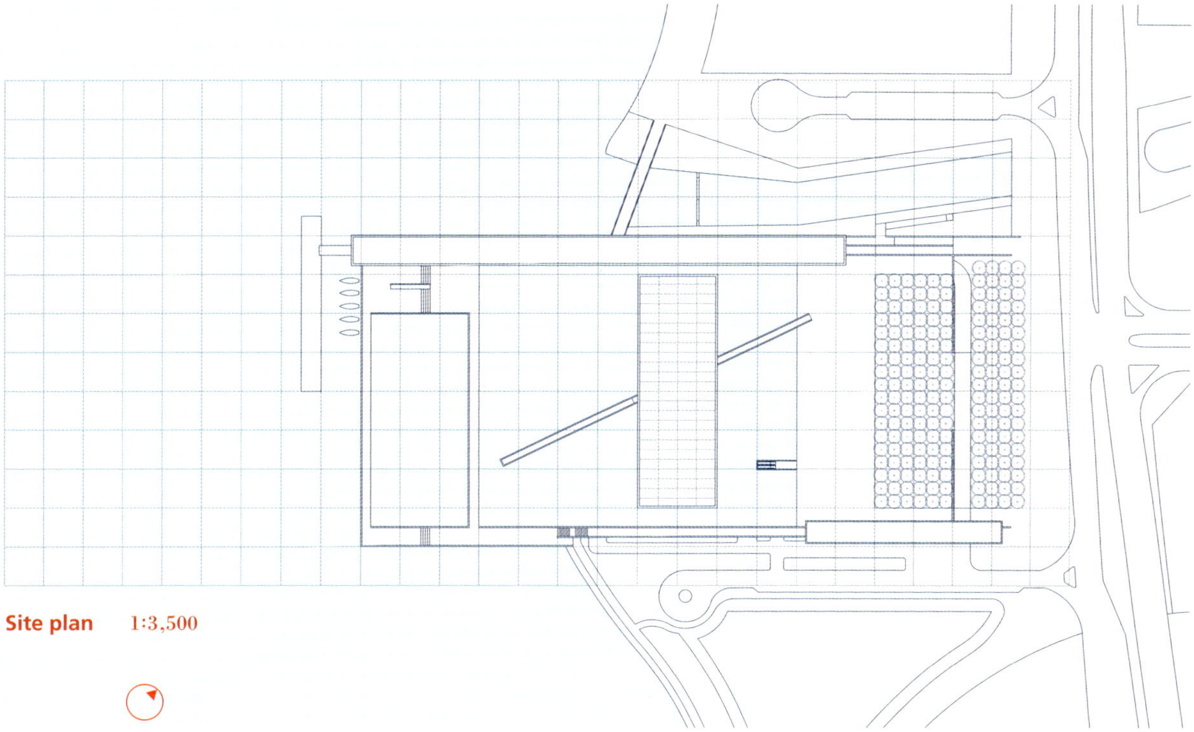

Site plan 1:3,500

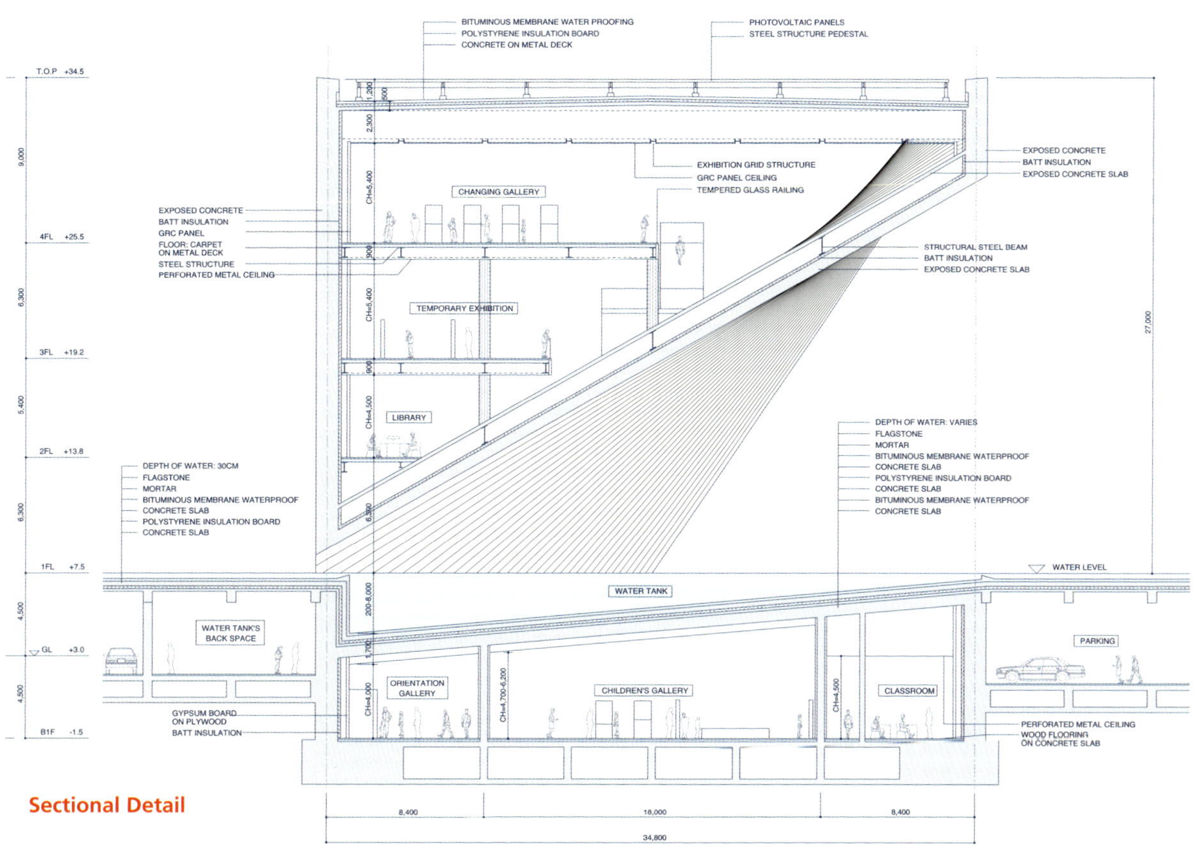

Sectional Detail

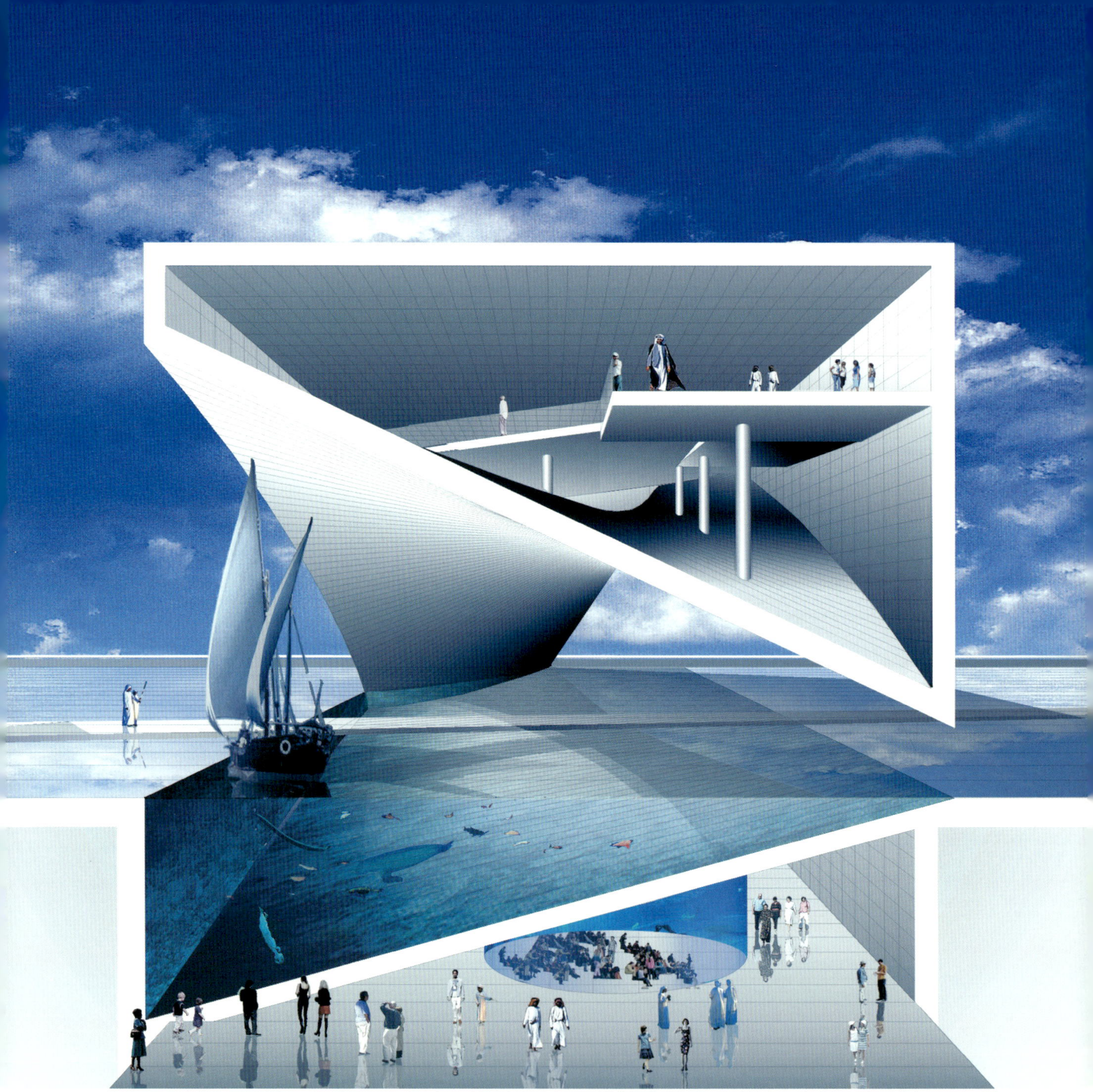

水面下には、地上にくり抜かれたヴォイドを反転したかたちの巨大な展示水槽が設けられる。

A huge water tank for exhibitions has been placed below the water, shaped as an inversion of the void that has been carved out above ground level.

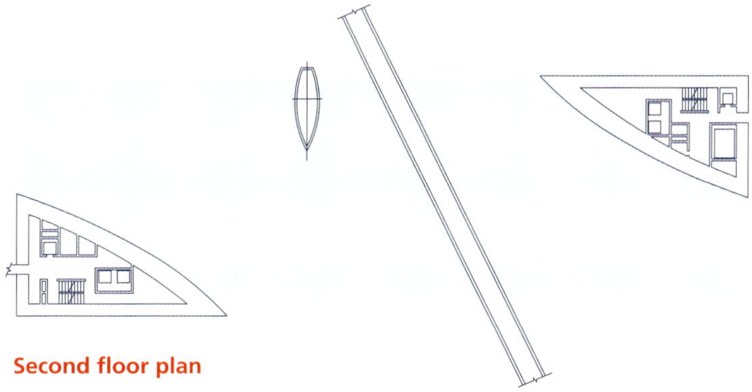

Second floor plan

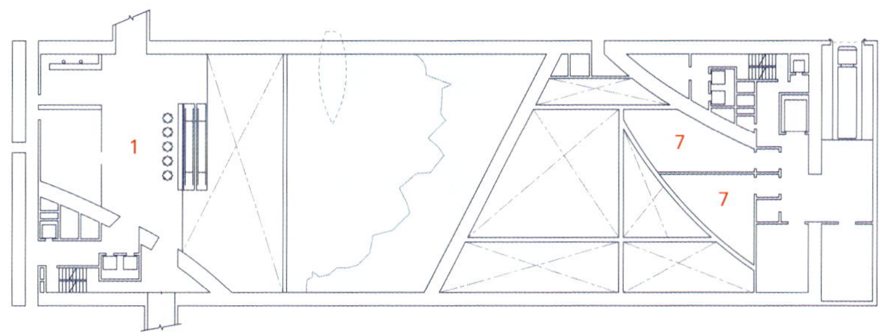

First floor plan

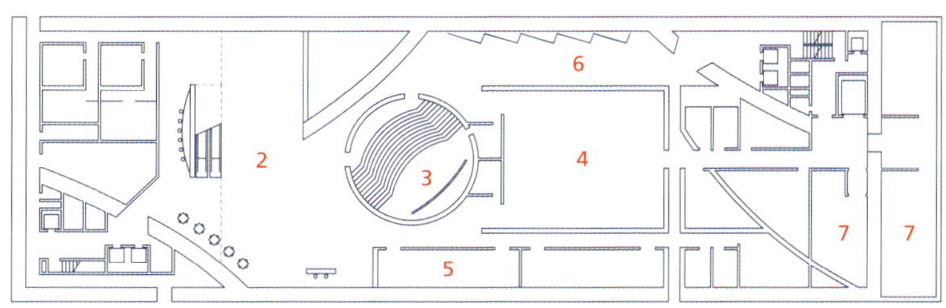

First basement plan 1:1,000

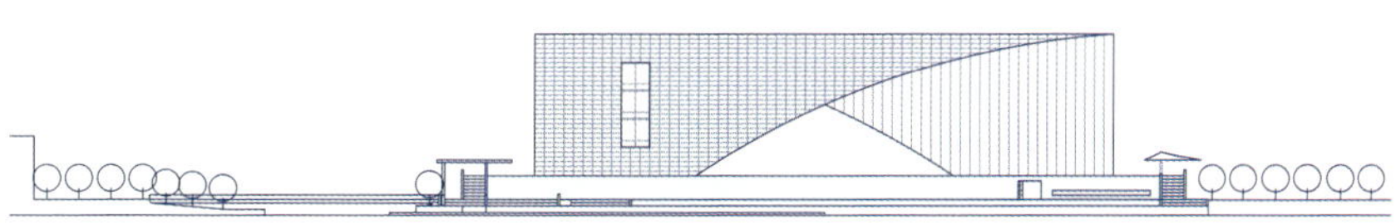

Elevation 1:2,400

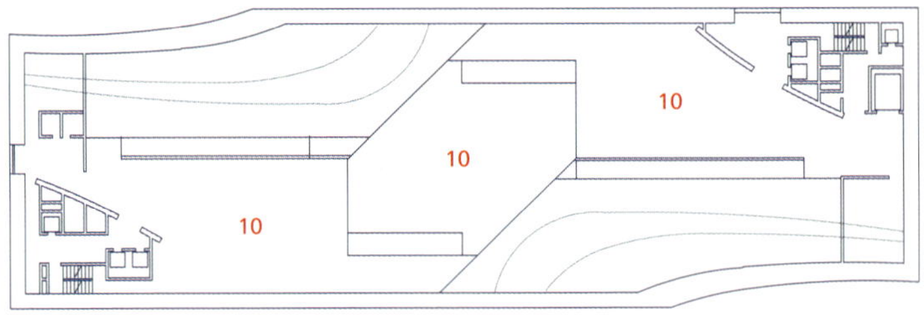

Fifth floor plan

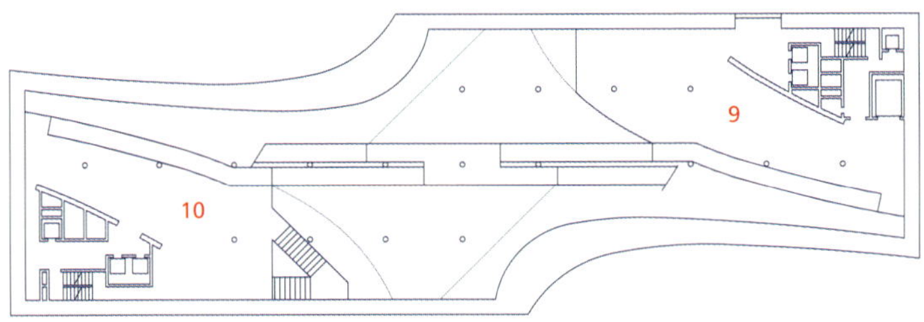

Fourth floor plan

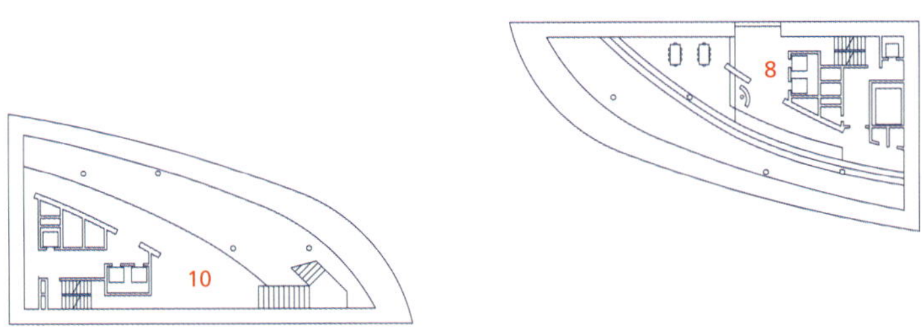

Third floor plan

1 entrance
2 lobby
3 AV theater
4 children's gallery
5 classroom
6 orientation gallery
7 collection storage
8 library
9 temporary exhibition
10 permanent gallery

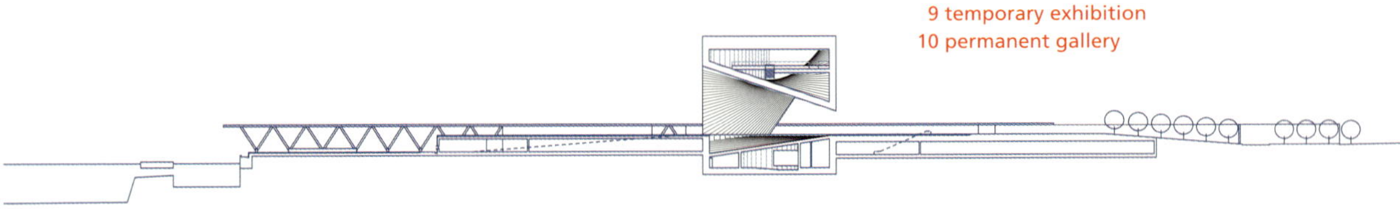

Section 1:2,400

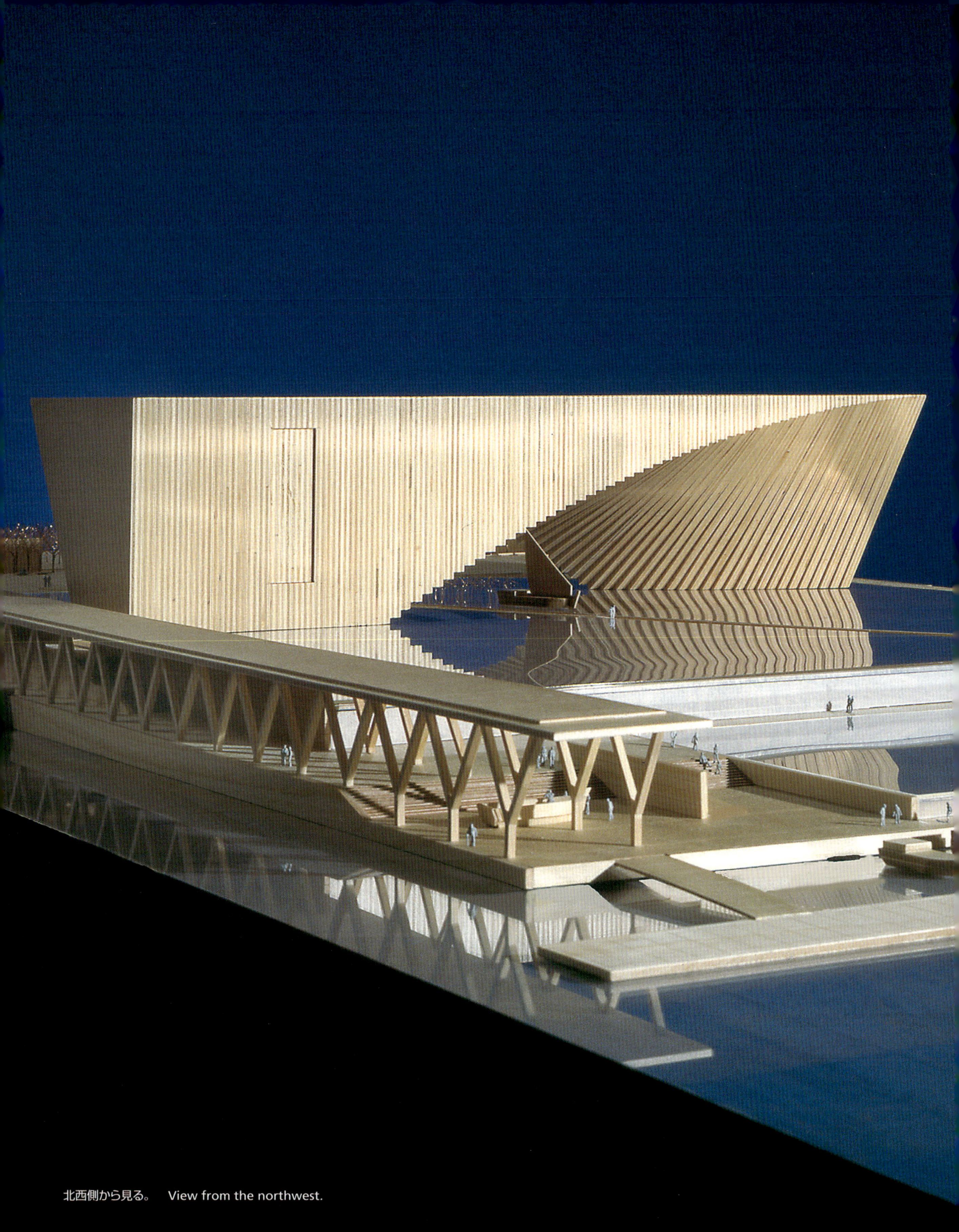

北西側から見る。　View from the northwest.

建物越しに望むアブダビの海景。　Looking out past the building to the Abu Dhabi seascape.

作品年表

1990-2008

Chronological Table of Projects

海外作品
Outside Japan

専用住宅／共同住宅／茶室
Houses, Housing and Tea House

国内作品
Inside Japan

未完プロジェクト
Unbuild Project

完成作品は竣工年、未完プロジェクトは
設計開始年に従って配置しています。

-1991

1990
ストックホルム現代美術館・建築美術館国際設計競技案
The Modern Art Museum and Architecture Museum, Stockholm, International Design Competition

1990
松谷邸増築
Matsutani House Addition

岩佐邸増築
Iwasa House Addition

伊東邸
Ito House

B-Lock 北山
B-Lock Kitayama

国際花と緑の博覧会「名画の庭」
Garden of Fine Art, Expo'**90** / Osaka

十文字美信仮設劇場
Temporary Theater for Bishin Jumonji, Photographer

S ビル
S Building

JR 京都駅改築設計競技案
The Reconstruction of JR Kyoto Station, International Design Competition

1991
大淀のアトリエ II
Atelier in Oyodo II

石河邸
Ishiko House

佐用ハウジング
Sayoh Housing

ミノルタセミナーハウス
Minolta Seminar House

姫路文学館
Museum of Literature, Himeji

ロック・フィールド静岡ファクトリー
Rock Field Shizuoka Factory

播磨ヘリポート
Harima Heliport

真言宗本福寺水御堂
Water Temple

TIME'S II
Time's II

甲南大学スチューデントサークルプロジェクト
Konan University Student Circle Project

奈良市民ホール国際設計競技案
Nara Convention Hall International Design Competition

1992

1992 年セビリア万国博覧会日本館
Japan Pavilion Expo '**92** / Sevilla

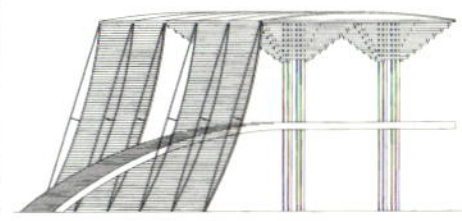

シカゴ美術館屏風ギャラリー
Gallery for Japanese Screen, the Art Institute of Chicago

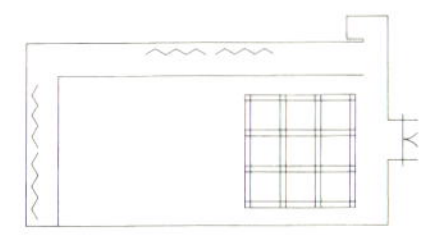

宮下邸
Miyashita House

大手前女子大学アートセンター
Otemae Art Center

熊本県立装飾古墳館
Forest of Tombs Museum, Kumamoto

ベネッセハウス ミュージアム
Benesse House Museum / Naoshima

姫路市立星の子館
Children's Seminar House, Himeji

1993

ヴィトラ・セミナーハウス
Vitra Seminar House

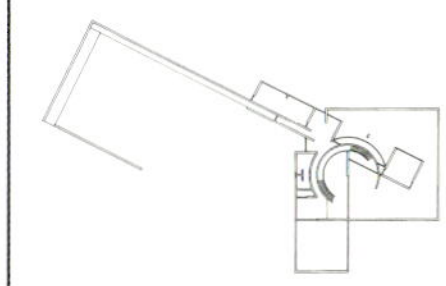

ギャラリー野田
Gallery Noda

YKK 津田沼寮
YKK Seminar House

六甲の集合住宅 II
Rokko Housing II

李邸
Lee House

兵庫県立看護大学アートセンター
College of Nursing, Art and Science, Hyogo

垂水の教会
Church in Tarumi

六甲アイランドプロジェクト
Rokko Island Project

1994

テート・ギャラリー
現代美術館国際設計競技案
Tate Gallery of Modern Art, International Design Competition

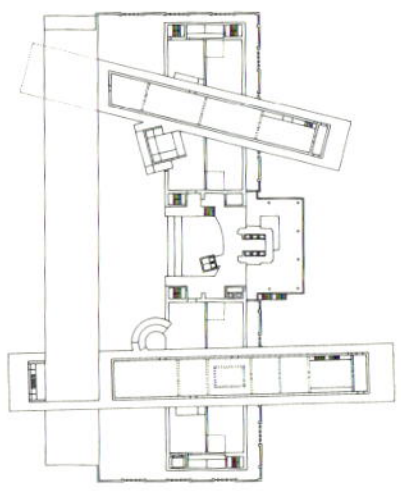

日本橋の家（金森邸）
"House in Nipponbashi" Kanamori House

大阪府立近つ飛鳥博物館
Chikatsu-Asuka Historical Museum, Osaka

京都府立陶板名画の庭
Garden of Fine Art, Kyoto

兵庫県木の殿堂
Museum of Wood

サントリーミュージアム
＋マーメイド広場
Suntory Museum + Plaza

紀陽銀行堺ビル
Kiyo Bank, Sakai Building

マックスレイ本社ビル
Maxray Headquarters Building

鹿児島大学稲盛会館
Inamori Auditorium

成羽町美術館
Nariwa Museum

1995

ユネスコ瞑想空間
Meditation Space, UNESCO

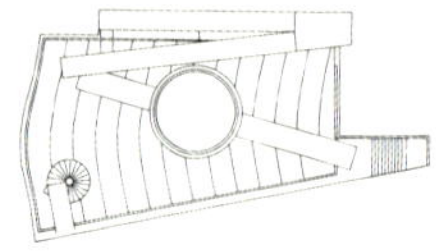

ローマ司教区教会
国際設計競技案
Vicariato di Roma, International Design Competition for the Church of the Year **2000**

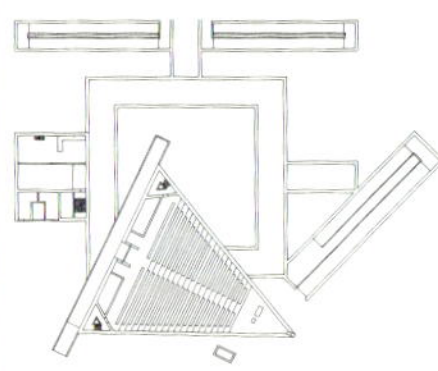

大淀のアトリエ・アネックス
Atelier in Oyodo Annex

海の集合住宅プロジェクト
Seaside Housing Project

丘の集合住宅プロジェクト
Hilltop Housing Project

播磨高原東小学校
Harima Kogen Higashi Primary School

綾部工業団地交流プラザ
Ayabe Community Center

市立五條文化博物館
Museum of Gojo Culture

ベネッセハウス オーバル
Benesse House Oval / Naoshima

大山崎山荘美術館
Oyamazaki Villa Museum

宇ノ気町立金津小学校
Kanatsu Primary School, Unoke

長良川国際会議場
Nagaragawa Convention Center

大谷地下劇場計画
The Theater in the Rock, Oya

1996

ストーン・スカルプチュア・
ミュージアム
Stone Sculpture Museum

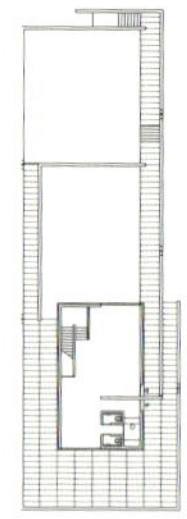

白井邸
Shirai House

ギャラリー小さい芽（澤田邸）
"Gallery Chiisaime" Sawada House

平野区の町屋（能見邸）
"Town House in Hirano" Nomi House

マンハッタンのペントハウス
Penthouse in Manhattan

スタジオ・
カール・ラガーフェルド
Studio Karl Lagerfeld

姫路文学館南館
Museum of Literature II, Himeji

上海釜山航路
フェリーターミナル
Shanghai Pusan Ferry Terminal

1997

モンテンルパ
社会復帰センター
Muntilupa Resocialization Center

ライン世界文化博物館
The Museum of World Cultures on the River Rhine

青木の集合住宅
Ohgi Housing

八木邸
Yagi House

シカゴの住宅
House in Chicago

播磨高原東中学校
Harima Kogen Higashi Junior High School

小海高原美術館
Koumi Kogen Museum

越知町立
横倉山自然の森博物館－
横倉山・牧野富太郎展示室
The Yokogurayama Natural Forest Museum, Ochi

TOTO セミナーハウス
TOTO Seminar House

1998

ネパール子ども病院
Shiddhartha Children and Women Hospital

渡辺淳一文学館
Junichi Watanabe Memorial Hall

ダイコク電機本部ビル
Daikoku Denki Headquarters Building

織田廣喜ミュージアム
Daylight Museum

朝日新聞岡山支局
Asahi News Paper Okayama Bureau

エリエール松山ゲストハウス
Elleair Matsuyama Guesthouse

1999

セント・ポール寺院聖台
国際設計競技案
A New Font for St. Paul's Cathedral, International Design Competition

アントワープ市立博物館
国際設計競技案
Museum Aan de Stroom, Antwerp International Design Competition

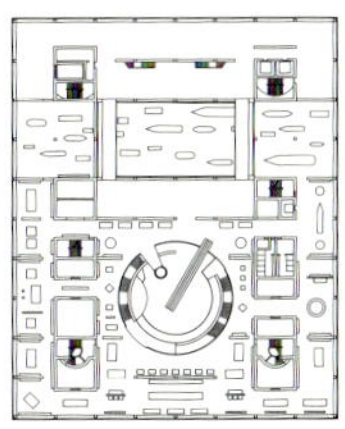

ネルソン・アトキンス美術館
国際設計競技案
Nelson Atkins Museum, International Design Competition

レイナ・ソフィア美術館
国際設計競技案
Museo Nacional Centro de Arte Reina Sofia, International Design Competition

パリ原始博物館
国際設計競技案
Musee du Quai Branly, International Design Competition

六甲の集合住宅 III
Rokko Housing III

光の教会／日曜学校
Church of the Light, Sunday School

南寺（直島・家プロジェクト）
Minami-Dera (Art House Project in Naoshima)

西宮市貝類館
Shell Museum of Nishinomiya City

淡路夢舞台
Awaji-Yumebutai (Awaji Island Project)

2000

FABRICA
（ベネトン・アートスクール）
FABRICA
(Benetton Communication Research Center)

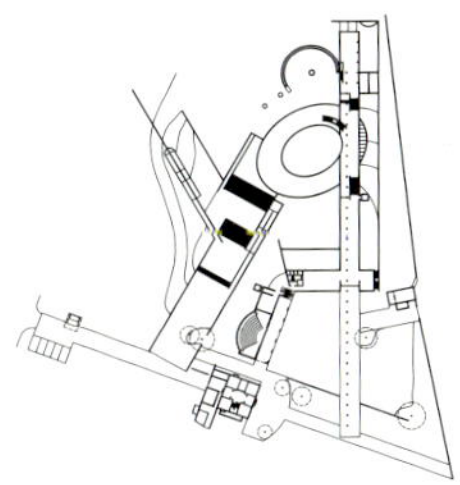

カルダー美術館
Calder Museum

BOSCH セミナーハウス
国際設計競技案
BOSCH Seminar House, International Design Competition

セント・ジョーンズ・
セミナーハウス
St. John's Abbey Seminar House

ダラスの住宅
House in Dallas

ロック・フィールド
静岡ファクトリー
（II 期増築＋ランドスケープ）
Rock Field Shizuoka Factory Study Center

南岳山光明寺
Komyo-ji Temple

ミュゼふくおかカメラ館
Fukuoka Camera Museum

新潟市立豊栄図書館
Niigata City Toyosaka Library

2001

ピューリッツァー美術館
Pulitzer Foundation for the Arts

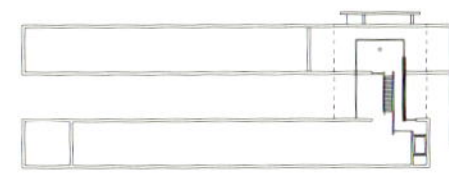

アルマーニ・テアトロ
Armani / Teatro

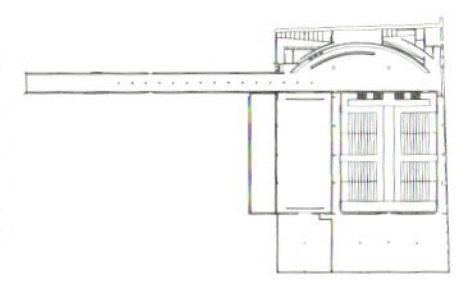

グラウンド・ゼロ・
プロジェクト
Ground Zero Project

クラーク美術館増築計画
Sterling and Francine Clark Art Institute Expansion Project

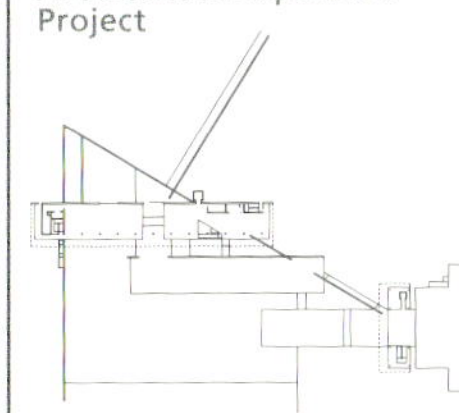

ピノー現代美術館
François Pinault Foundation for Contemporary Art

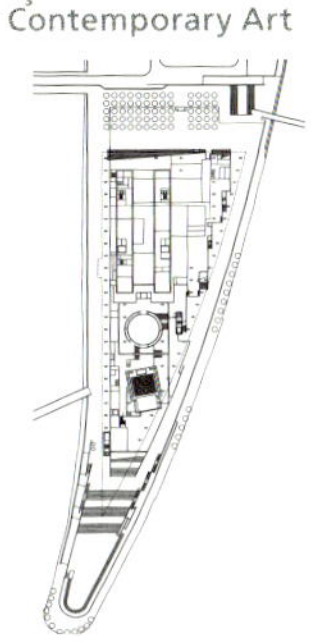

神宮前の集合住宅
Jingumae Housing

4×4 の住宅（東京）
4x4 House (Tokyo)

大阪府立狭山池博物館
Sayamaike Historical Museum, Osaka

神戸市水際広場
Kobe Waterfront Plaza

兵庫県立美術館
Hyogo Prefectural Museum of Art

国際芸術センター青森
Aomori Contemporary Art Center

司馬遼太郎記念館
Shiba Ryotaro Memorial Museum

宝塚温泉
Takarazuka Onsen (Spa)

四国村ギャラリー
Shikokumura Gallery

2002

フォートワース現代美術館
Modern Art Museum of Fort Worth

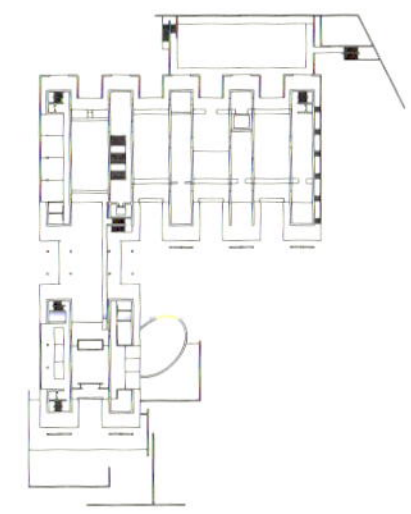

マンチェスター市
ピカデリー公園再生計画
Piccadilly Gardens Regeneration, Manchester

灘浜ガーデンバーデン
Nadahama Garden Baden

国際子ども図書館
The International Library of Children's Literature

アウディジャパン本社ビル
Audi Japan Headquaters

西田幾多郎記念哲学館
Nishida Kitaro Museum of Philosophy

コキュオフィスビル
COCUE Office Building

アサヒビール神奈川工場
ゲストハウス
Guesthouse, Asahi Kanagawa Brewery

尾道市立美術館
Onomichi City Museum of Art

加賀市立錦城中学校
Kinjo Junior High School, Kaga

2003

4×4 の住宅
4x4 House

西麻布の集合住宅
Nishiazabu Housing

マリブの住宅
House in Malibu

一戸南小学校
Minami Primary School, Ichinohe

野間自由幼稚園
Noma Kindergarten

ロック・フィールド
玉川ファクトリー
Rock Field Tamagawa Factory

2004

ホンブロイッヒ/ランゲン美術館
Langen Foundation / Hombroich

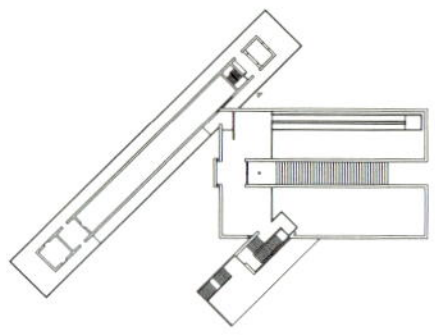

ICED TIME TUNNEL /
The Snow Show **2004**
ICED TIME TUNNEL /
The Snow SHow **2004**

森の教会
Chapel in the Woods

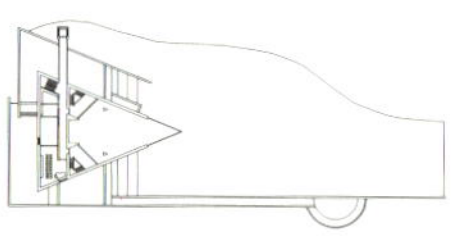

上海デザインセンター
Shanghai Design Center

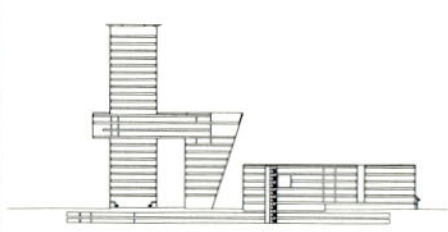

見えない家
Invisible House

仙川プロジェクトI
Sengawa Project I

仙川プロジェクトIII
Sengawa Project III

ゴールデン・ゲート・ブリッジの住宅
Golden Gate Bridge House

加子母村ふれあいコミュニティセンター
Kashimo-mura Community Center

地中美術館
Chichu Art Museum / Naoshima

県立ぐんま昆虫の森 昆虫観察館
Gunma Insect World Insect Observation Hall

絵本美術館 まどのそとのそのまたむこう
Iwaki Museum of Picture Books for Children

仙川プロジェクトII
Sengawa Project II

2005

テアトリーノ
Teatrino

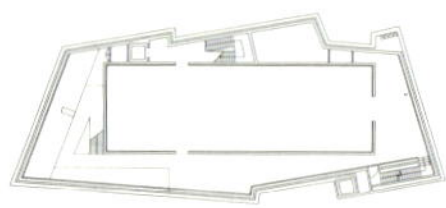

Hミュージアム
H Museum

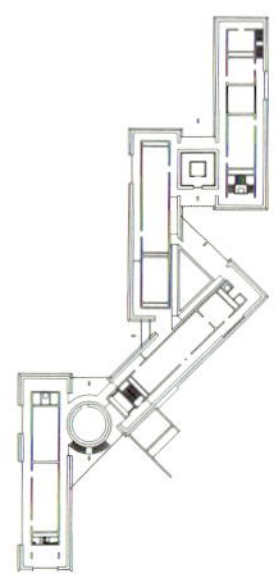

高槻の住宅
House in Takatsuki

ロック・フィールド 神戸ヘッドオフィス/神戸ファクトリー
Rock Field Kobe Headquater / Kobe Factory

hhstyle.com/casa
hhstyle.com/casa

2006

パラッツォ・グラッシ再生計画
Palazzo Grassi Renovation

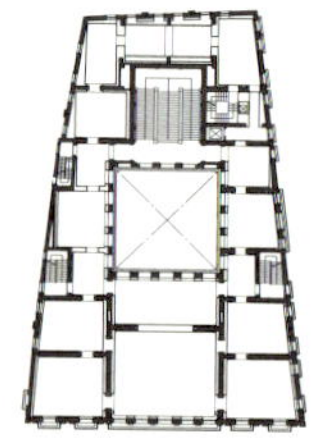

アブダビ海洋博物館
Abu Dhabi Maritime Museum

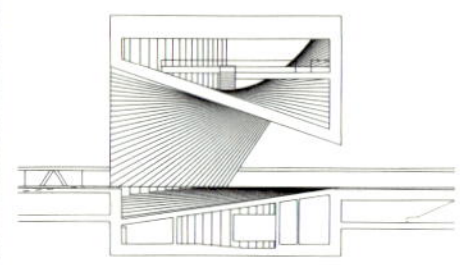

滋賀の住宅
House in Shiga

表参道ヒルズ(同潤会青山アパート建替計画)
Omotesando Hills (Omotesando Regeneration Project)

さくら広場
Sakura Hiroba

さくら広場(門真)
Sakura Hiroba (Kadoma)

直島ベネッセハウス パーク/ビーチ棟
Noshima Benesse House Park / Beach

坂の上の雲ミュージアム
Sakanouenokumo Museum

2007

プンタ・デラ・ドガーナ再生計画
Punta della Dogana Renovation

仙川プロジェクトV
Sengawa Project V

深井邸
Fukai House

回遊式住居
Walk-around House

21_21 DESIGN SIGHT
21_21 DESIGN SIGHT

竜王駅
Ryuo Station (JR-Line)

仙川プロジェクトIV
Sengawa Project IV

曹洞宗太岳院
Taigakuin Temple

2008 竣工予定

ノバルティス研究施設棟
Novartis WSJ-**352**

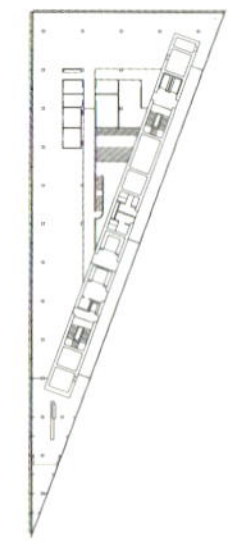

仙川プロジェクトVI
Sengawa Project VI

東急東横線渋谷駅
Tokyu Toyoko-Line Shibuya Station

東京大学情報学環・福武ホール
Interfaculty Initiative in Information Studies・Fukutake-Hall, the University of Tokyo

作品データ［掲載順］ Projects Data

アメリカ America

グラウンド・ゼロ・プロジェクト
Ground Zero Project

❶アメリカ合衆国 ニューヨーク州 ニューヨーク／
New York, New York, U.S.A.
❷モニュメント／monument
❸2001.12-2002.1
❿『a+u』2002.3、『新建築』2003.3

フォートワース現代美術館
Modern Art Museum of Fort Worth

❶アメリカ合衆国 テキサス州 フォートワース／
Fort Worth, Texas, U.S.A.
❷美術館／museum
❸1997.1-1999.9
❹1999.9-2002.10
❺44,370 m^2
❻9,240 m^2
❼14,820 m^2
❽地下1階 地上2階／1 basement 2 stories
❾鉄筋コンクリート造／reinforced concrete
❿『GA JAPAN』27 62、『a+u』1997.8 2002.3、
『新建築』1997.7 2003.5

シカゴ美術館屏風ギャラリー
Gallery for Japanese Screen, the Art Institute of Chicago

❶アメリカ合衆国 イリノイ州 シカゴ／
Chicago, Illinois, U.S.A.
❷展示室／gallery
❸1989.2-1991.4
❹1991.5-1992.5
❼160 m^2
❿『新建築』1993.1、『a+u』2002.3

クラーク美術館増築計画
Sterling and Francine Clark Art Institute Expansion Project

❶アメリカ合衆国 マサチューセッツ州
ウィリアムズタウン／Williamstown,
Massachusetts, U.S.A.
❷美術館／museum
❸2001.2-
❺570,000 m^2
❻1,210 m^2
❼8,260 m^2
❽地下1階 地上1階／1 basement 1 stories
❾鉄筋コンクリート造／reinforced concrete
❿『a+u』2002.3

ピューリッツァー美術館
Pulitzer Foundation for the Arts

❶アメリカ合衆国 ミズーリ州 セントルイス／
St. Louis, Missouri, U.S.A.
❷美術館／museum
❸1991.5-1994.12 (phase 1)、
1995.7-1997.10 (phase 2)
❹1997.11-2001.7
❺3,920 m^2
❻1,040 m^2
❼2,380 m^2
❽地下1階 地上2階／1 basement 2 stories
❾鉄筋コンクリート造／reinforced concrete
❿『a+u』2002.3、『新建築』2002.3、
『GA JAPAN』55、『GA DOCUMENT』58

森の教会
Chapel in the Woods

❶アメリカ合衆国 ワシントン州 ベルヴュー／
Bellevue, Washington, U.S.A.
❷教会／chapel
❸2004.1-2007.12
❹2008.1-
❺27,600 m^2
❻3,900 m^2
❼4,840 m^2
❽地下1階 地上2階／1 basement 2 stories
❾鉄筋コンクリート造／reinforced concrete

ヨーロッパ　Europe

1992年セビリア万国博覧会日本館
Japan Pavilion, Expo'92 / Sevilla

❶スペイン セビリア／Sevilla, Spain
❷パヴィリオン／pavilion
❸1989.9-1990.12
❹1990.9-1992.2
❺5,660 m^2
❻2,630 m^2
❼5,660 m^2
❽地上4階／4 story
❾木造／wood
❿『新建築』1990.6 1991.9 1992.5、『GA DOCUMENT』33、『a+u』2002.3

テート・ギャラリー現代美術館国際設計競技案
Tate Gallery of Modern Art
(International Design Competition)

❶イギリス ロンドン／London, U.K.
❷美術館／museum
❸1994.10-1995.1
❺35,610 m^2
❻13,660 m^2
❼25,200 m^2
❽地下2階 地上6階／2 basement 6 stories
❾鉄骨鉄筋コンクリート造／steel framed reinforced concrete
❿『GA DOCUMENT』43、『a+u』2002.3

セント・ポール寺院聖台国際設計競技案
A New Font for St. Paul's Cathedral
(International Design Competition)

❶イギリス ロンドン／London, U.K.
❷洗礼盤／font
❸1999.11-2000.2
❾ガラス／glass
❿『a+u』2002.3

ヴィトラ・セミナーハウス
Vitra Seminar House

❶ドイツ ヴァイルアムライン／Weil am Rhein, Germany
❷会議研修施設／conference center, seminar house
❸1987.4-1992.5
❹1992.6-1993.7
❺19,408 m^2
❻360 m^2
❼508 m^2
❽地下1階 地上1階／1 basement 1 story
❾鉄筋コンクリート造／reinforced concrete
❿『新建築』1990.8 1994.2、『a+u』2002.3

ユネスコ瞑想空間
Meditation Space, UNESCO

❶フランス パリ／Paris, France
❷瞑想空間／meditation space
❸1994.1-1995.5
❹1995.4-1995.10
❺350 m^2
❻33 m^2
❼33 m^2
❽地上1階／1 story
❾鉄筋コンクリート造／reinforced concrete
❿『GA JAPAN』18、『新建築』1996.3、『a+u』2002.3

FABRICA（ベネトン・アートスクール）
FABRICA
(Benetton Communication Research Center)

❶イタリア トレヴィソ／Treviso, Italy
❷教育・研究施設／education, research center
❸1992.4-1994.12
❹1992.10-2000.6
❺48,834 m^2
❻1,250 m^2
❼5,172 m^2
❽地下2階 地上2階(新築部分)、地下1階 地上3階(既存修復部分)／2 basement 2 stories (extention), 1 basement 3 stories (restration)
❾鉄筋コンクリート造(新築部分)、木造+レンガ造(既存修復部分)／reinforced concrete (extention), wood + brick (restration)
❿『新建築』1994.2 2000.1 2000.9、『GA JAPAN』46、『GA DOCUMENT』36 62、『SD』2000.10、『a+u』2002.3

アントワープ市立博物館国際設計競技案
Museum Aan de Stroom, Antwerp
(International Design Competition)

❶ベルギー アントワープ／Antwerp, Belgium
❷博物館／museum
❸1999.9-2000.6
❺12,000 m^2
❻18,670 m^2
❼15,000 m^2
❽地上5階／5 stories
❾鉄骨鉄筋コンクリート造／steel framed reinforced concrete
❿『a+u』2002.3

アルマーニ・テアトロ
Armani / Teatro

❶イタリア ミラノ／Milan, Italy
❷劇場、ギャラリー（改修）／theater, gallery (renovation)
❸2000.3-2000.9
❹2000.9-2001.7
❺9,700 m^2
❼3,400 m^2（テアトロ部分／teatro）、12,300 m^2（全体／whole）
❽地上1階(テアトロ部分)／1 story (teatro)、地下1階 地上3階(オフィス部分)／1 basement 3 stories (office)
❾鉄筋コンクリート造(新築部分)、鉄骨造(屋根部分)／reinforced concrete (extension), steel frame (roof)
❿『新建築』2001.12、『GA JAPAN』54、『a+u』2002.3

ヨーロッパ　Europe

マンチェスター市ピカデリー公園再生計画
Piccadilly Gardens Regeneration, Manchester

❶イギリス マンチェスター／Manchester, U.K.
❷公園／public garden
❸1999.1-2000.4
❹2000.4-2002.6
❺80,000 m^2
❻650 m^2
❼500 m^2
❾鉄筋コンクリート造／reinforced concrete
❿『a+u』2002.3、『新建築』2003.3

パラッツォ・グラッシ再生計画
Palazzo Grassi Renovation

❶イタリア ヴェニス／Venice, Italy
❷美術館（改修）／museum (renovation)
❸2005.6-2006.2
❹2005.9-2006.4
❺1,450 m^2
❻1,400 m^2
❼6,320 m^2
❽地上5階／5 stories
❾レンガ造、木造／brick, wood
❿『新建築』2006.9

ノバルティス研究施設棟
Novartis WSJ-352

❶スイス バーゼル／Basel, Switzerland
❷研究施設／pharmaceutical research
❸2004.4-2006.7
❹2006.8-2009.3
❺1,995 m^2
❻1,766 m^2
❼22,385 m^2
❽地下2階 地上8階／2 basement 8 stories
❾鉄筋コンクリート造／reinforced concrete

ホンブロイッヒ／ランゲン美術館
Langen Foundation / Hombroich

❶ドイツ ノイス／Neuss, Germany
❷美術館／museum
❸1994.7-2002.7
❹2002.8-2004.7
❺120,220 m^2
❻1,860 m^2
❼3,050 m^2
❽地下2階 地上1階／2 basement 1 story
❾鉄筋コンクリート造、一部鉄骨造／reinforced concrete, steel frame
❿『a+u』2002.3、『新建築』2005.1、『GA JAPAN』72、『GA DOCUMENT』79 83

テアトリーノ
Teatrino

❶イタリア ヴェニス／Venice, Italy
❷オーディトリアム、ギャラリー／auditorium, gallery
❸2005.6-
❺800 m^2
❼1,800 m^2
❽地下1階、地上2階／1 basement, 2 stories
❾鉄筋コンクリート造／reinforced concrete
❿『新建築』2006.9

ストーン・スカルプチュア・ミュージアム
Stone Sculpture Museum

❶ドイツ バード・クライツナッハ／Bad Kreuznach, Germany
❷美術館／museum
❸1996.9-
❺6,034 m^2
❻130 m^2
❼221 m^2
❽地上2階／2 stories
❾鉄筋コンクリート造、木造／reinforced concrete, wood

ピノー現代美術館
François Pinault Foundation for Contemporary Art

❶フランス スガン島／Ile Seguin, France
❷美術館、ホール／museum, hall
❸2001.1-2005.4
❺32,000 m^2
❻11,000 m^2
❼32,700 m^2
❽地下1階 地上5階／1 basement 5 stories
❾鉄骨鉄筋コンクリート造、鉄骨造／steel framed reinforced concrete, steel frame
❿『GA DOCUMENT』70、『a+u』2002.3

プンタ・デラ・ドガーナ再生計画
Punta della Dogana Renovation

❶イタリア ヴェニス／Venice, Italy
❷美術館（改修）／museum (renovation)
❸2007.5-2007.10
❹2007.10-2009.1
❺2,500 m^2
❻2,500 m^2
❼3,800 m^2
❽地上2階／2 stories
❾レンガ造／brick

アジア　Asia

ネパール子ども病院
Shiddhartha Children and Women Hospital

❶ネパール ブトワール／Butwal, Nepal
❷病院／hospital
❸1997.1-1997.10
❹1997.11-1998.11
❼1,073 m^2
❽地上2階／2 stories
❾鉄筋コンクリート造／reinforced concrete
❿『a+u』2002.3

上海デザインセンター
Shanghai Design Center

❶中華人民共和国 上海／Shanghai, China
❷事務所、ショールーム、ホール／office, showroom, hall
❸2004.7-2006.12
❺9,127 m^2
❻3,639 m^2
❼47,055 m^2
❽地下2階 地上24階／2 basement 24 stories
❾鉄骨鉄筋コンクリート造、鉄骨造／steel framed reinforced concrete, steel frame

H ミュージアム
H Museum

❶大韓民国／South Korea
❷美術館／museum
❸2005.09-
❺70,900 m^2
❻4,600 m^2
❼9,000 m^2
❽地下1階 地上2階／1 basement 2 stories
❾鉄筋コンクリート造／reinforced concrete

アブダビ海洋博物館
Abu Dhabi Maritime Museum

❶アラブ首長国連邦 アブダビ／Abu Dhabi, UAE
❷博物館／museum
❸2006.6-
❺61,000 m^2
❻25,400 m^2
❼33,300 m^2
❽地下1階 地上5階／1 basement 5 stories
❾鉄筋コンクリート造、鉄骨鉄筋コンクリート造、鉄骨造／reinforced concrete, steel framed reinforced concrete
❿『GA JAPAN』85、『GA DOCUMENT』97、『新建築』2007.6

凡例／**legend**

❶所在／location
❷用途／principal use
❸設計期間／design period
❹施工期間／construction period
❺敷地面積／site area
❻建築面積／built area
❼延床面積／total floor area
❽規模／scale in building
❾主体構造／structure
❿掲載誌

略歴　Profile
安藤忠雄　Tadao Ando

略歴	1941	● 大阪に生まれる
	1962-69	● 独学で建築を学ぶ
	1969	● 安藤忠雄建築研究所を設立
受賞	1979	●「住吉の長屋」で昭和54年度日本建築学会賞
	1985	● フィンランド建築家協会から、国際的な建築賞 アルヴァ・アアルト賞（第5回）
	1989	● 1989年度フランス建築アカデミー大賞（ゴールドメダル）
	1993	● 日本芸術院賞
	1995	● 1995年度プリツカー賞
	1996	● 高松宮殿下記念世界文化賞
	2002	● 2002年度アメリカ建築家協会（AIA）ゴールドメダル
		● ローマ大学名誉博士号
		● 同済大学（上海）名誉教授
		● 京都賞
	2003	● 文化功労者
	2005	● 国際建築家連合（UIA）ゴールドメダル
		● レジオン・ドヌール勲章（シュバリエ）叙勲
名誉会員	2002	● イギリス ロイヤルアカデミー オブ アーツ名誉会員
教職	1987	● イェール大学客員教授
	1988	● コロンビア大学客員教授
	1990	● ハーバード大学客員教授
	1997-	● 東京大学教授
	2003-	● 東京大学名誉教授
	2005	● 東京大学特別栄誉教授
		● カリフォルニア大学バークレー校客員教授
主な作品	1983	● 六甲の集合住宅Ⅰ（兵庫 神戸）
	1989	● 光の教会（大阪 茨木）
	1992	● ベネッセハウス ミュージアム（香川 直島）
	1993	● 六甲の集合住宅Ⅱ（兵庫 神戸）
	1994	● 大阪府立近つ飛鳥博物館（大阪 河南）
	1995	● ベネッセハウス オーバル（香川 直島）
	1999	● 六甲の集合住宅Ⅲ（兵庫 神戸）
	2000	● 淡路夢舞台（兵庫 淡路）
		● 南岳山光明寺（愛媛 西条）
		● FABRICA（ベネトンアートスクール）（イタリア トレヴィソ）
	2001	● ピューリッツァー美術館（アメリカ セントルイス）
		● アルマーニ・テアトロ（イタリア ミラノ）
		● 大阪府立狭山池博物館（大阪 大阪狭山）
	2002	● 兵庫県立美術館（兵庫 神戸）
		● 国際子ども図書館（東京 台東）
		● フォートワース現代美術館（アメリカ フォートワース）
	2003	● 4×4の住宅（兵庫 神戸）
	2004	● 地中美術館（香川 直島）
		● ホンブロイッヒ／ランゲン美術館（ドイツ ノイス）
	2006	● 同潤会青山アパート建替計画（表参道ヒルズ）（東京 渋谷）
		● パラッツォ・グラッシ再生計画（イタリア ヴェニス）
	2007	● 21_21 DESIGN SIGHT（東京 港区）

Profile

1941 ● Born in Osaka, Japan

1962-69 ● Self-educated in architecture

1969 ● Established Tadao Ando Architect & Associates

Awards

1979 ● Annual Prize, Architectural Institute of Japan "Row House in Sumiyoshi"

1985 ● The 5th Alvar Aalto Medal, The Finnish Association of Architects, Finland

1989 ● Gold Medal of Architecture, Académie d'Architecture (French Academy of Architecture), France

1993 ● Japan Art Academy Prize, Japan

1995 ● The Pritzker Architecture Prize, U.S.A.

1996 ● The 8th Premium Imperiale

2002 ● Gold Medal of the American Institute of Architects, U.S.A.

● Honorary Degree, Università Degli Studi di Roma, Italy

● Honorary Degree, Tongji University, Shanghai, China

● The Kyoto Prizes, Japan

2003 ● Person of Cultural Merit, Japan

2005 ● Gold Medal of Union Internationale des Architectes

● Chevalier de l'Ordre National de la Légron d'Honneur, France

Affiliations

2002 ● Honorary Academician, The Royal Academy of Arts in London

Academic Activities

1987 ● Visiting Professor, Yale University

1988 ● Visiting Professor, Columbia University

1990 ● Visiting Professor, Harvard University

1997- ● Professor, The University of Tokyo

2003- ● Emeritus Professor, The University of Tokyo

2005 ● Special University Professor Emeritus, The University of Tokyo

● Regent Professor, University of California, Berkeley

Representative Works

1983 ● Rokko Housing I, Kobe, Hyogo

1989 ● Church of the Light, Ibaraki, Osaka

1992 ● Benesse House Museum, Naoshima, Kagawa

1993 ● Rokko Housing II, Kobe, Hyogo

1994 ● Chikatsu-Asuka Historical Museum, Kanan, Osaka

1995 ● Benesse House Oval, Naoshima, Kagawa

1999 ● Rokko Housing III, Kobe, Hyogo

2000 ● Awaji-Yumebutai (Awaji Island Project), Awaji, Hyogo

● Komyo-ji Temple, Saijo, Ehime

● FABRICA (Benetton Communications Research Center), Treviso, Italy

2001 ● Pulitzer Foundation for the Arts, St. Louis, U.S.A.

● ARMANI / TEATRO, Milan, Italy

● Sayamaike Historical Museum, Osaka-Sayama, Osaka

2002 ● Hyogo Prefectural Museum of Art, Kobe, Hyogo

● The International Library of Children's Literature, Taito, Tokyo

● Modern Art Museum of Fort Worth, Fort Worth, U.S.A.

2003 ● 4×4 House, Kobe, Hyogo

2004 ● Chichu Art Museum / Naoshima, Naoshima, Kagawa

● Langen Foundation / Hombroich Museum, Neuss, Germany

2006 ● Omotesando Hills (Omotesando Regeneration Project), Shibuya, Tokyo

● Palazzo Grassi Renovation, Venice, Italy

2007 ● 21_21 DESIGN SIGHT, Minato-ku, Tokyo

クレジット Credits

Photography　写真

Mitsuo Matsuoka　松岡満男
pp.57-63 68-73, 75, 78-83, 90-97, 100-102, 104, 106-110, 114-117, 136-141, 144-145, 149, 198-201, 204, 205 above, 207-208, 214-221, 226-227, 318-325

Shinkenchiku-sha　新建築社
pp.111, 146-147, 152-158, 160, 162-169, 202-203, 205 below, 225, 242-247, 255-257, 278-282, 284-299, 356-359, 361-365

Tomio Ohashi　大橋富夫
pp.184-189, 191-193, 314-315, 384-385, 390-393

Yukio Futagawa　二川幸夫
pp.86, 170, 172-173, 210-211

Yoshio Takase　高瀬良夫
p.143

Masaya Yoshimura　吉村昌也　p.26

© 2002 EDAW/Photography by Dixi Carrillo　p.263-267, 268 below, 270-273

Len Grant Photography　pp.268 above, 269

Stephane Couturier　pp.174, 178-179

The Pulitzer Foundation for the Arts © Robert Pettus　p.67

© Kubach-Wilmsen Foundation　p.344

Jake Rajs/Getty Images　pp.24-25

James Blank/Getty Images　p.64

Pankaj & Insy Shah/Getty Images　p.382

David Steele/Gallo Images/Getty Images　pp.394-395

Other photographs courtesy of Tadao Ando Architect & Associates
上記以外の写真すべて安藤忠雄建築研究所

Drawings　図版

Tadao Ando Architect & Associates　安藤忠雄建築研究所

English Translations　英訳

Hiroshi Watanabe　渡辺 洋
pp. 12-23, 32-55

Thomas Daniell & Ellen Van Goethem
トーマス・ダニエル & エレン・ヴァン・ホーテム
Project descriptions and captions
作品解説、図版キャプション

Japanese Translations　和訳

Yasushi Zenno　禪野靖司
pp.84-85, 132-133, 258-259

Yukiko Komaki, Akane Moriya　小巻由紀子・守屋あかね
pp.352-353

The source of following drawings:
"TADAO ANDO DETAILS" volume 2 and 3
by A.D.A. EDITA Tokyo
以下の図版初出：『TADAO ANDO DETAILS』
２巻および３巻（A.D.A. EDITA Tokyo 刊）
pp.76-77, 98-99, 112-113, 212-213, 248-249, 250-251, 252-253, 308-309

Tadao Ando Architect & Associates
安藤忠雄建築研究所

Tadao Ando	安藤忠雄
Masataka Yano	矢野正隆
Fumihiko Iwama	岩間文彦
Kazuya Okano	岡野一也
Takaaki Mizutani	水谷孝明
Hironobu Wakayama	若山泰伸
Hidehiro Yano	矢野英裕
Kanya Sogo	十河完也
Yoshinori Hayashi	林　慶憲
Shimao Mori	森詩麻夫
Antoine Müller Moriya	アントワンヌ ミュレー 守屋
Tatsuhito Ono	小野龍人
Takeharu Suzuki	鈴木丈晴
Tomonori Miura	三浦朋訓
Kosuke Sakai	酒井康介
Kazutoshi Miyamura	宮村和寿
Shunri Nishizawa	西澤俊理
Eiji Hayakawa	早川鋭二
Daisuke Besshi	別枝大輔
Seiichiro Takeuchi	竹内誠一郎
Hiroyuki Tanaka	田中宏行
Kensuke Suto	須藤謙介
Chisato Kodaira	古平知沙都
Akiko Hayashida	林田安紀子
Kaori Soneda	曽根田香
Tamao Shichiri	七里玉緒
Yumiko Kato	加藤由美子